Rights of Passage

HELEN R. WOOLCOCK

RIGHTS OF PASSAGE

Emigration to Australia in the nineteenth century

WITHDRAWN

Tavistock Publications
London and New York

blished in 1986 by
k Publications Ltd
Lane, London EC4P 4EE

ed in the USA by
ock Publications
n with Methuen, Inc.
eet, New York, NY 10001

Typeset by M.C. Typeset Limited, Chatham, Kent
Printed in Great Britain
at the University Press, Cambridge

British Library Cataloguing in Publication Data

Woolcock, Helen R.
 Rights of passage: emigration to
 Australia in the nineteenth century.
 1. Voyages and travels. 2.
 Steamboats —— History —— 19th
 century. 3. Great Britain ——
 Emigration and immigration ——
 History —— 19th century. 4.
 Queensland —— Emigration and
 immigration —— History —— 19th
 century. I. Title
 910'.09162 G540

 ISBN 0-422-60240-X

Library of Congress Cataloging in Publication Data

Woolcock, Helen R.
 Rights of passage.
 Bibliography: p. Includes index.
 1. Australia —— Emigration and
 immigration —— History —— 19th
 century. I. Title.
 JV9124.W66 1986 325.94 86-943

 ISBN 0-422-60240-X

To Mother

CONTENTS

LIST OF PLATES

ACKNOWLEDGEMENTS

This study first appeared in 1983 as a doctoral thesis which was made possible by a Wellcome Trust Research Training Scholarship and Travel Grant. It has been revised during the tenure of a Hannah Post-doctoral Fellowship at the University of Western Ontario, Canada.

I am indebted to W.F. Bynum who supervised the thesis, urged me to prepare it for publication, and advised with the final script. The interest and support of family and friends, particularly Elvira Hobson, and cooperation from archivists and librarians in Brisbane, Canberra, and London have encouraged me in the task. I would also like to thank Steven Self of the University of London Computer Centre and, for their suggestions and comments, Oliver MacDonagh, F.B. Smith, Charles Price and Bryan Gandevia in Australia, Sir James Watt, Robin Craig and John Osborn, in England, and Ian Steele in Canada. At Tavistock, Gill Davies and Heather Gibson have skilfully steered me through the rites of publication.

H.R.W.
1985

PREFACE

Her Imperial Majesty personally chose the name for the British colony of Queensland, a vast and virtually unknown country occupying the north-eastern corner of Australia, some 12,000 miles from the motherland. The first governor was sworn into office under the summer sun of December, 1859. For the next four decades, until the federation of the Australian colonies on 1 January, 1901, Queensland maintained close maternal ties with Britain and regarded the older colonies as sibling rivals.

Having won separation from the parent colony of New South Wales, Queenslanders were confident of continued progress and determined that the new creation would succeed. The belief in progress had been cultivated by civilized, enlightened society, endorsed by the doctrine that there should be no limits to the acquisition of wealth and property by individuals prepared to work for it and, following the publication of Darwin's *Origin of Species* in 1859, was expressed in social evolutionary terms. These concepts moulded colonial policy and attitudes. In response to an address of welcome, the first governor summed up the prevailing sentiment:

> 'I rejoice to witness around me the obvious progress alike of material industry, of mental activity, and of moral and physical well being. Everything may be expected from such signs as these. They are strong proofs to our Queen and countrymen at home that the foundations of a mighty and flourishing province of the British Empire have already been laid in this part of Australia.'   (Quoted in Lack 1959a: Prologue)

Queenslanders were primarily concerned with material progress. The land waited to be explored and exploited. All who
contributed to its development expected to share the profits; 'the
whole adult community believed that the enjoyment of material
prosperity would be the reward of honourable industry' (Clark
1978:137). The self-made man became synonymous with colonial
success. But in 1859 it was obvious that a population of 25,000 and
7½d in the treasury were not sufficient to develop a country seven
times the size of Great Britain. The colony needed finance and
people. Since the aboriginal population did not share the white
man's aspirations and natural increase alone could not meet the
demand, the immediate solution was to look to the mother
country for a workforce and the capital to support it.

Experience had shown that a criminal, refuse or drifting people
did not provide the most suitable material for colonization.
Moreover, Queensland was conscious of its dubious past (transportation to the eastern colonies had ceased just twenty years
before), and the fact that Britain needed an outlet for its
overcrowded prisons, asylums and workhouses and for the
growing numbers of unemployed. The new colony would have
none of these. It wanted only those who shared colonial
expectations, could work hard and reproduce rapidly. Within a
few weeks of founding, steps were taken to attract such a
population, and a vigorous immigration policy with recruitment
concentrated mainly in Britain, and to a lesser extent in Europe,
came into effect. Apart from temporary interruptions, this policy
was maintained throughout the colonial period. The imperial
government encouraged emigration, but offered little or no
financial support for voluntary colonization. Queensland accepted
this responsibility and entered the migration market, already well
established by 1860, prepared to subsidize the introduction of
'suitable' colonists.

Mass migratory movements of the nineteenth century reflected
the belief in progress and expansionist forces – political struggles,
scientific and technological developments, and an unprecedented
population growth – operating at every level of western society
(see Cunliffe 1974). These forces created colonial empires, and
simultaneously concentrated and dispersed both peoples and
diseases. Ordinary men often appeared as pawns in the hands of
the powerful, yet national leaders recognized that only a contented

and healthy society served the interests of progress and civilization. Measures for monitoring public health had been introduced
to England in 1837 and were quickly adopted by the new colony.
The first Registrar-General in his 1860 Report wrote:

> 'Statistical Records are, year by year, attracting a larger share of
> public attention in all civilized communities, until they now
> form the best criterion by which to estimate and measure . . .
> the progress each has made in the march of civilization . . . they
> have disclosed startling and unexpected facts, bearing on the
> moral, sanitary, and social condition of every community
> which has authorized and provided for their compilation.
>
>   The most important of these records, at least, in a young
> country, are those which relate to human life . . . it is,
> therefore, a subject of sincere congratulation, that the Govern-
> ment of this Colony should have taken early steps to provide
> for the compilation and publication of a reliable record of its
> Vital Statistics from the first day of its separate existence.'
>
> (QVP 1861:871).

The detailed records of 'civilized' countries last century have
been analysed at length. By comparison, there exists a surprising
dearth of information for populations in transit. Certainly the
responsibility for collection, quite apart from the collation and
storage of such data, presented enormous problems. The
Registrar-General for England in his annual reports issued only
gross statistics for emigration from the United Kingdom –
numbers embarked, their country of origin and destination, as
well as the births and deaths of British nationals at sea. But it must
be remembered that Britain took a paternal, not a financial,
interest in the well-being of her emigrants. In fact, the average
convict transported to the Antipodes earlier in the century was
better documented and provided for than voluntary departees,
especially those who fled famine-ridden Ireland for North
America (see Bateson 1974 and MacDonagh 1961).

   Legislation to protect the emigrant trade had been introduced as
early as 1803, but persistent abuses and horrendous reports of
transatlantic voyages and their aftermath, forced revisions to the
law and culminated in the Passenger Act of 1855. For the next
forty years, this statute regulated the lives of hundreds of
thousands who sailed under the British flag. Although it allowed

for relatively effective public health at sea, contagious diseases continued to be a 'source of suffering, misery, and pecuniary loss' and, according to delegates to the Australasian Sanitary Conference in 1884, should never have broken out on ships sailing with healthy people (QVP 1885:III,495). Such a statement needed to be qualified; at that time smallpox was the only disease with a specific preventive. Nevertheless, governments and shipping companies were expected to provide medical care and enforce proven preventive measures such as immigrant inspection at embarkation and thorough sanitation en route.

By and large, no accusing finger could be pointed at the Queensland authorities. They soon recognized that the law guaranteed only minimal standards, and introduced more rigorous regulations, remunerated passenger personnel according to the numbers landed alive, and strictly supervised every phase of the system from recruitment and selection, through the voyage to arrival and employment. It is not surprising, therefore, to find an almost complete account of Queensland immigration among extant colonial records. In addition to official publications, some 90 per cent of the passenger lists, a mass of correspondence, and reports by health officers, immigration agents and ship-surgeons have survived. These, together with maritime and colonial records held in Britain, have allowed a detailed analysis of morbidity, births, deaths and the causes of death at sea for Queensland immigrants between 1860 and 1900. The vast travelling public also left a record of their experiences; diaries, journals and letters provide further insights into conditions and reactions during the voyage. While the authorities clearly outlined what they considered as essential for a safe, healthy and disciplined passage, immigrants did not always agree. For them, the process meant being 'uprooted . . . [and] compelled to adjust old habits and assumptions to new circumstances' (Crawford 1970:13).

The term 'healthy immigrants' extended beyond the merely physical to include the whole person. It was not enough that future colonists be young, robust and accustomed to physical labour, or that they were provided with a clean environment, good food and medical attention in transit. Character screening, discipline, mental and moral improvement were also integral aspects of a health-care programme designed to ensure that new arrivals not only landed alive and well, but were able to meet the challenges and demands of colonial life. Inevitably, weaknesses appeared in the system and resulted in sickness, death and disruption at sea, and the introduction of 'unsuitable' colonists. Such weaknesses also revealed the complex interrelationship of legislation and administrative policies, the nature and flow of emigration, shipping arrangements and technological advances, medical practice, passenger reactions, and circumstances beyond human control. This study examines each of these variables, its implications and effects, in order to determine how they influenced the Queensland immigrant health-care policy, and whether or not the programme's objectives were realized. Did the government succeed in its efforts to secure healthy and respectable colonists for the progressive development of this remote outpost of the British Empire?

The study also raises, and partly addresses, wider questions. How did the health of Queensland immigrants in transit compare with that of the landed populations from which they derived or into which they were absorbed? Was their record on a par with, better, or worse than that of other migratory populations during a similar period? Many descriptive accounts and analyses of nineteenth century voluntary migration, including its medical aspects, have been written (see, for example, Charlwood 1981, Coleman 1972 and Erickson 1976), yet none of these provides a critical and quantitative evaluation of passenger health. The study endeavours to deal with this issue, at least at an exploratory level. In the first place, it furnishes comprehensive and definitive 'vital statistics' for the Queensland immigration; second, it relates these statistics to comparable records for England and Wales, and the colony; and third, it compares results for the colonial immigration with those for the total United Kingdom emigration and the merchant marine during the second half of the last century. Despite the methodological and statistical problems that surfaced, this dovetailing of maritime medicine with demography has, I believe, added another dimension to migration studies and extended the scope of comparative and colonial history.

Finally, as the over-all picture of Queensland immigration emerged, it became clear that travel conditions, contrary to popular impressions of nineteenth-century migration, were far from 'frightful'. Certainly evidence from the first half of the century supports such impressions; but for one segment of the migratory public after 1850, life at sea was, on the whole, a safe, healthy and tolerable experience.

Note to readers: All quotes in the text are given *verbatim*, including spelling and punctuation errors.

Rights of Passage

GOVERNMENT POLICY

British aspirations, ideals and methods had a profound influence on colonial Queensland's development. Despite the distance, growing self-sufficiency and a non-European environment, the 'double attachment' to the mother country and the adopted land was strong (see Ward 1966:110). According to a nineteenth-century Antipodean historian, once Britons discovered a flair for colonization, they worked through the problems 'rather by mere instinctive doggedness in the right direction than by close attention to rules or the guidance of theorizing philosophers' (Jose 1901:v). This empirical approach, and the belief in progress,[1] shaped colonial policies. The land also moulded attitudes. Obsessed with its development, Queenslanders displayed a frontier mentality and a marked national identity. Moreover, immigrants outnumbered the native-born for almost the entire colonial period. In this pioneer community, aggressiveness and fear, recklessness and conservatism were all too often reflected in politics and policies (see Crawford 1970:59).

During the second half of the nineteenth century Britain dominated the world scene; war made no demands on her resources, free trade encouraged industrial growth and imperial expansion, and conditions for the labouring classes improved. But this apparent strength and stability had to be maintained in the face of Germany's emergence as an industrial, colonizing nation, French and Russian activities in the Pacific, and at home, an ever-increasing population which threatened to realize the worst Malthusian predictions. 'The British are . . . of necessity an emigrating people', Queensland's Registrar-General observed as he recorded that, in 1881, an estimated 931 persons were added daily to the United Kingdom (QVP 1882:1,869). The death rate was also decreasing as a result of public health reform and a steady rise in the standard of living which, in turn, raised the level of awareness concerning the distribution of property and labour.

In the early decades of the century the decision to emigrate tended to be a last resort, the only escape from an intolerable situation; but increasingly it became the route to a better, independent life which offered a just reward for labour and dimmed the spectre of poverty. Moreover, many with capital, however limited, were attracted by investment possibilities and the opportunity for a fresh start. Nor were those who made the decision impeded by the imperial government; emigration solved the problem of excess population, provided a safety-valve for discontented workers and helped to develop her colonies. Although the question of financing colonization and emigration received considerable attention, the British authorities maintained a policy of non-fiscal involvement, apart from a few instances of assistance for the parish poor. In an age of *laissez-faire* it was believed that state aid impeded self-help and private enterprise.[2] The colonies did not object to this attitude; it left them free to select and organize immigration according to their own terms.

Early policy makers knew exactly the type of colonist they wanted for Queensland. This colonist was not to be drawn from the 'convicted' or 'damaged' segments of Britain's population. 'If we give away our land' they asserted, 'we have the right to choose to whom we should give it' (QPD 1865:II,648). They even refused land grants to discharged naval and military officers since the records had shown that these officers were, by their previous training and life-style, poorly prepared for the demands of pioneer life (CO 386/76: 322–25, 328). In 1870 and again in 1886, when the British parliament considered a state-aid programme for removing the 'deserving poor' to the colonies, Queensland's Agent-General made it clear that his government would be unlikely to enter into any scheme which proposed settling Crown land with unwanted Britons, and which denied them the final control (see QVP 1871:896–97 and 1886:II,917). Similarly, attempts by private organizations to establish colonization schemes failed largely because of the government's fear that once selection was taken out of their hands, an undesirable population would be introduced. Assisted passages were also refused to anyone aided by guardians of the poor or public charities. However, by the close of the century when the quality of new arrivals had greatly improved, immigration policy was influenced as much by a growing sense of Empire solidarity as the necessity for continued progress and control.

Following the cessation of the Napoleonic Wars in 1815 emigration from Britain increased dramatically, and government involvement at the legislative level became necessary to control abuses. Such moves were linked with the development of British dominions overseas. In 1840 the Colonial Land and Emigration Commission was established to advise and assist the home government in matters relating to colonial policy and Crown land sales (a portion of the income from these was appropriated for immigration purposes) and to supervise the transfer of indentured or coolie labour.[3] In addition, the Commissioners organized emigration on behalf of the colonial authorities, disseminated relevant information and administered the passenger acts, a function which was assumed by the Board of Trade in 1872. As the colonies became self-governing, the need for the Commission diminished, and it finally wound up operations in 1878. But the lack of a central agency for coordinating colonial publicity was keenly felt, and the Emigrants' Information Office opened in London in 1886; it did an excellent job with its paltry subsidy. Thus, in order to control the emigrant trade, the imperial government, despite its parsimony, had to intervene. By the time Queensland entered the market in 1860, the administrative machinery was not only fully operational, but it was possible to benefit from the experience of the older Australian colonies. The new colony accepted the financial responsibility for immigration, and then began formulating a policy that utilized the current organization to suit its particular requirements.

Queensland's initial needs were material rather than political since separation from New South Wales had automatically bestowed responsible, representative government and given its citizens 'the most complete liberty to manage their own affairs' (La Meslée 1883:171). Her new leaders, however, were singularly unprepared for the demands of government; both the first governor and premier (he served as colonial secretary) were young and newly arrived from England; the first elected assembly were 'a band of enthusiastic amateurs' (Morrison 1966:21).[4] These leaders faced the formidable task of developing a land mass of 668,497 square miles, largely unexplored, half lying in the tropics, and bounded on the north and east by a 2,500 mile coastline (see Map A). The white population numbered one to every 22 square miles and was concentrated in the deep south-east in and around Brisbane, the colony's administrative centre. The treasury was empty. But Queensland was 'blessed with a healthy climate' and the future seemed bright; 'there was money to be made by the enterprising' (Newell and White 1967:60).

The vast tracts of unalienated Crown land provided the primary source of colonial revenue and a gilt-edged security for capital investment. Land-related policies, therefore, allowed governments 'an unusually energetic role in economic and social affairs' (Blainey 1968:166-67), yet they had to cope with the delicate task of balancing land, labour and capital. This task began with the arrival of the first convicts at Sydney Cove in 1788. As long as Australia remained a penal settlement, the home government guaranteed a regular workforce and funding. Then a trickle of free settlers started to arrive after 1815; they spread beyond the prison walls, developing the land with convict labour. Distance, however, was the great barrier to voluntary immigration; few could afford the fare. Colonial theorizers like Edward Gibbon Wakefield pondered the problem and advocated land inducements for settlers with capital; from the revenue it would be possible to bring in free, but carefully selected, labourers (see Wakefield 1829). Within a few years New South Wales 'went into the business of immigration in no half-hearted fashion' (Coghlan 1918:226), and introduced a system whereby emigrants were chosen for their potential as useful colonists, subsidized, and sent out in government-chartered vessels under the care of a Royal Navy surgeon. A bounty scheme soon followed, but generated so much scandal that, as soon as the Emigration Commission was established, it assumed supervision of the entire Australian migration. However, the colonial governments continued to subsidize the various schemes – assisted, free, bounty and remittance (settled colonists could nominate and introduce friends and relatives) as well as land grants for employers willing to defray the cost of importing labour.

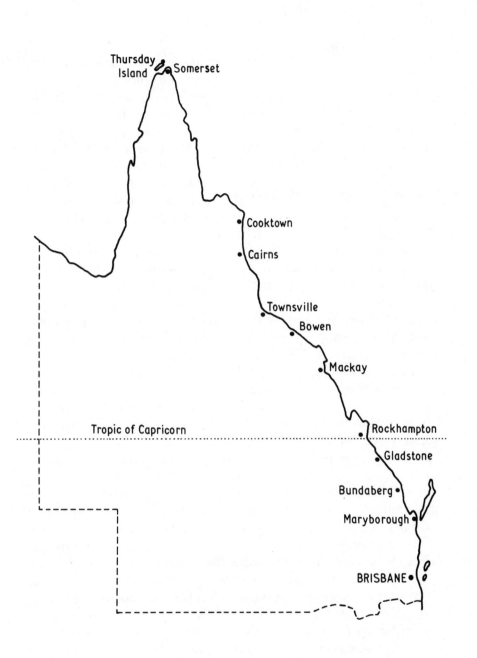

Map A Queensland ports

By the time Queensland drew up its first immigration policy, these schemes had been well tested. The home government maintained that the colonies ought to be grateful for any labour they received, but it was soon found that only selected immigrants and those with capital proved the most suitable. Consequently, most of the voluntary settlers before the gold rush of the early 1850s were English, middle-class farmers and merchants, the class most likely 'to lay the foundations of a solid economic and social organism' (Madgwick 1966:58). Even so, as the number of subsidized immigrants multiplied, inconsistencies and abuses in the system became apparent. Eligibility criteria had to be enforced, conditions of travel improved and steps taken to correct the male–female imbalance. The initial preponderance of single men not only exacerbated problems that were the natural consequence of a convict society, but increased the need for single, morally sound women.[5] Queensland recognized these difficulties and the necessity for such safeguards, but sometimes ignored them, so great was the demand for labour.

This demand had existed from the time the Moreton Bay district was opened to free settlers in 1840. Sixteen years earlier a penal settlement for 'double-dyed' (twice-convicted) felons had been established near Moreton Bay on the banks of the Brisbane River, 600 miles north of Sydney. With the closing of the settlement, the port became available and pastoralists and squatters, seeking new sheep-grazing country, began pushing northward in the wake of explorers. This rapid expansion raised an immediate cry for cheap, suitable labour. The introduction of Chinese and Indian coolies did not meet the need, and opposition from the southern colonies blocked attempts to renew transportation. Most Australians wanted to bury the past and create a future based on social solidarity and acceptability. Of necessity, this involved the voluntary immigration of Anglo-Saxons (see Lewis 1973:1 ff). Northern developers, therefore, had to rely on workers from the south. Then in 1848–49 voluntary immigrants began to arrive in Moreton Bay direct from the United Kingdom largely through the efforts of John Dunmore Lang, a Scottish cleric and an energetic colonizer. In 1838 he had brought in German missionaries, the first free settlers to the district, to evangelize the aborigines. Other Germans followed and quickly adapted to the land. Convinced that these northern settlements should be responsible for their own management, Lang campaigned vigorously for their separation from New South Wales, and determined to populate the new creation with sturdy, independent Protestants to counter-balance the Irish Catholic influx after the 1846–47 potato famine. The first of the three vessels chartered by him reached Moreton Bay from Scotland just two weeks after the arrival of the first shipment of government-subsidized immigrants organized by the Emigration Commissioners.

Northern development and the separation movement suffered a temporary set-back with the discovery of gold in south-east Australia in 1851–52. Overnight the country's image changed. Settlers flocked to her shores; and newly-gained financial independence paved the way for responsible government. Although Australia's population doubled, many gold seekers, once the fever subsided, drifted into the towns and showed little inclination to develop the land. New South Wales had to maintain state-aided, selective immigration. A steady trickle of these new colonists reached Moreton Bay but they by no means met the labour needs of the north. The only way to improve the situation was through separation and self-government. Spurred on by the discovery of gold at Canoona (near Rockhampton) in 1858, Queensland finally came into existence the following year. Even at its inception the colony was highly decentralized, with regional rivalry firmly entrenched and the belief in progress 'inseparably attached to the "moving frontier"' (Fitzgerald 1982:113). The land waited to be developed and labour had to be recruited.

Within six weeks of the colony's founding the premier announced that immigration would continue under the remittance regulations then in force for New South Wales. A few days later similar provisions allowed naturalized Queenslanders to introduce friends and relatives from Europe (QGG 1860,1:36,78–9). New arrivals under this scheme were subsidized and therefore had to meet certain eligibility criteria and travel under prescribed conditions. The premier also sent instructions to the Emigration Commissioners to continue direct shipments to Moreton Bay; but they, knowing nothing of the new arrangements, decided to forward Queensland immigrants to Sydney until advised otherwise. During the first year only one shipment reached the colony.[6] Communication problems, the inevitable result of Queensland's size and distance from the motherland, had to be tackled at once.

The colony had few paved roads, no telegraph system, no railways, only a fortnightly mail service with Sydney, and even less frequent contact between her towns and settlements. Although an occasional vessel from overseas kept Queenslanders in touch with the outside world, none of the seaports could accommodate a laden ship of 1,000 tons. Then inland exploration surged ahead, a hydrographic survey of the coast revealed harbours further north, though few navigable rivers, and in 1861 Brisbane and Sydney (the final destination of mail packets) were linked by telegraph and the sod for the first Queensland railway was turned.

From the outset railways were considered almost as vital for land development as immigration. All three – 'the trinity of hope' – were combined in a capital-absorbing network.[7] But railways, rather than opening up new areas, generally provided an outlet for established settlements, strengthened separatist tendencies, and emphasized regional differences. Three main lines were built inland from Brisbane, Rockhampton and Townsville and not joined along the coast until after 1901. The threat of triple division hung like a cloud over the colonial period. As Brisbane and the surrounding districts had struggled for independence in the 1850s, the central region with its major outlet at Rockhampton agitated for separation from southern Queensland in the 1870s, and during the last two decades of the century, a similar movement developed in the north with its centre in Townsville. Inter-regional rivalry was the product of many factors – climate, Queensland's size, the acentric position of Brisbane, the lack of communication facilities in the early years, the question of coloured labour and, perhaps most important, adherence to a British model of development. Northerners continually demanded labour and complained about the unfair distribution of immigrants, but the majority of new arrivals preferred to land in Brisbane where living conditions were more attractive; as one proceeded up the coast, the towns diminished in 'size and civilization' (Acton 1889).

Neither the railways nor the land policies achieved the desired results, yet successive governments pursued the original plans for development. Early leaders saw Queensland as 'a great property to be developed along sound business lines for the benefit of the colonists and prosperity' (Farnfield 1974:12). This development, despite the obvious differences of terrain and climate, was conceived in terms of the English yeoman farmer. The authorities seemed to ignore the pattern of pastoral occupation that had opened up Australia, and the fact that few areas in the colony, apart from the coastal lands, were suitable for agriculture. The thrust of legislation was to make land available for the 'small man' and inaccessible to the wealthy pastoralist (Shaw 1961:139). Not surprisingly, a 'class contest for land' developed (see Clark 1978:167). Moreover, new arrivals were often daunted by the prospect of going 'up country'; this was an untamed land, quite unlike anything they knew 'back home'. Pioneers needed experience, fortitude and good health.

Yet land settlement depended on immigration. Principles outlined by the Governor in his opening speech to the first parliament in May 1860 remained unchanged for the next thirty years; the colony's success, he declared, could be assured by a liberal land policy which had 'the effect of directing hither a permanent stream of immigration of the most desirable character', at minimal cost to the treasury (QGG 1860, 1:187–88). Immediately £5,000 was voted to cover expenses incurred by the Emigration Commissioners in despatching remittance immigrants and providing free passages for selected domestic servants, farm labourers and shepherds urgently needed in the colony. Since intercolonial arrivals exacerbated the male–female discrepancy, the only way to reverse this 'serious social evil' was to increase the European female immigration. The demand for 'respectable' single women, willing to undertake menial work, remained 'intense and constant' (ECR 1865:16). According to Blainey (1968:170), free fares for domestic servants acted as a 'vital bribe' to entice women to a man's land and boost the natural increase.

In August 1860 a select committee was appointed to review existing schemes for introducing colonists and recommend the 'best mode of inducing a cheap, healthy, and continuous flow of immigration to the Colony' (QVP 1860:635). Lang's views on developing Queensland by populating it with 'an industrious and virtuous' people and attracting capitalists as employers greatly influenced the deliberations of the committee (see COL/A10:60–2481). Their proposals were embodied in the Crown Lands Alienation Act of September 1860 (QS 24 Vic. no. 15). This provided for a land-order system of immigration which eliminated the need for government subsidy except for domestic servants.[8] It was a neat system, designed to maximize the colony's primary resource, minimize costs and augment the population. To secure its efficient working, Henry Jordan, one of the principal framers, resigned his seat in the Legislative Assembly and took up appointment in London early in 1861 as Emigration Commissioner for the colony, with instructions to promote the 'many advantages offered by Queensland' and supervise the selection and despatch of land-order immigrants (QVP 1860:636).[9] At the receiving end, an immigration agent and Board were appointed. The latter had no judicial functions; it inquired into alleged breaches of the law and the regulations, and advised the government. Thus, within a year of formal separation, the new colony had created its own immigration policy and the necessary machinery for administering it.

New immigration regulations came into effect on 1 January, 1861 and cancelled previous systems, but they retained conditional clauses relating to age, and made provision for arrangements similar to those which applied on the Commissioners' vessels. However, before the end of the year the system had been modified. In the first place, land orders were made available to continental immigrants and John Heussler was sent to Germany to conduct this emigration;[10] second, the remittance system was reinstated, with the Commissioners undertaking responsibility for this scheme; and third, because of abuses, colonial employers were no longer allowed to recruit labour through private agencies in England. The authorities soon realized that they had to keep a tight control over all aspects of immigration for it to succeed.

In London, Jordan's vigorous campaigning on behalf of Queensland quickly put the new colony on the map. Believing that the land-order system could be fully effective only if it was coordinated under one agency, he signed a contract with the directors of the famous Black Ball Line. They agreed to lay on first-class vessels to sail direct to any port in the colony designated by the government, abide by the conditions of travel stipulated in the regulations, and provide a free passage for any emigrant who forfeited his land order to the shippers. In return, they required that a certain proportion of the passengers on each vessel despatched under this agreement pay the full fare and be accepted unconditionally, without any eligibility screening, by the Black Ball agents. However, all 'free' passengers were screened by

Jordan: he was determined that no undesirable or refuse population should reach Queensland's shores. Others also took advantage of the land-order system and made similar arrangements, but
were not always as careful with the selection of immigrants or
provisions for the voyage. The Roman Catholic Bishop of
Brisbane, under the auspices of the Queensland Immigration
Society, introduced several shipments of distressed Irish
peasants,[11] and a private entrepreneur despatched a vessel from
Scotland. Jordan himself, under pressure from charitable concerns
and with the approval of the colonial government, sent out many
hundreds of unemployed and destitute cotton operatives and their
families, the majority of whom reached Queensland in 1863. The
American Civil War, by cutting off cotton supplies to the English
mills, diverted the attention of would-be emigrants to the new
colony where cotton cultivation was receiving much publicity and
encouragement.

Cotton growing raised the whole issue of coloured labour.
Since it was firmly believed that white people found it difficult to
survive, let alone work effectively in the tropics, Queensland's
leaders favoured coolie labour to develop the north. This proposal
was strongly resisted by many who saw such labour as 'diametri-
cally opposed' to the colony's best interests.[12] Nevertheless,
Polynesians (known as Kanakas) were brought in from the Pacific
Islands under private contract to work on the cotton plantations.
When these declined an increasing number of Islanders were
absorbed into the rapidly expanding sugar industry. Cane
growing began near Brisbane but moved to more suitable
northern coastlands. By the 1880s sugar had become a major
export and the peopling of the tropics 'a subject of lively
controversy' (see Bolton 1963:vii). Gradually it was conceded that
Europeans could tolerate living and working in these northern
areas; the 'myth' eroded as medical science revealed that disease
control rather than the climate was the problem. In Queensland's
multi-racial society, coloured labour was regarded as 'a merely
temporary expedient' (QGG 1885,36:947–48), the Chinese were
treated as hostile invaders, and the aborigines were either ignored
or exterminated. The colony, despite its climate and location, was
to be a white man's land with immigration directed towards
introducing a suitable European, and predominantly British,
population.

As the number of new arrivals rapidly increased, the government restricted land orders to those who travelled direct from Europe, placed the entire United Kingdom component under Jordan's supervision, and included a new category of assisted immigrants.[13] But there were problems; questions were being asked about the quality of the immigration. When the Colonial Secretary visited England towards the end of 1862, he investigated both Jordan's and the Commissioners' methods of operation. His preference for the latter recognized their years of experience but overlooked the fact that they conducted the smaller and less complicated remittance system. In spite of all Jordan's precautions and efforts to select 'the best class of honest, industrious, hard-working men, of good character and provident habits' (QVP 1863:II,446), each shipload arrived with a proportion of less than desirable colonists. It seemed all too easy to circumvent the selection procedure or use the system as a cheap route to the southern colonies. There were also reports of frightful conditions and a high mortality on some Black Ball ships. Finally, a large-scale trafficking in land orders developed, the expected influx of those with capital did not materialize, and the loss of land revenue at a time when finance was urgently needed for public works proved a serious handicap to colonial development.

Following the Colonial Secretary's return to Queensland, a select committee was appointed in April, 1863 to investigate the working of the land-order system, the questionable activities of Bishop Quinn's Society, and a petition from German colonists for another agent to replace Heussler who had resigned the previous year, leaving the selection of immigrants in the hands of the Hamburg shippers. A change of government prevented recommendations being implemented, but a new select committee, like its predecessor, concluded that land and immigration policies should remain 'closely integrated', and the land-order system ought to be trimmed rather than cancelled since the demand for labour seemed 'insatiable'. Accordingly, new regulations came into force on 1 January, 1864. These introduced a quota system for all government immigrants from Great Britain based on the relative populations of England, Scotland and Ireland and restricted the Continental immigration to remittance passengers. Thirty-acre land grants were offered to cabin and intermediate travellers while steerage full-payers received a non-transferable

£18 order. All steerage passengers (subsidized or full-paying) had to submit to selection, provisions for the voyage remained, and a number of vessels had to be despatched to the northern ports. A few weeks later the Colonial Secretary wrote to Jordan informing him that these new restrictions were designed to bring to a close the land-order system. Jordan immediately sailed for the colony and resigned in May 1864. Trying to implement a policy 12,000 miles from base, frequent changes and increasing restrictions in the regulations, reports of appalling conditions at sea and frustrated expectations on arrival, complaints about 'ineligible' immigrants and a falling off in British emigration, jeopardized the system for which he had worked with 'excessive, continuous, unremitting toil' (QVP 1864:II, 1018).

A select committee decided that the crisis had arisen owing to a failure in communication, over-enthusiasm, inexperience, difficulties with supervision, and indeed, the novelty of the whole operation. Yet many conceded that the land-order system had worked; a speech in the Assembly in July 1864 recorded that whereas 'we had scarcely enough labour to rub along with; now, we have a steady influx of population' (QPD 1864:I, 196). Jordan was exonerated, reinstated and returned to London as the Agent-General for Emigration with a mandate to implement the provisions of the first Immigration Act passed in September 1864 (QS 28 Vic. no. 17). This included the principle features of previous regulations, provided stricter controls on land orders and immigrant occupation categories, and added a penalty clause for fraud. However, no European agent was appointed, the Commissioners continued their limited operations, and the majority of immigrants continued to arrive under the land-order system. Unable to suggest a viable alternative, Queensland's leaders believed that the legislation, with its inbuilt safeguards, would attract the desired population.

As the first fruits of development appeared, the government forged ahead in an orgy of public spending with loans raised in London. Throughout 1865 they lifted restrictions on both the quantity and quality of immigrants in order to induce navvies and labourers of every description to take up employment in the colony. Vessels arrived groaning with human cargo and railway plant. Before long the authorities were disturbed by frequent complaints of defective shipboard arrangements, increasing mortality at sea and dreadful conditions on arrival, as well as the 'refuse class' who had been introduced at great expense to the treasury and were filling Queensland's gaols and asylums.[14] The Continental immigration also came under censure. Then hints of a recession in Britain filtered through, unemployment in the colony grew, and new arrivals drifted south looking for work. Yet the colony began 1866 confident of continued growth. When news of the collapse of the London loan market reached Brisbane, it came as a tremendous shock.

Both immigration and public spending were suspended in September and Jordan was recalled with instructions to close the London office. However, notification of his resignation was already on its way; his position had become increasingly untenable as a result of administrative changes and interference from Brisbane, confusion over the two modes of emigration and escalating complaints about the cost and conduct of the land-order system. It is not surprising, given the difficulties with distance and communication, the worsening recession in Britain, growing unemployment and, not least, the effect of climate, that the colony came to a standstill. Indeed, the climate played a vital role in the boom–bust cycles of colonial development. These swung from reckless overspending to a cautious recovery which attempted to make good the losses and consolidate previous gains. At first the land seemed to be bursting with untapped potential, but the brutal effect of drought, cyclones and floods on a primary-producing economy still had to be taken into account. Space and the tropics had been reckoned with but not the problem of coping with an under- or over-supply of water (see Jones 1931:288–95). As exploration pushed north and west, hopes of finding an inland sea and good grain-producing areas receded; and what looked like sheep-grazing country often proved more suited to cattle. Everything thrived in 'good times', but the situation could change dramatically; 'taming the land and its resources, in the name of progress, would [prove] a bitter and terrible struggle' (Fitzgerald 1982:53).

The events of 1866 dealt a severe blow. Yet within twelve months signs of recovery, stimulated by the discovery of gold one hundred miles north of Brisbane, became apparent and optimism revived. Queensland's leaders proceeded cautiously; they decided to retain the London office, provide passages for immigrants already selected and continue the offer of land orders to full-paying passengers. During the post-mortem period, the immigration policy was thoroughly overhauled. Although its success in augmenting the population could not be denied, 'the small farmer remained conspicuous by his absence' (Shaw 1961:138). Nevertheless, the belief persisted that colonial progress depended on a class of small property holders to develop the land, curb the squatters' advance and employ labour: 'Parliament . . . [went] back to the land, even if no one else did' (Shaw 1961:139). And so the second round of immigration began with the offer of liberal inducements, in the form of 'homestead grants', under the Crown Lands Alienation Act of 1868 (QS 31 Vic. no. 46). The acting agent in London was instructed to despatch monthly vessels with full-paying and remittance passengers, school teachers and a limited number of subsidized domestic servants and farm labourers.

In February, 1868 a select committee recommended the full-scale resumption of immigration, but a change of government prevented the necessary legislation reaching the statute books until September, 1869 (QS 33 Vic. no. 9). The new act was a carefully prescribed measure; it repealed previous legislation and allowed the government full control over every aspect of immigration. Full-payers were offered non-transferable land orders with a residency clause attached, provision was made for other categories to repay their fare, the quota system was retained, and a penalty clause covered violations of the regulations during the voyage. The act also provided for an immigration board at each Queensland port and the establishment of depots to receive new arrivals, facilitate their employment and disseminate information. European immigration was resumed with the appointment of an agent resident in Germany and responsible to the new Agent-General who reached London early in 1870. He was expected to supervise the entire emigration to Queensland and publicize the colony, concentrating his efforts particularly in the agricultural districts. As the new decade dawned, policy makers prepared for another wave of development, but this time it would be carefully monitored and controlled. There was also the prospect in the near future of improved communication facilities between London and Brisbane.[15] In their grand isolation, however, they could not anticipate the effect of their policies or of events beyond their control.

By the time the colony found its feet, the full impact of the 1866 crisis was only being felt in Britain. The appeal of Queensland as a brave, new country had been tarnished, and the confidence of intending immigrants and investors badly shaken. It was not restored either by continuing reports of a trying climate, difficulties settling the land and limited inducements offered under the new legislation. Few farm labourers could afford the required £1 deposit, let alone contribute towards the passage. For those able to pay the full fare, the non-transferable land order was of little value if they had no intention of taking up the land. Besides, conditions for the average rural worker in Britain had recently improved; and for the small capitalist, the larger land grants, shorter distance and cheaper travel made emigration to North America decidedly more attractive. On the Continent, however, initial response to the efforts of Queensland's agent was encouraging; a shipping contract secured the regular despatch of vessels from Hamburg. Interest also extended to southern Germany, Denmark and Scandinavia, Switzerland and northern Italy where earlier attempts to attract silk growers to Queensland had aborted. Recruiting agents were appointed in these areas.

Unfortunately the sailing of the first vessel from Hamburg coincided with the outbreak of the Franco-Prussian war in mid-1870. Young men of the class most sought after by the colony were conscripted, and finding an alternative port after the blockade of the Elbe proved impossible. Neither did the situation improve when hostilities ceased; the new German government did not favour emigration, was wary of schemes involving indented labour, and not only made it extremely difficult for foreign agents to recruit in the country but threatened to expel them. Despite these difficulties, the Queensland authorities were loathe to withdraw their operations since European immigrants generally adapted well to the land and proved 'useful and valuable colonists' (QVP 1875:II,608). Although the agency had to be closed in January, 1874, free passages to the colony were made available to all those who could afford the fare from Europe to an English port. Continued pressure to resume direct travel led to the appointment of another agent in 1875. He was able to effect the necessary arrangements through an authorized German emigration agent and shipping firm, and extend recruitment to other Continental countries. The Queensland government was encouraged to persevere (see QVP 1877:II,883–87), and for the next three and a half years, immigrants sailed direct to the colony from Hamburg.

Also in the early 1870s problems arose with the British emigration. The full extent of conditions back home took some time to register with the colonial authorities; immigration recovered slowly and was difficult to control. The Agent-General was charged with having failed to carry out his commission and resigned in 1871, accusing the government of administrative interference and a 'niggerdly attitude' (QVP 1871–72:711). The entire system was again thoroughly investigated and, in the following year, three new pieces of land-labour legislation appeared. The new Immigration Act (QS 36 Vic. no. 5), though cautious and conservative, was more tempered than its predecessor and allowed greater flexibility in its execution; the land laws offered improved benefits for the selector. This legislative triad was intended to provide for long-range, coordinated development; but the needed boost for immigration came primarily from the discovery of rich gold fields in the north of the colony in 1872–73, and from agricultural unrest in England. Although gold seekers poured into Queensland, the government found it necessary to continue subsidizing new arrivals willing to work on the land. However, as the economy improved, they offered further inducements and lifted certain eligibility restrictions under an amending land order act in 1874 (QS 38 Vic. no. 8). But family-size limits had to be quickly restored owing to an unduly high death rate on vessels carrying large numbers of children;[16] the introduction of navvies for a revived public works programme was suspended for the same reason; and the system remained riddled with abuses. It was therefore decided to abolish land orders altogether and rely on a liberal land grant policy to attract colonists with capital. The new 1875 statute (QS 39 Vic. no. 1) also lowered remittance fees, cancelled outstanding passage-money repayments, and retained assistance for selected classes of immigrants. Despite signs of another recession, the government felt compelled to pour in aid to keep up a steady influx to the colony.

The mini-boom conditions of 1872–75 were only temporary. Thousands of Chinese had been attracted to the gold fields and as the yield tapered off, they looked for other work. At the same time an increasing number of Kanakas and immigrants, many of them single men, were landed at the northern ports to work on the sugar plantations. When the crop failed at the end of 1875, unemployment rose sharply and public works programmes had to be hastily organized. The situation was further complicated by the fact that established employers preferred 'old chums' and married couples without children. Immigration itself was dogged with difficulties; reports, sometimes exaggerated, of scandalous arrangements on vessels and of the 'worst possible description' of new arrivals became more frequent, and improved conditions in the United Kingdom and competition from other colonies reduced the reservoir of suitable candidates. Then during 1875, evidence of long-standing corruption and malpractice in Queensland's London office came to light. The government struggled unsuccessfully to resolve these problems. Inefficiency in both London and Brisbane and a lack of coordination gave rise to allegations of a costly system that introduced only inferior people. London maintained that constant changes in the regulations confused and deterred would-be immigrants, while Brisbane pointed out that loopholes in the selection procedure permitted abuses and increased the number of those who could not or did not intend to work on the land.

Although communication links had improved, the distance still made it difficult to supervise the system as a whole. Travelling conditions remained less than satisfactory, criticism was levelled at the mode of despatch and reception of immigrants, and many ships arrived during the hottest and most unhealthy months at ports where the labour demand was least. Kanakas glutted the market and new arrivals had to be given aid or transferred to areas where employment was available. It seemed absurd that the government should grant relief while subsidizing immigration. As the familiar pattern of falling revenue and rising unemployment emerged and the spectre of drought crept over the land, the colony once again found itself in the grip of depression; but this time it was not as dramatic or severe. Continental immigration was the first to be terminated, in January, 1879, followed two months later by the closure of operations in London. The authorities, however, had the situation under control and within a few weeks issued directions for 'improving the quality of emigration' (see QVP 1879:II, 172–73). These incorporated a comprehensive range of safeguards to prevent abuses and the introduction and maintenance, at public expense, of a class 'regarded as a very questionable benefit to the community' (QVP 1879:II,172). Strict elegibility criteria were outlined together with detailed arrangements for departure and the voyage. Before the close of the year, immigration had been resumed and the Agent-General's office reorganized. Compared with the 1866 crisis, recovery proceeded more rapidly and less cautiously after 1879; the colony grew and within a few years had been overtaken by the 'intellectually drunken conception of . . . "illimitable" resources' (Fitzpatrick 1969: xxviii).

The year 1880 marked an important milestone for Queensland immigration; the authorities signed a contract with the British India Steam Navigation Company for the conveyance of mails and full-paying passengers to the colony via the Suez Canal and the Torres Straits. This arrangement soon extended to include subsidized immigrants. Also that year the remittance scheme was revived and as prosperity returned, more free and assisted passages became available for selected domestic servants and farm workers. Continental nominees were offered free travel from England in government vessels. Although European agents were appointed, plans to re-establish direct immigration failed. By the time the new and decidedly liberal immigration act reached the statute books in 1882 (QS 46 Vic. no. 7), conditions for its operation could only be described as favourable. Hints of a recession in the United Kingdom coincided with reports that a 'Mountain of Gold' had been discovered in central Queensland and that labour was urgently needed. The shorter voyage and better shipping accommodation were already attracting 'a more eligible class', cable linkage between London and Brisbane effectively reduced the distance and allowed greater control over immigration, and the new land laws offered excellent inducements. The Agent-General was instructed to sent as many suitable immigrants as were forthcoming.

It was hoped that these positive factors, and more particularly the bounty system made possible under Clause 17 of the 1882 Act, would finally achieve the desired results for immigration. The object of the scheme was 'to obtain a class of emigrants, who by industry and frugality, [had] earned and saved a portion of their passage money' (QVP 1884:II,619). Only applicants of 'good fame' who had not previously resided in Australia and intended to settle permanently in Queensland were accepted. But as ever, abuses soon crept in and steps had to be taken to prevent agencies and philanthropic societies using the scheme to off-load 'imbeciles, criminals, and other objectionable characters' on the colony (QVP 1883–84:1380). The other subsidized classes still had to submit to selection, but no repayments were required and the Agent-General was authorized to reimburse pre-embarkation expenses for 'deserving cases'. All who travelled in government vessels were guaranteed full protection and half the new arrivals had to be landed at the northern ports. Penalty clauses relating to residence, impersonation and fraud were also included. The 1882 act repealed previous legislation and remained in force for almost forty years; government policy had finally achieved a measure of maturity and stability.

Queensland in the early 1880s attracted much attention, and its reputation as 'the favourite colony for immigrants' stimulated boom conditions. Trade increased, government loans were floated, and the vast spending on public works and immigration created an artificial prosperity. The number of new arrivals reached a record level in 1883, and at one point the influx was so great they could not be absorbed. The Agent-General had to cancel additional vessels, suspend the services of the emigration lecturers, and refuse all new applicants until the pressure was relieved. Successive reductions of subsidized immigrants were ordered; but the bounty passengers, despite difficulties with the scheme, continued to be encouraged in the belief that they represented the class most needed in the colony and were introduced at minimal cost to the treasury. When a new government took office in November, 1883, it found the immigration loan not only exhausted but overdrawn, and the economy resting on a very shaky foundation; 'over-optimism [had] led to over-expansion' (Shaw 1961:168).

Yet nothing could alter the deep-rooted conviction of Queensland's leaders, whatever their political persuasion, that land-linked immigration was vital to the colony's progress. The Crown Lands Act of 1884 offered extremely liberal inducements, and an amending immigration act of the same year allowed increased concessions for indentured labour to cope with the threatened cessation of the Kanaka trade. Sugar growers suggested replacing the Islanders with Europeans and the authorities agreed that 'Under the peculiarly favourable circumstances of the Queensland climate European labourers are physically able and will, if properly treated, be found willing to do all the necessary field labour in connection with this industry' (QGG 1885,36:947–48). In 1885 a Continental agent was appointed to recruit workers, but he met with such opposition that he was soon recalled. However, the Queensland and Italian governments finally worked out an agreement for indentured labourers. The continuing importance of immigration was further underscored by the four-year appointment of a new Agent-General who, while holding office, retained his seat in the colony's Upper House.

Although a steady stream of new arrivals reached Queensland, economic forebodings and irregularities in the system resulted in a further amendment to the legislation in 1886 (QS 50 Vic. no. 8). This stepped up government intervention, restricted remittance and indentured immigrants, and abolished the bounty scheme which, while successfully boosting the population, had, instead of increasing the rural landowner sector as intended, augmented the urban business class. All attempts to implement the land development policy seemed to abort, including the reintroduction of land orders in 1886; this provision mostly benefited steerage travellers. Then all classes of full-paying passengers began falling off as the recession became entrenched in Britain and the colony. The termination of the shipping contract in 1887 allowed the authorities to impose strict limits on the number of subsidized immigrants. However, they did not cancel assistance completely, despite rising unemployment and growing labour unrest. In fact, the remittance system, after years of 'sweeping condemnation', was seen as a valuable means for promoting 'success and prosperity' (QVP 1888:III,154). Over the next few years immigration simply wound down; shipments were reduced, publicity curtailed, and assistance restricted to selected domestic servants, agricultural workers, nominees and indented labourers. These included several hundred Italians who arrived in December 1891 to work on the sugar plantations.[17]

The full impact of the drought that had set in in 1883, the floods of the early 1890s, crop failures and trade losses, labour troubles and political turmoil, falling prices, unemployment and poverty, finally registered; and in 1892, the government suspended all subsidized immigration. The whole system, apart from land orders for full-payers and remittance passengers who arrived entirely at the expense of colonists nominating them, ground to a halt. Immigration numbers reached their lowest level in the 1893–95 period. But as the colonial growth rate began to stagnate, the need for more people once again became an issue; 'immigration from the more thickly inhabited countries must be encouraged by every possible means', the Registrar-General noted in his 1894 report (QVP 1895:III,296).[18] The first moves came early in 1896 when the government voted £5,000 to publicize the liberal land grants available to full-paying passengers. Then special discount passages were offered to agriculturalists who travelled on British India steamers, and in January 1897, free ship-kits were provided for full-paying and nominated immigrants who sailed direct to the colony as third-class passengers. This was soon followed with assistance for selected domestic servants and farm labourers. Lecturers were appointed to promote the colony in the United Kingdom, and special agents recruited in Europe. By the turn of the century, increasing numbers of Scandinavians and Italians were arriving via Sydney.[19] This drive for population was spurred on by the prospect of Federation and the 'White Australia Policy', a crude summary of which appeared in the *Bulletin* – 'The cheap Chinaman, the cheap Nigger, and the cheap European pauper to be absolutely excluded' (quoted in Clark 1957:447). The colonial period finished as it had begun, with the promise of prosperity and the cry for more people of respectable Anglo-Saxon origin.

Queensland's immigration policy may have been founded on idealistic principles, but it was moulded by more mundane considerations. This tension between idealism and pragmatism was reflected in unrestrained spending in good times and severe restrictions in recession, and in short-term policies rather than long-range planning. Any evidence of progress stimulated immigration, in spite of an awareness that it persistently fell short of its goal to develop the land. Conditions in the home countries, in Queensland and on the high seas left their mark on the policy and its administration, yet it was the level of government involvement that created a carefully controlled system and secured a highly selected population for the colony.

EMIGRATION AND IMMIGRATION

Queensland's immigration policy may not have achieved the desired pattern of land development, but the fact that almost a quarter of a million souls reached the colony's shores from Britain and Europe between 1860 and 1900 had far-reaching consequences. Australia has been described as a 'nation of immigrants', yet Queensland last century was '*the* immigrant colony of Australia' (Lawson 1963:1). According to the 1881 census, only 40 per cent of its population were native-born; and even at the time of Federation, twenty years later, they had gained only a slight lead over those originating outside the colony. Moreover, government subsidy and control meant that the majority of the immigrants had been hand-picked.

Perhaps the most significant result of the immigration policy was a population growth, unparalleled by that of any other Australian colony (see Cumpston 1927:586–88). The twenty-fold increase from 23,520 in 1859 to 498,249 in 1900 (QVP 1901:II,1369) represented a growth rate six times greater than that for the total Australian population during the same period. By contrast, England and Wales increased by a little more than 60 per cent. Natural increase (the excess of births over deaths) was responsible for 40 per cent, and net immigration (the excess of immigrants over departees) for 60 per cent of the colonial population growth.

The Britons and Europeans who constitute the focus of this study, however, represented only part of the total increase; a considerable number of them moved away from Queensland.[1]

Colonial society was in a state of constant flux, ever adjusting to a high mobility and assimilating new arrivals not only from Britain and Europe but also from the Australasian colonies, the Pacific Islands and Asia. Over half the total immigration were other Australians; each colony acted 'like a sieve', with a 'perpetual motion to and fro' across its borders (Rogers 1907:166). While Queensland policy makers were busy plugging the loopholes in the legislation to prevent subsidized immigrants going south, mineral discoveries and employment opportunities attracted southern colonists north; and these, as the Registrar-General pointed out, proved an asset since they were already acclimatized (QVP 1887:III,311). Gold discoveries also attracted the Chinese, but their numbers decreased sharply following exclusionist legislation. They, together with the Polynesians and other aliens, composed only 9 per cent of the immigration in the last decade compared to 25 per cent during the 1870s. Unlike the aborigines, they were included in all enumerations and estimates of the colonial population.

Birthplace figures show conclusively that a large part of the total immigration originated in Britain or the Continental countries; this sector constituted 63, 55, 43, 42 and 29.5 per cent of Queensland's population at each successive decennial census between 1861 and 1901 (scc QVP 1902:II,943). Although the Continental component never rose above 10 per cent, its contribution to colonial development was highly valued. The predominance of those born in Britain reflected not only Queensland's close ties with the motherland but also the impact of socio-economic trends in the receiving and sending countries. If we compare the rate of inflow for direct arrivals from Britain and Europe with the annual population increase for the colony (see Woolcock 1983:56), we find a definite correspondence, with peaks during the boom years of 1864–66, 1872–75 and 1881–83 when vast sums were borrowed and spent and controls were relaxed to encourage an influx of new colonists. Queensland's population was strongly influenced by immigration. So too was colonial development. Although this depended primarily on British institutions, capital and people, securing the right kind of people demanded careful organization blended with a sensitivity to real, rather than supposed, requirements in the colony and recruitment potential in the homelands.

By 1860 global migration, whether forced or free, was a fact of life. Much has been written on the forces underlying the decision to uproot from one land and replant in another. The effect of wars and political struggles, industrialization and the rural–urban shift, unjust land laws and changes in land tenure, the rising population and unemployment, religious and racial persecution, famine and grinding poverty, or simply a restlessness and the desire for change – all these, and many more 'push' factors were at work. The British colonies and America offered the necessary 'pull' factors and the opportunity for a fresh start in life. Appleyard (1964:53) has pointed out that, while demographic and economic conditions together with government policies influenced both the volume and direction of migration, the final decision to migrate rested with the individual. Hope and optimism, stimulated by the possibility of becoming independent and self-sufficient, motivated many. The new colony had land for the asking and, compared with 'home', the wages were high.

The Agent-General in 1871 described Queensland's immigrants as

'men and women [who] have been moved to seek their fortune in a distant though not foreign land under circumstances which have led them to believe that they may find greater happiness and comfort there than they can attain in the country of their birth, where competition is so keen, where the strain of life is so severe, and where the reward of labour seems to them to be uncertain.'

(COL/A156:71–1528)

In a similar vein, the colonial agent in Germany in his 1874 report noted that 'The wish to have a farm of their own, and to work for themselves, has . . . formed the principle inducement for emigration' (QVP 1875:II,734). But Schindler (1915:71) maintains that the Germans' desire, unlike the British, was 'less to rise socially than to get rid of the nightmare of political disturbances'; Walker (1964:191) agrees. Most Germans, it seems, came from depressed farming areas, travelled in family units and settled in Queensland determined to preserve 'the standards and attitudes' of the Fatherland (see Waterson 1968:131). Yet, regardless of their roots, there were always a number of emigrants who viewed the process as an adventure and gave little thought to what lay ahead; some wanted to improve their health; others were 'sent' to avoid disgrace or resolve a crisis. A case in point was the 'wild' young man whose family hoped that he would have 'sobered down' after a few years farming in Queensland (Hume and Fowler 1975:137). The colonial authorities discouraged such as these.

When Queensland was created in 1859 only a few officials in the Colonial Office and a handful of relatives and friends in Britain and Germany were aware of her existence. Yet within a short time, the new colony was on the map. According to Lacour-Gayet (1976:218), 'The name, or something, acted like magic and 50,000 new immigrants settled there.' Certainly less simplistic factors were responsible, but almost 60,000 people arrived from Britain and Europe in the first and another 56,000 in the second decade. The latter figure more than doubled in the 1880s but was decimated in the 1890s, the decade of the depression. Official statistics record that 240,210 immigrants reached Queensland during the colonial period (see Table 1, p. 346). Initially there were two factors in her favour – the American Civil War and the colony's cotton-growing potential. Still, a lion's share of the credit must go to Henry Jordan. By his efforts and dynamic, almost charismatic appeal, he laid the foundation and established the pattern for emigration to the colony.

Jordan believed in Queensland and the immigration policy; he capitalized on the current situation and mounted a publicity campaign which served as a model for the next forty years. He contacted 'men of influence' and newspapers, delivered public lectures, wrote and published handbills and pamphlets advertising the colony, answered thousands of letters and personal inquiries, and encouraged satisfied colonists to share their experiences with others 'back home'. But, most important, by operating the land-order system through one shipping firm, he was able to advertise regular monthly sailings to Queensland and have the Black Ball agents do the spade work of recruiting. Jordan, however, was determined to prevent the 'sweepings' of England's streets sailing for the colony (see QVP 1866:1067–068; 1867–68:II,81). All those selected through his office, received his personal attention. He tried to present a realistic picture for future Queenslanders by emphasizing not only the attractions but the hard work and difficulties. Within three years of his arrival in

London, Jordan claimed to have conducted the largest non-pauperized emigration ever established from Great Britain (QVP 1864:1017). An old colonist recalled how emigrants sent out in the early years were known as 'Jordan's Lambs': 'A magnificent lot of hardy pioneers they were, no wasters, no drunkards, no unemployable were to be found amongst them' (RHSQ, Immigration).

In nothern Germany, John Heussler followed a similar pattern by contacting the civil authorities, promoting the colony and signing a shipping contract. But he worked under less favourable conditions – a greater ignorance of Queensland, official resistance, doubts concerning female emigration, and a fear that labour arrangements for the colony would reduce new arrivals to semi-slavery (see Kleinschmidt 1951). Before Heussler could consolidate his efforts he had to return to Queensland, leaving all arrangements in the hands of shipping and local agents. This proved most unsatisfactory, for at that time many were turning to emigration as an escape from increasing political unrest, conscription and worsening conditions. During hostilities between Germany and Denmark (1865–67), more than 500 Danes left for the colony in vessels from Hamburg. The Continental agent appointed in 1870 immediately encountered opposition, the Franco-Prussian War and problems associated with the building of a new German nation. He was recalled in 1873. Further efforts to encourage emigration to the colony during the remainder of the 1870s met with only limited success; recruitment activities in the early 1880s failed altogether. Over the years local agents tried to stir up interest in Scandinavia and Denmark, but significant numbers did not sail for the colony until the end of the century. When an emigration from northern Italy was finally organized in 1890, it had to be abandoned because of the depression. For many reasons – official opposition, adverse publicity and competition from other countries – Queensland failed to secure a firm footing in the European emigrant trade. This was disappointing since Continental immigrants generally were accustomed to farming under poor conditions and became the 'agrarians' ideal settlers'. Moreover, the majority were 'energetic', law-abiding and Protestant (see QVP 1900:V,632 and Waterson 1968:134).

The colonial government had no option but to concentrate their recruiting activities in the United Kingdom. Henry Jordan had worked single-handed, but subsequent Agents-General could not cope with the increasing demands of lecturing and writing, public relations and administration. The first regional agent-lecturers, for England, Scotland and Ireland, were appointed in 1874. Such appointments usually went to men who had a first-hand and recent knowledge of the colony. Their function was two-fold. First, they established local recruiting agencies where applicants for assistance were selected and processed (doubtful or complicated cases were referred to the regional lecturers or the London office). The number of local agencies could be augmented or reduced according to demand and by 1876, 370 such agencies were operating throughout the United Kingdom. Second, they kept the local agents up to date with the progress of the colony and changes in the regulations, and promoted Queensland, especially in the agricultural counties, by disseminating information, addressing public meetings and attending markets and country shows. Personal contact, however, proved the most effective method of recruitment. A hierarchy of functions thus developed. The Agent-General, with his staff at the Queensland emigration office in London, supervised the entire operation in Britain and was answerable to the Colonial Secretary in Brisbane. He represented Queensland at the Colonial Office and was expected to use every means available to promote the colony's best interests.[2] The regional agent-lecturers were responsible to him, and below them a network of local agents acted as the direct link with prospective colonists. Although full-paying passengers (and some bounty immigrants) made arrangements directly with the shipping agents, land-order warrants were issued only by the London office.

Most countries receiving immigrants maintained a similar organization; competition from this source often interfered with Queensland's efforts. Furthermore, the United States offered unconditional entry and, after two centuries of immigration, the 'pull' of established friends and relatives. Unless the colony was quick to adjust agents' fees, inducements and other perks, it could easily lose its share of the market. Other factors also influenced recruitment – constant policy changes, conflicting methods of operation, adverse reports from the colony, the volume of trade between Queensland and the home country, and the state of the British economy, particularly as it affected rural areas: agricultural labourers were notoriously difficult to recruit. As agents ventured into places unaccustomed to the idea of emigration, they found poverty, a deep-rooted attachment to the soil and opposition from local employers (see QVP 1867–68:II,77). And finally, there was the element of fear, often aroused by a series of disasters at sea. This, together with the whole range of human emotions, could dampen the desire to emigrate. Yet, despite all the obstacles, thousands of people dug up their roots and sailed for the colony.

These emigrants represented only a fraction of the ten and a half million who left the United Kingdom between 1860 and 1900, 28 per cent of whom were foreigners passing through British ports. Of the remaining seven and a half million, two-thirds were absorbed by the United States, 11 per cent went to British North America, 14 per cent emigrated to the Antipodes, and most of the other 8 per cent sailed to the Cape Colony.[3] The migratory habits of the British were well recognized: 'The people of these islands are more moveable than other nations, and large numbers of them are always abroad . . . generally in ships at sea, in the great commercial entrepôts, and in the capitals of Europe, in our colonies, or in the States of America' (Census 1861:III,4). Queensland captured less than 3 per cent of the British and Irish emigration.[4] Although this seems an insignificant proportion, there exists a direct relationship between the rate of outflow from the United Kingdom and the rate of inflow to the colony, with corresponding high points in both (see Figure 2.1). Carrothers (1929:227) maintains that outflow usually reached a peak following a period of depression, while a slump in the receiving country had a more immediate effect on the inflow. Minor fluctuations in the rate of immigration as well as the general trend after 1883 suggest specific reactions to conditions in Queensland. The latter also determined the level of recruitment activity.

On the other hand, the volume of flow of the Continental immigration tended to reflect the European political climate rather than developments in the colony or the efforts of Queensland's agents. Also, the pattern of the total German emigration differed from the British. After 1850 German emigrants came mostly from east of the Elbe and the lower classes predominated; of the one and a half million who emigrated between 1871 and 1885, 95 per cent went to the States and 1 per cent to Australia; the outflow was heavy during the Franco-Prussian War and its aftermath, fell off between 1874 and 1879, and then began a steady increase with a

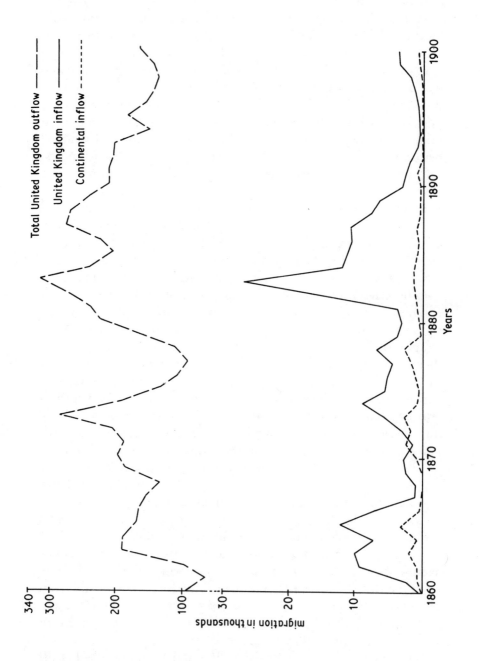

Figure 2.1 Emigration to Queensland, 1860–1900

gradual improvement in the quality of the 'Auswanderer' (see Walker 1964:165,175 ff.). However, the majority (almost 70 per cent) of Queensland's European immigrants sailed between 1861 and 1879. The constant trickle arriving via British ships in the 1880s and 1890s depended on government funds and the ability of naturalized colonists to assist with the passage money. At its best, this immigration was a mere drop in the bucket of the great 'Auswanderer' movement. In 1873, when 'a complete emigration fever was raging . . . (with) an almost alarming tendency to quit the Fatherland' (QVP 1877:I,884), only 1.6 per cent of all those sailing from Hamburg and Bremen were destined for the colony. Even so, the Continental influx represented 10.75 per cent of the total direct overseas immigration to Queensland between 1860 and 1900; this proportion reached almost 20 per cent during the 1870s.[5] By 1891 Queensland had the largest European-born population of all the Australian colonies (QVP 1893:III,859 ff.).

An examination of the remaining 90 per cent – the United Kingdom sector – demonstrates some of the factors involved in recruiting colonists, and indicates that there were difficulties imposing the quota system. The proportions for the three divisions of the United Kingdom emigration to Queensland bear a greater resemblance to the general outward movement than they do to their relative populations. Between 1861 and 1901, the English and Welsh population rose from 69 to 78 per cent, the Scottish remained at approximately 11 per cent throughout the period, and the Irish dropped from 20 to 11 per cent. The corresponding proportions for the emigration were 53, 10 and 37 per cent while England and Wales contributed 58.5, Scotland 13.5 and Ireland 28 per cent to Queensland's immigration.[6] These figures reveal a compromise between the quota system and the reality of emigration trends; so do fluctuations within each division.

During the 1860s, when so many 'sons and daughters of Erin' became the victims of famine and land eviction orders, more than half the outflow were Irish; but they composed only one-fifth of the population of the British Isles and a little less than a third of the immigration total. Jordan was accused of discrimination against the Irish when he criticized Bishop Quinn's Society and tried to apply quotas. Certainly the efforts of the Society and the high proportion of remittance passengers raised the number of arrivals from Ireland above that intended by the government;[7] but the percentage was even higher in the 1870s despite a sharp fall in emigration from Ireland and the continued decline of her population. The Agent-General in 1874 admitted he had despatched more Irish than the quota allowed (QVP 1875:II,628); there were difficulties recruiting in England and Irish labourers were forthcoming. Although the downward trend for the Irish population and emigration continued, the dramatic decrease in the numbers leaving for the colony related to the fact that Queensland vessels sailed only from English and Scottish ports after 1880.

Throughout the period, except for the last decade, the proportion arriving from England and Wales remained a little below 60 per cent. This was consistently less than the English–Welsh component of the population, but similar to the emigration pattern after 1870. The 1860s were distorted by the Irish migration which seems to have had little impact on the relative proportion of the Scottish population. However, the Scottish immigration showed considerable variation over the four decades, registering 12 per cent in the first, falling to 7 per cent in the second and then more than doubling in the 1880s when an all-out recruiting drive coincided with land reorganization in the Highlands. On the whole, Scotland's agricultural population was reluctant to emigrate unless changes in tenure and a series of poor seasons forced a decision. When a Scot left his country he usually did so 'in calculating contentment' (see Donaldson 1966:206).

A comparison of the immigrant pattern and Queensland's population shows that the English sector of the latter remained less than its immigrant counterpart, while the reverse generally held for the Scots and Irish. It is impossible to determine whether fewer Irish and Scots went south or more were attracted north; but it would seem that they felt more at home with the Queensland environment and society than the English. The Scot's concept of agriculture 'well fitted them for soil-breaking in the colonies' and those tenents of Calvinism which equated prosperity and individual virtue readily adapted to the selector's role so encouraged by the Queensland government (see Waterson 1968:135–36). The fact that so many Irish were nominated meant that they tended to remain with relatives and friends; some were so poor they could not move beyond the port of arrival. MacGinley (1974:17) concludes that a large part of the Irish immigration between 1885 and 1912 were 'young, unmarried, unskilled people of predominantly rural background'. There is reason to believe that this also applied to Irish arrivals during the previous twenty-five years. Despite the differences between the migratory and colonial populations, sufficient similarity exists to assume that the characteristics of the one may be found in the other. Since details of the religious affiliation of immigrants are so patchy, the 1881 census figures have been selected to provide a general estimate. From the 90.5 per cent belonging to the Christian religion, a fairly predictable pattern emerges – 38 per cent were Church of England, 28 Roman Catholic, 11.5 Presbyterian, 9 Lutheran and the remaining 13.5 per cent belonged to other Protestant denominations (QVP 1902:II,943). The large Irish-Catholic segment made its presence felt in colonial society and on the high seas.

Conditions in the homelands and the colony influenced recruitment and were reflected in the rate of flow, the volume and the composition of the migration to Queensland. Selection also played a role, though it had a greater impact on the quality of the immigration. Yet both selection and quality were partly determined by the economic status of the new arrivals. Only 15 per cent of the organized inflow paid the full fare to the colony.[8] The authorities were frequently disturbed by the fact that so few with capital came to the colony or settled the land. Indeed, the ratio of full-payers to subsidized immigrants fell from one in six in 1865 to one in twelve in 1873 (QVP 1875:II,627). A slight improvement in the 1880s was attributed to the introduction of steamships and the efforts of lecturers to publicize Queensland's potential among the well-to-do. The ratio increased with the suspension of assisted immigration in the 1890s, and by the end of the colonial period, the government agreed that full-payers, whatever their connection with the land, were 'a desirable acquisition' provided they possessed the 'energy and determination to succeed in a new country' (QVP 1899:I,1258). However, two-thirds of the full-payers travelled as steerage passengers; only 5 per cent of the total immigration could afford cabin-class fares. We may conclude, therefore, that very few new arrivals were in a position to employ labour and that the majority expected to be wage-earners.

Subsidized immigrants fell into several categories: almost a half were given a free passage, assisted and remittance immigrants each represented approximately 25 per cent, and there was an insignificant number of indentured labourers. These figures indicate that almost three-quarters of those sponsored by the government (two-thirds of the total immigration) did not have to pay their fare to the colony. The proportion of free passengers reached a peak in the 1870s when problems with recruitment and corruption in the London office led to a relaxation of the regulations and gross abuses in the system. The higher percentages for remittance immigrants during the first and last decades may be attributed to the emigration conducted by the Commissioners between 1860 and 1865, and the favouring of this class towards the end of the period. Many of these people were 'exceedingly poor' and 'much below the standard' of ordinary emigrants (QVP 1884:II, 598, 668), and included the free-nominated passengers – those who paid their way from the Continent to an English port where they received a free passage to the colony. Although bounty immigrants travelled second-class, they have been included with the assisted category since the government contributed to their fare. The payment required by those who were partly subsidized varied according to the availability of funds and the demand for labour.

Crowley (1951:333) has estimated that the Queensland treasury paid an average of £19.3.0 for each government immigrant between 1860 and 1919. In fact, almost £4.25 million – three-quarters of the total Australian expenditure on immigration – was poured into the system during the colonial period. This enormous sum represents a cost of approximately £17.12.6 for each new arrival from Britain and Europe, irrespective of whether they paid their fare or were assisted. The average amount exceeded £21 both in the 1860s, largely because of the Commissioners' relatively expensive operation, and in the 1890s when the volume of migration fell dramatically; it reached its lowest level (£14.2.6) in the 1880s, thereby confirming the government's claim that the bounty system attracted a better class of immigrants at a reduced cost. How much capital these immigrants brought with them is a moot point.

When full-scale immigration resumed under the 1869 act, provision was made for the establishment of a savings bank which allowed passengers to deposit money in England and recover it in the colony. The deposits, however, gave only a general estimate of the economic status of immigrants since many at first were 'too suspicious to entrust their money out of their own keeping' or too poor to contribute (QVP 1876:II,1053). Gradually more availed themselves of the facilities, and by 1884 the Agent-General was able to report that 'the total collection in proportion to the number despatched [was] higher than that for any previous year' (QVP 1885:II,782). The record was reached in 1885, with an average deposit of £2.10.0 for each immigrant. Officials noted that the increase reflected 'the improved social status of the emigrants' (QVP 1883:II,419); health, respectability and the bank deposit became the standard criteria for assessing future Queenslanders. When the SS *Bulimba* departed in January 1883, the Agent-General remarked that, although the emigrants presented a poor appearance, the amount they deposited made them more acceptable (QVP 1883–84:1368). The rising standard of living in the home countries and a better regulated selection procedure accounted for the growing number of favourable reports after 1880. Such reports justified immigration expenditure.

Investment meant involvement. The authorities worked hard to develop a system that would optimize the outlay and guarantee success for the immigration policy. Selection was seen as fundamental to the whole process; it would have been impossible without it to secure 'suitable' colonists. From the outset the procedure not only outlined the criteria which subsidized emigrants had to satisfy, but also included specifications for the voyage. The remittance regulations introduced soon after separation required, in addition to restrictions on age, family size and occupation, that applicants be 'of sound mental and bodily health, and good moral character', and show on arrival that they had been 'properly found during the voyage', having sufficient clothing and sailing under conditions which promoted comfort, safety and health (COL/A4:60–1056). The first Queensland regulations, issued in January, 1861, retained the age limit of forty years for men and thirty-five for women, added a residency clause which excluded previous colonial inhabitants, and stipulated that all applicants for a land order must travel direct to Queensland from Europe only in vessels which adhered to the requirements laid down for the Commissioners' ships (QGG 1861,2:15–17).

Soon after making arrangements for the regular despatch of immigrants, Jordan recognized the need to adopt a comprehensive procedure which would screen applicants for assistance, assess the suitability of those requesting land orders, and set limits on the numerous charitable societies sponsoring emigrants. The Black Ball Line, without his consent, had despatched seventy-three workers through the East London Weavers' Aid Society, and he feared that a 'combination' might develop between the shippers and such societies and inundate the colony with 'a refuse class' (COL/A19:61–2377). Teething troubles in the early years constantly demonstrated the need for centralized control and a standardized selection procedure. The Emigration Commissioners had, for many years, used application forms – one for single and married men and another for single women – in selecting subsidized immigrants for the Australian colonies. These forms included information relating to age, present and previous occupations, income, place of birth and residence, the receipt of parish relief, and previous residence in the colonies. It was obligatory that the form be signed by 'two respectable householders' ('Publicans or Dealers in Beer or Spirits' were excluded) who could testify that the applicant was 'honest, sober, industrious, and of general good character' and, to the best of their knowledge, did not have a criminal record. A medical practitioner had to certify that those named in the form were not

> 'apparently mutilated or deformed in Person, nor . . . afflicted with any disease calculated to shorten life, or to impair physical or mental energy . . . that they have all had the small pox or have been vaccinated, and are entirely free from every disease usually considered infectious or contagious; and that all the male adults are capable of labour in their callings.'
>
> (COL/A28:62–1303)

Finally, a magistrate or clergyman of the parish to which the applicant belonged declared that the statements were authentic and the referees 'worthy of credit'.

Regulations attached to the application forms clearly stated the eligibility criteria: age limits were forty years for men and thirty-five for married women, couples could not be separated or leave behind children under eighteen years, no widows or widowers with young children would be accepted, the men had to agree to work for wages. Only single women aged between eighteen and thirty-five years, of 'unexceptionable character', sound in body and mind and with written evidence that they had been 'in service' need apply; those with illegitimate children were definitely not eligible. Government subsidy was not intended as a charity. Jordan introduced similar forms and regulations. Although the Queensland remittance system allowed a maximum of sixty years for men and women, the land-order scheme retained the previous limits and restricted occupational categories for assisted immigrants to unskilled mechanics, domestic servants and labourers. Further revisions more clearly defined these categories and brought all steerage passengers, whether full-paying or assisted who sailed in Black Ball vessels, under the same procedure (QGG 1862,3:501–02 and 1863,4:989–91). In these early years, eligibility for assistance largely depended on the applicant's occupation and his or her ability to contribute to the fare. Apart from exceptional cases, subsidized immigrants were required to deposit £1 with the London office for every statute adult (the 1855 imperial passenger act defined a statute adult as anyone twelve years of age and over or two children between one and twelve years), and in return they received a ship-kit containing bedding and mess utensils. All passengers were expected to pay their fare to the port of embarkation.

Regulations issued under later immigration acts included similar provisions. Sometimes 'Directions' attached to the application forms stated that preference would be given to particular categories such as 'young married couples without children, families with a large proportion of daughters over 14 years of age, and female domestic servants of good character' (see QS 33 Vic. no. 9). Although full-payers did not have to undergo screening, they were denied a land order if, for any reason, they were considered unsuitable. Remittance immigrants completed less detailed forms, but certificates of health and respectability, stating that they were free from infectious disease and were not 'lunatic, idiot, deaf, dumb, blind, or otherwise infirm' were required (COL/A106:68–1533). Continental immigrants receiving assistance agreed to abide by the shipboard regulations and work for wages on arrival. They had to submit a character reference signed by an authorized person who had known them for three years and could testify that they had never been convicted or imprisoned for 'any crime . . . riot, assault, or drunkenness' or received parish relief. A medical certificate declared their physical and mental fitness (QS 33 Vic. no. 9).

Health and character requirements remained constant throughout the period, but clauses relating to previous residency and
intent to settle permanently were applied with increasing severity.
It was usual for selection regulations to be altered according to the
demand for labour, the treasury, or abuses within the system.
During the economic squeeze of 1879, the Executive Council
issued detailed and circumscribed 'Directions' outlining precisely
who was eligible for assistance (see QVP 1879:II,172–74); yet
three years later, the only restrictions for bounty passengers were
an age limit of fifty-five years for married couples and thirty-five
for single men and women, and the stipulation that they adhere to
the residency clauses and produce for the shipping agents evidence
of respectability and 'sound bodily and mental health'. However,
the shippers had to forfeit the bounty and carry at the reduced rate
anyone found violating the regulations. Despite this safeguard, it
was feared that philanthropic concerns might take advantage of
the scheme to off-load 'imbeciles, criminals, and other objectionable characters' on the colony (QVP 1883–84:1369–373,1380).
Any evidence of a deterioration in the required standards during
both lean and full times called for an immediate investigation of
the criteria and the procedure by which they were applied.
Selection may have been used to regulate immigrant numbers, but
its primary function was to control their quality. In principle, 'any
person of good character . . . able and willing to work with his
hands' was acceptable (QVP 1877:II,1173): the aged, the destitute
and the defective were not.

It was one thing to establish selection criteria but another to
ensure they were effectively enforced. Henry Jordan laid the
foundation. Sensitive to criticism and aware of defects and abuses,
he adapted existing methods and focused his efforts on crucial
aspects of the process. In response to the allegation that he had
created a 'cumberous machinery', he asserted that immigration
would fail to achieve its end without good selecting agents to
screen applicants and well-paid surgeons to care for immigrants
during the voyage (QVP 1867–68:II,86). The following method
generally applied throughout the period. A would-be emigrant
contacted the Queensland office or a local agent; if he seemed to
fulfil the requirements for a free or assisted passage, he was issued
with an application form. Once the necessary particulars were
complete and the health and character certificates obtained (birth

and marriage certificates were required after 1872), the form was returned to the London office or an authorized selecting agent for approval and registered with the Agent-General. Shipping agents received a commission for each full-paying passenger and emigration agents received a fee for each subsidized immigrant processed by them. Fees varied according to the category of immigrant, funds available, labour demand and competition from other colonies.[9] Doubtful applications were referred to the Agent-General for his sanction. Candidates were distinctly warned that the completion of a form in no way entitled them to a passage, and to make no preparations until they received an affirmative reply and the contract ticket for the passage. Remittance immigrants required a ticket and the confirmation that their colonial sponsors would accept full responsibility for them.

Jordan personally processed all applicants for an assisted passage and kept a file on each; no one was ever approved 'without proper investigation into his antecedents' (QVP 1867:I,226). Despite periodic and alarming complaints, especially after Jordan was instructed to relax the regulations to allow a free flow of labourers to the colony, he could claim at the end of his appointment in 1866 that the procedure he established provided 'a perfect check' to the introduction of a refuse class (QVP 1867–68:II,86). Almost a decade later, when agencies were operating throughout the United Kingdom, the Agent-General asserted that 'no other emigration service sends more carefully selected emigrants than our own' (QVP 1875:II,615). This kind of statement was repeated whenever doubts concerning selection arose. But no such claims could be made for the Continental emigration. Prospective colonists arrived in Hamburg from several countries and, under German law, foreign emigration agents were forbidden to have direct contact with them or control the selecting agents approved by the German government (QVP 1877:II,1141; COL/A158:71–1971).

A system of reporting coordinated officials in Britain and Brisbane. A London office representative was present at the embarkation inspection and rejected or demanded the full fare from any one who had falsified his documents or was found unsuitable; while in transit the surgeon-superintendent recorded immigrant health and behaviour; on arrival, local officials filed a report of the muster and time in the depot. Follow-up information frequently completed the picture: someone was found border-hopping, a domestic servant had turned to prostitution, or a young man had died of consumption soon after arrival. All reports were forwarded to the Agent-General with instructions, whenever necessary, to provide an explanation or take remedial action. As a result, the government might cease operating through a particular agency or adopt extra safeguards. Jordan, for instance, introduced the ruling that medical certificates could be obtained only from practitioners approved by the Agent-General (QVP 1866:1090). At one time a portion of the agents' fees was withheld until colonial officials advised that the new arrivals were acceptable (QVP 1879:II,173). Following the great influx of 1883, an additional testimonial was required for single women, and doctors received 'a confidential circular on the importance of a rigid examination' for all applicants (QVP 1885:II,781).

The extent to which recruitment and selection influenced Queensland's immigration can be better appreciated by analysing this population in greater detail. Although half the new arrivals were given a free ticket to the colony, the fact that they, and the other government immigrants, had to buy a ship-kit, provide themselves with a certain quantity of clothing, and pay their fare to the port of embarkation effectively excluded the unemployed. Only under exceptional circumstances were these provisions waived or the unemployed accepted. Work experience and colonial labour needs were key factors in selection. A listing of 112,837 free, assisted and remittance immigrants between 1861 and 1893 shows that 45 per cent were connected with the land as agriculturalists, pastoralists and miners, 19 per cent were industrial workers (artisans, mechanics, navvies and general labourers), 32.5 per cent were domestic servants, and the remaining 3.5 per cent were not specified.[10]

During the 1860s when hundreds of navvies poured into the colony, the majority (40 per cent) of the new arrivals were classed as industrial labourers. This proportion dropped sharply in the next decade, but recovered slightly with the building boom of the early 1880s, and then slumped to 4 per cent between 1891 and 1893 as the depression advanced. Land-related workers show a reverse trend with their greatest inflow during the 1870s when agricultural unrest in England and the Continental immigration reached their highest levels. The Germans were 'pre-eminently small farmers with a passionate love of grain and grape' (Waterson 1968:127). The domestic servant proportion increased steadily from 25 to 44.5 per cent throughout the period in response to an ever-present demand and the certainty of a free passage. A number of government-sponsored school teachers arrived and some ship surgeons remained, but official returns do not list the occupations of full-payers or what proportion belonged to the professional classes. Generally, men with only an 'intellectual education' and middle-class women employed as governesses were advised against going to the colony; the emphasis was on people who would roll up their shirt-sleeves and take to work with their hands (QVP 1890:II, 1552).

The difference between occupational categories for the immigration and the colonial population during the first two decades suggests that new colonists misrepresented their occupations in order to qualify for government assistance, or changed it according to the work available. In 1882 the immigration agent complained that some mechanics who shipped as farm labourers demanded their trade on arrival or threatened to go south (COL/A338:82–3055). Contrary to immigrant trends between 1861 and 1881, the colonial agricultural sector declined while the proportion of industrial workers increased, no doubt as the result of mineral discoveries. Also the domestic servant class in the colony grew from 50 to 63 per cent, a figure considerably higher than that for the immigration. It is impossible to determine to what extent rising literacy levels influenced the occupational structure, but they would have contributed to an improvement in the quality of new arrivals. A sample of fourteen voyages taken from the 1885 passenger lists (IMM/120) indicates that 65 per cent of the immigrants were literate. This proportion corresponds to the 1881 Queensland census figures which show that 60 per cent of the population could read and write. The majority of new colonists may have been unskilled labourers or artisans, but they were clearly not drawn from the lowest orders of society (see also Borrie 1954:16). In the first place, they could, of their own volition, decide to emigrate; and second, they had to measure up to colonial requirements.

This latter consideration, more than any other, was responsible for the peculiar demographic features of the Queensland immigration.[11] The proportion of the 241,740 passengers who sailed direct to the colony from British and European ports for each successive decade between 1860 and 1900 was 24.5, 23.5, 47.5 and 4.5 per cent. In the first half of the period 85 per cent sailed under the British flag and 15 per cent under the German. Immigrants were usually classified according to the type of passage (saloon, second cabin, intermediate and steerage), their sex, marital status and statute-adult age (see Table 2, p. 348). The payment, space available and provisions for the voyage were calculated on the basis of this classification; infants travelled free. Even though complaints relating to passenger list 'irregularities' were frequent, especially during the 1860s, it has been possible to trace details for 99.6 per cent of the immigration. The Agent-General forwarded copies of the list by overland mail following the despatch of each vessel. Sometimes these copies went astray, did not arrive on time, were incomplete or disagreed with lists carried on the vessel. The arrival muster, together with the surgeon's or captain's statement of births and deaths at sea proved the most reliable method for checking immigrant numbers.

In this study, saloon and second cabin travellers have been, where possible, combined as a cabin class; intermediate and steerage passengers as well as stowaways were listed as a steerage class; and the remaining 8.5 per cent could not be categorized (this figure rose to 33.5 per cent in the 1860s). Of the categorized numbers, 95.8 per cent travelled steerage, though this figure dropped to 88.8 per cent in the 1890s. It was definitely a lower middle- and working-class immigration. The fact that less than 1 per cent on German and more than 5 per cent on British vessels during the first two decades could afford a cabin passage (the German figure did reach 3 per cent in the 1860s), supports the observation that the Continental immigration was generally poorer than the British. Some 321 successful stowaways have been recorded; only two were women, and 70 per cent sailed during the 1880s when better records were kept and steamships offered an easier voyage. Stowaways were usually given a free passage or put on the ship's articles.

Despite efforts to recruit single women and redress the male–female imbalance in the colony, the statistics indicate that immigration aggravated the problem. Embarkation figures for the whole period registered 57.5 per cent for males and 42.5 per cent for females – approximately a 3:2 ratio. The female proportion, however, did increase from 40 per cent in the first decade to almost 50 per cent in the last as emigration for single women became more commonplace. Furthermore, as Queensland developed, so did its reputation as a marriage market. When a contingent of domestic servants, leaving England for the colony in 1890, were asked their reason for emigrating, most admitted it was to find a husband (ANL, *Daily News*, M 468). During the second half of the nineteenth century the female population of England and Wales slightly exceeded the male; but the colony was a man's land. Here the female sector increased only from 39.7 to 44.3 per cent between 1861 and 1901. Sex ratios for both the sending and receiving countries were clearly affected by the predominantly male migration. A similar situation prevailed in the other Australian colonies where it was found that masculinity was particularly high among non-subsidized immigrants (see Crowley 1951:313). The Queensland figures lend some support to this finding; 61 per cent of the cabin passengers were male compared to 57 per cent for the steerage. The male preponderance was also more evident on German (61.5 per cent) than British (58.3 per cent) vessels, despite conscription for military service. Incidentally, steerage females outnumbered males in the 1890s when subsidized passages were primarily reserved for domestic servants.

A little less than a quarter of the total inflow were married; the majority (56 per cent) were single adults and the remaining 20 per cent were children under twelve years. The single-adult proportion increased from 50.5 to 72 per cent over the four decades; and although the male–female ratio for this sector began at 2:1, it had almost balanced by the 1890s. Single men represented 35 per cent of the total immigration, with this figure rising to 41 per cent for cabin passengers. The latter group, however, constituted only a fraction of the whole, yet they generated more than their fair share of problems on the high seas. Few single women travelled cabin class. German vessels registered 10 per cent less than the British for their single-adult sector, but single males greatly outnumbered females, especially during the 1860s. Walker (1964:187) has observed for this period that many German emigrants were men who went ahead to prepare for their families. Moreover, the German authorities were wary of inducements for single women (CO 386/78:70–1).

On the other hand, the proportions for married people and children were greater for the Continental than the British emigration. This supports other observations (see Walker 1964:186 and Waterson 1968:127) that the 'Auswanderer' was family orientated. However, it must be remembered that the 1860s and 1870s were troubled years when the German government guarded with 'the greatest jealousy the departure of young men until they . . . completed their term of military service' (QVP 1878:II,4). A distinctive feature of the immigration as a whole was the decline in the married and children's sectors, particularly in the last decade. Sex ratios for the children were almost equal, with a slight leaning towards the males, while the reverse held for the married people. This female weighting was more obvious on British than German vessels and most marked among cabin passengers. It was a common practice for husbands to travel alone to the colony and when they were established, nominate their family or send home the fare.[12] This would account for the relatively high percentage of married women in the cabin class; yet comparatively few children travelled under these more favourable conditions. The Queensland immigration, then, was predominantly single and male, and appears to have included families rather than communities. Yet the evidence suggests that few would have embarked not knowing another soul on board.

Determining family size presented difficulties since it was not always possible to isolate the nuclear from the extended family or distinguish single-parent families. Some children travelled with a guardian; others were listed with the full-payers if the number in the family exceeded the limit allowed for assisted passengers; those over fourteen years were berthed in the single-adult compartments separate from their parents. Although the reliability of the data may be questioned (approximately 50 per cent of the married people have been sampled), an estimate of family size is important since it illustrates selective patterns in the immigration. Almost one-third of the married sector travelling as couples were childless; some became parents during the voyage. Decadal proportions for couples with children were 62.5, 69, 70 and 63 per cent. Of the 20,000 family units examined, 86 per cent included both parents. Most of the remaining 14 per cent were mothers; but a few fathers sailed alone, usually with their older children.

Single-parent families reached as low as 8 per cent in the 1870s, but rose to 44 per cent in the last decade when remittance immigration was relatively high.

The three families with twelve children were an exception. The proportion of families with one child was 31 per cent, with two children 26 per cent, with three to five children 36 per cent. Only 7 per cent had more than six children. Small families (one and two children) increased by 10 per cent over the four decades, despite a temporary regression in the 1880s. The government preferred married to single immigrants because they showed a greater tendency to settle; they gave most encouragement to couples with minimal or no parental responsibilities since large families created 'misery and disappointment, and almost fruitless outlay' (QVP 1864:949). Family restrictions applied primarily to free passengers. In the early 1870s, for example, only one child under the age of twelve was allowed free; all others had to pay the full fare (QVP 1872:1437). European families seem to have been hardest hit by this regulation; the proportion of one- and two-children families increased from 50 per cent in the 1860s to 63 per cent in the 1870s while comparable British families remained at 57 per cent for both decades. The records suggest that larger families belonged to full-paying or remittance passengers; many of the latter were Irish. Sometimes a nurse or servant accompanied a saloon family to care for the children; but a mother travelling steerage in 1897, fortunately in a better-class steamship, had sole charge of her children, all ten of them under the age of twelve.

The structure of Queensland's immigration was determined more by age restrictions than any other factor. Although a record of the ages of 91.4 per cent of the whole have survived, some of these on account of ignorance or misrepresentation are doubtful, especially before 1872 when birth and marriage certificates were required. One man, on a voyage in 1861 where several passengers far exceeded the age limit, had 'the appearance of being not less than eighty'; there was a couple who gave their ages as 39 and 34 years in order to qualify for assistance, but admitted on arrival that they were 58 and 44 years old; another immigrant whose contract ticket gave one figure and the passenger list another, had no idea of his age (COL/A23:61–3023; COL/A48:63–3077; QVP 1863:II,463). Despite discrepancies, recording errors and unknown ages, the data provide a sufficiently accurate estimate of immigrant age patterns, the most striking feature of which is the predominance of young adults (see Figure 2.2). Almost 60 per cent of those for whom their age is known were concentrated in the 15 to 29 year category; this sector showed a steady increase from 57 to 66.5 per cent over the four decades. Indeed, 82 per cent of the immigrant population were under thirty years of age. This proportion, when compared with the decennial census figures from 1861 to 1901, exceeds the same category for England and Wales by 20 per cent and for Queensland by 15 per cent. As a result of introducing such a high percentage of people of marriageable age, the colony's population tended to be younger than that for the motherland. As Henry Jordan pointed out: '"the doctrine of population" in Queensland, means immigration of the classes which increase and multiply' (QVP 1877:II,678). Apart from the 1890s, the age pattern for each decade remained relatively constant.

In view of the berthing arrangements, it is convenient to consider the immigration as two separate populations – adults (15 years and over) and children (zero to 14 years). In the adult sector, 77.5 per cent of the males and 75 per cent of the females were aged between 15 and 29 years. A further breakdown reveals that 53 per cent of the married women and 44 per cent of the married men fell within this age range compared with 88 per cent for single women and 89 per cent for single men. However, one-third of the adult single women and one-quarter of the men were under twenty years of age. Thus we may conclude that the married people were older than the single adults, that married women were younger than married men, and that the single men and women were comparably aged, apart from the high percentage of teenage girls.

Cabin and steerage figures for the under-thirty adult group demonstrate similar trends, though the lower percentages for the cabin passengers indicate that they were, across the board, older than their steerage counterparts. Also in this age range, the proportion of steerage single females exceeded that for single males by 2.2 per cent; three-quarters of the adult single women travelling steerage were aged between 15 and 24 years. This fact alone was sufficient to move the Queensland authorities to use every possible precaution and provision for the girls' welfare. Both British and German figures followed the steerage pattern, but the European immigration was the older of the two. Mean age

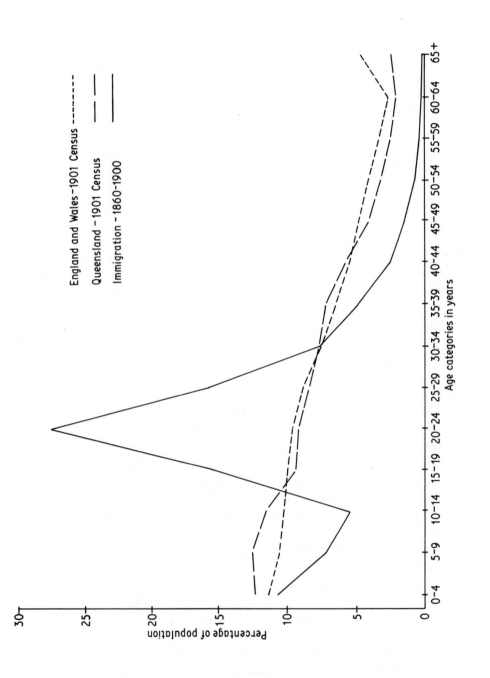

Figure 2.2 Immigrant and landed populations: age structure

differences confirm these findings. For British cabin passengers, the married men were three years older than married women and eleven years older than the single men for whom the mean age was 25.4 years (single women were slightly older). Each British steerage category was younger; the average ages for married men and women being 31.6 and 29.6 years, and for single men and women, 22.9 and 21.8 years. Apart from married men and single women in the cabin class, the corresponding German mean ages were all higher. Thus, compared to the British, European immigrants during the first half of the period were not only poorer but older.

Children under the age of fifteen years represented almost a quarter of the total immigration, a figure which altered little during the first three decades but dropped sharply in the last. If we look at the proportions for children of the total inflow according to sex (21 per cent males, 26.5 per cent females), passage (19.5 per cent cabin, 23 per cent steerage) and nationality (22.5 per cent British, 29 per cent German), we can see that they formed a significant sector of the travelling population, a sector that had to be reckoned with in all shipping arrangements. Some of the implications of sailing half way round the world with children are illustrated by an analysis of their age structure. The majority (46.5 per cent) were under five years of age and almost one-third of this group (14.5 per cent of all children) were infants; five- to nine-year-olds accounted for 30.5 per cent and children in the ten- to fourteen-year-old category for 23 per cent. Most of the families would have included infants and young children. It is not surprising, therefore, that the mean age for the total immigration was 21 years, with only 1 per cent older than 65 years. Married couples ranged from 16 and 17 years to 72 and 84 years for women and men respectively, while the oldest single passenger was an 84 year old widow, travelling steerage.

Immigration to Queensland during the last four decades of the nineteenth century represented only a fraction of the total outflow from Great Britain and Europe, but it bore many of the characteristics of this exodus, reflected the impact of conditions and events in both the sending and receiving countries, and certainly influenced the composition of colonial society. Those who sailed from Hamburg were poorer, older and included more married couples and children and fewer single people than their

British counterparts. Among the 90 per cent from the United Kingdom, the English and single men predominated. On the whole, it was an influx of young adult manual workers who travelled to the colony wholly or in part at government expense. This meant that they had been recruited and carefully selected with the one intention of developing the colony through hard work and natural increase. Selection largely determined the nature of the immigration; it also screened the health (both moral and physical) of future colonists and ensured that travelling conditions were in their best interests.

SHIPPING
ORGANIZATION

Emigration to Queensland involved long-range planning, a life-changing decision and a 12,000 mile voyage which severed links with the homeland and provided a transition period between the past and the future. As far as the colonial authorities were concerned, the voyage determined the success or failure of their efforts to secure suitable immigrants. Providing for safe and healthy conditions at sea absorbed much of the financial outlay, demanded a high level of coordination and embraced legislators, administrative officers, imperial and colonial interests, technology, public health and the shipping trade.

A reliable mode of transport to convey large numbers of people over long distances as efficiently and economically as possible was funadmental to the immigration system. In 1860, only the sailing ship was considered since it dominated the Australian run. When the Queensland government introduced regular steamship sailings twenty years later, steam quickly displaced sail on the colonial route. Of the 1,317 direct passenger voyages to Queensland between 1860 and 1900, 68.3 per cent were under sail; they represented 59 per cent of the total immigration and almost the full complement (98.5 per cent) of the colonial embarkees in the first twenty years.[1] During this period, approximately 10 per cent of the voyages and 15 per cent of the immigration left from Hamburg on German sailing vessels. In the 1880s three-quarters of the passengers arrived by steamer; this proportion rose to 99 per cent in the last decade. The sailing ship, therefore, was the primary means of transport for Queensland immigrants during the first half of the period and the steamship in the second; but the steamer proved the more attractive and efficient of the two and, in economic terms, compared favourably.[2]

At the beginning of the nineteenth century, few could have predicted that the sailing ship, having held undisputed supremacy on the seaways of the world for thousands of years, would be so rapidly displaced. Even with the writing on the wall, it achieved a final moment of glory by acquiring a finesse, size and speed unknown in shipping history. The previous three hundred years had seen little change in function, design or construction. The East Indiaman, the typical British merchant vessel, was a warship adapted for passengers. When the East India Company's monopoly was broken in 1813 and the Napoleonic Wars came to an end two years later, the merchant ship was freed to develop along new and innovative lines, stimulated by a dramatic and sustained increase in passenger and cargo traffic (see Divine 1960:22). Emigration, an expanding colonial empire, a time of relative peace and a rising standard of living made travel available to all classes of society during the nineteenth century. The United States also responded to the challenge and forged ahead refining design and introducing specialization to the trade. By the 1840s it was seriously competing with the British on the transatlantic run. Out of the Boston shipyards came the famous Mackay-designed clippers which stunned the world and set a new trend in sailing ships.

The average net weight of passenger-cargo vessels between 1800 and 1850 has been estimated at 300 tons (see MacDonagh 1961:47); but within a few years some of the largest ships under sail had reached 2,500 tons. As the size increased, the shape of the hull changed, introducing a yacht-like appearance; the vessel lengthened relative to the beam, the bow was extended forward, and the blunt stern-end was sharpened. Vested interests also lay behind the change. The system of tonnage measurement introduced in 1773 assumed that the depth of the hull was half its width, so shipowners built their vessels with a small beam and greater depth to increase capacity while keeping port dues and similar charges to a minimum. These deep, narrow ships were usually fitted with three decks – a main and two passenger. The

Plate 1   The British emigrant ship, *Kapunda*

1854 Merchant Shipping Act, however, controlled this practice with new regulations for tonnage measurement.[3] The speed and manoeuverability of sailing ships were greatly enhanced by the increased size and amount of sail, adaptations to the rigging, and the new-style hull with its copper coating to prevent an encrustation of barnacles and seaweed. Although the large, fast, full-rigged ship looked magnificent driving through the seas, it became 'about the most dangerous vehicle ever invented by man' (Thornton 1945:57).

From the beginning of shipping history, wood had been used as the basic construction material. The introduction of iron seemed to contravene the laws of nature: iron did not float. In time, the most hardened traditionalists had to concede that it was lighter, more durable and allowed a greater carrying capacity than wood. Composites – iron-framed vessels with wooden planking and decking – first appeared, but soon gave way to an all-iron hull, decks, bulkheads and lower masts. Although the iron age of shipping was firmly established by 1870, before the end of the century iron had been superseded by steel.

Sailing ships on the Queensland route between 1860 and 1900 illustrate these developments (see Plate 1). Out of a total of 577 vessels, 490 (85 per cent) were solely wind propelled and of these, thirty-one were German. Most of the ships (72 per cent of the German and 82 per cent of the British) sailed to the colony only once or twice. However, twenty-six of the British vessels made five or more voyages, with the *Corinth*, a neat little barque of 614 tons, completing the London–Moreton Bay run fifteen times between her maiden voyage in 1872 and her last in 1885. She usually carried government cargo consignments and, in all, brought only 101 passengers. By contrast, the *Indus*, in seven voyages from 1870 to 1877, conveyed 3,261 immigrants to Queensland. The closest contender, the *Royal Dane*, carried 3,054 passengers and was the larger of the two vessels, registering 1,615 tons. Its dimensions (222 ft × 44.4 ft × 19.4 ft) suggest that it was designed with speed, capacity and safety in mind. Both ships belonged to the Black Ball fleet and together had clocked up more than forty years of sea-going experience by the time they entered the colonial trade.[4]

The *Montmorency*, a 668 ton wooden ship, was the first overseas vessel to reach the new colony. She carried 301 immigrants and dropped anchor in Moreton Bay in October, 1860 after 110 days at sea. Over the next forty years the standard of sailing vessels on the Queensland run gradually improved. Approximately 23 per cent of the British ships were built before 1860, but the majority (almost 70 per cent) came out of the yards in the next two decades; only 8 per cent were constructed after 1880. All but 10 per cent of the pre-1860 vessels were wooden; they averaged 919 tons and their mean dimensions (175 ft × 33 ft × 21 ft) gave a length-beam ratio of 5:1 and a beam-depth ratio of 3:2. These figures indicate that none of the 'coffin' ships was used in the Queensland trade. Both the colonial government and the Commissioners refused to charter such vessels since mortality statistics at sea during the gold-rush years of the early 1850s had shown that deaths on ships with two passenger decks far outnumbered deaths on single-decked vessels (see Welch 1969:15–18). The older ships varied in size from small craft of 307 tons to the large Black Ball clippers of almost 2,000 tons. Vessels constructed during the next twenty years were more uniform in size but slightly smaller, with an average of 849 tons; the dimensions (189.3 ft × 32.2 ft × 19.7 ft) resulted in similar proportional ratios. Only 26 per cent of these vessels were wooden, 8 per cent were composites, and the remainder were iron. Steel replaced the former two categories in ships built between 1880 and 1899. Consequently, both their mean tonnage (1,151 tons) and the superficial measurements (220.7 ft × 35.1 ft × 20.9 ft) increased. A glance over the figures for British sailing ships on the Queensland route shows that the major innovation was in construction material rather than design; most (55 per cent) were built of iron.

German sailing ships constructed before 1860 and used on the Hamburg–Brisbane run were not only larger than their British counterparts, but two-thirds of them were iron. Those built during the next two decades were all of iron and slightly smaller. The length-beam-depth ratios were similar to those for the British vessels. However, at least one of the German ships, the 711-ton *Wandrahm* which sailed to the colony during the 1860s, had two passenger decks. All the German vessels were selected for their immigrant-carrying capacity, whereas a percentage of the British ships were primarily for cargo and carried only a few passengers.

Changes in sailing ships in the second half of the nineteenth century improved their capacity and safety rather than their speed.

It is true that stunning records were set under the competitive conditions of the China tea races, but delivering a shipment of passengers or cargo to the colony created different demands. During the gold rush, first to California in the late 1840s and then to Australia in the early 1850s, speeds were greatly enhanced as a result of design refinements, increased canvas and, most important, the adoption of 'Great Circle Sailing'. Both the researches of Lt Maury of the United States navy into wind and current patterns, and Towson's Tables, published by the British Admiralty in 1847, demonstrated that the shortest distance on the globe is the arc of a large circle (see Charlwood 1981:20ff). Captains on the Australian run saw the value of this information and altered the traditional route; they bypassed Cape Town and heading south, entered the 'speedway for sailing ships' created by the westerly winds – the Roaring Forties and Howling Fifties (see Blainey 1966:4). The new route reduced the passage time by a fifth.[5]

During the colonial period voyages to Queensland by sailing ship averaged 109 days (approximately three and a half months), with passage times for the four decades (111, 107, 109 and 114 days) remaining relatively constant. Nevertheless, the range was enormous. In March 1883, the *Maulsden*, a 1,500-ton iron ship, left Greenock, doubled the Cape in 39 days and arrived in Maryborough 'after a phenomenal passage of 69 days' (RHSQ Shipwrecks). By contrast, a 'short ship', one with less than thirty steerage passengers, took 204 days. The record for an immigrant ship was 196 days and goes to the *Erin-go-Bragh*, a Black Ball vessel and the first chartered by Bishop Quinn. This 'crazy, leaky, old tub' took a fortnight crossing the Irish Sea from Liverpool and finally sailed from Cork on 7 February, 1862 (Davies 1937:312). Half way through the voyage, she began shipping water and was twice forced into port (at Cape Town and Hobart, Tasmania) because of sickness and a shortage of provisions and water. More than six months after departure, she limped into Moreton Bay and was promptly quarantined for ten days (see Boland 1963–64:317–18).

Immigrant vessels – those carrying more than thirty steerage passengers – usually did the voyage in less time than short ships since their relative size allowed it and their human cargo demanded it. During the 1860s British immigrant ships took an average of 107 days, but reduced this to 103 in the 1870s and to 99 days in the 1880s. The change to iron was primarily responsible for the improved performance, and resulted in a mean time of 104 days for the three decades. The extra distance from Hamburg added another week to the mean passage time for German vessels (112 and 110 days for the two decades), while short ships sailed at a more leisurely pace and averaged 112 days over the entire period. Under favourable conditions some vessels could reach 16 or 17 knots an hour without difficulty and cover more than 300 miles a day. Once the new southern route was established, sailing ships remained the most viable and economical form of transport on the long Australian haul, years after the steamship dominated other major seaways.

The seaworthiness of a vessel, its age and the nature of the cargo largely determined its speed and safety. After 1854 the imperial government introduced more stringent regulations for the registry and survey of its ships, particularly passenger carriers. It would appear from the records that relatively few newer vessels were used in the Queensland trade. Only 26 of the 459 British sailing ships took their maiden voyage to the colony and over half (57 per cent) had weathered the high seas for ten years or more at the time of sailing. The *Indus* was thirty years old when she delivered her last shipment of passengers in 1877. Mean ages for the British ships in the first two decades (11 and 12 years) indicate that they were slightly older than the German ships (9 and 11 years). However, the average age at sailing for British vessels in the 1880s dropped to ten years, while short ships became significantly more aged over the four decades.

The quantity and type of cargo often contributed to the ageing process. Although the trend towards specialization had been apparent for years, the merchant vessel retained its dual purpose as a cargo and passenger carrier until the end of the century. It was designed primarily for cargo, but usually provided limited, permanent accommodation for cabin travellers on the upper deck. Temporary fittings between decks for immigrants on the outward passage were thrown overboard on arrival to make way for a consignment of wool or other produce from the colony. Legislative prohibitions, the number of passengers, hull depth and the demand for goods from the home countries regulated the general cargo taken on the outbound voyage. During the 1860s when Queensland immigration was heavy and large quantities of railway plant were required, vessels sat deeply in the water, groaning and rolling under the strain in rough seas. An old wooden ship with a heavy and poorly secured cargo was not only unsafe, but could create misery for the hundreds of souls on board. In the early part of the century shippers gave little thought to the comfort of their human cargo, but attitudes gradually changed and minimum standards for immigrant vessels were established; Queensland introduced additional regulations to ensure the safety of her future colonists. Although there were no dramatic developments in travel under sail between 1860 and 1900, the steady improvements guaranteed increasingly favourable conditions for Queensland immigrants using this mode of transport.

Steam had been applied to water transport as early as 1788, but it took another twenty years for the first success with a paddle steamer. Before long it became a familiar sight on inland waterways, in the coastal trade and on the Atlantic. Then, following the repeal of the British navigation acts in 1849–50, trade, the merchant navy, and ship building rapidly expanded; and as the United States' supremacy with the sailing ship began to wane, the British steamship took its place. By 1865, yards in the United Kingdom were turning out more steam than sailing ships (see Palmer 1971:44). When the Queensland government signed the first contract with the British India Company in 1880, the steamship bore little resemblance to the 'floating smoke-box' that had earlier battled through the seas, arriving days after its wind-driven rivals (see Armstrong 1964:23). However, the steamer was not dependent on tides or winds, and the one advantage it had been able to offer from the outset was a regular service for mails, high-class cargo and passengers wanting to reach their destination in a given time. As marine engineering developed, the screw propellor replaced the paddles, the compound superseded the single engine, and wood, then iron and finally steel appeared in construction. By 1900 the steamship carried no sail, had fewer and shorter masts, included a super-structure of cabins and state-rooms, and was steered from a high bridge mid-ship rather than a low stern position (see Blainey 1968:270). Technological advances, together with the opening of the Suez Canal in 1869 and the establishment of coaling stations, soon gave steam the edge over sail and transformed nineteenth-century shipping.

Plate 2   SS Dorunda

Only two paddle and three auxiliary steamers sailed to Queensland during the first half of the colonial period. Auxiliaries did not depend solely on steam, but carried sail to utilize the 'free' wind power and reduce coal consumption (see Coates 1900:108–11). According to the surgeon-superindendent, the 85 day voyage of the SS *Great Victoria* in 1865 was a huge success (COL/A75:66–48). The following year the Black Ball Line chartered the SS *Great Pacific*; but, with a passage time of 107 days, it seems unlikely that the ship used her engines. Then, in 1874, the famous SS *Great Britain* sailed to the colony in 67 days. Unfortunately, the voyage was not conducted to the satisfaction of the Queensland authorities, the surgeon collapsed and died on arrival in Moreton Bay, and the experiment was never repeated (COL/A192). It was not until the SS *Merkara*, a British India vessel, sailed down the Queensland coast in April 1881, that a regular steamship service was established. This 1,996-ton (368.2 ft × 37.2 ft × 28.5 ft) iron screw-steamer, built six years previously, made a record of thirty-one voyages to the colony between 1881 and 1896, and averaged 57.2 days from London to Moreton Bay. She carried a total of 8,300 passengers.

Eighty-two steamships served Queensland during the second half of the colonial period (see Plate 2). Approximately one-fifth of these were built between 1860 and 1879, with a mean tonnage (1,629.5 tons) almost doubling that for the corresponding sailing vessels. The average dimensions (331.6 ft × 35.8 ft × 24.8 ft) were also larger and produced a greater length-beam and a marginally smaller beam-depth ratio (9:1 and 3:2). All were constructed of iron. More than half the steamers built during the last two decades were steel; the average tonnage (1,986 tons) increased and the dimensions (329.7 ft × 41.3 ft × 24.3 ft) represented a change in hull design, with a reduced length-beam ratio and a slightly larger beam-depth ratio. Although both sailing and steam ships increased in size over the four decades, the latter were more spacious and efficient; they were also less weather-beaten. The majority (55 per cent compared to 43 per cent for sailing ships) were under ten years old at the time of sailing, but their average age increased from seven years in the 1880s to ten years in the 1890s. Incidentally, the SS *Great Britain*, built in 1842, was the oldest vessel to reach the colony. The mean passage time for immigrant steamships was 58 days; this clipped the length of comparable voyages under sail by 46 days (seven and a half weeks). However, the record (48 days) was only three weeks short of that set by the *Maulsden*, while the little 287-ton paddle steamer *Queensland*, purchased for the colonial coastal trade in 1862, coaled at numerous ports along the way and took four days longer than the *Erin-go-Bragh*.

A steerage passenger to Queensland on the SS *Duke of Norfolk* in 1900 would have found it difficult to imagine sailing as an immigrant on the *Montmorency* forty years earlier. The steel, screw-propelled steamship was almost four times the tonnage, three times the superficial dimensions and reduced the passage time by half. This 2,438-ton steamer was not designed exclusively as a passenger liner, but the steerage accommodation was permanent rather than temporary, refrigeration supplied fresh food for all classes and eliminated the need for a deck farmyard to supplement provisions on the cabin table, electric light replaced oil lamps and candles and, incorporated in the design, were safety features such as transverse water-tight bulkheads to minimize the risk of sinking in the event of a collision or hitting a submerged rock. Moreover, no ballast was required to offset heavy masts and rigging, and steam winches speeded up cargo-handling (see Knox-Robinson 1978:18).

Along with these developments came improved navigational aids. In sailing ship days, navigation depended on basic equipment – a compass, chronometer, one or two sextants, a sounding line and a log line – and on its 'sister science', astronomy (see Charlwood 1981:18–19). After 1852 all iron-built vessels had to carry an azimuth compass since iron created a new magnetic field and distorted directional readings. Captain Cook had demonstrated an efficient method for calculating the ship's longitude with a chronometer, but the accuracy of this expensive item deteriorated after two or three months at sea. If foggy or stormy weather made it impossible to use the sextant for estimating latitude, then the captain had to rely on 'dead reckoning' using the log line to determine the speed and the distance covered between two known points; but such calculations could not take into account the effect of winds and currents (see Edwardes and Parsons 1975:41). Although the sounding line gave some idea of depth, its use was limited in poorly charted seas. As trade and passenger traffic increased, so did the demand for hydrographic surveys and more accurate, detailed charting of coastal and oceanic waters, winds and currents, and for aids such as lighthouses and light ships, signalling and side lights for the vessel. Yet, however sophisticated the equipment, a captain always depended on the sharp eyes of the look-out and his own knowledge of the seas. By and large, navigational conditions for steamers to the colony were superior to those for sailing vessels, but the Red Sea and the intricacies of the Barrier Reef along the Queensland coast could be hazardous. A severe dust storm in the Red Sea in 1886 reduced visibility to a few yards and the captain of the SS *Dacca*, a British India vessel, literally 'felt' his way along (COL/A473:86–5780).

When we consider the possibilities for disaster at sea, it is remarkable that only three Queensland-bound vessels in the 41 years and 1,317 voyages were wrecked. A British Royal Commission in 1873 reported that 0.47 per cent of all registered passenger ships leaving United Kingdom ports between 1847 and 1872 were lost, often with no survivors (BPP 1873:xxxvi 315,335). Queensland's 0.2 per cent, although it covers a later and longer period, nevertheless suggests an improvement on the general rate of loss. The first to go down was a German vessel, the *Wilhelmsburg*, 'one of the finest and largest of the fleet of Messrs T.C. Godeffroy and Son' (COL/A51:64–652). It was caught in 'fearful gales' and sunk off the Dutch coast on 3 December, 1863 with the loss of 257 of the 282 immigrants on board. The other two were British vessels, but all passengers and crew survived. The *Netherby*, a Black Ball ship (see Plate 3), was wrecked in a storm off King Island in Bass Strait at the south-eastern corner of the Australian mainland in July, 1866,[6] and, as a result of poor navigation, the SS *Dacca* foundered on a reef while steaming through the Red Sea in May, 1890 (QVP 1891:IV,25).

Other Queensland vessels were involved in accidents and distress at sea which caused delays but no loss of life. The *Flying Cloud* in 1866 collided with a ship as she left the London docks; immigrants remained on board for a month while repairs were effected (COL/A79:66–1209). In 1897 the SS *Duke of Devonshire* hit a rock near Thursday Island at the northerly tip of Queensland, but all the passengers were safely conveyed to their destination by coastal steamer and the vessel was refloated (QVP 1898:II,691). Official records and diaries frequently describe rather terrifying experiences of 'near collisions' and vessels which almost capsized,

Plate 3 The wreck of 'The Netherby

ran aground or were severely disabled during a storm. Several were lost on the home-bound voyage (see Davies 1935:319–25 and Cotton 1957:1283–94). Passengers, especially on sailing ships, took a lively interest in the navigation and progress of the vessel; a fair wind did much to improve the temper of all on board.

Developments in nineteenth-century shipping demanded legislative control. A perusal of the *British Statutes* between 1850 and 1900 indicates that maritime-related bills were constantly before the House in an attempt to balance shipping requirements and imperial interests, trade and technological advances and, not least, the welfare of ordinary people – passengers and crew. 'The laborious process of improving the conditions of voluntary emigration began . . . with the passenger act of 1803' (Mac-Donagh 1961:54). This dealt with health and hygiene, fraudulent shippers and masters, and the overloading of unseaworthy vessels; but it fell short in its enforcement, a problem which continued to dog later legislation. Although the act was intended to prevent abuses and deter emigration, this was not possible with the growing social distress following Waterloo. A series of amendments finally resulted in a new act in 1827 which swept aside all restrictions on passenger traffic. As disasters at sea escalated with frightening rapidity, the pendulum swung in the opposite direction to produce the curative 1828 act. The next two decades witnessed a struggle between *laissez-faire* and increased controls, state functions and individual rights, local and central government responsibility. But in the final analysis, it was the terrible toll exacted by cholera and typhus (particularly among the Irish), shipwreck and shipboard abuses, that brought about improved minimum standards for the emigrant trade.

At first the customs officer was the chief executor for the passenger legislation; but in 1833, an emigration officer was made responsible for the welfare of emigrants sailing from Liverpool. He identified the problems and pressed for increased berthing space and height between decks, better discipline and segregation of the sexes, as well as a clean water supply, a balanced dietary and adequate medical care – all provided by the shipping brokers or owners. Officers (ex-naval men on half pay) were appointed to other ports the following year, but none of them received any formal training, status or powers of enforcement. In the wake of systematic colonization and the establishment of state-aided emigration to the Antipodes, conditions at sea so deteriorated that an Agent-General for Emigration was appointed in 1837 to oversee the officers. Two years later, the Durham Report from Canada exposed the shameful excesses of the Atlantic trade and placed the blame at the officers' feet. The Colonial Land and Emigration Commission commenced operations the next year.[7]

There was an immediate improvement as breaches of the law were investigated, officers received instruction and passenger lists, sent ahead to the port of arrival, prevented over-crowding. But the Canadian authorities insisted that pre-embarkation abuses (diseased lodging houses, poor provisions and delayed sailings) and a lack of superintendence at sea constituted the primary areas for remedial action. Their proposals, together with recommendations from the Commissioners' reports, were embodied in the 1842 act which 'for its day, [was] a superlative piece of social legislation' (MacDonagh 1961:147). This required brokers and agents to be licensed and all passage agreements to be made on a prescribed form, provided for a minimum diet and 'sweetened' water supplied by the shippers from the contract date of sailing, forbade the sale of liquor at sea, raised the minimum height between decks to six feet, increased deck thickness and controlled overcrowding by allowing a passenger–tonnage ratio of 3:5 and nine square feet per adult (fourteen years and over) for berthing. More important, the act included enforcement clauses. Its apparent success was evident in the declining maritime death rate and a checking of the worst abuses until the Irish potato famine reached its climax with the unprecedented emigration and fearful epidemics of 1847.

Amendments to the act during the next two years brought more vessels under legislative control. Official surveyors checked the seaworthiness of ships covered by the law, and all emigrants were examined for infectious diseases before embarkation. An accelerating public health awareness found expression in clauses providing for additional berthing space, sufficient food, water and cooking facilities, and professional medical care. The Commissioners were authorized to establish emigration depots. Despite these advances, administration of the law, except for enforcement of the numbers clause, remained relatively ineffective since the volume of emigration grew at twice the rate of the executive corps. At the same time, their functions multiplied and became more specialized. They had to inspect supplies, vessels and passengers, supervise disciplinary arrangements on board, select suitable surgeons and masters, arbitrate in violations of the act, and attend to the 'paper work'. Also, the introduction of steam travel called for more technical and specialized knowledge and action, and the emigration officer, lacking both training and expertise, found himself increasingly at a disadvantage; the chasm between the law and practice widened.

The 1852 act, a direct result of a select committee inquiry the previous year, increased state responsibility and intervention. Penalties were introduced for ships sailing without a clearance or using other than main decks for passengers; all single men above the age of fourteen years had to be accommodated separately; provision was made for meals, berthing and sick bays, an adequate number of privies, lighting, ventilation, safety appliances and navigational aids; every vessel with more than 500 passengers had to carry a surgeon. Port authorities were empowered to make by-laws covering embarkation, entry to passenger docks and licensing of porters; masters had to enter into a bond with the brokers, and the discretionary powers of executive officers were augmented. Finally, under orders-in-council, the Commissioners could regulate not only discipline, but all matters relating to sanitation, provisions, health and safety during the voyage.

By mid-century, it was generally accepted that the emigrant had rights and that the state must intervene to protect them. In return emigrants were expected to submit to regulations designed for their well-being; the British vessel became a floating welfare state with reciprocal rights and privileges far exceeding those for any landed community. There was, however, a noticeable difference between voluntary migration covered only by the legislation and state-aided immigration financed by a colonial government. Two distinct types of passenger voyage evolved – those inspected by the emigration officers and those which the Commissioners were paid to organize and supervise.

Better kept statistics, reports from the United States, the degenerate state of the merchant marine and a series of disasters on the Atlantic in 1853, all provided fuel for another inquiry. Within two years the 1855 Passenger's Act (18 & 19 Vict. c. 119) had been passed. This statute consolidated fifty years of legislative response to evils in the emigrant trade, incorporated developments in the shipping industry and public health, and asserted the right of the state to intervene on behalf of those who, for a brief period, became stateless and defenceless. Britain's growing industrial and political strength meant that areas of social responsibility, including the safe conduct of her people to every part of the globe, could not be ignored. The act remained in force for forty years. It covered vessels carrying more than thirty steerage passengers, embraced all aspects of emigrant protection and served as the basis for regulations and shipping contracts under which almost 90 per cent of Queensland's immigrants sailed to the colony.[8]

As MacDonagh (1961:294 ff.) points out, the greatest innovation was the delegation of authority by parliament. In addition to their previous statutory powers, the Commissioners could issue orders-in-council requiring any vessel to carry a surgeon, prohibiting emigration from a particular port, and reducing the passenger complement, though it was expected that such authority would be exercised only in the event of an epidemic. Emigration officers were given absolute discretionary powers; it was their function to determine if passenger fittings and arrangements were adequate, the cargo and its stowage were dangerous, and if the navigational and safety equipment as well as the number of crew were sufficient. They appointed medical officers to examine emigrants at embarkation, decided what monies were recoverable from the shippers on behalf of the passengers, licensed and registered runners, and checked documents for the voyage (passenger lists, registration forms for births and deaths, and copies and abstracts of the act). When the officer was satisfied that the vessel, its master and owner had fully complied with clauses relating to seaworthiness, bonds and provisions for passenger welfare, he issued a Certificate of Clearance. Anyone connected with the trade was, to a lesser or greater extent, at the mercy of this unqualified, overworked and underpaid officer.

The new act began well and had established an encouraging record by the time Queensland immigration began. Nevertheless, large shipping companies and colonial governments soon recognized that the law allowed only minimum standards; they detected weaknesses in the system, noted the limitations and incompetence of the executive corps, and introduced additional safeguards. However, Queensland's regulations, while based on the law, were designed to enhance conditions at sea for a highly selected and much-needed population rather than protect a vulnerable class. During the next forty years the law itself underwent certain modifications. In 1856 the Commissioners issued an order-in-council with revised 'rules for preserving order, for promoting health, and for securing cleanliness and ventilation' during the voyage. These were updated following an amending act (26 & 27 Vict. c.51) in 1863. A further order, issued during the 1866 cholera epidemic, stipulated that all vessels with fifty or more passengers had to carry a medical officer. The 1863 act tidied up the legislation by cancelling exemptions for mail vessels and cabin passengers, bringing more steamships under its provisions, improving the dietary scale and increasing the master's bond. In the late 1860s, emigration from the British Isles plateaued and epidemic diseases diminished. These factors, together with the recession and a growing organization and independence in the passenger-cargo trade, reduced the need for a large executive corps.

Meanwhile, all aspects of merchant shipping, particularly those relating to management and manning, came under review. Concern for seamen, their poor reputation, terrible working conditions and high mortality rate, followed in the wake of passenger legislation. The Merchant Shipping Acts of 1867 and 1871 reflected this concern by improving facilities for sailors, regulating safety features and introducing penalties for unseaworthy and overloaded vessels. Despite resistance from shipping interests, subsequent legislation concentrated on this three-pronged attack. An 1872 statute transferred the measurement of tonnage and the administration of the passenger acts to the Board of Trade, and the much-reduced staff of the Emigration Commission took their place with the Board's inspectors. These men were the product of a trend towards specialization and had long been responsible for technical matters relating to steamships and the survey of vessels. No new measure or device was adopted until it had been scientifically tested, and its operation could be supervised by competent personnel; the expert had replaced the amateur. Although the functions of the emigration officer were retained, he increasingly sought advice on the adequacy of emigrant fittings, provisions and arrangements.

While passenger legislation remained unchanged, a succession of shipping acts continued to raise standards at sea and indirectly benefit the travelling public. The 1888 act, for example, made it mandatory for all emigrant vessels to be fully equipped with life-saving equipment. Men behind the large liner companies and shipbuilding firms found it was in their best interests to encourage such improvements. In 1894 passenger and shipping legislation finally merged; the Merchant Shipping Act (57 & 58 Vict. c.60) was a comprehensive and extensive synthesis of four decades of maritime law. It covered the registry, survey, measurement, cargo, navigation and safety of every class of vessel, and provided for wrecks, salvage and special courts of enquiry, as well as the management of crews. Clauses relating to the safety, discipline and health of passengers were retained; but by defining an emigrant ship as one carrying more than fifty steerage passengers, a greater number of vessels were exempt from the law. Conditions of travel had so improved by the time subsidized immigration to Queensland resumed in 1898, that the colonial authorities no longer considered it necessary to supplement the legislation.

Emigration and shipping were so inextricably linked during the nineteenth century that, as the emphasis shifted from emigrant protection to shipping improvement, the gains in one were consolidated in the other. Either way, passengers to the colony reaped the benefits. Yet these applied primarily to immigrants sailing under the British flag. The colonial government included the Queensland regulations and certain clauses of the passenger acts in all German shipping contracts, but these did not adapt well to Hamburg maritime law. For example, this law defined a statute adult as any person over the age of fourteen or two children between four and fourteen years, and allowed only twelve superficial feet for each such adult. Also, provisions for decency and discipline, safety, cleanliness and medical attention, water and foodstuffs, were inferior to the minimum British requirements (see QVP 1866:1015–022). Fortunately, only 7.2 per cent of the total immigration sailed under these less than satisfactory conditions (see Tables 3 and 4, p. 349).

Some 42.4 per cent of the Queensland-bound voyages were subject to the terms of the passenger acts, but these voyages represented 89 per cent of the immigrants. On short-ships, the only passenger might be the captain's wife, yet a fair proportion sailed with the maximum number allowed. Since these ships were exempt from the law, they did not have to employ a surgeon or subscribe to the fixed dietary and general arrangements for emigrant vessels. Their passengers, most of whom were full-payers and travelled cabin class, were covered by a private contract with the shippers or their agents. Comparatively few steamers sailed as short-ships during the 1880s, but in the last decade, they accounted for 70 per cent of the voyages and 43.6 per cent of the passengers, owing to the withdrawal of government assistance and the response to the more liberal numbers clause in the 1894 act. The majority of short steamers carried mails and therefore kept to a regular schedule, but short-ships under sail, not being tied in this way, could afford a more leisurely passage. Life on a short-ship differed greatly from that on emigrant vessels; the small proportion of passengers – 1.6 per cent by sail and 2.2 per cent by steam – did not have to cope with the pressures of a closely confined, regulated and stratified community.

The management and supervision of immigrant vessels to the colony not only differed from short-ships, but from one voyage to the next. Regulations sanctioned by the colonial authorities for government-chartered vessels came into effect in the early years of the land-order system and remained in force until 1892; they covered 86.4 per cent of the passenger act voyages. This meant that 87.1 per cent of future Queenslanders sailing on British emigrant vessels (both sail and steam) received care and protection in addition to that prescribed by the law. The 4.2 per cent travelling in ships chartered by the Commissioners on behalf of the government were also covered by similar regulations. However, the Commissioners did not accommodate a cabin class on their vessels or embark passengers at Scottish or Irish ports for lack of adequate facilities at these ports. While their ships were well managed, their operation was too limited to meet colonial immigration requirements. Shipping owners or charterers were directly responsible for the remaining 8.7 per cent of immigrants sailing on passenger act vessels. Although these ships (twenty-four in 1861–63 and five bounty vessels in 1883–84) had been inspected and passed by an emigration officer, they were so poorly managed that the Queensland authorities brought all such vessels under their regulations.

Immigration to the colony was a strictly controlled business. It had to be to ensure that the health of the thousands selected and subsidized by the government was maintained during the voyage.

Passenger legislation laid the foundation, but colonial initiative and shipping improvements raised the standard of living at sea. Despite 'the stringent regulations and special preparations' which deterred many shipping firms from becoming involved in the Queensland trade, a number of well-known companies were willing to do business. When Henry Jordan arrived in London in 1861 he

> 'saw several large shipping firms and proposed to them that they should put on a ship to the colony . . . One and all . . . at once refused. They did not know the name of the Colony . . . there was no trade to Moreton Bay . . . and a passenger trade without freight would not pay. And as for my proposal that I should pay them . . . with land orders, they quite laughed at the idea.'
>
> (QVP 1864:988)

He finally met John Taylor, a new and junior partner with the Liverpool based Black Ball Line whose founder, James Baines, had captured a large share of the Australian trade during the previous decade. In 1858 Thomas Mackay, his partner, opened an office in London, and it was here that Jordan negotiated, on behalf of the government, with John Taylor for the Line's exclusive operation of the land-order system.

This was an innovative and risky venture since payment for free and assisted passages was in kind and the return cargo was limited and uncertain. Jordan's only guarantee was a constant flow of immigrants. The first sailing in 1861 augured well and regular departures during the following year encouraged the firm to purchase extra vessels (several of these were American clippers which became available at bargain prices during the Civil War) and sign a formal contract in February 1863 (see QVP 1864:938–39). Under the agreement the shippers received a nominal payment, in addition to the land order, for each subsidized statute adult landed alive in the colony. In return they agreed to make available their large staff of agents to publicize Queensland and recruit colonists, comply with the regulations, and contribute to the surgeon's salary and gratuities for assistants and crew involved with passenger care (see QVP 1863:II,436). The company needed the Queensland trade and Jordan could not conduct his emigration without its administrative support and the assurance of regular sailings. This interdependence was summed up in Thomas Mackay's claim that, in common with the colonial government, the firm's 'one wish' was to draw attention to Queensland by fostering 'a continuous and healthy stream of immigrants' from the capitalist and working classes (QVP 1864:937).

Although thousands departed for the colony under the agreement, constant criticism was levelled at the entire organization – the Line's monopoly, problems associated with carrying four distinct classes and, not least, unsatisfactory conditions of travel. Many felt that the old American softwood vessels were unsuitable as emigrant ships. When Jordan discovered that the government had decided to terminate the contract and open tenders for a new one, he feared for the future of the system and immediately sailed for the colony with John Taylor. Both defended the operation and pointed out that the firm's agencies could not be used by the Queensland Emigration Service under any other contract. A revised agreement was signed in September, 1864. This provided a more stable financial base and included additional regulations for discipline and health care at sea (QVP 1865:660 and 1867–68:II,94). Jordan and Taylor returned to London satisfied with the new arrangements, but in the next couple of years the firm and the colony ran into difficulties; both were working on a huge credit. In 1865 the system again fell into disrepute largely because of the uncontrolled influx of navvies for public works, and in 1866 the crash came. Barnard's Bank which financed the Black Ball Line collapsed, followed quickly by the Agra and Masterman Bank which undergirded Queensland's projects.

The company went into liquidation, but came through the disaster and refloated operations. Mackay and Son took over the London-based part of the business and, despite a much reduced emigration, continued to lay on ships under the former agreement which was renewed in September, 1866 and January, 1868. But after the passing of the 1869 Immigration Act, the writing was on the wall. A conservative government controlled the system, cancelled the Line's exclusive rights and, placing the trade on the open market, called for tenders for individual sailings (QVP 1871:902). The *Indus*, the last ship to fly the Black Ball flag, sailed for the colony as the Line suspended payments in April, 1871. The 'enterprising venture' on which they had embarked ten years before had not paid off, but out of the trial-and-error period and as a result of the firm's support and willing compliance with the regulations, a method of operation emerged which set the pattern for the colonial immigration system. Almost 60 per cent of all the voyages in the first decade sailed under Black Ball contracts. The Line was proud of its record, having conveyed more than 'forty thousand souls to [the] colony, without the loss of a single life, except from natural causes' and established a mean passage time similar to that for voyages to Sydney and Melbourne. Such achievements, the directors believed, could only be attributed to their 'fine, airy ships, with small cargo capacity but possessed of great sailing powers' (QVP 1871:904).

During the 1870s, conservative policy, problems with the Queensland Office in London, a growing colonial trade, and fluctuations in the volume of emigration affected shipping arrangements and intensified government intervention. When the authorities insisted that all vessels be classed as A1 at Lloyds, it was pointed out that a seaworthy vessel might not be suitable for emigrants. So they agreed to charter only ships passed by the Commissioners or Board of Trade (see QVP 1871:906). Each new contract incorporated the regulations and involved a method of payment by which the shippers received the first moiety at departure and the second after the vessel's arrival in the colony when the number landed alive and fulfilment of the terms of contract had been verified. However, finding suitable vessels became increasingly difficult as the Board of Trade stepped up their surveillance after 1872; fewer firms were prepared to undertake the expense and effort of outfitting emigrant ships. Also, single-voyage tenders prevented coordinated planning between shippers, provision merchants and fitters (see QVP 1873:997–98).

Finally, the government grasped the situation and allowed a one-year contract which went to Taylor, Bethell and Roberts of the London Line in July, 1873. The Agent-General extended this agreement for a further twelve months on the grounds that the company knew the trade and was prepared to abide by the regulations; but his action was not approved since complaints concerning the quality of the immigration, 'irregularities' and mismanagement were multiplying (see QVP 1875:II,611). Shortly after tenders had been invited in June, 1875 for three-year contracts for different sectors of the service, the fraudulent conspiracy involving members of the London Line, several of the staff of the London office and the provisions contractor was exposed. Needless to say, the firm's tender was rejected. Between 1872 and 1875, they had introduced almost the total complement of government immigrants to the colony. The contracts finally went to three other firms – Anderson and Anderson, McIlwraith, McEacharn and Company, and Thomas Law – all of whom remained with the colonial trade.[9] Shipping arrangements were, if possible, more closely monitored after the upheaval, but conditions on sailing vessels improved and demonstrated the benefits of long-term agreements.

After considerable opposition and much wrangling, the government signed an eight-year mail contract with the British India Steam Navigation Company on 6 May, 1880; and the following year arrangements were made for the conveyance of immigrants in the regular monthly steamers.[10] Although Queensland's location and the demands of the northern ports finally forced the issue, the establishment of a northern shipping route had been debated for years (see QVP 1865:953 and Austin 1949:229). An attempt to initiate a mail steamer service in the 1870s failed partly on the grounds that the route through the Suez Canal and the Torres Straits was considered climatically unsuitable for immigrants (QVP 1873:998); but the first few successful British India voyages proved otherwise and by the time tenders were invited for the bounty scheme in 1882, all such objections had been overruled. Since it was intended that bounty passengers – the government paid £10 for each and the shippers offered a reduced second-cabin passage – be carried separately from regular immigrants, the original contract stipulated that cargo sailing ships of not more than 600 tons be used. The shippers agreed to adhere to the terms of the passenger acts and the 1882 Immigration Act and were responsible for all voyage arrangements, including the survey and outfitting of vessels (see QVP 1883–84:1369). Then the scheme was extended to steamers and an agreement was signed with British India (see QVP 1884:II,606–07); but reports of gross mismanagement on bounty vessels quickly led to a modification of the contracts. In future, the Queensland regulations would be enforced on all vessels carrying more than fifty bounty passengers (see QVP 1883–84:1383–384). A limited number of sailing ships served the northern ports until 1889, but British India monopolized the steamship service. When immigration was at its peak, they chartered and virtually absorbed the Ducal Line vessels; their rate of £16 per adult altered little during the two decades and compared favourably with sailing ship charges for the whole period. During the late 1890s, the Gulf Line appeared on the Queensland run, but used the southern rather than the northern route.

Problems with the German immigration were not confined to recruitment and selection; the Queensland authorities found that shipping contracts could not be effected with the degree of control and reliability they had come to expect with the British firms. In 1861 Heussler negotiated an agreement with Godeffroy and Sons, and on his return to the colony eighteen months later, left the responsibility for the immigration in their hands with no disinterested party to supervise the operation.[11] The final Godeffroy contract terminated in 1866. During the 1870s the government was not only forbidden to intervene in shipping arrangements, but was restricted to a choice of two firms licensed to conduct the German emigration. The Queensland agent signed an agreement with Knorr and Company in May, 1870 (see QVP 1872:1433), and twice renewed it before cancelling it prematurely in November, 1873. The last German contract was negotiated with the better-known Sloman and Company in April, 1877 (see QVP 1877:II, 1175–191). When difficulties arose in the 1880s with the despatch of Continental immigrants via English ports, the government tried but failed to arrange a steamer service from Bremen or a Mediterranean port of call for British India ships. It was not until the late 1890s that Queensland immigrants could travel in Nord-Deutscher steamers to Sydney where they transshipped to Brisbane.

Apart from the opening up of the northern route, improved port facilities in both the United Kingdom and Queensland enhanced the conduct of the colonial immigration. In 1860 London handled the bulk of the cargo trade and Liverpool was the chief port of departure for transatlantic and Antipodean passengers. A more efficient method of port management, the building of new docks, and the provision of an emigration depot to replace disease-ridden and morally shady lodging houses, eliminated many of the problems associated with embarkation at Liverpool, but it remained a difficult process; sailings were at the mercy of the tides and the port was large, overcrowded, often fog-bound and had dangerous sand bars (see Chandler 1973). This partly explains why only 4.1 per cent of Queensland's total immigration left from Liverpool, with the majority using the port during the first decade. Colonial officials also found it more convenient to supervise the departure of vessels from the southern English ports. But the fact that London had no depot was considered a major drawback, especially for single women. The Brisbane bureaucrats urged that adequate provision be made 'to avoid . . . the evil of placing young girls in such a questionable position for even one day' (COL/A131:69–3359).

Plymouth offered depot facilities and became a popular port for Queensland departures largely because collisions and choppy conditions in the Channel could be avoided (see QVP 1884:II,596). Sailing ships frequently embarked cabin passengers and cargo in London and called three to four days later at Plymouth for the immigrants. Even after steamships entered the trade, this arrangement continued until an emigration depot was opened at Blackwall in London in 1884. But an increasing number of Queensland-bound vessels left directly from the Thames, despite the limited facilities and the Channel delays. As a result, almost half the British passenger act vessels sailed from London, a quarter departed from Plymouth and a further 3 per cent called at the two ports. If the Southampton and London–Cork sailings are added, we find that 80 per cent of the emigrant vessels left from the southern English ports. Only seven (1.2 per cent) ships departed from Cork and another 3.4 per cent used it as a second port of call after London or Liverpool. The Irish complement was encouraged to travel via England, and after 1880 had no alternative. Once, in 1874, a despatch was organized from Belfast, but this proved so expensive that it was decided to use Glasgow, despite its limitations, for the northern Irish and English as well as the Scottish passengers. A little over a tenth of the immigration left from the Clyde. Conditions for the Hamburg embarkees were also poor, with no emigration buildings and sailings dependent on the Elbe tides or the season. Continental immigrants relying on a passage from one of the English ports suffered the greatest inconvenience.

Setting out across 12,000 miles of 'unfenced salt meadows' was a daunting business and usually a memorable experience – one of confusion, excitement and apprehension. Frequently the time of departure did not improve the situation. Almost a third of the voyages began during the most favourable months from April to June, only 20 per cent left in the worst of the winter between January and March, and the other half were distributed over the remaining six months. While sailing ships preferred to schedule their departures during the summer, steamships were, by and large, not dependent on the weather conditions. A sailing vessel leaving the London docks had to be towed down the Thames to Gravesend where another pilot came on board to negotiate it through the English Channel. In the early years, immigrants boarded directly in London, but later travelled by river steamer to embark at Gravesend. Then, in the late 1880s, a rail journey from Blackwall to Gravesend came as a welcome improvement, especially in 'cold, foggy and unfavourable weather' (QVP 1892:II,811).

Sometimes a sailing ship could be weeks anchored off the Downs or sheltering in Plymouth Sound waiting for a fair wind; but once clear of the chops of the Channel, the captain assumed full control until Queensland was safely reached. Out into the Atlantic, the vessel headed towards the South American coast but could be further delayed in the 'doldrums' while immigrants sweltered under the equatorial sun. Veering away from South America, they continued sailing south-east, bypassing the Cape of Good Hope, until they picked up the Westerlies and began easting down the next 8,000 miles. In these southern latitudes passengers had to live through the coldest and most terrifying part of the voyage with snow storms, heavy seas and the threat of icebergs. After rounding Tasmania at the southerly tip of eastern Australia, the captain fetched north towards sunny Queensland. Sometimes he attempted the shorter route through Bass Strait (it was on King Island at the entrance to the Strait that the *Netherby* was wrecked). All the sailing vessels and the few auxiliary and paddle steamers as well as the Gulf Line ships used the southern route (see Map B).

Unless the life of those on board was threatened by a shortage of water or provisions, epidemic disease, mechanical difficulties or a mutinous crew, a vessel did not stop between the home and colonial ports. Only twenty-four sailing ships (this involved 6 per cent of the passengers) were forced to make such a stop. The government did not treat these lightly and thoroughly investigated the circumstances. They disapproved, for example, if a ship

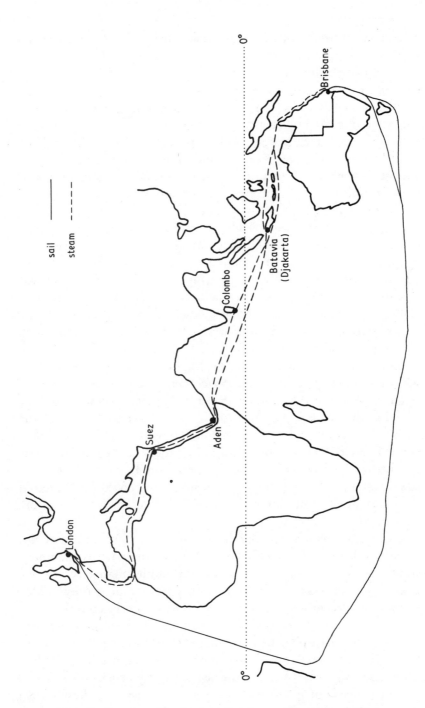

Map B London, England to Brisbane, Queensland: route

had to put into a southern Australian port since the immigrants might be tempted by its 'superior attractions' and change their mind about settling in Queensland (see QVP 1871:908). Strict precautions were also observed on steamship voyages, with only cabin passengers allowed ashore at coaling ports. Three steamers had to make an emergency stop; yet very few were delayed through poor management, collisions or mechanical problems. Apart from 'stress of weather and other unavoidable causes', almost 94 per cent of the immigrant voyages (both sail and steam) were trouble-free, a testimony to the careful selection of vessels and the supervision of arrangements.

A British India steamer leaving London or Plymouth encountered few of the problems of a sailing ship trying to clear the English Channel; but she could be tossed about in the Bay of Biscay before entering the Mediterranean Sea. The first stop was usually Port Said or Suez at the southern end of the 103-mile Canal. Between here and Aden (a distance of 1,300 miles), the calms, strong headwinds and heat of the Red Sea created much discomfort, and were often followed by monsoons in the Indian Ocean. The call at Colombo or Batavia (Djakarta) came as a welcome relief. The ship then proceeded through the Indonesian Archipelago, past the southern coast of New Guinea to Thursday Island at the northerly tip of Queensland. After coaling here, she steamed down the coast in the sheltered passage between it and the Great Barrier Reef, disembarking passengers at the various ports before finally dropping anchor in Moreton Bay. An important advantage of this route was that immigrants could be landed at their intended destinations and not be lured by the more developed colonial towns.

The inner passage proved ideal for steamships but was not popular with sailing vessels on account of the narrow channels, sudden shifts of wind, cyclones, and difficulties manoeuvring (see Lack 1959b:130–54). Over the years, hydrographic surveys added to the knowledge of coastal waters, and the timely completion in 1881 of new and corrected Admiralty charts benefited the new overseas steamer trade. British India vessels remained 'wonderfully free from accident' (see Halls 1978:93). Between 1859 and 1885, fourteen new ports were established along Queensland's coast to serve the needs of inland pastoralists and miners (see Lewis 1973 and Bird 1968). Producers pressed for railway development from river-sited, tidal ports and ignored the advantages of natural harbours. By the mid-1880s, port weaknesses were evident; few could handle vessels of more than 2,000 tons, lighterage was extensively used, and problems related to dredging, wharf facilities, pilotage and coastal lighting were exacerbated by lack of funds, administrative changes and the size of the colony, to say nothing of floods and cyclones.

Brisbane, the chief and most southerly port, was not only remarkable for its eccentric position in the colony, but also its navigational problems. Large ships and ocean steamers had to be offloaded in Moreton Bay and passengers and their luggage trans-shipped twenty-five miles up river to the immigration depot. Further north lay Maryborough, sited on a deep, barless river and Bundaberg, with its difficult entrance; both had to wait for mineral discoveries and the growth of the sugar industry before being adequately developed. Although Gladstone had a natural harbour, it was superseded by Rockhampton, situated on the 'hazardous' Fitzroy River. Here immigrants continued to be trans-shipped to town even after a deep water port had been built in Keppel Bay. The situation was similar at Townsville, the foremost port in north Queensland, where an artificial harbour had to be constructed. Bowen, a little to the south of Townsville, was gradually eclipsed as Mackay grew along with the sugar industry. To the north, Cairns and Cooktown developed and waned in response to inland gold discoveries. More than 1,100 miles of coastline lay between Cooktown and Brisbane (see Map A, p. 5).

Although shippers preferred Brisbane on account of its better facilities, contracts usually stated that a proportion of the immigrants must be landed at the northern ports. Not only did the majority of short-ships discharge their passengers and cargo in Brisbane, but this port was also the primary destination for 41.6 per cent of all immigrant (passenger act and German) voyages. A further 3.5 per cent of these voyages shared their shipment between Brisbane and another port, 15 per cent terminated at the central ports, and only 5.2 per cent were destined for the north. Steamships disembarking passengers down the coast accounted for the remaining 34.7 per cent. They also carried 40 per cent of all who embarked on immigrant voyages. Between 1881 and 1892, Brisbane received 60 per cent of all new arrivals; this figure rose to almost 70 per cent for the whole period.[12] The town could create a most favourable impression, especially during the winter months. A French traveller described his arrival: 'The day was perfect: not a cloud in the sky, just hot enough to be pleasant and just enough breeze to give a delicious freshness to the air . . . it made one think spontaneously of an earthly paradise' (La Meslée 1883:71).

The colonial authorities, as well as emigrant guidebooks, advised that, in view of weather hazards and adjustments facing 'new chums', vessels should avoid arriving in the hot season (see, for example, QVP 1875:II,644 and Chadfield n.d.:5). Queensland spans two climatic zones, temperate and tropical, and receives abundant coastal rains throughout the year, with maximum falls in summer and autumn (November to April) when the whole area is under the influence of the south-east trade winds. These blow continuously over the north, but the southern regions receive some relief when the Westerlies move in between May and October (winter and spring). Some attention was given to the government recommendation since almost one-third of the immigrants arrived during the three coolest months – June, July and August. This proportion was as high as 38 per cent in the 1860s, but dropped to 30 per cent in the next decade and decreased yet further during the second half of the period. Departure times of sailing ships depended on colonial demands, vessel availability and weather conditions, but the more even distribution of arrivals in the 1880s and 1890s indicates that steamers were tied to a mail contract and a regular schedule.

Arrival times also affected passengers required to undergo quarantine. Any vessel entering a colonial port with infectious disease, or even the suspicion of it, on board was refused pratique by the health officer, detained for a few days to check developments, or immediately ordered into quarantine. The shippers maintained passengers during the seven to ten 'lay' days (these were allowed under contracts for disembarkation), but after that they were responsible only for the full-payers while the government met the expenses for subsidized immigrants. A total of 78 vessels (53 sailing and 25 steam representing 6 per cent of all voyages) did not receive a clean bill of health. Seventy per cent of these were fully quarantined, for another 17 per cent quarantine occurred during the voyage or involved only a segment of the immigrants, while the remaining 13 per cent had pratique delayed but were not quarantined. These three procedures involved some 13 per cent of the total immigration – 14.8, 15.6, 12.2 and 0.9 per cent for each decade. Three German vessels accounted for 15 per cent of those detained in the 1860s; but this figure more than doubled in the 1870s, with 8 of the 53 vessels from Hamburg affected. Although the average time spent in quarantine did not alter appreciably for the first two decades (32 and 31 days), it definitely decreased in the 1880s (16 days for sail and 21 days for steam).[13] The record goes to a Black Ball vessel, the *Rockhampton*, which reached the colony in May, 1866 with an epidemic of typhus fever on board; the last passengers were finally released from quarantine more than three months after arrival. Fortunately, they were detained during the winter. However, a third of the 78 vessels (and immigrants) were released or delayed during the hottest months of the year, January to March.

Developments in nineteenth-century shipping unquestionably favoured Queensland's immigration. When the new colony began, imperial trade was expanding, a solid legislative foundation for emigrant protection had been established, steam was rapidly displacing sail, port facilities were receiving attention, and a campaign had begun to improve navigation and the standard of the merchant marine. Over the last four decades passengers increasingly benefited from these developments and reached their destinations more quickly, safely and comfortably. Conditions on Queensland immigrant vessels were further enhanced by the efforts of the government to secure the cooperation of reputable shipping firms and to enforce regulations which raised the minimum legal standards for maritime travel. Major difficulties in the organization of shipping related to the German immigration and to those vessels not covered by the regulations. Nevertheless, most of the passengers selected and subsidized by the Queensland government, sailed in ships which were chartered, outfitted and managed according to detailed specifications for the safety and welfare of future colonists.

PASSENGER ARRANGEMENTS

'We shall leave no stone unturned to realise your highest expectations' Thomas Mackay of the Black Ball Line reassured Henry Jordan after working with him for almost five years to establish a satisfactory system for conveying immigrants to Queensland (QVP 1866:1045). Such expectations were generated by government efforts to secure conditions of travel for colonial immigrants that would maintain and even enhance their potential as 'suitable' colonists. Jordan knew that difficulties with any aspect of the voyage could jeopardize the entire system, and therefore determined to make his emigration service 'superior' to all others (QVP 1864:1018).

At first it was believed that the provisions of the 1855 act would afford sufficient protection; but as disturbing reports of conditions on the Black Ball vessels reached London from the colony, the need to improve voyage arrangements became imperative. Jordan consulted with the Commissioners before drawing up the first Queensland shipping contract. Their twenty years' experience supervising emigration to the Australian colonies had shown that no 'scheme of assisted migration would be permanently satisfactory which [was] not within the complete control of the governments of the States concerned' (Coghlan 1918:2,876). The contract, and the regulations it incorporated, closely adhered to the Commissioners' model and came into force with the sailing of the *Light Brigade* in February 1863 (see QVP 1863:II,436). 'By having our own ships' Jordan informed the authorities in Brisbane, 'we can secure economy, quality, and the best equipment' (QVP 1867–68:II,80).

During the next few years Jordan maintained a close surveillance of the whole operation, modified the agreement by adding further safeguards, and compiled a set of *Instructions to Surgeon-Superintendents*, commonly known by the colour of its cover as the 'Blue Book'.[1] These *Instructions* were the detailed version of the regulations which formed the basis of all subsequent shipping agreements; they were enforced with little alteration until 1892, and dealt with every aspect of the immigrant health and welfare from embarkation to employment. Less than 40 per cent of all passenger ships to the colony were subject to the regulations, yet this figure represented four-fifths of the total number of immigrants (77.5 per cent in Queensland government vessels and 3.8 per cent in the Commissioners'). Another 7.7 per cent of the immigrants were covered solely by the provisions of the passenger acts, 7.2 per cent sailed under the German law, and 3.8 per cent travelled in short-ships (see Table 4, p. 349). Thus the great majority of future colonists were provided with planned health care as they travelled. At the close of the colonial period the Agent-General claimed that it had always been 'the desire and intention of the Government and the people of Queensland to do their very utmost in the interest of all persons invited to their colony, and for their protection both before and after arrival' (QVP 1900:V,625).

The regulations were drawn up on the assumption that if healthy people were placed in a healthy environment, then disease and death would be minimized. Convinced by the results of public health reform, the authorities believed that, 'in contrast to the powerlessness of curative medicine, the power of preventing disease is about the happiest possession of science' (QVP 1876:II,476), and that 'all social improvements must have their root in cleanliness' (QVP 1878;1,959). They were, to a man, confirmed sanitarians; effective sanitation was the cornerstone not only of 'cleanliness and comfort' but also of 'health and morality'. The duty of any 'civilized' government, they asserted, was 'to protect its subjects . . . from insidious attacks of disease . . . assaults of crime, or from accidents' (QVP 1862:447). This applied to colonists on land and at sea.

The 1855 act allowed five tons and fifteen superficial feet on the upper passenger deck for each statute adult. It was found, however, that the numbers accommodated on Queensland immigrant vessels varied depending on the tonnage, dimensions and decking, whether sail or steam, and indeed, on the volume of outflow. In 1863, for example, 713 passengers of all classes crowded onto the *Beejapore*, a 1,347-ton wooden ship, while less than a hundred sailed in vessels of comparable size when immigration was at a low ebb. The SS *Dacca*, a steel 2,545-ton vessel, in 1884 embarked 746 passengers, but four years later carried only six. In calculating passenger ratios, officials recognized that

> 'The tonnage . . . gives a general . . . view, of how the ship is loaded. The carrying capacity . . . is fixed by the superficial space on the passenger deck, and vessels of a like build will come out about the same, whilst vessels differently pooped will give a different result.'
>
> (QVP 1877:II, 1140)

Several times the authorities questioned the numbers embarked, but alleged breaches of the passenger acts could not be sustained. Although conditions on the *Rockhampton* in 1863 called for a full-scale investigation, the emigration officer who had supervised arrangements pointed out, in reply to a charge of overcrowding, that a nine-foot square steerage cabin allowed 'ample space' for twelve persons and exceeded the legal requirements (QVP 1864:1020–021).

The first Queensland agreement stated that emigrants were to be 'carried only on one deck, except the poop' and that no ship would be accepted if there was a deck house, the poop extended beyond the after part of the aft-hatchway, or the height between decks was less than 6 ft 4 ins (the minimum height under the 1855 act was 5 ft 6 ins). In later contracts, the height was raised by 6 inches, and the minimum set for steamships was 7 feet (see QVP 1883–84:1402–403). Many vessels allowed a greater height, with some measuring 9 feet between decks. Under revised regulations the superficial space allowed for berthing was also increased to 16 feet for single men and women and 18 feet for each statute adult in the married compartment. As far as can be determined, vessels bound for the colony not only carried less than the statutory numbers, but their passenger ratios improved over the four decades.[2]

An average complement of 354 immigrants (adults and children) embarked on government-chartered sailing vessels between 1860 and 1890, with the numbers decreasing slightly over the three decades. The tonnage per passenger (3.1, 2.9 and 3.2) and the superficial area (28, 22 and 23 feet), when compared with the corresponding ratios for the Commissioners' and privately organized vessels (3.0 tons and 16 feet for both) indicate that the latter vessels allowed less space during the 1860s. The large Black Ball ships and the number of cabin passengers no doubt contributed to the difference. The mean complement for the Commissioners' vessels was 313, and for private, 406 passengers. However, the numbers decreased and the space per person increased on private sailing ships in the 1880s. It is not surprising, given the allowance under the Hamburg law of 11 superficial feet (this was increased to 12 feet in 1868), that German vessels were more crowded than their British counterparts, offering only 2.0 and 2.4 tons per person in the 1860s and 1870s. But the space (19 feet and 16 feet) certainly exceeded the legal allowance. Immigrant steamship figures for the 1880s show an increased mean complement per voyage (447 passengers for government and 522 for bounty ships) and also a greater capacity – 4.5 tons and 33 superficial feet per person on government steamers. In the 1890s, low immigration and the introduction of larger vessels combined to provide the most spacious conditions for the entire colonial period. An emigrant guidebook, published soon after Federation, declared that the voyage to Queensland was 'the safest and pleasantest . . . in the world' (Gibbs 1903:101).

Short-ships throughout the period carried an average of 7.5 passengers per voyage under sail and 26.9 under steam. Most of these passengers enjoyed saloon accommodation which entitled them, under the 1855 act, to 36 superficial feet for each adult. The *Alfred Hawley*, a little 420-ton wooden barque, made several voyages to the colony with cargo during the 1860s. She had four permanent first-class cabins, each fitted with the barest essentials – a bunk and mattress, wash-stand, slop-pail and lamp. Passengers supplied their bed-linen and added other items to improve the decor and comfort; they dined at the captain's table, relaxed in the saloon lounge and promenaded on the main deck (see Hume and

Fowler 1975). The lone, male steerage traveller mentioned on one voyage probably shared the crew accommodation and food. A first-class passage on any kind of vessel offered relative space, privacy, freedom and ever-increasing amenities, including cabin and table service. Compared to the steerage, saloon passengers dined sumptuously. The daily menu on the *Selkirkshire* in 1882 was fairly typical:

> 'We have three or four courses to dinner every day and everything of first class quality today we had two kinds of soup, roast fowl, boiled fowl and sailors corned beef, mashed potatoes, carrots and turnips, cauliflower, then tarts and pudding, for desert almonds, raisins, nuts, figs, and other things breakfast is a substantial meal to potatoes, beefsteak, curried lobster, whiting, and other things to numerous to mention . . . about 4 in the afternoon the steward brings us a cup of tea, and a biscuit, then about eight o clock we have a kind of tea supper.' (Thomson 1882)

The farmyard carried on sailing ships provided fresh supplies for the cabin table, but on steamships provisions could be taken on at each port and stored on ice or under refrigeration. The cost for such a passage could range from £45 to £65. On the SS *Great Victoria*, for example, a saloon traveller paid £60 to £65 with 'Beds, bedding, linen and every requisite supplied (except wines and spirits) for £5 extra' (Coates 1900:127–28).

For approximately half this amount second-class passengers were allowed 20 superficial feet of space and were accommodated in somewhat cramped but private cabins, either in the aft-section between decks or in the poop. They were provided with steward service, messed separately (but supplied all tableware) and were served fully-cooked meals which, though lacking the first-cabin luxuries, offered more variety than the steerage menu. The second-class kept themselves apart from the immigrants, and were sometimes invited to participate in saloon activities and entertainments. An intermediate traveller paid £18 to £22 for his or her passage (this class was eliminated on most vessels to the colony after 1870). The difference between the intermediate rate and the £15 to £18 fare for a steerage full-payer allowed a little more privacy and berthing space. Messing arrangements were similar for both classes. Children between one and eleven years paid half the adult fare; there was no charge for infants under one year. Any number of guidebooks outlined 'Helpful Hints' for second-class and intermediate travellers, from suitable clothing to the best method for securing the slop-pail (see Chadfield n.d.:10–18).

A passenger act ship could not be cleared for sailing unless she had been surveyed and certified as seaworthy before the cargo was loaded. The decks had to be at least one and a half inches thick and firmly secured; the vessel had to be 'manned with an efficient Crew', and carry the prescribed navigational equipment and safety devices – life-boats, life-buoys, anchors and a fire engine 'in proper working order'. Additional specifications for vessels chartered by the Commissioners and colonial government required that they be classed as A1 at Lloyds, be kept 'tight, strong and substantial, properly masted, rigged, and stowed' throughout the voyage, carry the *Commercial Code of Signals*, *The Mercantile Navy List* and updated charts of the relevant seaways, use side-lights and fog-signals, and sail no further south than latitude 47° from April to September and 53° from October to March. The cargo and its stowage were checked. Certain articles were forbidden – 'Gunpowder, Hides, or any other commodity likely, by reason of its nature, quality or quantity to be detrimental to the safety or health of the Passengers'. Thus, only limited quantities of iron and salt (this was believed to 'vitiate' the air) were allowed (see COL/A66:65–1199). Steamships under charter also required the 100 A1 Lloyd's classification, and had to be iron or steel built.

Government ships were also selected for their suitability as immigrant carriers. Could they be adapted to provide adequate steerage accommodation for three to four hundred men, women and children of 'varied antecedents'? Such a population represented a broad spectrum of British society and often included a number of 'foreigners'. Apart from the small percentage of full-payers, the majority were assisted to the colony, but all were brought together for several months with their expectations, anxieties and 'seeds of disease', cut off from land in a neither-here-nor-there existence, and had to be kept safe and sane until they reached the colony. A married woman described the shipboard community in a letter to her parents: 'It is like being in a village, the time flies along while we are chatting . . . There are all classes, all trades, and one or more from nearly every County, and every religion' (Cook 1883:6). The situation on a steamship differed somewhat with the shorter, punctuated voyage. A traveller under sail observed the difference: 'Three months at sea . . . welded us into a community. The passengers did not spend their time counting the days to the next port, as passengers on a steamer do. They settled down to a daily round' (Hale n.d.:62). Disruption demanded continuity in novel and often difficult circumstances.

Having to house, feed and organize this community within the confines of a long rectangular space between decks required careful planning. The Commissioners arranged their vessels 'with a proper regard to the health and comfort of emigrants, as well as for the preservation of good order amongst them' (ECR 1865:351–53). A similar policy was adopted for Queensland government ships, but had to be adjusted to meet the particular demands of carrying more than one class of passengers. The authorities urged that 'precedence' must not be given to first-class travellers on their vessels (see QVP 1876:II, 1024–025). For example, the deck area reserved for the saloon had to be made available for a daily exercise session for the single girls. Young 'gentlemen' were therefore advised to travel by short-ships or warned that they could be refused a passage on government vessels. Substantial and well-secured bulkheads divided the steerage into three distinct areas. Single males fourteen years and over occupied the foremost compartment towards the bow; by law, each had to be berthed separately. Married couples and their children under the age of fourteen were accommodated in the central area, adjoining the single female compartment which was located aft, nearest the stern. This section included girls over fourteen, single women, and wives travelling alone, with or without children. Since they were the most vulnerable group afloat and the most needed in the colony, particular attention was directed towards their care and protection (see Plate 4).

Before installing fittings between decks, the whole area was scraped, disinfected and painted; the scuppers were adjusted to drain off unwanted water. Two-tiered berths were then arranged, usually athwart ships, along the sides of the vessel. A space of three to nine inches had to be left between any berth and the side of the ship, and due allowance was made for proximity to hatchways and privies. The lower bunk, fitted with removable boards for cleaning purposes, had to be at least 6 inches from the floor and separated from the one above by thirty or more inches.

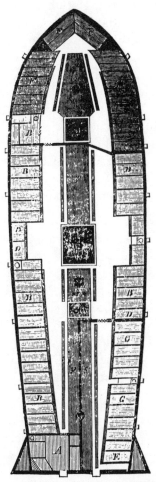

PLAN OF EMIGRANT SHIP BETWEEN DECKS.

A. The hospital for females, fitted up with six bed-places (one of which is pre pared and devoted to accouchements), and containing necessary conve niences.

B. The hospital for males, with four bed places, &c.

Between A and B are forty-eight bed places, six feet by three each, for married people above, and for their children below, every one furnished with bedding, pegs on which to suspend their clothes being placed to every upright stancheon, and each bed place divided from the next adjacent by stout planks from the deck below to the deck above. From the men's hospital (B) a bulkhead goes across the ship to separate that part of the vessel forward which is appropriated to single men and youths, whose bed places range from the hospital (B) round the bows to the termination of the bulkhead on the starboard side at C. Of these the number is forty-six, and as every one sleeps alone they are six feet by two. Between C and D are twenty-four bed places for married people (as on the opposite side), a bulkhead then goes half way across the deck, and runs in amidships to the stern, enclosing the apartment of the single females to F, and containing twenty-four bed places, each six feet by three, as two are required to sleep together.

F F are tables, the entire length of the ship, with fixed seats on each side of them, and beneath which are plate-racks and battens to hold the breakers (small casks) containing the daily allowance of fresh water, and hanging shelves are secured between the beams. Seats are also fixed at the outer extremity of every bed-place. The narrow interstices on either side are water-closets for females alone, as those for the men are upon the upper deck. It will be seen that the sleeping boxes are all athwart-ships, except the main hatchway (in the middle of the plan), where they are placed fore and aft, to afford more room. Numerous scuttles admit light and air, and the bulkheads are so constructed as to allow a free circulation of the breeze from windsails, &c.

Thus it will be manifest that the single women have an enclosed apartment to themselves, and so have the single men—one abaft and the other forward; the married couples filling up the intermediate space.

Plate 4 Plan of emigrant ship

This scarcely permitted sitting up, but children generally occupied the lower bunk. Double berths, 37 inches wide, were installed in the middle and aft compartments to accommodate a married couple, four children under twelve years, or two single women. Single-male bunks, 21 inches wide, were built double with a one-foot high dividing board. The length of berths varied, ranging from 6 feet to 6 ft 9 ins; all were fitted with foot and head boards 11 inches high. Narrow benches, attached to the end of berths facing the middle of the compartment, had rails underneath to hold water-pots and other utensils.

Provision for 'comfort', however, may be questioned after reading a married immigrant's account of accommodation on the *Beejapore* in 1863:

> 'the Berth clark . . . conducted me below . . . to a small place not larger than a small pantery & told me that me & my family would be allowed to share that with another man & his family making twelve of us in the whole . . . i could distinguish that there were four shelves on which we were to sleep
> measureing it afterwards i found this to be its utmost sise nine feet long by six feet wide & seven feet high . . . there were two broad shelves along one side & two along the end leaving a space of six feet by three feet to hold our Boxs, food & other necessarys . . . this was more than the law allowed'
>
> (Good 1863)

Space was even more at a premium for German immigrants; in the early years everyone was accommodated together in one long dormitory between decks.

Apart from swinging cots or hammocks in the single-men's compartment of some ships, regular bunks were constructed of wood until the introduction of iron berths in 1886. These not only provided single berthing for both the fore and aft sections, but could be dismantled and reused, reduced the incidence of vermin, and allowed better cleaning. Although communal living was a fact of life at sea, the authorities did not approve of open berthing in the married compartment; they were concerned for the integrity of the family unit and insisted that families be located together, whenever possible, in a 'room', usually created by extending the partition between berths to within ten inches of the deck above and fitting the bunks with front curtains or the entry space with a door. The Agent-General in his 1873 report observed that family 'cabins' did not prove inimical to health and greatly contributed to 'privacy and decency' (QVP 1875:732). However, Johnson's patent berths, first installed on the SS *Chyebassa* in 1881, seemed to be the answer; each could be well ventilated, had a separate entrance and dressing area, and day-bed type bunks folded up to allow for cleaning and for dining privately (see BMJ 1881:II,580). These cabins became commonplace on steamships and were so arranged that they eliminated the large central communal area so familiar on sailing ships. Tables with forms either side ran down the middle of the vessel (the forms could be detached and the tables swung out of the way). Here the immigrants messed and shared together, quarrelled and entertained each other. Steamships provided communal facilities, but the life-style was different (see Plate 5).

The emigration officer determined whether the light and air between decks was sufficient. If the vessel carried more than one hundred passengers, he could insist that 'an adequate and proper ventilating Apparatus . . . [be] fitted to his Satisfaction'.[3] Queensland shipping agreements detailed the specifications: in addition to hatchways and stern ports, side scuttles about fourteen feet apart had to be cut near the upper deck and fitted with glass; depending on the passenger complement, air shafts and funnels were to be installed and so arranged to 'prevent communication', presumably between males on the upper deck and the single women below; and skylights were to be cut in the upper deck if insufficient natural light reached the steerage compartment. Covered sperm-oil or candle lamps were used between sundown and 10 p.m.; safety lamps, one for each hatchway, were kept burning during the night. Fire regulations prohibited the use of naked lights below deck. By the late 1880s many steamships had electric light – 'a great boon and much safer' commented one surgeon (COL/A510:87–5989).

Queensland ships experimented with a wide variety of ventilating devices to direct in fresh and extract foul air. The apparatus designed by Dr Edmonds, a naval surgeon, was installed on several vessels (see BMJ 1864:II,376); but most arrangements functioned only with a fair wind and proved useless in stormy weather. It was not until readily available steam provided mechanical power for the rotary fan that the supply and exhaust

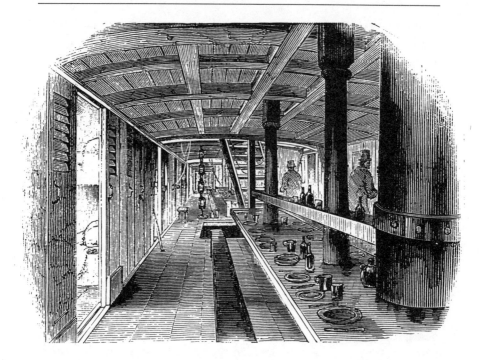

Plate 5 Between decks

system came into general use (see Roddis 1941:124). Before that, wind sails placed at the hatchways, cowls over the ports and mushroom ventilators were the most effective. The bulkheads dividing each section were usually constructed with double-louvred panels to permit a through current, and full deck awnings for use in the tropics became mandatory for all vessels, especially steamers using the northern route. By 1887 the despatching officer could report that all Queensland emigrant ships were so ventilated that, even if the hatches had to be battened down, between decks received an uninterrupted supply of fresh air (COL/A494:87–1041). Scuttles and ports were usually closed at night, but the hatchways remained open or covered with a booby-hatch in all but the worst conditions; the single-female hatch was provided with an iron grating, fitted with a padlock, for night use. One system, typical of Victorian ingenuity, operated in conjunction with the water-distilling apparatus; it provided drinking water, steam fuelled the galley, motivated the ventilator, supplied hot water for the bathrooms and wash troughs, and flushed the privies. The consequences of a breakdown in any part of this system need no elaboration.

Fresh water at sea was a precious commodity: the process of making salt water drinkable stands as one of the greatest advances in maritime history.[4] About the time the Queensland immigration began, the Commissioners approved two types of 'condensing machines' – Dr Normandy's device 'impregnated the water at the moment of distillation with super-oxygenated gas' before removing 'the disagreeable odour and flavour by means of animal charcoal' (L 1863:I,399), and Graveley's apparatus was said to produce eight to ten gallons of 'beautifully pure water' every hour (BMJ 1861:II,570–71). The Commissioners' and government vessels had to carry water-distilling equipment, sufficient fuel and spare parts, in addition to a reserve supply of fresh water in casks. The full allowance under the 1855 act was 130 gallons for each adult on the Australian voyage; but the Queensland regulations required 214 gallons and then halved this amount in lieu of the distilling device. The daily adult quota, exclusive of water for cooking, was three quarts and could be increased in the tropics if the supply was sufficient. By contrast, German vessels during the 1860s were not fitted with a 'condensing machine' and allowed 'one bottle' (one to two pints) a day per adult. Also, the Elbe water in the ships' casks was of questionable quality.

Pure water and pure air were the primary targets of public health reform in the nineteenth century, together with the provision of adequate sanitary facilities. The legal requirement for emigrant ships guaranteed a minimum of two privies, with an additional two for every one hundred passengers up to a maximum of twelve. On Queensland vessels, privies had to 'be arranged on deck with as much regard to decency and convenience as possible, taking every care that those intended for women are not too near the forecastle' (COL/A268:78–4478). The needs of women and children at night and during bad weather were also taken into consideration. Construction details and plumbing arrangements for water-closets and bathrooms were carefully specified in order to make them secure and leak-proof. The emphasis was purely functional: zinc fittings and baths were prohibited since they lacked durability, while two, even three, seater privies were allowed. Although the law made no provision for baths, the regulations required that at least one be installed, preferably near the hospitals for delousing purposes. For the majority of passengers, irrespective of class, bathing was a luxury, a rare and sometimes resisted experience; yet within the confines of a vessel, the need for personal cleanliness was obvious. Facilities gradually improved, first for women and children, and later for the men who generally improvised on deck, washing under the pump, dowsing each other with buckets of water or bathing in the sea during calm weather (see, for example, Qualtrough 1859). One enthusiast described the procedure: 'We take a line & a bully soup tin and draw water and wash ourselfs all over every morning' (Blasdall 1862).

Emigrant ships had to provide hospitals or sick-bays which allowed eighteen superficial feet for every fifty passengers, and were properly fitted and equipped. Queensland contracts stipulated that the hospital space be twice the statutory dimensions, that it include dispensary accommodation and be located only on the main deck. The shippers installed a male and female and sometimes a lying-in hospital, each supplied with a portable water-closet and screen, beds and bedding, a lantern and water filter, and other requisites. The doctor's dispensary, where he attended to out-patients and compounded his remedies, might be a saloon cabin appropriated for the purpose. Also located on deck, as far aft as possible, were the immigrant galley and bakehouse, built as one or separately, situated well away from the crew and first-class galleys, and supplied with specified utensils and purpose-built ovens.

The main deck was a busy and cluttered area, with privies and bathrooms, cookhouses and farmyard, the rigging and wheelhouse machinery, spars and long boat, as well as structures to accommodate the distilling apparatus, extra equipment and sometimes the sailors. In this area the crew worked and the passengers relaxed. To ensure sufficient free space for immigrants, the law prescribed that five superficial feet be made available for each statute adult. The poop deck had to be kept free since it was reserved for the single women's recreation period and the saloon passengers. Single men and families were allocated separate areas on the main deck, but were not restricted to specific times. In fact, the men were encouraged to sleep on deck in the tropics. Safe access from below required that gangways and ladders (at least two) for each hatch be the correct length and gradient and be fitted with hand-rails.

On most vessels heating was a problem because of the fire hazard. However, wooden ships were generally better insulated against the extremes of heat and cold than those built of iron or steel. During cold weather swinging stoves were allowed between decks; but on steamers, the 'wild heat' generated by the boilers and engines made adjacent living areas extremely uncomfortable, especially in the tropical latitudes. The storage of passengers' luggage was another important provision. A separate room or section of the hold was reserved so that luggage was readily accessible and would not be damaged during cargo handling. Similarly, the rations, 'medical comforts' and small stores had to be carefully stowed and protected. Outfitting an emigrant ship took at least nine days and was checked several times during this period by an emigration officer; but once a vessel was passed, no alterations could be made unless a private agreement was reached with the shippers (see QVP 1864:1020–021 and 1867:224).

According to the law sailing ships for the colony had to be provisioned for 140 and steamers for 80 days.[5] Since the dietary had been sufficiently augmented to eliminate the need for immigrants to supplement the rations, the shippers supplied only the legal quantities, but the first contract introduced an improved dietary. This was modified over the next thirty years to accommodate new food processing and preserving techniques (see, for example, CO 386/179:257), a changed mode and route of travel, and current medical opinion. Not only was the government scale 'much more liberal than a mere compliance with the requirements of the Passenger Act would demand' (ISS 1875:61), but remaining foodstuffs could not be used on subsequent voyages (see QVP 1876:II, 1025–026). As early as 1871 steerage passengers for the colony were said to be 'the best supplied [people] in any ships conveying Emigrants' (COL/A159:71–2015).

The basic weekly allowance for each statute adult included animal foods (salt beef 8 oz, pork 24 oz, preserved meat 24 oz, suet 6 oz, butter 6 oz), breadstuffs (biscuit 42 oz, flour 56 oz, oatmeal 16 oz, peas three-quarters of a pint, rice 8 oz), preserved vegetables (8 oz each of potatoes, carrots and onions), and groceries (raisins 8 oz, tea 1 oz, coffee 2 oz, sugar 12 oz, molasses 8 oz). Mixed pickles, mustard, salt and pepper added flavour, and 3 oz of the all-important lime juice were issued twice weekly in the tropics. A nutritional analysis indicates that the dietary, while it may have lacked variety, was 'adequate'.[6] Within limits, the surgeon was authorized to issue substitutes and order a change of diet if the weather or general health of the passengers required it. Children between four and twelve years received half the above rations; special provision was made for one- to four-year olds and infants over four months. The surgeon issued what nutriment he considered suitable for babies under four months, and hospital patients were issued with an extra quart of water a day. In 1884, following a proposal from three medical members of the Immigration Board, the dietary was modified to include increased flour and reduced biscuit, the substitution of tinned meat for salt pork and fresh for preserved potatoes, the addition of cheese and jams, and increased amounts of tea, sugar and raisins. For children it was suggested that sago replace raisins and that a supply of unsweetened, preserved milk be added since it proved 'useful in checking an outbreak of diarrhoea' (COL/A390:84–3637). Immigrants welcomed the greater variety.

The needs of Continental passengers and those who, for religious reasons, could not eat meat were also accommodated; sauerkraut, extra potatoes and dried fish were included. On the other hand, the wine ration allowed under German law was prohibited. Both the 1855 act and the regulations strictly forbade not only the sale of liquor to steerage passengers but also its consumption, except for medicinal purposes. As some compensation for the lack of fresh foods, new meat, bread and vegetables were issued while in port, for two days after sailing and immediately on arrival. The authorities also investigated compaints and, whenever possible, acted on suggestions for improvement. The liberal dietary was probably far superior to what the majority of immigrants were accustomed. 'It is like living on first class rations to a lot that are here', observed one young man; while another declared they were eating 'like Fighting Cocks' (Lumb 1885 and Blasdall 1862).

Since ration distribution was open to malpractice, the government provided the responsible officer (usually the purser or third mate) with detailed instructions, a list of the exact quantities to be issued and a reliable pair of scales. The shippers employed an immigrants' cook, or more than one depending on the numbers, and a baker; such appointments were subject to the surgeon's approval and control. The cook lit the fires each morning, prepared the basic foods (porridge, stews, soups and vegetables) and distributed them at the meal times; the baker issued fresh bread three times a week. But many of the rations were supplied directly to the immigrants to prepare pies and puddings, cakes and buns according to their favourite recipes; these were delivered to the cook or baker for the final stage of production. While no passengers were allowed in the bakehouse, the galley fires were available for their use at certain times of the day. Those with some experience of food preparation definitely had an advantage over the uninitiated; hunger drove many a young man to acquire the basic culinary arts as quickly as possible. To assist in this, Queensland ships carried several copies of a book, *Enquire within upon Everything*, containing detailed information on 'various modes of cooking all kinds of food' (ISS 1875:61). Immigrants usually took with them a supplementary supply (nuts, dried fruits, cheese, tinned fish, preserves, eggs and dessicated milk) to relieve the monotony of the regular dietary or 'tempt the appetite' when they felt unwell. One travellers' guide suggested that such items be stored in tins and bottles 'to preserve them from the dampness . . . and also from rats or mice' (Chadfield n.d.:18).

Medical comforts, an essential part of the provisioning, included foodstuffs suitable for invalid or special diets, 'stimulants' and ample quantities of soap; they were issued under the doctor's direction for the use of sick passengers, the preservation of health and the prevention of disease. Pregnant or nursing mothers, for example, received a daily half-pint allowance of stout or porter. Initially, the surgeon had sole control of these supplies, but the large quantity of liquor proved too great a temptation for some of them; the master and surgeon assumed joint responsibility for the 'comforts'. A fully stocked medicine chest (in addition to the captain's supply), medical stores and equipment were also placed on board. The required amount of every item, from beef extract to castor oil, was carefully calculated according to the length of voyage and the number of passengers and crew. Immigrants, however, took no chances and carried their own selection of home remedies and patent medicines. Although treatment was available, a clean, well-ordered and disease-free environment was of primary importance. Due provision was therefore made for cleaning and disinfection; the small stores included an impressive array of brooms, brushes and mops, scrapers and shovels, rubbish bins and buckets as well as huge quantities of holystone and whiting. Charcoal stoves hung from the beams and hot sand spread over the floor kept the 'tween decks area dry; disinfecting and antiseptic agents purified the atmosphere. Every contingency was anticipated and strict sanitation had to be observed since there was no escape for the floating population. On the other hand, because it was so contained, such a community presented the perfect opportunity for implementing public health principles to a degree not possible on land.

As long as Queensland chartered vessels, a colonial representative at the home port checked that the contract terms were fulfilled. By 1866 Jordan could boast that he had secured 'a perfect system of supervision' (QVP 1867–68:II,74). A despatching officer, appointed by the Agent-General and approved by Cabinet, was expected to attend daily at the docks for a week before departure to inspect supplies, weighing some cases and opening others to check their quality (QVP 1867:229–30 and 1879:II,173–74). If any part of the outfitting failed to meet requirements, he could demand a replacement or the necessary repairs and alterations. The surgeon-superintendent supervised the medicines, medical comforts, hospitals and dispensary and was requested to point out any arrangement he believed might endanger health. The shippers were liable to a £300 penalty should they refuse a 'Demand for Survey' or if supplies were in any way deficient. In 1881, shortly after the introduction of steamships to the Queensland run, the SS *Durham* was declared by an independent survey of vessels on berth for various colonies to be 'by far the best, and left nothing to be desired' (QVP 1882:II,537). Outfitting and provisioning a Queensland immigrant vessel realized the Utilitarian ideal – safe, functional and sanitarily-sound conditions intended to promote the greatest good for the greatest number.

Once an applicant for emigration received his contract ticket, he could proceed with preparations for departure. 'Directions' issued to subsidized immigrants clearly stated that they had to make their own arrangements for reaching the port of embarkation, and could be refused a passage on the grounds of unfitness, falsified documents, failure to arrive at the appointed time (usually two to three days before the scheduled date of departure) or for any other cause, such as insufficient clothing for the voyage. The 'Directions' detailed the minimum quantities of shirts and shifts, shoes and stockings, and 'exterior clothing' required, and recommended extra flannel since the journey might take four months and passed through extremes of climate.[7] Revised 'Directions' in 1882 allowed the Agent-General to modify requirements for steamships; lighter, but equally durable garments and a hat were introduced. Guide books suggested that travellers wear old clothes during the voyage and consign them to the deep when dirty or worn out, keeping the new for arrival.

Immigrants also provided their bedding, toilet articles and table utensils; these items could be purchased at the port, singly or as a 'ship's kit'. Assisted and remittance passengers had the choice of two, one costing 10/6 and the other 20/-; those travelling free deposited £1 with the Queensland Office and received the 10/6 kit – a bed and two sheets, a water bottle, wash basin, plate and pint drinking mug, a knife, fork and two spoons, and 3 lb of marine soap. Continental immigrants had to pay £1.9.0; the extra 9/- covered expenses during the mandatory four days in port before sailing (see QVP 1871:928). At least one free passenger seemed well satisfied with his kit: 'We . . . are allowed a full supply of cans etc for victuals, then there is the private cans & knife & fork, spoons bag & brush. I was told a lot of bad news about these tin cans, but . . . they are a credit to the Queensland government' (Lumb 1885). Feather beds were strictly prohibited, and only saloon passengers could take furniture on board. However, immigrants were encouraged to include small tools of trade in their luggage; the allowance of twenty cubic feet for each adult had to be divided into two or three closely packed and clearly marked boxes, one of which could be kept in the berth. Thus, departure for the colony involved emigrants in a good deal of preparation, and demanded of them resources that no 'refuse class' could meet.

On arrival at the embarkation port cabin passengers booked into a hotel while completing final arrangements; ordinary immigrants stayed in near-by lodging houses and received subsistence money if there was no depot or they could not go directly on board. The depots provided food and bunks and facilities for muster and inspection. At Birkenhead (Liverpool) emigrants dined in a ground floor mess-room and slept in rock-like beds in a communal dormitory on the first floor (see

Charlwood 1981:84–5). Glasgow, Queenstown (Cork) and London lacked even these provisions. When an Emigrants' Home opened at Blackwall (London) in 1884, it was hailed as a 'great improvement' on the Plymouth depot; travellers were 'better fed, better cared for, and far more comfortable' (QVP 1884:II,596). 'Its nautical furniture and berths in place of beds, [gave] the emigrant a foretaste of life on board ship' (ANL, *The Queen* M 468). Before leaving Hamburg, Continental immigrants travelling via England had no option but to stay in vermin-ridden lodging houses; on arrival in England they were met by private agents who, for a fee, organized accommodation and forwarded them to the port of departure. However, after 1884 they could land directly at the Blackwall depot.

All steerage passengers and their luggage had to be inspected before departure. On the first day the surgeon-superintendent checked the clothing supply and the despatching officer searched the luggage for prohibited items (spirits, firearms and offensive weapons). In later years immigrants were issued with a canvas bag to hold articles needed during the voyage and clothing for the first few weeks at sea. On the second day, the inspection muster took place; one by one emigrants passed before the ship's surgeon and a Board of Trade doctor, approved by the Agent-General.[8] Then the despatching officer and an emigration official questioned each in turn to determine if they were *bona fide* and respectable. The colonial authorities regularly instructed responsible personnel to refuse a passage to anyone 'not in sound bodily or mental health, or . . . unsuited to the requirements of the Colony' (QVP 1879:II,173–74 and 1883–84:1369–370). Staff at the emigration depot also 'closely scrutinized' embarkees and reported 'doubtful characters'. One young man departing in 1885 figured out that, 'if you behave yourself you are well treated & if you dont . . . they give you back the £1 you paid & you are done for . . . They say if a man starts making a row here he will be more bother than he is worth out there' (Lumb 1885). Once formalities were completed, immigrants faced the next stage – an eight- to sixteen-week 'holiday', cut off from the world, freed from decision making, but regulated by unfamiliar rules and a handful of unknown people.

The organization of Queensland vessels followed a precedent established for convict transports and the Commissioners' ships; the surgeon-superintendent was entrusted with the health, welfare, and discipline of future colonists. As the senior administrative and medical officer for the voyage, he assumed full responsibility for passengers as soon as they embarked. Immigrants were berthed in family units and, if possible, next to friends or 'persons of a similar class' so that they could be grouped in 'messes' of six to ten adults to facilitate cooking and cleaning arrangements. The surgeon checked that lower berths had been allocated to women in the late stages of pregnancy and that little children were kept away from hatchways and other dangerous areas. Abstracts of the 1885 act and the regulations, the 'Rules . . . for preserving order, promoting health, and securing cleanliness and ventilation on board', and copies of the dietary and rations were posted up in 'conspicuous places' in the saloon and other compartments of the ship. Immigrants were left in no doubt concerning their rights and responsibilities. Unless prevented by sickness, they were expected to be out of bed by 7 a.m. and, in the next hour, dress, roll up their bedding, thoroughly sweep between decks (including the area under the bunks) and throw the dirt overboard. Breakfast was served between 8 and 9 a.m., dinner at 1 p.m. and supper at 6 p.m. Cooking fires which had been lit at 7 a.m. were extinguished by 7 p.m. and three hours later, immigrants had to retire to their berths.

Each mess was responsible for the cleanliness of their section and cooking equipment. Five men (over fourteen years) for every one hundred passengers were rostered daily to carry out the general cleaning duties; each morning the team set to work scraping or dry holystoning the passenger deck, cleaning ladders, hospitals, round-houses, and water-closets, washing out coppers and pumping water into cisterns and tanks. Twice a week immigrants took their mattresses to the upper deck to air and shake them, and removed and dry scrubbed the boards of the lower bunks. Two other days were allocated for washing clothes and bed linen. Sundays provided a change of routine: at ten in the morning passengers presented themselves 'in clean and decent apparel' for a roll-call on the poop deck; thereafter the day was observed as religiously as circumstances permitted.

For the safety and health of all on board, naked lights and smoking, loose straw and hay, washing and drying of clothes were forbidden between decks. Married men had to take their turn on a night watch 'to guard against danger from fire and other causes, to attend to the hatchways, scuttles, and ventilators, to prevent irregularities, and for the general security' of passengers. Nine men (the ruling later extended to include single men) covered the three watches from 8 p.m. to 8 a.m.; they were expected to report every half hour to the officer on duty (ISS 1875:20 and COL/A535:88–1318). The authorities, knowing they could not be 'too careful of human life', insisted that order and morality be preserved. No communication was allowed between immigrants and crew; sailors were restricted to the forecastle which, together with the ship's cookhouse, was out of bounds to passengers. The temperance clauses had to be rigidly observed since many embarked with 'habits of drunkenness'; medical comforts could not, on any account, be used as rewards or inducements for cleaning duties. In addition, various kinds of misbehaviour were 'strictly prohibited':

> 'all immoral or indecent acts or conduct, taking improper liberties or using improper familiarity with the female passengers, using blasphemous, obscene, or indecent language, or language tending to a breach of the peace, swearing, gambling, drunkenness, fighting, disorderly, riotous, quarrelsome, or insubordinate conduct, also all deposits of filth or offensive acts of uncleanliness in the between decks.'
>
> (Order-in-council 7 January, 1864 Rule 20)

Under the 1855 act passengers were liable to a £2 fine or one month's imprisonment for 'insubordinate or riotous conduct' or refusing to obey the surgeon; he could take disciplinary action, but not inflict corporal punishment. Life at sea was regulated and disciplined, with social boundaries and territorial rights kept intact to provide a degree of continuity and cohesion for this temporary existence. One disruptive element could place at risk the health and safety of hundreds of lives.

An executive corps, mostly appointed by the surgeon-superintendent, assisted with the maintenance of law and order at sea. Initially, the master selected a matron from among the married ladies to supervise the single women if there were more than five on board, but under government contracts she was directly responsible to the surgeon. Then, within a few years, as a result of continuing scandal, mounting pressure and the example of other emigration services, the Queensland authorities decided to entrust the matron's appointment to the British Ladies Female Emigrant Society, with the approval of the Agent-General (QVP 1864:920). In time a permanent staff – mostly of mature, married women or widows – was established. A survey of matrons between 1870 and 1889 shows that their age at the time of sailing ranged from 25 to 75 years and gradually increased; their mean age for this period was 38 years.[9] At least five are known to have made more than twenty voyages. Jane Chase was an experienced ship's matron when she joined the Queensland service in 1873. During the next two decades this 'sensible motherly woman' watched over the single-female compartment on twenty-five vessels bound for the colony. Mrs Gaudin also rendered faithful service. After making the journey twenty-one times in seventeen years (1867–83) she decided to settle in Queensland. Her business venture failed, however, so she sought reappointment and supervised a further seven shipments of domestic servants and wives (COL/A410:84–9084).

The matron was responsible for the welfare of single women over fourteen years and unaccompanied mothers and their children. In her role as policewoman, guardian, governess, nurse and even midwife, she organized the cleaning, food preparation and meal-times, needlework and other 'useful' activities, school lessons, Bible instruction and general entertainment, and supervised the Sunday visiting period. However, her primary duty was to prevent communication between 'the girls' and any man on board, except the doctor, and provide around-the-clock protection, in the compartment (the key of which she kept always with her) or during the recreation period on deck. Depending on the number in her charge, she could appoint sub-matrons from among the single women to assist her. They received a £2 gratuity which increased to £3 for those who performed nursing duties.

Cooperation with the surgeon was essential, for the matron depended on his support and was answerable to him for the management of the women. Only he could alter the regulations and allow the girls, for example, to remain on deck after sundown in the tropics. One surgeon went so far as to protect their deck area with a five-foot screen, but admitted it interfered with the ventilation (COL/A526:87–9215). At an appointed time a bell summoned the young women to their sleeping places where they remained under lock and key for the night. The matron's unenviable task required tact, firmness, kindness and much patience. In return for her services she was given a separate cabin in the compartment, meals sent from the saloon table, a £5 gratuity for the satisfactory performance of her duties, a second-class return passage and free accommodation in the colony while she waited for a home-bound vessel. Permanent matrons, however, received a £25 gratuity which increased £5 for each voyage up to a maximum of £40; those who failed to meet the required standard were not reappointed.

Unless a schoolmaster was travelling to the colony under contract to the government, the surgeon appointed a teacher from among the passengers to conduct day classes (9 a.m. to 12 noon and 2 to 4 p.m.) and organize a Sunday School for children between 4 and 14 years, and arrange an evening class for young adults. An immigrant who saw the school as 'a capital idea' for keeping the children 'out of arms way' quite missed the point; the teacher's function was to improve the educational level of those under his care, to provide religious (but strictly non-sectarian) instruction, to supervise the library and to assist the surgeon. The government supplied the necessary books and materials, and for his services he received a £5 gratuity. Children were expected to arrive punctually and in a 'cleanly state' for classes. Each day began with a scripture reading; pupils were then instructed in the basic 'three Rs', with the curriculum sometimes extending to history and geography. The teacher kept a daily record of progress and conduct; a week or so before arrival, examinations were held followed by a prize-giving and a 'breaking-up' party. Evening classes were less structured, with tuition often on a one-to-one basis or involving language instruction for Continental immigrants. The schoolmaster submitted a report, in duplicate, to the surgeon at the voyage end.

The organizational unit for intermediate and steerage passengers was the mess. Each group was numbered, and selected a captain to collect their daily rations, water and cooked food at the appointed times, and be responsible for cleaning up after meals. This position could be held for the voyage or shared. A married woman explained the procedure:

'Fred is Capt one week, & Mr Holroyd, who is in the next

berth, takes the next week. There are 33 messes & as many as 10 or 12 adults to some . . . when they go for their food they wait their turn, and if not there, be served last.'

(Cook 1883)

Constables acted as 'watch dogs' for the community. 'There are men appointed as police to keep order and see that the place his clean' ran one simplified version of their functions (Anon. 1883). The surgeon selected 'big powerfull men' – one for every fifty passengers; each wore a badge inscribed, 'Constable H.M. Queensland Government', as his mark of office, was exempt from general cleaning duties and received a £3 gratuity. Some were allocated special functions and granted an additional £2; the water-closet constable kept the privies 'perfectly clean' and mess constables, either married men or women, carried food for the single-female compartment, 'thus obviating the necessity of any passing backwards and forwards of the unmarried women to the ship's-galley, which must not on any account be allowed' (ISS 1875:16). Also, single women were not permitted to act as servants for the cabin passengers. Occassionally a lamp constable was appointed. One of them reported on arrival that 'there was not a lot of lamp in better trim . . . and I well deserve my money' (COL/A296:80–3806). He received a gratuity.

Where else, but within the confines of a ship, would it be possible to regulate with such detail and oversight the life-style of a community? Yet this was not all. The Queensland authorities, recognizing the potential for good or evil of the hours of leisure at sea, applied the maxim quoted by one schoolmaster: 'When men have nothing to do, they are sure soon to do something worse' (COL/A68:65–1640). A library containing two to three hundred volumes of 'an instructive and amusing description' was placed on board each vessel. Books could be borrowed at fixed times, a register was kept and fines were exacted for over-due returns. In addition to copies of Dr Lang's works and the various government handbooks and publications, weekly lectures organized by the surgeon, included at least two or three on Queensland, 'its natural resources, and . . . prospects', in order to correct erroneous impressions the immigrants might have and to prepare them for colonial life by pointing out

'The honourable estimation in which labour is held in the

Colonies; the necessity of industry, perseverence, and temperance in order to success [sic]; the wisdom of taking immediate employment, without standing out for high wages . . . and the folly of expecting to obtain employment generally in the towns.'

(ISS 1875:30)

The surgeon was also encouraged to discuss popular medical topics since these, he was assured, would 'please and benefit the Passengers' and increase his influence on board.

The Church of England service had to be read publicly each Sunday on British vessels, but attendance at divine worship was not compulsory. Since so many Irish and non-Conformists emigrated to the colony, other denominations were permitted to meet, in a manner 'consistent with the general order of the ship', and guaranteed 'protection from interruption'. The fact that the Queensland government, unlike the Commissioners, made no provision for a 'Religious Instructor' reflected their essentially utilitarian and materialistic policy; prosperity depended on physical and moral integrity and the office of surgeon-superintendent was considered sufficient safeguard for both during the voyage. According to Ward (1966:87–8), immigrant attitudes were similar; the prospect of 'doing well' sustained them, rather than the consolations of religion.

Sundays, as well as providing a change of pace, might include a special treat for the children such as sweets issued from the medical comforts. 'Fancy a government giving the best mixtures to children', commented one surgeon's wife (Thomson 1882). Christmas, birthdays and such occasions called for a celebration and extra provisions, but passengers were forbidden to join in Neptune's ceremony when crossing the equator or to climb in the rigging to view such events. On ordinary days they were expected 'to be as much as possible in the open air, taking regular exercise, pacing the deck, reading, working, or amusing themselves innocently' (ISS 1875:20). Activities covered a wide spectrum – journal writing and mending clothes, sports of every description (including cricket), plays, lectures and debates, concerts and dances. Immigrants enjoyed sorting through their clothes and reminders of home whenever luggage was brought up from the hold. Indeed, within the rigid structuring there was considerable opportunity for self-expression.

As soon as the Queensland authorities received notification that a vessel had been despatched, preparations for arrival began. When a ship reached port, the pilot went on board and the master hoisted the blue visiting flag. While this was flying, no one could leave or communicate with the vessel except the health officer who was obliged to inform the authorities immediately of the state of health on board.[10] If all was clear, disembarkation got under way; but if the officer had any doubts, he sought advice from the Colonial Secretary or delayed pratique while the immigrants, crew and their effects were disinfected; 'the passengers are landed on Peel Island, a pleasant place a few hours' steaming from Brisbane, where they undergo a species of cleaning and a good blow', Dr Bancroft informed other colonial representatives at the 1884 Australasian Sanitary Conference (QVP 1885:III,508). If infectious disease was present, the health officer quarantined the vessel and instructed the master to hoist the yellow flag, proceed to the station anchorage, land the sick with adequate medical attendance and disembark passengers and their luggage as soon as possible. After 1880 the health officer at a northern port was authorized to remove the sick from the steamer to a local quarantine ground and allow the ship to continue down the coast flying the yellow flag (a signal lamp was used at night). Any officer having contact with an infected ship had to remain in isolation until his clothing was burned or disinfected.

Since the outbreak of plague in the Levant in the early fourteenth century, quarantine had been an internationally recognized practice to protect a country from 'the invasion of contagious or infectious disease consistent with the least possible interference with the liberty of individuals and . . . restriction to commerce' (QVP 1885:III,534; see Creighton 1891–94:I,145 ff.). The first English quarantine law was passed in 1710, but it was the 1825 act which formed the basis for similar legislation in the Australian colonies. As British trade increased, so did complaints that the law caused 'unnecessary impediments to international and commercial intercourse, without affording any adequate protection to the public health' (BMJ 1861:II,213). A series of international sanitary conferences throughout the nineteenth century endeavoured to reconcile these interests and recommend the most effective and least disruptive method of protection. Non-uniform laws for the Australian colonies created their own problems, and in 1884 and 1896 delegates met to draw up a federal policy, but this did not come into effect until after 1901.

The first vessels reaching the new colony from overseas were subject to the New South Wales legislation until Queensland passed her own Quarantine Act in 1863 (QS 27 Vic. no. 9). In the early 1870s the quarantine system came under attack and in March 1873 regulations were issued detailing the duties of the health officer, master and surgeon of the ship, the station superintendent and the pilot, and laying down rules for the care and discipline of immigrants (QGG 1873,14:335–38). In 1878 the Queensland Board of Health (formed in 1872) recommended that the law be modified in favour of partial quarantine and medical inspection currently operating in Britain. This immediately met with strong opposition from the health officer who contended that any relaxation would endanger the colony because of its close proximity to south-east Asia and remove one of the most powerful inducements to 'cleanliness and health' on board immigrant vessels (see QVP 1878:I,455–63). Minor revisions to the regulations followed in 1879, but the arrival of the SS *Dorunda* with a severe epidemic of Asian cholera among the passengers triggered off panic legislation in 1886 (QS 50 Vic. no. 25). This new law retained full quarantine, clarified ambiguities in the 1863 act and introduced regulations which accommodated steamships and updated the procedure (see QGG 1886,39:1933–937).

Management of the five quarantine stations along the coast often added fuel to the debate. Each site had to afford complete isolation, be sufficiently protected from the fury of the Pacific Ocean, be well drained, and have an adequate water supply, a convenient landing place and good communication with the mainland. Meeting all these conditions proved virtually impossible; the Moreton Bay station moved four times between 1860 and 1876. Peel Island, with its moderate temperatures and high, well-drained ground 'open to every breeze', was finally selected as the permanent site (see COL/A220:76–171). Despite its infrequent use, the station had to provide basic amenities, buildings had to be maintained (this seemed an unnecessary expense) and required a caretaker. The local telegraph operator for Moreton Bay who acted in this capacity allowed conditions to so deteriorate that the public, stirred by the passing of the first Public Health Act in 1872, demanded immediate action. As a result of the 1873 quarantine regulations, a resident superintendent was appointed and the government began improving facilities; a hospital, kitchen, and quarters for the surgeon, cabin passengers and single women were erected, while the married people were accommodated in the old buildings or tents, and the single men remained under canvas. Provision for the northern stations was even more spartan; the sub-immigration agent supervised the necessary make-shift arrangements and supplied tents. Such parsimony seems out of character with the investment in immigration. Apparently, expenditure for quarantine and for a public health programme (see Barclay 1971:3–12) did not square with the concept of colonial development; it took the authorities years to grasp the fact that maintaining a vigorous and healthy population required more than careful provision for the voyage, legislation to prevent the entry of disease, and a spacious country with a fine climate.

When the immigrants with their luggage, mess utensils and supplies had been landed at the station, the master of the quarantined vessel burned or threw overboard all the passenger fittings, disinfected the ship and ordered the crew to wash and air their clothes and bedding. After a prescribed period the ship was inspected and if all was in order, it was released and the cargo off-loading began. For the immigrants, quarantine became an extension of the voyage. The girls, under the matron's continuing supervision, were housed between the surgeon's quarters and the married accommodation; tents for the single men were erected 'some distance away'. The station superintendent and the constables assisted the surgeon in regulating the daily routine and maintaining discipline. Immigrants were divided into messes of fourteen, and two from each took it in turn to collect the rations and help with food preparation. Three or more men (each received a £5 gratuity) were selected to cook the meals 'in a proper manner' and serve them at stated times. The station supervisor was responsible for the provisions and medical comforts, checking their quality and issuing the daily quotas of flour, meat, vegetables, tea, sugar, salt and soap. Supplies were fresh but basic, and did not include such luxuries as coffee, butter and preserves. Local residents, however, usually sent down special 'supplements'; but officials examined all packages and confiscated any alcohol. The cabin passengers remained entirely separate.

Although quarantine allowed greater physical freedom, the

regimented life-style remained. Contact with the mainland was prohibited, the sick and their attendants were kept isolated, and the single women were locked in at night and not allowed to communicate with the other groups during the day. Immigrants were expected to rise at 5.30 a.m. in the summer or 6.30 a.m. in the winter and retire to bed by 9 p.m. (later regulations were a little more relaxed with rising times a half hour later and 'lights out' at 10 p.m.). The first week of quarantine passed quickly enough; passengers were kept busy washing and boiling, disinfecting and drying the clothing and bed linen used at sea; the luggage was fumigated. Then they settled down to the familiar routine of food preparation and meal times, airing and scrubbing, washing and bathing, while trying to adjust to a different climate and the surprises of 'bush life'. Under these circumstances, added to which were the frustrations of delay, it was essential to secure 'order, discipline and morality'. Offensive weapons had to be placed in custody; riotous conduct, fighting, 'bad' language, disobedience or obstructive behaviour could be penalized; anyone absconding from the station was liable to a fine or imprisonment. The surgeon kept a medical case-book and the station supervisor wrote a daily diary.

Needless to say, all concerned wanted a speedy release. The surgeon forwarded a certificate to the health officer when the passengers, or a section of them, had completed the formalities and were shown to be free of infectious disease for the prescribed period. As soon as official approval for release was granted, immigrants began packing up, but were not allowed to leave the station until all was in order. Finally, they were mustered and taken by river steamer to the immigration depot or town wharf.

A vessel arriving from 'beyond the seas' free of infectious disease was admitted to pratique immediately. The health officer examined any sick passengers and ordered their admission to hospital or allowed them to remain on board until fit to land. While still in the bay, the immigration officer arrived to muster the new arrivals, record their complaints, supervise the transshipment, inspect the vessel, its fittings and arrangements, and check all documents relating to the voyage (see QVP 1863:II,465). If any grievance was sufficiently serious, the agent urged that it be submitted to him in writing, and on his return to town, he convened a meeting of the Immigration Board, appointed under the law and authorized to

> 'investigate any complaints respecting the non-fulfillment of any contracts entered into for the conveyance of immigrants or respecting the conduct of any surgeon officer or other person on board any immigrant ship as well as any other matter which may be referred . . . to such a Board for inquiry and shall when requested give advice to immigrants on their arrival and assist them in obtaining employment'.
>
> (QS 28 Vic. no. 17, Clause 19)

Official documents – the surgeon's report, the purser's broaching book and the medical log-book, together with the health officer's and immigration agent's reports – were used in evidence and witnesses were called. The minutes of all such inquiries were submitted to the Colonial Secretary. A board could be appointed at any port and consisted of not more than six members; it had no judicial powers but recommendations made to the government were usually implemented and could lead to prosecutions under the passenger, immigration or quarantine acts.

After a five- to six-hour journey up river, immigrants were reunited with relatives and friends or landed at the depot. This came as no surprise to those who had been through quarantine, but for direct arrivals it could be a shock. In the early years the Brisbane building sometimes had to accommodate immigrants from two or three vessels arriving about the same time; the northern ports had no permanent facilities and instead rented a warehouse or used tents. After the select committee inquiry of 1863 a sum was voted for improvements, but legal sanction for the establishment of coastal and inland depots to serve as reception and employment centres did not come until 1869. While new arrivals waited to be hired, they received lodging, food and medical attendance for one week at government expense. A matron and a wardsman saw to their needs, segregation was maintained, any misbehaviour and all 'irregularities' were reported. Immigrants, however, were free to visit the town and make their own arrangements for housing and employment, but the single women had to return by sundown and were given full protection for the night (in the later period girls arriving in Brisbane were accommodated in separate lodgings). If work was scarce at the port where they landed, immigrants generally agreed

Plate 6   New immigration buildings, Kangaroo Point, Brisbane

to be transferred, with all expenses paid, to another depot where labour was in demand. Although earlier depots functioned with 'every regard paid to economy', conditions did improve. In 1882 the immigration agent made his first tour up the coast inspecting quarantine and reception facilities (see COL/A357:83–1574), and five years later the new Brisbane depot, superbly located, built of brick and stone and equipped with every amenity, was opened; but by this time immigration was on the wane (see Plate 6).

Apart from inadequate quarantine and arrival facilities, the colonial government spared no effort to secure a controlled and effective immigration system, designed to provide optimum care for a highly selected population. Each Queensland immigrant vessel offered 'the quintessence of Socialism' – complete state coverage for the well-being of all on board (Rogers 1907:163). Presumably Gandevia (1978:49) was referring to earlier emigrant ships to Australia when he claimed that, despite 'some official supervision' and improvements, conditions of travel were 'never as comprehensive or effective as in the convict transports'. Surely no government could have been more concerned or involved with passenger arrangements. The Agent-General and his staff in the United Kingdom and Europe, the surgeon-superintendent and his sub-officers at sea and the immigration agent and his department in Queensland coordinated with imperial officers, shipping agents, merchants and outfitters, the captain and crew, and colonial employers to provide an all-inclusive health care programme, from selection to employment. In return for the effort, expense and legal coverage, Queensland immigrants were expected to abide by the rules, benefit from the voyage and contribute to colonial progress on arrival.

SURGEONS

The Queensland regulations explicitly stated that the surgeon, rather than the captain, was responsible for the welfare of immigrants on government vessels. He was 'invested . . . with supreme authority on board in everything not connected with the sailing of the ship' (ISS 1874:1), was answerable to the colonial authorities and acted as their chief executive officer during the voyage. Much of the success of the immigration policy depended on him. Even on privately organized ships, the surgeon was a central figure since anyone contemplating a voyage to the colony would undoubtedly have considered the consequences of illness or injury in mid-ocean.

Both the law and the large numbers traversing the high seas last century demanded that a proportion of the medical profession, at any given time, be employed in a maritime rather than a landed practice. As specialization and a heightened professional awareness percolated through the medical world in the latter part of the century, the status and conditions of employment for ship-surgeons came under review. A writer to the *British Medical Journal* in 1881 divided the surgeons into two categories:

'There is, first, the youth just qualified; he may be possessed of a good deal of book-learning, and a good deal of dissecting-room lore, but he is almost necessarily ignorant of the routine and the requirements of life on board ship. He is also not unfrequently deficient in tact, and in knowledge of men and manners . . . The second class consists wholly . . . of the "bad hats" of the profession. These men are to be found hanging about the druggists' shops and steamboat offices of every large seaport town . . . I have found them . . . dull, drunken, and dirty.'

But he hastened to add that there was a third class,

'unfortunately a relatively small one, composed of men of mature age and experience, who have adopted the sea as a profession, and have stuck to it for years. Such men are generally to be found in the colonial emigration services, and in the crack ships across the Atlantic, or through the Suez Canal.'

(BMJ 1881:II, 1035)

As passenger legislation evolved during the first half of the century and abuses at sea were exposed, it became increasingly evident that, without someone to administer the law during the voyage, it would be rendered ineffective. The obvious choice was a surgeon:[1] he could represent the passengers' interests against unscrupulous shippers and masters, protect immigrants from their own ignorance and shortcomings and provide health care. After all, the most humane master was employed by the shippers, an emigration officer had only limited oversight, and a chaplain was liable to sectarian bias; but an impartial, qualified medical practitioner could fulfil the requirements. Moreover, as public health reform escalated and the medical officer became a key figure in the administration of laws designed to improve the nation's health, it seemed reasonable to apply this approach at sea.

Career surgeons had been employed on East India Company ships (see Roddis 1941:303), and in 1814 surgeon-superintendents were first appointed to convict transports and made responsible for the welfare of convicts, their dietary, accommodation, exercise and discipline (see Charlwood 1981:157–58). The first passenger act of 1803 made provision for an adequate medicine supply and a properly qualified medical man for every vessel carrying more than fifty passengers. Although subsequent legislation modified this provision, the 1855 act stated that a *bona fide* doctor must be appointed to every ship with more than fifty passengers and an anticipated voyage time exceeding eighty days under sail or forty-five with steam, or if the total complement (crew and passengers) was greater than 300 persons. But the perennial question remained. How could the surgeon's position be made sufficiently secure and remunerative to attract competent men (see MacDonagh 1961:197)? The Commissioners resolved the problem by introducing a system of selection and incremental payment (according to the number of satisfactory voyages) for doctors recruited by them. They not only raised their salary, but improved their status and extended their functions to include administrative and disciplinary duties. The surgeon-super-intendent became, in effect, a sanitary inspector, medical officer, emigration official and moral guardian; he was furnished with a detailed and comprehensive job-description.

Gradually the Commissioners built up a staff of reliable surgeons, and by 1869 could claim that 'the qualifications and moral character' of the medical officers had contributed to the very satisfactory mortality rate on their vessels during the previous ten years (ECR 1870:13). By creating an elitist class of ship-surgeons, the Commissioners provided a model for the colonial governments. Under the first Queensland regulations (QGG 1861,2:15–17), all ships bound for the colony with more than twenty immigrants had to provide a qualified medical man who was required to keep a journal. However, conditions on the early vessels so shocked officials and the general public that it was decided to adapt the role of surgeon-superintendent to all government chartered ships, and invest him with the authority needed to maintain discipline and health during the voyage (see QGG 1863,4:989–91). Instructions drawn up for his guidance, reminded the surgeon-superintendent of 'the very responsible and highly important position in which he was placed':

> 'The sole medical care of so many persons, is of itself, a responsible charge, but this responsibility is greatly increased from your having the governance and care of the *whole* of the Passengers intrusted to you, and it is to the Medical Officer that they will have to look as their guide, adviser, and protector throughout the voyage.'
>
> (ISS 1875:3)

The surgeon's 'moral influence' was considered of equal, if not greater, importance than his medical duties, since experience had shown that firm control on board promoted health and minimized disease. In exercising his authority, he was instructed to tolerate no interference, but expect full cooperation from the master and officers (the fact that he signed the ship's articles in no way lessened his status or power); he had to uphold the rights of passengers and prevent 'unnecessary association' between the crew and those in his charge and at the same time, preserve cordial relations with 'the servants of the ship-owners' so that they would set a good example and work together for 'the maintenance of morality, health, good order, and good feeling in the ship'. Furthermore, he must treat the passengers with 'impartiality, justice and kindliness' while demanding strict compliance with the rules. Anything less could undermine respect and confidence in him and tend towards disharmony among so many people 'of different classes and creeds, brought into very close association for a considerable period'. Finally, the surgeon was reminded that, because passengers on Queensland ships included full-paying and cabin classes, they were 'superior' to those travelling on regular emigrant vessels and ought to be disciplined with 'discrimination and courtesy' (see ISS 1875:4–6). In theory, the health-care programme for Queensland immigrant vessels should have been in good hands.

A medical officer was appointed for each of the 610 (558 British and 52 German) immigrant voyages, and the names of all but ten (nine British and one German) have survived. In addition, seventy-seven (almost 11 per cent) of the short-ships carried a doctor. Information is thus available for 332 medical men who cared for passengers on 677 voyages to the colony.[2] One of the surgeons travelled as an assistant on a short-ship in 1895, and another, a Mr Collis, embarked on the *Bayswater* at Liverpool in 1864 in a 'semi-state of intoxication'. A few hours later the captain found him drunk and 'incapable of rising from his bed he comblained of face ack'. The following day he remained in bed suffering from 'nervous debility & violent vomiting'. When the vessel reached Greenock, Mr Collis was still in bed, 'craving drink' and asking the purser 'to broach the Medical Confirds wich was refused to him'. After three days he was removed from his filthy cabin and a replacement doctor proceeded to the colony (Official Log, NMML). Captains were responsible for health care on the 630 short-ships without a medical practitioner.

Voyages covered by a surgeon were distributed as follows: government (71.2 per cent), Commissioners (4.3 per cent), private immigrant ships (5.6 per cent), German (7.5 per cent) and short-ships (11.4 per cent). Two-thirds of the 677 voyages were served by medical men who made the voyage two or more times. Nevertheless, some 70 per cent of all the surgeons undertook the responsibility only once; this proportion ranged from 60 per cent for government appointees to almost 90 per cent for private and short-ship doctors. Actually, the record for the former group is cast in a better light when we note that less than 40 per cent of them superintended 80 per cent of the vessels sailing under the Queensland regulations.[3] The colonial authorities clearly intended their medical officers to form a permanent staff for the immigration service, and in time accomplished this end; thirty-eight of the surgeons on the eighty-six government ships in the 1860s made the voyage only once, but this proportion (44 per cent) fell to 24 per cent in the next decade, to 15 per cent in the 1880s, and to zero for the last decade. The incompetent and unsuitable were not re-employed. Most of the single appointments to private immigrant ships were made in the early 1860s when the infant colony was struggling to establish an efficient and stable system.

A considerable number of doctors applied for the position as a convenient method of emigrating to Queensland. When Henry Jordan burst upon the English public with his intense advertising campaign, it is not surprising that medical men would be among those attracted to the colony. In fact, between 1860 and 1900, almost 40 per cent of all the ship-surgeons registered with the Queensland Medical Board in order to practice in the colony; many settled permanently. There were other motives for seeking an appointment; a few fresh out of medical school joined ship to travel or gain experience before taking up a practice on land; others saw the voyage as an opportunity for a change, an escape from personal pressures or as a means for improving their health. In 1873, James Rouch FRCSE, a surgeon with a distinguished academic record, 'began to show signs of kidney disease and went on a voyage to Queensland'; but he rapidly deteriorated while at sea and died within a week of arrival (*Plarr's Lives* 1930:246–47). Some were returning to the colony after further training or a visit home; yet for many, their Queensland service was part of a chosen maritime career.

During the first two years of the land-order system, surgeons were appointed and remunerated by the shippers; it was their poor performance that triggered off the government's decision to establish and pay their own medical staff. Jordan selected the first appointee under the 1863 shipping contract. He was Theodore Byrne, thirty-seven years old, married, qualified in medicine and surgery, and had spent some years in the Royal Navy. Byrne made a second voyage before settling in the colony in 1866. By this time, after carefully screening applicants and rejecting the unsuitable, Jordan had built up a nucleus of reliable men. His procedure for appointing surgeons was adopted when immigration resumed in 1869 and was retained, with little modification, for the next two decades. As immigration declined during the late 1880s, the permanent staff was gradually reduced and the few who remained in 1892 appear to have been absorbed by the large shipping companies. Although 108 of the 179 surgeons selected and appointed through the Agent-General's Office did not seek or were refused re-employment, the remainder superintended an average of 5.3 vessels (this figure rose to 6.4 in the 1880s). The nineteen surgeons who were appointed six or more times supervised half the government voyages; eleven of these accepted responsibility for more than ten shipments and spent a significant part of their professional life in the Queensland service.

Charles Woodward served the colony for twenty years. He was born in Dublin and trained at the Royal College of Surgeons (Ireland) where he qualified in 1867; four years later he became a licentiate of the Kings and Queens College of Physicians. Then in 1873, at the age of twenty-seven, Woodward first sailed to Queensland. After nine voyages the government appointed him as their despatching officer at Plymouth (QGG 1879,25:1056), a post he held for almost two years; in 1881 he rejoined the medical service and made three more voyages under sail before changing to steamships. His record remained trouble-free until August, 1883; sailing down the Queensland coast he became seriously ill with 'a modified form of smallpox' and had to be quarantined for six weeks (COL/A370:83:5209). The following year a single-female passenger who had been made to pay the full fare when Woodward recognized her as a former colonist, brought trumped-up charges against him 'out of petty spite' (COL/A387:84–2820); in 1885 he unsuccessfully applied for the position of medical superintendent at the benevolent asylum near Brisbane. After continuing with the immigration service for another five years, he was dismissed over an incident involving the destruction of passengers' luggage (COL/A581:89–756,939,4795,5053). Although he appealed and was reinstated, his days were numbered; immigration was much reduced and appointments became irregular. He was finally made redundant in 1892 and accepted employment with the British India Company (British India Register of Surgeons, NMML). During the previous twenty years, Woodward made twenty-seven voyages, was responsible for the welfare of 11,615 immigrants, delivered 55 babies, registered 112 deaths and landed in the colony 99.5 per cent of the number embarked in his vessels, a record which compared favourably with over-all rates during the same period.

A government surgeon was expected to join the ship several days before departure to check all the medical and passenger arrangements and examine the immigrants. At embarkation he received a sheaf of documents and forms, together with such items as the library for which he was personally responsible. The first few days at sea were crucial for establishing order, a sense of community and who was in control. He rearranged the berthing where necessary, organized the messes, appointed sub-officers and began supervising the daily routine, the distribution of rations, the quality of the cooking, baking and water supply as well as the condition of the general-use areas. If the cook, baker, the man operating the distilling apparatus or any of the sub-officers died or failed in their duties during the voyage he must appoint a replacement.

The health of passengers, the surgeon was informed, depended on two factors – the 'careful observance' of the imperial regulations, particularly those relating to 'perfect cleanliness and thorough ventilation', and his own 'skill and resources' in preventing and treating disease. He was, however, presented with a list of 'valuable' suggestions for the diagnosis of infectious diseases, isolation and disinfection, visiting and care of the sick, and the use of the hospitals on board. Final instructions drew his attention to methods for reviving 'suspended Respiration' if a person was recovered after going overboard, and to measures for preventing or dealing with a fire at sea. In every particular, the medical officer was told what to do and how to do it. Was this prompted by the reputation of ship-surgeons in general, the utilitarian approach of the Queensland authorities or the poor profile of mid-nineteenth century medicine? The latter offered little uniformity of opinion or specifity of treatment, and the profession was groping towards an improved status. It is not surprising, therefore, that such commonsense directives were considered necessary.

It had been amply shown on the Commissioners' ships that moral-improvement activities and the control of liquor supplies promoted discipline and a good tone on board. These areas came under the surgeon's jurisdiction; he was not only expected to restrict the consumption of alcohol among cabin passengers and prohibit it altogether for the immigrants, but he had to determine if security arrangements for the girls were adequate and mete out punishment to anyone breaking the rules. The schools, library, Sunday services, weekly lectures and general activities were his responsibility. In addition, there were the clerical duties – preparing a passenger list, keeping a medical and disciplinary log, recording the daily temperatures between deck, registering births and deaths and listing the possessions of those who died, completing the classified summary and writing an official report of the voyage and time in quarantine, detailing the 'health, discipline and arrangements' of the ship. He recorded unsuitable immigrants, noted any interference or non-cooperation by the master and officers, and signed certificates of competence for the passenger personnel. All documents were submitted to the Colonial Secretary's Office on arrival, and duplicates were forwarded to the Agent-General. Should the vessel be forced to make an emergency stop during the voyage, the medical officer had to contact the British Consul and send a report of the circumstances to London. Carrying out these many functions with the cooperation and support of the master and his officers, the matron, the constables and the dispensary assistant demanded, quite apart from the surgeon's medical expertise, some degree, however minimal, of managerial and administrative skill.

The surgeon-superintendent's mandate allowed him almost unlimited authority on board. His power base was consolidated in the 1860s, reached a peak in the 1870s but was trimmed towards the close of that decade; payment and re-employment were made subject to an assessment of his performance and 'the satisfaction of the Agent-General' (COL/A254:78–797). This meant that the surgeons were no longer 'free agents'. With the introduction of steamships, his jurisdiction was restricted to steerage passengers only and his license to demand structural alterations to the fittings was withdrawn (COL/A334:82–1593). Nevertheless, he retained his position as chief executive officer, a status that was never accorded to the surgeon of a German vessel. Prussian law would not allow any situation that potentially detracted from the master's supreme command. In 1865, the health officer urged that instructions, adapted to 'German pecularities', be issued to surgeons on Queensland vessels out of Hamburg (COL/A71:65–2063). An inquiry the following year confirmed that medical officers were not only appointed without any reference to their 'character or professional acquirements', but received no status except 'by courtesy of the captain' (QVP 1866:1016). If the two did not cooperate, then the surgeon 'might be almost just as well left behind' one of them observed (COL/A76:66–429). The situation did not improve during the 1870s.

Since Hamburg law required that a sailing vessel carry only a medical attendant or a nurse (neither should be prone to seasickness) to check medicines and keep between decks clean, the emigration agent was forbidden to put up abstracts of the Queensland regulations unless those clauses relating to the surgeon's authority were scored out (QVP 1871:927–28 and COL/A185:73–1157). The captain was fully responsible for the ship, crew and passengers. To some extent this applied on privately-organized British immigrant ships – the early Black Ballers, the first bounty vessels and passenger carriers at the end of the colonial period. The 1855 act authorized the medical officer, aided by the master, 'to exact Obedience to all Rules and Regulations . . . prescribed by any . . . Order in Council' (18 & 19 Vic. c.119 s.60), though surgeons on these ships usually performed only medical duties. Yet the situation varied; on one bounty vessel the doctor was informed that his sole function was to 'physic the passengers' while another was encouraged to assume the role of a surgeon-superintendent and maintain 'morality, good order, and discipline' (COL/A391:84–3784).

The terms of employment also varied according to whether a surgeon was appointed by the shippers, the Commissioners or the Queensland government. On the Black Ball ships in the early 1860s the remuneration was less than £40 a voyage; even thirty years later, surgeons on British India vessels received only 1/– a month for each passenger.[4] Apparently shipping company doctors relied on gifts from grateful passengers to supplement their pittance; yet this practice had begun to die out by the mid-1870s (BMJ 1876:I,32). Generally, the office of ship-surgeon was not taken seriously; many were young and inexperienced or old and incompetent. The emigration officer checked their qualifications but ignored their experience and expertise. However, as improvements in passenger travel during the closing decades of the century coincided with the growth of scientific medicine, specialization and professionalism, the status of ship-surgeons was much debated in medical circles, the media and parliament. Since medical officers on land were civil servants, it was argued that, in view of the similar functions involved, appointments at sea should be the responsibility of a government medical marine service rather than the shippers (see, for example, BMJ 1881:II,992,998; BMJ 1883:I,1245; BMJ 1884:II,1164). Despite intense lobbying, this proposal was rejected; ship-surgeons did not achieve a status higher than that of a fourth-ranking officer. In the late 1890s, when the regulations and the role of the surgeon-superintendent no longer applied on Queensland immigrant vessels, the medical officer had to accept an inferior rank; this placed him in 'a very difficult position' (see QVP 1900:V,671).

Although conditions for privately employed surgeons varied enormously – some of the larger shipping companies established a permanent medical staff – medical men appointed by the Commissioners and the colonial emigration services were in a class apart. In 1862 the Commissioners paid their surgeons 10/– for each adult for the first two voyages, 12/– for the second two, 14/– for the third two, then increasing to a maximum of 20/–, as well as a free, first-class return passage (QVP 1863:II,440). The first Queensland appointees received only 5/– for each statute adult landed alive in the colony, a £50 gratuity, a separate saloon cabin and a first-class return passage.[5] In order to retain suitable men, Jordan urged that incremental payment be introduced; an increase of 2/6 for each voyage up to a maximum of 15/– was finally granted, with payment conditional on the 'faithful discharge' of his duties as outlined in the *Instructions*. During the boom years of the early 1880s, the head-money was raised to 10/– for the first voyage and increased for subsequent voyages to a maximum of 20/–, to attract sufficient surgeons and to be able to compete with other colonies; but as immigration declined, both amounts were reduced and complaints by senior surgeons relating to irregularities in the appointment procedure and terms of employment became more frequent.

Another bone of contention was the fee for quarantine services. For years a daily rate of £1.1.0. was considered the 'usual payment', but this was raised to £2.2.0. in the late 1880s. Some surgeons were allowed a leave of absence from the service, a few requested financial recognition when they retired, and at least one suggested that, whereas each death meant a loss of head-money, each live birth should be remunerated (see COL/A158:71–1944). Following a difficult voyage involving extra duties, the surgeon generally received an extra gratuity; while others, because of their questionable performance, had their payment delayed or deducted. For Dr Bonthron the experience of superintending a Queensland vessel proved a personal disaster; after being subjected to an Immigration Board inquiry and having to borrow money for his wife's return fare, he told the authorities in no uncertain terms that he should have remained in Britain where he could have commanded 'hundreds of pounds' during the same period (COL/A47:63–2884). Another surgeon refused appointment since 'the small number of Emigrants' would not bring him sufficient income (COL/A61:64–3180). Although the records are peppered with complaints, requests for an extra allowance and evidence of obvious injustice, a regular surgeon-superintendent in the Queensland service was well paid. Even for a first voyage he received £150, with all expenses paid and the possibility of perks from the saloon passengers. The income for a senior man might be as high as £400 a ship and £600 a year, a sum which was comparable with that for other senior government officers (the immigration agent's yearly salary was raised to £500 in 1864). No wonder such appointments were 'much sought after' (see BMJ 1883:II,659).

While at sea the surgeon lived as well as anyone on board. In 1882 the shippers took on extra provisions – 'one additional sheep, one pig, 2 dozen fowls, 1 dozen ducks. fruit, biscuits, and many other things' – and prepared 'a *nice* cabin and another little room next to it' for the doctor and his bride (Thomson 1882). Others did not fare as well. In 1864 Dr Miller's health began to fail after weeks of having to cope with a constantly wet cabin floor and the 'intolerable' smell from an adjoining communal privy (COL/A58:64–2372). Twenty-five years later the surgeon on the SS *Dorunda* reported that his cabin was 'not habitable in heavy seas'; while another claimed that the temperature in his cabin was 'always three degrees higher than in any other part of the ship' (COL/A627:90–9167 and COL/A502:87–4494). A single surgeon might have to share his accommodation with an officer or another passenger; if a doctor's wife accompanied him, she paid the first-class rate (the captain's wife was charged only £1 a week). The surgeon's quarters at the quarantine station scored the greatest number of complaints. On the whole, doctors seemed satisfied with the dietary, though a few questioned the quality of the alcoholic beverages and one indignant surgeon insisted that he had to survive on steerage rations; salt meat was served with every meal, there were 'No preserved Salmon, Sardines, Lobsters, or Anchovies. No bacon, Raisins, Figs, Almonds, Nuts, Wine' and even 'the biscuits were musty' (COL/A42:63–1741). Another, who fell out with the captain, absented himself from the cabin table and then complained that his dietary did not conform to the contract (COL/A34:62–2639).

It was one thing to offer attractive terms of employment, but it was another finding men of the right calibre. Yet, despite competition from other emigration services and the limited number of qualified, experienced and competent practitioners prepared to forego a landed practice for the hazards and demands of a life at sea, the Queensland authorities did not hesitate to penalize or dismiss unsuitable surgeons and demand 'a more careful choice' by the Agent-General; they wanted 'men of good professional qualification and high moral character' whose performance matched their remuneration (QVP 1863:II,408). It was not enough that surgeons be 'fully certified as professionally qualified'. The selection procedure introduced in 1863 required that they be married, morally upright, 'of temperate habits' and willing to remain with the service (QVP 1863:II,408).

When several of the first appointees 'proved unworthy of their trust', Jordan pointed out that he had to begin with 'untried material', and that the Commissioners not only had problems with 'troublesome and . . . dissolute' surgeons but their ships did not carry full-payers who saw themselves as independent of discipline. Furthermore, by refusing to sanction the incremental salary he recommended, the government made it more difficult to attract competent men (QVP 1864:1018–019). But he gave the matter his 'utmost attention' and checked every applicant's 'professional requirements . . . and antecedents' (see COL/ A73:65–3111 and QVP 1866:1071). By 1866 Jordan had built up a permanent staff of 'high class' men who met the desired standard – and practised 'the strictest sobriety'. Apart from a few poorly screened and last-minute appointees, such a staff seems to have been maintained; it was generally found that mature men who had both maritime and professional experience gave the best service. The shippers responsible for privately organized vessels were requested to pay particular attention to the appointment of the medical officer (see QVP 1883–84:1377).

Contrary to the general impression, the majority of surgeons on Queensland ships were neither young and inexperienced nor old and incompetent; their average age at the time of sailing was 34.5 years. Mean ages for the four decades (35.7, 32, 34.8 and 36.3 years) reflect Jordan's insistence on mature men in the 1860s, the recruitment of younger surgeons in the 1870s, and their increasing age in the 1880s and 1890s. Both the youngest (19 years) and the oldest (65 years) were appointed to Black Ball ships before the introduction of the Queensland regulations in 1863; 85 per cent were aged between 25 and 44 years. When a father applied on behalf of his son, he was informed that the government did not allow 'a youth just out of College' to be given charge of an emigrant ship (COL/A352:83–315). In 1876 the Immigration Board recommended that Dr Newell, despite a satisfactory first voyage, a BA degree, two diplomas from the Royal College of Surgeons (Ireland) and a Dublin MD, should not be re-employed because he was 'far too young'. The Agent-General ignored the recommendation and appointed Newell to another ship in 1878. But this was his last; he was 'more or less drunk' for the entire voyage (COL/A249:77–5868; COL/A261:78–2308). That same year Dr Lightoller kept a measles epidemic under control during his first voyage, but was told by officials on arrival that a man 'of riper years and more experience' ought to have been selected in view of the grave responsibilities of the position (COL/A266:78–4074).

The birthplace of the surgeons is of interest since the distribution of those from the United Kingdom (England and Wales 60 per cent, Scotland 15 per cent, Ireland 25 per cent) is similar to that for the passengers and suggests emigration as a motive for joining a Queensland ship. Britain supplied most (78 per cent) of the surgeons, 15 per cent were born in Europe and the remaining 7 per cent originated in the Australian and other British colonies. Apart from their origins, the question of whether or not ship-surgeons should be married was vigorously debated. The Commissioners accepted a man regardless of his marital status (one of their surgeons met and married an Irish immigrant lass who took his fancy during the Queensland voyage he superintended); but the colonial authorities believed that a married man would be more mature and responsible, keep the 'fair sex' in perspective and command greater authority. It was pointed out, however, that the ruling made little difference and could prevent a suitable man being appointed (see COL/A81:66–2049). In 1865 the Immigration Board recommended that the stipulation be abolished on the grounds that married men showed no greater morality and often accepted appointment 'under pressure of unfortunate circumstances attributable to past misconduct' (COL/A65:65–864). Although no consensus was reached, a couple of reports the next year resolved the issue: one superintendent proposed marriage to three of the single women and another, 'not withstanding his old age (63 years) and grey hairs . . . carried on an illicit connexion' with one of the young girls (COL/A82:66–2347 and QVP 1866:1023). Both men were married. Almost 40 per cent of the voyages were covered by a surgeon known to be married at the time of sailing, with this figure possibly rising to 75 per cent; only 4 per cent were known to be single. The proportion of vessels with a married surgeon dropped from 60 per cent in the first to 16 per cent in the last decade. It was not unusual for a doctor's wife and family to accompany him.

Previous maritime experience was definitely a factor in favour of selection. Slightly more than 70 per cent of the voyages with a surgeon (this figure reached 85 per cent in the 1880s) had the benefit of his familiarity with conditions at sea. Their previous experience involved service with the navy, an immigrant or coolie ship, or travel as a passenger. Less than 10 per cent of the vessels were left to a complete novice (the remaining 20 per cent are uncertain). One doctor strongly recommended that no raw recruit should superintend a vessel unless the master or chief officer had sailed previously with immigrants (COL/A358:83–1992). A record of the surgeons' experience prior to their first Queensland voyage not only shows that 42 per cent of them had served with the merchant marine, but that most of them had been in practice for some time. The period between a surgeon's first medical qualification and his voyage (or voyages) to the colony averaged nine years, and ranged from young men fresh out of training to the practitioner with forty-four years in the profession. Fewer than half (43.3 per cent) the voyages were covered by a surgeon with less than five years in practice.

Surgeons on the Queensland route were, by and large, mature, married men, employed by the colonial government, of English extraction, experienced in their profession and having the additional advantage of previous maritime service. Nevertheless, not one of them was legally eligible for appointment unless he held a recognized medical diploma that entitled him to become a registered practitioner.[6] The surgeons for whom their qualifications are known (90 per cent), held at least one legitimate diploma prior to their first voyage to the colony; 18.6 per cent held only one, 72.2 per cent had two or three, and 9.2 per cent held four to six qualifications. Some 60 per cent were licensed to practise both medicine and surgery. A breakdown of the figures shows that two-thirds of the doctors held one or two basic medical diplomas or degrees from a College of Physicians or University (a further nineteen added an MD degree); 91 per cent held a surgical certificate, diploma or degree, the majority being licentiates or members of one of the three Royal Colleges in the United Kingdom (sixteen were elected as Fellows or received a Master's degree); 30 per cent qualified as apothecaries; 21 per cent recorded a midwifery diploma (this specialty was often included as part of the surgical training). Twenty-two of the doctors held degrees outside medicine, in Arts, Science and Theology. Medical officers, both British and German, on Queensland immigrant vessels appear to have satisfied the legal requirements.

A follow-up study which includes the time of their colonial service and a ten-year period after their last Queensland voyage reveals that only 7.8 per cent completed further training or upgraded their qualifications; this is consistent with their maturity and experience. Most of those who added to their qualifications did so in another area of expertise. In 1885 Dr W.F. Taylor superintended his third vessel on his return to the colony after completing a Diploma in Public Health and a commissioned report for the government on 'Water Supply and Sewage Disposal' in Great Britain (see QVP 1885:III,553–94). The time between the first and last qualification for the surgeons ranged from 0 to 41 years, but averaged 3.6 years; two-thirds received their diplomas within a two-year period, and only 10 per cent extended the interval beyond ten years. However, the time at which the doctors qualified is important; 30 per cent gained their first diploma before 1860 (the earliest was in 1822), half qualified between 1860 and 1879, and 20 per cent trained in the 1880s and 1890s. Corresponding figures for the last qualification are 16, 54 and 30 per cent. The majority, therefore, trained and qualified before 1880. It was during the last twenty years of the century that modern, specialized and scientific medicine began to take shape. Queensland's ship surgeons largely belonged to the transitional period when the miasmatic and germ theories of disease coexisted, constitutional and hereditary aetiology received new impetus from evolutionary thought, and sanitary science dominated medical practice.

Many establishments throughout the United Kingdom offered medical training but only a limited number were authorized to hold examinations and grant diplomas. The general trend among aspiring practitioners was to train in one place, or even several different institutions, and to qualify from another. Queensland ship-surgeons were no exception. However, almost three-quarters (72.5 per cent) of them trained in one location only, while 68 per cent held diplomas from at least two 'medical Corporations' listed under the registration acts. More than half (54.4 per cent) completed all or part of their training in England (of these 80 per cent 'walked the wards' in one of London's large teaching hospitals and only seven attended an English university); but slightly less than half the doctors (49.5 per cent) held English qualifications. When we look at the Scottish figures, we find the reverse to be the case: 29.5 per cent attended a Scottish university, medical establishment or both (Edinburgh was the most popular place) and 47.2 per cent held Scottish diplomas. Clearly, the examination facilities offering in Scotland attracted many who had trained elsewhere. The number with Irish qualifications (19.8 per cent) also fell short of the proportion (22.4 per cent) who did all or part of their training in Ireland; four-fifths of these centred on Dublin; three went to an Irish university. Most of the medical officers on the German vessels had passed the German Staats examination. There were a few British and colonial men who held an MD from one of the internationally famous universities – Berlin, Paris and Leiden. A handful trained and qualified in Australia (Melbourne and Sydney) and North America (New York and Ontario). Within this diversity there was considerable uniformity – more than 90 per cent of Queensland ship-surgeons were the products of British medical education (see Plate 7).

Their working experience also suggests a strong British emphasis. Prior to their first voyage to the colony, 56 per cent of the doctors for whom information is available practised solely in the United Kingdom, with two-thirds of these based in London or one of the English counties. These figures would certainly have been influenced by the fact that the Queensland Agent-General's Office was in London. Of the other 44 per cent who pursued their career further afield, more than half lived for a time in the British Isles. Although 70 per cent of the doctors are recorded as having had only one place of residence before sailing to Queensland, the evidence indicates, despite its limitation, a greater mobility, and reveals a wide spectrum of professional experience – in private practice, in hospitals, as a medical or health officer, in medical education, as the doctor for an Insurance Association, Friendly Society or Lodge, as a railway, colliery, factory or prison surgeon, in the defense forces at home and overseas, and in the merchant marine. Four are known to have had another profession. After qualifying in divinity as well as medicine and surgery at Glasgow University, Dr Finlay spent the next twenty years as a curate in several London parishes. Whether he saw patients privately is not known, but in 1881 he was appointed to a Queensland ship. The captain questioned his medical ability and noted Finlay's fondness for drink. Although he was given a first-class certificate, he never sailed again, but remained wandering from one medical officer post to another in the far north and west of the colony.

The colourful career of the well-known Dr Kevin Izod O'Doherty provides a contrast (see Pike 1966). Transported to Van Dieman's Land (Tasmania) for his political activities in Ireland during the 1840s, O'Doherty served his sentence and then returned to Dublin to study medicine. He qualified as a Fellow of

List of Surgeons employed in the Queensland Immigration Service, showing number of Voyages performed by each, up to 31ˢᵗ May 1889

Nº	Name	Date of Sailing 1ˢᵗ Voyage - (The earliest procurable from Registers)	Number of Voyages	
1	Woodward C.R.	February 1ˢᵗ 1873	25	
2	Hickling Thomas	October 19ᵗ 1873	23	
3	Goodridge Edward W.G.	June 9ᵗ 1882	11	
4	Dunkley William W.	July 4ᵗ 1882	12	R.D.M
5	Sedingham A. Napier	December 1ˢᵗ 1882	10	
6	Goodall Joseph	January 7ᵗ 1883	11	R.D.M
7	Marshall James	April 12ᵗ 1883	10	
8	Ford-Webb Charles	December 6ᵗ 1883	10	
9	Poland James Henry	June 26ᵗ 1884	9	
10	Smith Kenneth		8	
11	Collins C. Tenison	January 13ᵗ 1885	6	R.D.M
12	Goodridge William D.B.	July 6ᵗ 1887	4	R.D.M
13	Wolfe J.L. de	March 7ᵗ 1888	1	R.D.M
14	Gardner David	December 22ⁿᵈ 1888	1	R.D.M

Not known whether intends applying for another Ship

W.E. Parry Okeden
Immigration Agent

Immigration Office ⎱
Brisbane 12ᵗ June 1889 ⎰

There are no other means than the above of giving information asked for. W.E.P.O.

Plate 7 Surgeons employed in the Queensland Immigration Service

the Royal College of Surgeons (Ireland) in 1857, two years later was awarded diplomas in medicine and midwifery, and in 1862 emigrated to Queensland where he established himself in private practice, accepted several medical officer appointments and became deeply involved in the affairs of the infant colony. Within five years he had been elected as a member of the Legislative Assembly. Trollope no doubt had O'Doherty in mind when he wrote, 'It may occasionally happen that a gentleman who has been unfortunate in his youth forces his way up to some place of note, in the legislature or elsewhere, and then a whisper is heard abroad that the gentleman came to the colony in the old-fashioned way' (Trollope 1875:I, 109). O'Doherty's political career extended over many years, including those in the Upper House. During this time he helped frame Queensland's education system, and served on several Commissions, the Central Board of Health and the Medical Board. In 1886, after a visit to Ireland, he returned as surgeon-superintendent on the SS *Duke of Westminster*. He was then sixty-two; and although he continued to serve the colony for many years, he never regained his place as a leading medical and public figure. One of his sons, Edward, went to Ireland to study medicine and was given oversight of a vessel when he returned to the colony in 1882. There were other family names on the Queensland route – the Harricks brothers, the Scatchards, and Edward and William Goodridge. William disliked steamships and when sailing vessels were taken off the colonial service in 1889, he transferred to coolie transports.

The task of a regular ship's doctor differed greatly from that of a surgeon-superintendent. The one involved treatment of the sick only; the other required, in addition to professional ability, a judicious management of people, the capacity to apply the principle rather than the letter of the law and, above all, adaptability. Some treated their responsibilities as a burden, most took them in their stride, and a few circumvented or ignored them. A last-minute appointee found himself 'quite unprepared to grasp the multifarious duties' devolving upon him; another surgeon, whose 'thankless labours' allowed him to snatch only one meal a day and a few hours sleep at night, observed that 'a man would need to be more than *mortal* to be able to act so as to seem to do *one half* of his work' (COL/A193:74–550; COL/A47:63–2884). No wonder an experienced superintendent advised against appointing young, raw recruits; 'What does he know of discipline, who had never been under it himself?' he asked (COL/A73:65–3111). Dr Underhay's case was most unfortunate. In 1865, during his first (and only) voyage, he took the *Instructions* far too literally, ran foul of the captain and was victimized by the passengers. They 'sent him to Coventry', lampooned him in song, and two of them poured treacle over his face while he slept (see Hurle 1967:30,31,32). He had to resort to writing up his medical log 'in haste and secrecy in the dead of night' and, in a state of near paranoia on arrival, reported 'a most unhappy voyage' (COL/A72:65–2787,2818).

The surgeon's health, the outbreak of an epidemic, hazardous or trying weather, lack of cooperation from the master and officers, and insubordinate immigrants could, singly or combined, make or break a voyage. Dr Hickling's description of the situation during the cholera epidemic on the SS *Dorunda* in 1855 boggles the mind; he finally 'dropped with exhaustion' (see QVP 1886:III,754–92). Dr Senftleben, who sailed with the *Alardus* from Hamburg in 1872, was denied all authority. The captain permitted the single men and women to mix freely; infected cask water caused a severe outbreak of dysentery and forced the ship into port en route; the second officer, who acted as the purser and distributed the rations, sold more than 1,200 bottles of gin and brandy to the passengers. Then the vessel had to put into Melbourne; the captain had mysteriously disappeared a few days before, the chief officer was dying of tuberculosis, and the surgeon refused to continue with the second officer in charge. After five days in quarantine, the *Alardus* proceeded to Moreton Bay where Dr Senftleben submitted his thirty-six-page report: 'I cannot help remarking' he wrote, 'that my health and spirits have suffered more during this voyage than in the last campaign in France which I was in the whole time with one of the most exposed field regiments of the Prussian Army' (COL/A185:73–1157).

The surgeon's duties began with embarkation – a time of 'hopeless confusion' with the doctor 'being called in all directions' while trying to supervise medical arrangements for the voyage (COL/A73:65–3111). Once on board he kept to a regular daily routine. The following schedule is fairly typical:

'6 A.M. Pumping,
Decks, Serving out bread and Breakfast

9 A.M. Hospital
10 A.M. Visits
for Cleanliness between decks Ventilation etc
11 A.M. Visits
for Sick between decks Women & children
12 Mid-day
Medicines, Wines and Comforts.
12.30 Luncheon
2.30 P.M. Visits
Between decks after Passengers dinners &
on alternate days with the Master.
6.30 P.M.
Rounds and Hospital
9.30 P.M. Watches seen to.
Names called of Constables and Watch
10 P.M.
Night Rounds for turn in
Lights Out.'

(COL/A193:74–550)

Many surgeons did not begin their day until the breakfast supervision at 8 a.m. or even 10 a.m. when it was usual to combine their medical rounds with the 'tween decks sanitary inspection. These might be as perfunctory or as thorough as they wished. The diary of a Black Ball voyage in 1862 describes how the 'old idiot' of a doctor was finally prevailed upon to visit a sick lad in the steerage compartment; he stood as far from the patient as possible to ask a few necessary questions before beating a hasty retreat with 'his coat tails in one hand & a handkerchief in the other to slash the vermin from of his sanctified person' (Blasdall 1862).

Certainly the 'live stock', smells and close confines of the immigrants' berths would have been a deterrent, but the surgeons' reports indicate that most of them regularly checked between decks and attended the sick. One of the permanent doctors during the last years of the Queensland service actually visited the hatches 'several times' in the night to see if the men on watch were doing their duty (COL/A458:86–1999). Passengers often expected too much of the medical officer and imposed on him. Dr Lightoller in 1878 began 'to wish the voyage was at an end'; the married people seemed to think he had 'nothing else to do but look after them alone' (quoted in Charlwood 1981:307). On arrival in the colony, the immigration agent expected the doctor's assistance with the final muster, but several steamship surgeons objected to 'running all over' the vessel for immigrants and having to control employers who met the ship at each coastal port. Undoubtedly, most of the government doctors would have disagreed with the claim that they chose the colonial service 'as an easy and certain way of obtaining a competence, with a minimum of work or annoyance' (BMJ 1881:II, 1035).

Although every passenger ship was supplied with sufficient medicines and hospital equipment, the doctor had to provide his own surgical instruments. The person he appointed to work under his supervision in the dispensary, and assist with out-patients and those in hospital, usually had some experience with the medical world – a 'pharmaccutist', an unorthodox practitioner, a medical student or a 'man of the cloth'. 'Dr' Patrick Smith, the hospital assistant on the *Maryborough* in 1865, subsequently qualified from the University of Sydney, practised in Brisbane and superintended two vessels during the 1880s. If a surgeon became incapacitated, he had to leave the care of the sick to the assistant, a nurse, the captain or a relative. Sometimes a medical man among the passengers was willing to be involved. On the *Light of the Age* in 1864, the Rev. Mr Cass who had trained in medicine took over when Dr Mackay became ill; he received the £25 deducted from the surgeon's gratuity (COL/A50:64–387).

An assistant's duties could be most demanding. One superin-tendent suggested that a nurse also be appointed from among the married women to apply poultices, administer injections, attend to women in childbirth, prepare invalid diets and assist mothers with the care of their sick children (COL/A67:65–1307). How-ever, such appointments were made only under extenuating circumstances; if extra duties were required of an assistant, he was recommended for a bonus. Since they sailed as immigrants, one assistant recommended that, instead of the £5 gratuity for satisfactory service, better accommodation near the dispensary and prepared meals would allow them to work more effectively and handle trivial complaints (COL/A332:82–1154). Some of them earned every penny of their payment; one attended to more than 230 cases during the voyage, while another, on the *Star of England* in 1863, virtually took over from the surgeon who was 'a thoroughly slothful man' (COL/A28:62–1261; COL/A45:63–2372). On the other hand, incompetence or misbehaviour could result in dismissal or the forfeit of his gratuity; one lost his job after he sent a note to one of the single women (COL/A412:85–252). In 1884 an assistant in his ignorance administered a lethal dose of castor oil and laudanum to a female passenger who suffered from 'anascara and general dropsy' and had embarked hoping to improve her health; she did not survive. Both the surgeon and assistant were denied a gratuity (COL/A392:84–4132).

A doctor's reaction to the voyage was one indicator of how he coped with his responsibilities. While some did not read the *Instructions* carefully and others emphasized one duty in preference to another, the more experienced found that attention to good order and discipline from the outset, lessened their burden and allowed time for relaxation, even enjoyment. Life on board sailing ships tended to generate extremes of reaction, but the evidence suggests that, whatever the mode of transport, the surgeon's approach and his ability to maintain morale also facilitated his task. Organizing the school, library, lectures and entertainment did not come easily for some, while others seemed to thrive on it. Dr Scott offered a full weekly programme – '*Sunday* Masses, prayers, Sunday School . . . *Mon* Concert *Tues* Discussion class *Wed* Lecture *Thurs* Religious meeting *Fri* Recitations and readings' – and found time to paint the scenes for the Christmas play. For him the time at sea was a 'superlative holiday trip' (COL/A75:66–48). More realistic was another surgeon's comment that, despite the heavy 'Sanitary, Disciplinary and Medical' duties, the voyage was pleasant (COL/A360:83–2085). There were the fights and arguments to arbitrate, refractory passengers to punish and the 'paper work' to finish. 'With so many people . . . always wanting something', lights-out at 10 p.m. could not come soon enough; but he could find time to relax – playing the flute at a concert, writing an article for the ship's newspaper or settling down with a book and fishing line. The doctor's wife also contributed to life on board by assisting with the school or organizing a choir. Some surgeons took an analytical interest in the job and submitted to the authorities suggestions for improving arrangements and fittings; one or two offered to write a handbook for use in the emigrant trade. Although no one surgeon produced a revolutionary design or a medical breakthrough, their over-all contribution to the quality of life on Queensland ships cannot be ignored.

The surgeon-superintendent was expected to be the typical mid-Victorian untrained expert. Some proved highly competent, others failed dismally, but accordingly to the records, the majority gave satisfactory service. Again Gandevia (1978:49) must have been referring to the early days of voluntary emigration to Australia when he maintained that regular ship-surgeons, compared to those on convict transports, were generally 'less well qualified, less experienced and more inclined to alcohol', and 'never acquired the same authority'. Not only were Queensland superintendents invested with a great deal of authority, but they and their colleagues on non-government vessels generated surprisingly few complaints. Only 235 comments could be found in the numerous reports available. Of these, almost one-tenth commended the surgeons, 23 per cent referred to some aspect of their work, and the remaining two-thirds (159) were complaints. These represented 28.9 per cent of the surgeons, but only 7 per cent of the voyages covered by a medical practitioner. A gradual decrease in the average number of complaints per surgeon (1.9 in the 1860s to 1.0 in the 1890s) points to progressive improvements in the service, the growth of a permanent staff of reliable medical officers and the trimming of the surgeon's power base.

Immigrants contributed 39 per cent of the complaints, officials on arrival (immigration agent, health officer and members of the Immigration Board) added 34 per cent, captains 7 per cent, and the sub-officers (matron, teacher, constables and doctor's assistant) 2 per cent; the remainder included other immigration personnel and surgeons who were displeased with their terms of employment. Apart from unspecified complaints (7 per cent) and those submitted by surgeons relating to their salary and appointment (4 per cent), the greatest proportion (63 per cent) were concerned with failure to maintain discipline and the remaining 26 per cent referred to the surgeons' incompetence, either professionally or as an administrator. Disciplinary problems included 'a lack of control' which was generally believed to result in poor sanitation, increased morbidity, a slackening of morals and a lowered morale. The surgeon's attitude and behaviour towards the passengers, his intemperance and immorality, breaches of the law and the regulations, a failure to assert his authority, or simply an inability to cope because of 'constitutional defects' also came under this heading. However, the less complimentary statements throughout the reports were balanced by such comments as 'an excellent disciplinarian', 'a most efficient, exemplary officer', 'the doctor knows his people', 'always concerned for the physical and moral welfare of the Emigrants', 'a very intelligent and qualified man', 'greatly respected', and 'the immigrants were loud in their praises of him'. The various complaints and commendations leave the impression that the surgeon's personality, his attitude towards others and his ability to command respect and exercise authority were considered more highly than his medical competence.

Charges by the captain or officers against the doctor invariably resulted from incompatible personalities, a conflict of authority, or the surgeon's refusal to recommend them for the government gratuity. Sometimes the doctor was accused of interfering in matters that were not his concern, but here lay a fine dividing line, particularly if the ship's equipment was likely to endanger passengers. When allegations were substantiated, three options were available – the master, the surgeon or both could be dismissed from the service, or they might have part of their gratuity deducted, or the Agent-General was advised not to allow them to travel together again. Nevertheless, cooperation was mutually advantageous; on more than one occasion the doctor and his constables were called to intervene in a threatened mutiny among the crew. Although the more mature surgeons rarely had difficulties, the master sometimes gave a young, raw recruit a hard time; he might disagree with a diagnosis, forestall treatment, threaten, dominate or ignore him. Any surgeon who allowed himself to be treated in this way was generally considered unsuited to the job. On his first voyage in 1864, Dr Sandiford found himself at the mercy of the master who, it seems, kept him in ignorance of the quarantine laws and insisted that he give false answers concerning the health of the ship. Sandiford was prosecuted, committed for trial and imprisoned for six months. When the 'mental anguish' of being thrown together with 'felons of the deepest dye' caused a rapid deterioration in his health, the sentence was commuted (see COL/A59:64–2518,2657). But the incident served as a warning to future surgeons to exercise their authority, abide by the law, and follow the *Instructions*.

Occasionally a matron did not 'hit it off' with the doctor; or he regretted his choice of a constable or schoolmaster. However, allegations by the sub-officers, since they depended on the surgeon for their gratuity, proved a serious indictment of his failure to control himself, his staff or those in his charge. On the other hand, passenger complaints were often without foundation or the result of personal antipathy. Saloon travellers objected to a superintendent restricting the sale of liquor, those in the steerage who had been punished for misconduct complained of injustice, abuse or cruelty, and charges of neglect or mismanagement were frequently lodged by the relatives of immigrants who had died en route. Under such circumstances conflicting evidence was inevitable and required particular discernment by the immigration agent or Board.

In several instances lack of control was associated with intemperance. The surgeon, as a saloon passenger, received a daily liquor allowance and, notwithstanding precautionary measures, could also avail himself of medicines and medical comforts. On a few voyages, passengers knew that 'stimulants' had been misappropriated. Although this 'weakness' did not show itself until the ship was well out at sea, a surgeon's reputation as 'an habitual sot' or 'an opium eater' could be firmly established by the time of his arrival. This meant that he was incapable of attending to the sick. Indeed, one besotted surgeon collapsed into the patient's berth and another was discovered, totally inebriated, in a female toilet. Several apparently discharged their duties, despite regularly resorting to the bottle. Dr McLean began well, but his performance slowly worsened until, on his seventeenth voyage, he was declared 'unfit for professional duty'; the 140 days' supply of medical comforts had been consumed in eighty. He was dismissed, but received full payment in view of his long service (COL/A263:78–3219). Whether a surgeon was overtly alcoholic or guilty of occasional insobriety, the authorities considered 'intemperance – of *whatever degree* – as a serious disqualification' (COL/A70:65–2274). Since accumulated evidence had shown that drunkenness was responsible for most of the loss of life and property at sea, they could not be too careful in their choice of a man on whom so much depended.

Apart from the problems with drink, an overbearing captain or illness, some medical officers did not have the 'slightest idea' or intention of maintaining discipline. They failed to establish a routine or check the constables, indulged in undue familiarity with the single women or allowed blatant immorality, used coarse and blasphemous language, lost their temper or adopted a harsh, even brutal, attitude towards the immigrants. A few issued medical comforts as 'rewards for trifling services rendered by the passengers' (COL/A320:81–3866), while others were too strict, 'injudicious' or simply lacked commonsense. 'Wanting in the most essential moral qualifications, for such a responsible office' was the typical bureaucratic assessment (see, for example, COL/A48:63–3141). An immigrant expressed it another way: 'a more weak-minded fool than the doctor has sildom lived' (Good 1863).

The fault did not always rest with the surgeon; passenger attitudes and prejudices could undermine his control. A petition in 1865 for better supervision on German vessels noted that the medical men appointed were 'not of a character calculated to inspire confidence' (COL/A70:65–2251); but a decade later, immigrants on the *Fritz Reuter* regarded their superintendent as a 'tormentor' when he tried to instill order and cleanliness between decks (COL/A271:79–729). An Irish doctor encountered personal prejudice among his shipment of Lancashire cotton operatives in 1863, and Dr Cambell who had previously worked for the Imperial Service claimed, after facing an Immigration Board inquiry, that on Queensland government ships the surgeon was 'on probation' rather than the passengers (COL/A78:66–901). Diaries and official reports suggest that immigrants, aware of their rights yet unaccustomed to being 'governed' by a doctor, willingly accepted the free medical treatment but often had difficulty submitting to his authority. 'The ships doctor . . . seems to know more about dispensing religion than medicine' wrote one young man (Blasdall 1862). The surgeon sometimes walked a tightrope; but a father-figure approach, consistent with governmental paternalism, generally gained him respect and acceptance. 'I endeavoured to rule the passengers by kindness and moral force in preference to physical and degrading punishment, and am thoroughly satisfied with the result' remarked one surgeon (QVP 1876:II, 1170).

The authorities dealt firmly with any medical officer whose deliberate or unintentional neglect of his duties was known to be responsible for sickness, deaths and disorder on board. One was dismissed and half his gratuity mulcted for jeopardizing the immigrants' health when the water supply ran low and he failed to insist that the master put into the Cape of Good Hope (COL/A76:66–476). Professional incompetence and neglect usually involved the allegation that treatment had been withheld or delayed or was inappropriate. A married man on the *Gauntlet* in 1873 claimed that Dr Freeman, by refusing medical comforts, 'got six of as strong children as we ever seen over Board' (COL/A187:73–2064). Another medical officer should have reberthed several small children who were located too close to the engine-rooms and died of heat exhaustion while travelling through the Red Sea (COL/A346:82–5225). A man, too ill to attend his wife, reported on arrival that she died because the surgeon refused to treat her in her bunk (COL/A396:84–5055). A group of mothers on a voyage in 1865 were so incensed by the 'murder' of a child, they grabbed hold of the doctor and clipped his beard (COL/A63:65–57).

There were times when it was physically impossible for a doctor to handle all the requests for attention; yet some of the complaints were clearly justified. An undisputed case of incompetence involved a young man who was permanently disabled because the surgeon failed to diagnose an obvious leg fracture and treated it instead as an 'ugly hurt' (COL/A341:82–3179). Incidentally, the surgeon was dismissed from the service on a charge of drunkenness. Although all accusations were investigated, there is no evidence that any doctor was prosecuted for criminal negligence or mismanagement. Claims that they failed to isolate patients with infectious disease, institute preventive measures or provide adequate care, were successfully refuted by pointing to non-cooperation by the master or passengers and calling on a wide range of medical opinion to support their position. But if a surgeon refused to submit his log, or it was found to be poorly kept, with omissions, misspelt diagnoses or inaccuracies, his professional ability was suspect and he was regarded as unsuitable (see, for example, COL/A304:80–6815).

The efforts of the most conscientious and qualified man could be impaired by physical and mental unfitness. Surgeons were subject to a variety of ills – severe headaches, exhaustion from overwork, mumps, fractures, an infected finger, sore throat, 'catarrhal fever and gastric derangements', 'severe rheumatism',

neuralgia, smallpox and typhus. One became 'temporarily de-
ranged' and suffered total amnesia for part of the voyage; at the
time there were thirty cases of typhoid fever on board (COL/
A371:83–5330). They also suffered their share of seasickness: 'The
doctor his as bad as anyone on board' observed a sympathetic
fellow traveller (Anon. 1883). In all, six surgeons died while in
charge of passengers. The death rate for the Queensland surgeons
(1.8 per cent) was, in fact, higher than that for the total
immigration (1.4 per cent). Were they exposed to greater health
hazards, or should they too have been physically screened? The
first went down with the *Wilhemsburg* in 1863. Three years later
Dr Pedgrift contracted typhus from the immigrants and died a
week before arrival. His replacement (Dr Levett) who had been
seconded from another ship which reached the colony at the same
time, suffered a fatal accident while supervising quarantine. Then
in 1878 Dr Mark, on his second voyage to Queensland, died of
tuberculosis, and Dr Spence succumbed to gastritis while superintending his fourth ship. In 1895 a British India surgeon committed
suicide five days after leaving London. Thirteen others died
shortly after completion of the voyage; for five of them the cause
is unknown, three were drowned during the return passage, two
died of tuberculosis, two of organic disease and one of 'fever'. The
combined mortality record supports the assumption that a few of
the surgeons applied for a ship in order to improve their health.
The authorities, however, were displeased if a doctor's illness or
death adversely affected the passengers' health.

In return for faithfully discharging his duties, the surgeon
received a first-class certificate, full payment, the guarantee of
another appointment, and perhaps a testimonial from the passengers. However, a satisfactory voyage was not always sufficient;
the immigration agent, for a variety of reasons, might not approve
of a medical officer. We have seen that some surgeons were
thought to be too young. In 1882 Dr Tennant was denied a
certificate on the grounds that he refused to assist with the final
muster, the ship's library was poorly kept, he took several days to
answer complaints and the general tone on board 'did not create
confidence in him' (COL/A332:82–1198). If an Immigration
Board inquiry sustained charges against a surgeon, he was
immediately dismissed from the service with all or part of the
head-money mulcted and sometimes the return passage denied. In

a few instances the £50 from the shippers was the only payment a surgeon received. He had the right of appeal either directly to the Queensland government or through the Agent-General, and in some cases was reinstated with full payment.

The records show that at least two surgeons were prosecuted for violations of the quarantine act, and that charges were laid against two others under the passenger and quarantine acts. Apart from these instances, forty-five (25 per cent) of the 179 government appointees are known to have been dismissed. Twenty-eight of these dismissals occurred in the 1860s and represented 17.6 per cent of all immigrant voyages for that decade. This proportion fell to 5.7 per cent in the 1870s and to 2.7 per cent in the 1880s. Only one surgeon was dismissed in the last decade. Most of the reasons for dismissal resolved into one of four categories – failure to maintain discipline, intemperance, neglect of sanitary and medical duties, and misconduct. The colonial authorities in their haste to eliminate inefficient and unsuitable officers sometimes appeared harsh, even unjust, in their judgements; but the success of their efforts was reflected in the decreasing frequency of complaints against the surgeons and in the gradual improvement in the service.

Follow-up information, covering their years on Queensland vessels and for a ten-year period after the last voyage, has been traced for almost 90 per cent of the surgeons and provides further insights into the men who cared for immigrants as they sailed to the colony. During this period the majority seem to have remained in one country, but the location is of interest. Compared to the pre-service figure of 2 per cent for those who originated or resided in Australia, we find that 44 per cent lived for a time or settled in Queensland and 24 per cent located in one of the Australasian colonies. Many of the doctors clearly accepted appointment in order to emigrate or investigate employment and living possibilities in the Antipodes. Their follow-up career patterns are also of interest. Most of them held two or more positions during the time, but the proportion employed as medical or health officers rose from 22 per cent before, to 45 per cent after their Queensland service and the number holding other government appointments trebled. In 1874 Dr Winstone, a former surgeon-superintendent on one of the Commissioners' vessels to the colony, became the medical examiner for the Board of Trade at the Port of London. A first-class certificate for a Queensland voyage would have been a distinct advantage when applying for such an appointment. Many of those who settled in the colony held medical officer posts; in fact, thirteen of the thirty-six gazetted in 1885 had served on immigrant ships (QGG 1885,37:2235). However, the number who continued with the merchant marine fell from 42 to 21 per cent. Twenty-five of the surgeons held public office in Queensland, including the three – Dr K.I. O'Doherty, Dr J.J. Mullen and Dr W.F. Taylor – who became members of the colonial Legislative Council.

The over-all professional profile for Queensland's ship surgeons indicates that the majority, before and after their time in the Queensland service, were accustomed to working for an employer; being answerable for the welfare of immigrants in transit was another variant of a familiar pattern. The main difference lay in their terms of employment – those who were employed by the shippers, and those who had to handle a dual role and exercise discretionary powers on behalf of the Queensland government. The records show that the latter were, on the whole, carefully selected and drawn from the more reputable members of the medical fraternity. While most of the surgeons spent only a fraction of their career in the Queensland service and all but a few remained rank-and-file practitioners, their profile suggests they not only took an active interest in their profession as members of a medical society and writing articles for medical journals, but became involved at many levels of society. Certainly those who settled in Queensland seem to have contributed to the health and progress of the colony.

Dr Henry Scott illustrates the varied career and catholic interests of the 'average' Queensland ship-surgeon. Between 1865 and 1866 Scott successfully superintended three vessels. He was married and met the requirements for age, qualifications and experience. His date of birth is unknown, but by 1855 he was a member of the Pharmaceutical Society of Great Britain. Four years later he qualified as an apothecary in London, and satisfied the examiners in Glasgow in medicine, surgery and midwifery. He became a licentiate of the Royal College of Physicians (London) in 1861. Scott was English and did his medical training at the Westminster Hospital in London where he received a prize in chemistry. Before applying to the Queensland service, he worked at an ophthalmic hospital and a maternity charity. His report for each voyage detailed the health and conduct of the passengers and crew, noted shipboard arrangements and offered suggestions for improvement. Immediately after his third journey he joined the merchant fleet stationed at the Chincha Islands and was commissioned by the Peruvian government to set up a fever hospital and report on an earthquake. Following his return to England, he became a district medical officer and by 1877 had settled in private practice in Hertfordshire. Scott's individuality, enthusiasm and humanitarian concern filtered through his reports and are reflected in the wide range of his publications:

> '"On Tubercular Consumption;" "On Diseases of Women and Children;" "Counsel to a Young Wife;" "Report of the Earthquake in Peru, 1868;" and of Essays and Pamphlets on "Vaccination;" "Suggestions for Improved Dwellings for the Poor;" "Clitoridectomy;" "Medical Competition;" "Female Medical Colleges;" "Cheap Food;" "Medical Clergy;" "Schemes for Tariffs of Medical Fees;" "Third Class Railway Carriages;" "Medical Apprenticeship;" "The One-Faculty System;" "Medical Relief for the Poor;" "Improved Apparatus for Cooking;" "The Amalgamation of the Societies Scheme;" &c.'
> (*Medical Directory* 1872)

Few of the doctors on the Queensland ships had such a prolific pen; yet many, like Scott, appear to have had a genuine concern for the welfare of immigrants in their charge. While a small number were drawn from the dregs of their profession, the majority, though ordinary men, represented an 'upper-class' of ship-surgeons. Those appointed by the colonial authorities were well remunerated, but had to meet stringent standards to remain with the service. As the government's executive officer at sea, the surgeon-superintendent was responsible for a vital stage of the immigration programme and had to therefore conform to colonial expectations; on him, more than any other person, depended the health of selected immigrants as they sailed to Queensland. By and large, the permanent staff of medical officers on Queensland immigrant vessels met the requirements and satisfactorily discharged their duties.

CREWS

Careful arrangements and provisioning for the voyage, and the surgeon's oversight and attention were designed to keep immigrants healthy as they travelled to the colony, but their safety at sea basically depended on seaworthy vessels and the men who sailed them. At the time Queensland staked her claim for a share of the emigration market, the British merchant marine were already working towards a 'steady development in technical and commercial efficiency, which turned the ill-manned and unenterprising marine of the 'forties into the imposing, self-reliant institution of seventy years later' (Thornton 1945:80). Whether or not the colonial authorities were aware of this transformation is immaterial; they were primarily concerned that the performance of the captain and his crew on a Queensland-bound ship in no way interfered with, but contributed to, the welfare of all on board.

Every account of nineteenth-century shipping records that sailors before 1850 were a sorry lot – 'rum-soaked' illiterates, untrained and inefficient, the ill-used outcasts of society. They lived hard, worked harder and died young; a seaman's health was usually broken after twenty years' service (see Course 1965:195). Apart from the highly-reputable captains of the East India Company and the large shipping firms which adopted a similar apprenticeship system, most masters worked their way up through the ranks. Many were intemperate, poorly-educated, 'rule-of-thumb' navigators who treated their men with the same brutality they had known. Efforts to consolidate emigrant protection not only revealed a close relationship between shipwreck and mortality on the one hand, and unscrupulous shippers and alcohol on the other, but had also exposed the degenerate state of British crews and their deplorable working conditions. Legislation designed to upgrade the merchant marine proceeded steadily during the second half of the century, despite resistance by shipping interests in parliament to any move that would make shipowners liable for loss of life at sea, and increase the rights of their employees. Britain was, in fact, one of the last countries to formulate a code of maritime law, and her seafaring men were among the last of the working classes to benefit from the industrial revolution and social reform.

The Merchant Seamen's Act of 1835 (5 & 6 Will. 4 c. 19) allowed a measure of control in that it provided for the registration of crews (including apprentices) with the customs officer at the beginning and end of a voyage. Then the following year, a select committee report (BPP 1836 xvii 373) recommended the establishment of a Mercantile Marine Board to coordinate all aspects of the British merchant navy. However, the proposals contained in the report proved too radical and were not implemented for several years. In the meantime, passenger legislation absorbed attention, but increasing and alarming reports of the poor performance of British seamen forced through an act in 1844 (7 & 8 Vict. c. 112) which introduced the ticket system and the articles of agreement. This meant that no man could join ship unless he signed an employment contract; in effect, the master's unlimited power was curtailed. The act also laid down certain basic conditions for the crew, including a supply of medicines and the daily issue of lime juice after ten days on a salt meat diet. An order-in-council in 1845 instituted voluntary examinations for masters and mates; it also stipulated that, on voyages south of the equator, the master must hold a first-class certificate, be at least 21 years of age and have had a minimum of six years' experience at sea; the first officer had to be 19 years old, with four years' experience. When applying for a ship, both were required to submit proofs of their experience and of their 'habitual sobriety'. These regulations allowed improvements on the Australian run and were steps in the right direction, but they merely scratched the surface of a deeply entrenched problem.

Then the repeal of the navigation acts and the beginning of free trade opened up a new era for British shipping. The time was ripe for reform. A statute, passed in 1850 (13 & 14 Vict. c.93), struck at the root of the problem – the lack of coordination and organization within the merchant navy. It sanctioned the creation of a Marine Department under the Board of Trade with local boards to administer the law, conduct compulsory examinations for first-class certificates (these could be cancelled through incompetence or misconduct) and establish shipping offices to control the hiring and discharge of seamen, keep a record of their character, conduct and ability, and supervise their payment. The act also controlled crimps – boarding-house keepers who fleeced the men and worked in collusion with the masters to make up a crew – and included regulations relating to the accommodation, dietary, health and discipline of sailors. This long-overdue legislation began to effect real changes, but its minimum standards encouraged 'a general level of officially approved mediocrity' (Thornton 1945:45). The more reputable shipping firms recognized this and were able to show that it was possible to enhance their commercial viability by offering training and better conditions for their men. This, in turn, stimulated further legislation.

Although more than thirty acts relating to merchant shipping were passed between 1850 and 1900, evasion of the law continued to be the major impediment to progress during the first half of this period. The Board of Trade, despite the powers vested in it, did not have sufficient personnel to absorb, interpret and enforce the legal alterations and additions. It was largely left to private concerns and colonial governments to determine standards, supervise shipping agreements and penalize any breach of contract. Since over-all maritime efficiency and safety showed no real improvement, a Royal Commission was appointed in 1873 to investigate marine insurance and the shocking loss of life at sea. Their report concluded that 30.5 per cent of losses between 1856 and 1872 were due to natural causes, 4.5 per cent to unseaworthy, overloaded vessels and the remaining 65 per cent to bad navigation, mostly caused by ignorance and drunkenness. It seemed that poor quality crews rather than the shippers were largely to blame (see BPP 1873 xxxvi 315,335). In the face of such evidence, it is not surprising that the Queensland government closely monitored her shipping contracts and the performance of the masters and their men. Incidentally, only one British passenger vessel bound for the colony went down, without loss of life and as a result of foul weather conditions, during the period under investigation.

Subsequent legislation only temporarily reversed the situation. Following the allegation in 1884 that the lives of one in three British seamen had been lost in the previous twelve years, another Commission was appointed; this time the blame shifted from incompetent and negligent masters and their crews to shipowners and the condition of their vessels. Parliamentary intervention continued under mounting public pressure, competition from rapidly industrializing countries and specialization within the industry. Improved facilities for passengers and subsidized immigration also contributed to the reforming process. Moreover, seamen themselves, supported by a vigorous campaign concerned for their interests, became more organized and pressed for their rights. By 1900 the majority of British ships were well-found and well-managed and their officers, engineers and men 'had established . . . a reputation which was unrivalled for sound navigation, technical skill and loyal service' (Thornton 1945:93). However, these improvements had only an indirect spin-off for Queensland; from the outset, the colonial authorities demanded efficiency, competence and cooperation from the masters and crews engaged for her vessels.

Rapid advances in German shipping in the latter part of the century also had little impact on immigration to the colony from Hamburg between 1861 and 1879. Nevertheless, the loss of only one vessel in fifty-two voyages, and that due to natural causes, is some reflection of the standard of German crews on vessels to Queensland. Unfortunately only two reports pertaining to these crews have survived. According to the surgeon's account of the *Alardus* voyage in 1873, the performance of the master and his officers was far from satisfactory (see COL/A185:73–1157); an inquiry into mortality on the *Wandrahm* in 1866 revealed that the master, although a good seaman, was uneducated and unsuited as the commander of an immigrant ship because of his attitude to the passengers, the first officer was excellent, the purser and cook did not discharge their duties faithfully, and the remaining crew were 'a fine body of men, all young and powerful, and fond of their business' (see QVP 1866:1019).

The Emigration Commissioners set the precedent for manning standards on Queensland immigrant ships. They found that if a captain was carefully chosen, he would be more likely to engage a reliable crew. Each contract for vessels chartered by the Commissioners specified that

> 'The Master, Officers, Crew, Passengers' Baker, and Cooks, shall respectively be approved by the Commissioners or their Agents, and if at any time objected to by them shall be removed. The said party of the second part shall be responsible for the conduct, acts, and defaults of the Master, Officers, Crew, Baker, and Cooks of the Ship.'
>
> (COL/A66:65–1199)

When Jordan was refining details for the immigration service, he formally established that the Agent-General would retain the power to veto the appointment of any captain he considered unsuitable as commander of a government ship. If, during an interview to discuss vessel and voyage arrangements, the Agent-General did not approve of the master, he could, in writing, request a replacement. He also went a step further and secured, under penalty of dismissal, the captain's recognition of the surgeon-superintendent's authority as well as his promise to cooperate with the surgeon and to cause his officers, purser, stewards, cooks and baker to assist in maintaining order and discipline (see QVP 1867–68:II,71–2 and ISS 1875:40–5).

The directors of the Black Ball Line agreed to these conditions; John Taylor acted as their spokesman when he reported to the Queensland government select committee in 1864 that

> 'We have at all times tried to use our best judgement in selecting commanders . . . but we found the . . . difficulty . . . existed . . . in at once finding a number of men, who were good seamen, fit to undertake the practical care, as far as seamanship was concerned, and also possessing the demeanour peculiar to a class of men who can keep in order 300 or 400 people cooped up in a passenger ship. Of course, we only retain those men in the service, who we find desirable to do so.'
>
> (QVP 1864:1054–058)

The selection procedure remained in force until 1892; even the captains of the British India steamships had to be approved by the Agent-General. The masters of German vessels were also subject to certain controls, despite their position of 'supreme authority';

the Queensland authorities, by withholding the gratuity or recommending his dismissal, made it clear that the man in command must be experienced, sober and 'a judicious disciplinarian' (see QVP 1876:II, 1029). But on privately organized ships, whether these carried a few or hundreds of souls, the captain and his crew were answerable only to the shippers, since none of them could claim a government gratuity.

The Commissioners' agreements also stipulated that each vessel must be 'always manned with an efficient Crew', with the required number calculated according to the ship's tonnage and the passenger complement (see COL/A66:65–1199). A similar clause appeared in the Queensland contracts (see, for example, QVP 1877:II, 1175–176 and 1880:II, 1053–058). Indeed, anyone involved with sea transport knew that safety depended as much on the crew as it did on the vessel, its master and the navigational equipment. Legislation to improve the performance of British mariners concentrated on three particular areas – competence, terms of employment and working conditions. Examinations and the issuing of certificates of competence for masters and mates on overseas vessels was one of the first moves. An act in 1862 (25 & 26 Vict. c.63) extended this provision to marine engineers and made it obligatory for ocean-going steamers to carry one certified and experienced engineer with a first-class record for conduct and sobriety. Although the change from sail to steam initially produced a shortage of men capable of handling the new mode of transport, many quickly adapted and appreciated the reduced physical demands.

Systematic training for seamen was another step in the right direction. In 1850 the Board of Trade set up schools, and as early as 1857 the Mercantile Marine Service Association offered formalized training based on the Admiralty system. However, a more comprehensive programme became available through Devitt and Moore, the firm of London brokers, well-known in the Queensland trade. Thus it became increasingly common for officers, rather than working their way up through the ranks, to serve an apprenticeship. This usually involved a four-year indenture under which a lad of fifteen years or younger went to sea contracted to a master. In return for food, accommodation and instruction 'in the art of a mariner', his parents or a guardian outfitted him and paid a fixed sum which was recovered as 'wages' for his labour during the four years. A seventeen-year-old immigrant described the contract: 'They have to pay £30 down as a premium and it costs them a good round sum to fit them with the necessary things . . . They get £5 the 1st 2nd and 3rd years and £15 in the 4th year so they get back the £30 and their trade' (Lumb 1885). At the end of the fourth year the apprentice was released to sit the second officer's examination; and if the indenture expired at sea, he could sign on as an able seaman or third mate. Steamships introduced a similar training system during the 1880s.

Apprentices were accommodated separately, but they ate the same food, worked the same shifts and did the same duties as the men in the forecastle. More often than not they were self-taught, snatching a few hours with their textbooks whenever possible. Mellor Lumb (1885) also took note of the working conditions for the middies on his vessel: 'a young lad say about 14 years of age who has been brought up to every luxery in a good home . . . comes on Board and has to be on duty every four hours', and he added with feeling, 'they fare a lot worse than us Emigrants'. An old Queensland seaman recalled his student days on a sailing ship when he and three other lads shared an 8 ft by 6 ft deck house which remained awash with six inches of water in bad weather; they 'were always hungry and stealing cabin stores was considered no crime' (RHSQ Shipping, Moxon: n.d.). Desertions were fairly common, given such circumstances, a harsh master or difficult companions. After serving eighteen months of his indenture on the Australian run, a young man jumped ship in 1864 and wrote home apologizing to his parents:

> 'I am sorry to tell you that I have run away from the Golden South . . . Ever since I joined the ship I was very unhappy being the youngest of the six middies, there was one big fellow in particular that used to give me plenty of kicks, he was going to be made 3rd mate going home & I should have had a regular dog's life with him, so I thought that if you had known how I was situated, that you would not have minded me running away.'
>
> (Upher 1863–65)

Two to five lads were included in the crews of Queensland vessels carrying apprentices; their names appeared in the crew list but they did not sign the ship's articles of agreement.

This formal contract set down the terms of employment for the crew. No man could sign the agreement until it had been read over and explained to him by the superintendent of a shipping office; and no vessel was given a clearance unless the articles were complete. Formerly, when insufficient hands volunteered, a man might wake from a 'hang-over' to find himself afloat and employed as a 'sailor'. The introduction of the ticket system and the articles effectively eliminated this, but the practice of issuing an advance note for the first month's pay in order to attract a crew was not abolished until 1880. The superintendent was also present at the end of the voyage when the men received their discharge certificates and wages from the master. On Black Ball vessels in the early 1860s the usual rate for a 'man before the mast' was £2 to £3 a month (see Stammers 1978:259); even forty years later, an able seaman on a sailing ship only received £3, and on a steamer £4 a month (see Course 1963:261 and Knox-Robinson 1978:24). The large number of foreign sailors employed on British vessels partly accounted for these low wages. Several of the steamship lines (this included British India) carried British officers and an Indian lascar crew – firemen, greasers and trimmers who were totally unskilled and easily exploited.

At the time of hiring, officers and engineers presented their certificates of competence, and each crew member rated himself as he signed on, knowing that he would be severely penalized if his performance did not match the rank for which he contracted (stowaways were usually put on the articles). Aware of the consequences of violating disciplinary clauses in the agreement, the crew signified their willingness 'to conduct themselves in an orderly, faithful, honest, and sober manner, and to be at all times diligent in their respective duties, and to be obedient to the lawful commands of the said Master . . . in everything relating to the said Ship and the Stores and Cargo' (Crew List and Agreement, *Scottish Bard* 1884, NMML). For his part, the master agreed to pay the wages marked against each man and provide the weekly scale of rations stated in the agreement. If a sailor believed he suffered because of a breach of contract, he presented his grievance to the captain; the difficulty a master had in hiring or keeping a crew was indicative of his reputation for justice and seamanship. The master was also required to keep an official log of the voyage, and was liable to criminal prosecution should he fail to enter the wages, conduct and competence of each crew member, sickness, deaths and all particulars relating to a deceased sailor, as well as passenger births, marriages and deaths. All such entries could be used in a court of law, including those relating to 'every collision with any other ship'.

All offences listed in the disciplinary clauses of the agreement – desertion, neglecting or refusing to join ship, quitting without leave, wilful disobedience, assaulting a master or mate, damaging the ship, embezzling the cargo or smuggling – were legally punishable with a fine or imprisonment. In addition, the Board of Trade issued disciplinary regulations which could be incorporated in the contract and covered such matters as drunkenness, assault of anyone on board, and possession of spiritous liquors and offensive weapons. Violation of any one regulation cost the offender 5/–, with this amount being doubled for the second and subsequent convictions for intoxication. Although the ship's logs for colonial voyages prior to 1875 record relatively few entries on this account,[1] the official Queensland reports indicate that drink persisted as a problem among the crew for most of the period. Certainly this was true for the marine as a whole. Other rules dealt with smoking and the use of safety matches, profane and obscene language, observing the sabbath, airing bedding, washing clothes and cleaning the decks at specified times.

Steamship agreements modified these regulations and added others – 'no animals, birds, or reptiles' were allowed on board without special permission, the crew must wear the company's uniform, no cash advances would be made during the voyage, the firemen and seamen were expected to 'render mutual assistance in the general duties of the vessel when required'. There was one clause which applied on all emigrant ships, sail and steam: 'Any man found below among the Emigrants or having any intercourse with them in conversation or otherwise or molesting them in any way at any time whatever shall forfeit one month's pay' (see Agreement, *Alexandra* 1873, NMML). Agreements for government ships specifically prohibited contact with the single women. Although the regulations aimed at increasing crew efficiency, their primary effect on immigrant vessels was the segregation of the shipboard population into two separate and distinct communities, each with their prescribed territory and laws. The only permissible contact between the two was through, or with the consent of, their officially appointed representative – the master in the case of the crew and the surgeon-superintendent for the passengers. Both the captain and the surgeon of a government vessel were only too aware of the implications should they allow any infringement of the regulations.

Each reforming statute that dealt with the terms of employment for seamen weighed heavily on the side of discipline. When the first measures appeared in 1850, sailors rose in protest and formed the 'Penny Union' (each member paid 1d a week). During the next fifty years many such unions, representing almost every sector of the marine, were formed to consolidate their position, protect their interests and campaign for better conditions. In time, much-needed, on-shore facilities came into operation – a Savings Bank, Sailors' Homes and provision for the care of diseased, injured and aged mariners. At sea, technological refinements, penalties for undermanning and improved accommodation, dietary and medical care raised the standard of living and reduced risks for the crew. There was one interesting innovation; after recognizing for more than a decade that colour blindness made it impossible to distinguish the different side-lights on vessels, and was in part responsible for shipwrecks and collisions, compulsory sight tests were introduced for masters and mates in 1887 (see BMJ 1876:II,690). Six of the Queensland ships are known to have been involved in collisions during the forty years, but the reasons were not recorded.

Although mariners campaigned for an eight-hour day, the traditional routine of dividing the crew into two watches and alternating their on- and off-duty at four-hourly intervals, remained. This routine allowed time for little else besides sleeping, eating and, in bad weather, trying to dry out. However, work demands changed with the advent of the steamship; being a mechanical vehicle, navigation required brains rather than brawn, except for the men who toiled in the engine and boiler rooms. Moreover, the functions of each rank and conditions of employment were comparable to landed occupations. On sailing ships, life was often sheer survival. The men sang as they worked, coordinating their movements to the familiar strains of sea shanties and dulling the harsh edge of reality with reminders of the grog and their 'Nancy' at the journey's end. When the weather was favourable, there were moments for relaxation – fishing, dancing to a fiddle on deck or celebrating such time-honoured traditions as crossing the Line and 'hoisting the dead horse'.[2]

Sailors were accommodated in the forecastle, high in the bow, in cramped, insanitary quarters which received the full force of the seas. Generally the cook and baker slept in the galley. During one home-bound voyage, the missing aft-hatch grating was finally located in the cook's berth, but he refused to relinquish it since he was 'up to his knees in stinking water' (Official Log *Monarch* 1865, NMML). Petty officers (boatswain, carpenter, sailmaker) and apprentices were berthed in deck houses; cabins for the captain, officers and chief steward were located aft in the stern. Other stewards slept where space was available – on cabin tables, in the male hospital or on deck (see COL/A145:70–1993). Crew areas, as a rule, were fitted with bunks, except in the forecastle where swinging hammocks could be rolled up to allow more room. During the tropical nights, sailors slept on deck.

The nine superficial feet allocated for each seaman under the 1850 act was scarcely sufficient to promote hygienic conditions; it took another seventeen years before the space was increased to twelve feet. This provision did not alter for the remainder of the century, and was considerably less than the fifteen superficial feet minimum allowed for passengers. There was, however, only one recorded instance on Queensland-bound ships when the crew complained of overcrowding; the surgeon sanctioned the use of the male hospital until it was needed by the passengers (COL/A217:76–181). On the whole, the men accepted their lot, but others protested on their behalf: 'Gentlemen do not house their dogs with such a disregard of health, comfort, and decency as is shown in the housing on board ship of English sailors' fumed a writer to the *Lancet* (L1866:I,374). An amending act in 1867 (30 & 31 Vict. c.124) dealt with working conditions for the crew. The accommodation had to be securely constructed, properly lit and ventilated, protected from the sea, weather and 'effluvium' from the cargo or bilge, kept free of stores and be regularly surveyed by a Board of Trade inspector. Their area also had to include one or two privies solely for the crews' use. This regulation appears to have been observed on British immigrant vessels to the colony even before 1867, but on the early German ships toilets were shared by sailors and passengers alike. For obvious reasons, bathing facilities were ignored throughout the period; yet much of

Plate 8   Heavy weather in the Channel

the sickness among firemen and stokers was attributed not only to the high temperatures in which they worked, but also to a 'suppressed' function of the skin caused by encrusted grime and perspiration (see BMJ 1879:I,600).

While the captain and officers ate well, the men survived on the 'pound and pint' rations. An early account of the naval dietary described the 'putrid salt beef (called Irish horse), salt pork, and musty bread. The biscuit moved like a piece of clock-work . . . owing to the myriads of maggots that infested it. The butter looked and tasted like train oil thickened with salt' (quoted in L 1862:I,180). The merchant marine would not have fared any better; little wonder the health of seafarers broke down so rapidly. One of the first improvements was the provision that, if the men knew they were being cheated, they could legally demand a survey of the supplies, and if necessary be compensated up to 4d a day (17 & 18 Vict. c.104). The 1855 passenger act clearly stated that the crew rations must not be inferior to those for the passengers and that they must be stored separately. The weekly scale of provisions for each seaman on the *General Caulfield* in 1864 (see Crew List and Agreement, NMML) consisted of 7 lb bread or biscuit, 6 lb salt beef, 3¼ lb salt pork, 2 lb flour, 1 lb peas, 1¼ oz tea, 12 oz sugar and 2 oz raisins – a calorie-concentrated diet. The beef and flour were issued on alternate days to the pork and peas; the daily water allowance was seven pints in the hot and six pints in the cold weather. A similar scale was listed in the *Scottish Bard* agreement for 1883 (NMML) except that reduced quotas for the peas and tea had been complemented with rice and coffee, and the raisins were omitted; fresh meat and vegetables could be issued at the master's discretion. A 'grog' (rum and spirits) allowance was definitely prohibited. This last stipulation applied on most immigrant ships and was a frequent source of discontent among the crew. As might be expected, Queensland shipping contracts allowed a more varied and nutritious dietary, with such items as preserved meat and potatoes, raisins, suet, mustard and vinegar added to the basic foods (see, for example, COL/A268:78–4478). The absence of complaints and the extra rations suggest that sailors on the government vessels were better fed than the average British mariner.

Although the issue of lime or lemon juice had been legalized as early as 1844, the apparent incidence of scurvy began to increase alarmingly during the early 1860s. It was found that masters sometimes ignored the law, sailors refused the ration, or supplies were rendered ineffective through substitution or adulteration. At one stage potash was substituted for lime juice, 'with very doubtful results' (BMJ 1867:I,117). To counteract the disturbing trend the Board of Trade published a circular in 1866 which outlined methods for preserving and packing the juice, and instructed that 'each man should have at least four ounces . . . a week, and should take it as part of the daily food'.[3] They further urged that, in port and for as long afterwards as possible, fresh meat, vegetables and fruit be supplied, adequate quantities of preserved vegetables and plenty of 'good water' be carried, and that greater care be given to cleanliness and ventilation. These instructions became mandatory under the 1867 act. Sailors took every opportunity to supplement their rations with fresh fish; but only on steamships and with the advent of refrigeration was it possible to provide a more balanced dietary for the crew as well as the immigrants. The lascar crew on British India steamers lived on curry and rice (see QVP 1886:III,789).

As the century progressed, the emphasis gradually shifted from the quantity to the quality of the dietary until both were brought under the jurisdiction of an Inspectorate of Ship's Provisions set up under the 1892 act (55 & 56 Vict. c.37). However, a minimum scale was not legalized until 1906, fifty years after a similar provision for passengers. While the quantities allowed under each agreement were intended to meet the work demands of seamen, so often the quality, monotony and cooking of the provisions negated their nutritional value and energy supply. A cook prepared food for the captain's table, the immigrants expected to receive their basic commodities in a 'properly cooked state', but the crew were divided into messes of fifteen to twenty men, one of whom was chosen to collect the rations and prepare the food (see Roddis 1941:143). He received no bonus, was usually inexperienced, worked without supervision, organized special diets for sick sailors – hence the name of 'Doc' – and was abused for the chronic shortage and inedible food. In time the large steamship companies not only employed cooks for the crew, but established a full catering service to accommodate all on board.

Improved medical care also contributed to rising standards in the merchant marine. The minimum legal scale of medicines and medical stores was printed in the *Mercantile Navy List* together with directions to the captain for the treatment of cholera and 'What to Avoid' during the epidemic season – overcrowding, dampness, filth, unwholesome food and water, an excess of food and alcohol, and purgatives. Between 1850 and 1867, the Board of Trade adopted the scale issued by the Admiralty; the revised list first appeared in the *London Gazette* of 13 December, 1867. It was not until the mid-1860s that the reformers turned their attention to the health and hygiene of seamen. Many sailors signed on in broken health, infected with disease and infested with vermin. In order to deal with this problem, the 1867 act introduced penalties for any crew member who, through his own default, became ill and incapable of work during the voyage. Furthermore, should incapacity be shown to be the result of negligence on the part of the owner or master, they were required to meet all expenses such as doctor's and hospital charges. Provision was therefore made for the medical inspection of seamen if the captain demanded it and paid the required fee. Needless to say, many preferred to take the risk and the clause became a dead letter for the smaller shipping concerns. Even under the all-embracing 1894 Merchant Shipping Act, the onus for examination remained with the master or owner. There was, however, no option for Queensland government vessels; their crews had to be medically checked before embarkation (see QVP 1875:II,641).

The scale of medicines issued under the 1867 act was based on the newly revised *British Pharmacopoeia* and included a comprehensive range of astringents, purgatives, stimulants, analgesics and disinfectants to deal with common crew complaints – respiratory tract and chest infections, gastric and enteric disorders, venereal diseases, joint and muscular pains, injuries and sepsis. Surgical instruments and first-aid equipment were also placed on board together with supplies of farinaceous foods, preserved meats, vegetables and soups, port and brandy suitable for invalid ('slop' or 'slush') diets. Queensland contracts after 1869 specifically stated that the cook was not to be responsible for these diets for either the passengers or crew (see, for example, COL/A268:78–4478). Knowing how the medicines might be used, the Board of Trade published *The Ship-Captain's Medical Guide*, compiled by Dr Harry Leach (medical officer for the Port of London), as an aid in the diagnosis and treatment of disease. Any master of a foreign-going British vessel proceeding to sea without a medicine chest, medical stores and the prescribed quantity of lime juice, all properly packed and stowed, was liable to a £20 fine; but only after 1894 did it become obligatory for a ship with a crew of more than one hundred to carry a qualified medical practitioner. Throughout the colonial period a *bona fide* ship-surgeon, rather than the captain, was responsible for the health of seamen on Queensland immigrant vessels. Thus, in every respect, working conditions for crews on these ships seem to have been superior to prevailing standards for the merchant marine as a whole. After all, immigrant welfare largely depended on 'good order' among the 'ship's servants', and this could not be achieved without discipline and adequate working conditions.

What do we know of the sailors on the Queensland ships? Information has been traced for some 50 per cent of the crews for all passenger voyages to the colony; and despite its limitations, this sample allows a discussion of the composition, health, behaviour and competence of the men. The first two decades, when sail dominated, are best documented, except for the German voyages. However, crew numbers for half the vessels out of Hamburg are known, and these show that German immigrant ships to the colony between 1861 and 1879 were manned with an average of twenty seamen, carried a mean complement of 325 passengers and averaged 667 tons. Apart from the master, there were two or three mates, a carpenter and sailmaker, a cook and steward (sometimes their duties were combined), ten to eighteen 'men before the mast' and usually two apprentices. On one voyage in 1876, there was no carpenter and crew numbers were such that immigrants had to go aloft to help with the rigging (COL/A227:76–2426). The available statistics indicate that British immigrant vessels under sail to Queensland were better manned than the German; during the first two decades the British ships averaged 1,062 tons and carried a mean crew of thirty-nine and a passenger complement of 365 (by German standards the number of crew relative to a similar tonnage would have been thirty-two).

The Queensland contracts for immigrant sailing ships allowed twenty men for the first 500 tons, between twenty-three and thirty-five for another 500 tons and two for each additional 100 tons (see COL/A268:78–4478). It is clear that vessels adhered to this specification; for the period between 1860 and 1889 they averaged 39.5 crew members for ships with a mean of 1,066 tons and 366 passengers. At least two-thirds of the crew had to be deck ratings (able seamen, ordinary seamen and boys), and one of these must be able to operate the water-distilling apparatus. In addition to the number considered necessary for safe navigation, the shippers had to engage 'a competent Baker and a Cook' to serve the needs of the immigrants, and a second cook if the numbers exceeded 300 statute adults. The average sailing ship crew comprised three or four officers, including the purser, three deck petty officers (bosun, carpenter and sailmaker), a 'donkey man' who distilled the water, eighteen or nineteen able seamen, four or five ordinary seamen and boys, two apprentices, three cooks, including the saloon cook, two or three stewards who were reserved for the cabin classes, and sometimes a storekeeper, assistant purser or clerk. The shippers might also employ a butcher; there was a confectioner on one vessel.

Short-ships under sail to Queensland between 1860 and 1900 averaged 648 tons and eight passengers, with a mean crew of 18.6 men. Although the major reduction was in the deck-rating category (twenty-three for immigrant compared to ten for short ships), the number of apprentices carried was, in fact, higher. Economy rather than the law dictated manning levels for cargo-carrying short-ships. With fewer hands, crew duties were more varied and less specialized. There were usually two mates (one for each watch), a bosun or carpenter, one of the able seamen functioned as the sailmaker, and the cook as well as preparing meals, waited on the table and provided cabin service for the captain, officers and saloon passengers. A young lady travelling to the colony by short-ship in 1868 was most impressed with the cook; just as a meal began, the soup upset and, 'with the most beautiful resignation', he cleaned up the mess, relaid the table and produced more soup (Hume and Fowler 1975:150). The perform-ance of this crew member very often regulated the quality of life on board.

As steamers became more efficient, the amount of sail they carried decreased and so did the number of deck ratings. This meant an increase in the new class of marine labourers – firemen, greasers and trimmers – who were accommodated within the traditional hierarchy as engine-room ratings. Engineers ranked as officers (four or five were employed on steamers to Queensland);

engine-room petty officers included the boilermaker, refrigeration mechanic and gunner. A comparison of crew members for short and immigrant steamships (65 and 75 respectively) indicates that the tonnage, which was similar for both categories, determined the basic manning level, while the passenger complement accounted for the difference in crew size. The fact that British India vessels carried European officers and took on Asians as regular hands (each group signed a separate agreement) introduces certain distortions. Means for the European and lascar sectors from a sample of steamship voyages between 1881 and 1890 are thirty-four and ninety respectively; voyages that do not distinguish the two average 110; but for steamships carrying a solely European crew, the mean of sixty-nine suggests that it was cheaper to carry a multi-racial complement. Both the accommodation and dietary for the native seamen were inferior to that for their European counterparts, yet they worked well and, according to an experienced surgeon-superintendent, gave less trouble than a white crew on immigrant ships; they did not drink or question authority (QVP 1900:V,654).

The wide socio-cultural spectrum represented by Queensland-bound sailors was partly reflected in their performance. Masters and senior officers were British; they lived under relatively favourable conditions, but their work involved responsibility and exposed them to particular pressures both from the men and passengers. For the regular seaman life was hard, rough and often dangerous, whether he slaved in the galley, mended the sails, repaired the woodwork or engines, worked aloft, steered the vessel or stoked the boilers. In the engine room men worked by the light of parrafin lamps in torrid conditions while unprotected machinery 'spat steam and oil' (Blake 1956:215). A sailor shared twenty-four hours of each day with men of every class and nationality; there was no escape. As a rule, he stoically accepted his lot, but resisted discipline. Of the 287 complaints registered against the crew, from the master to the lowest rank, only 20.5 per cent had to do with incompetence and the remainder with misconduct, ranging from discourteous behaviour towards an immigrant to outright mutiny.

Although the Queensland authorities were primarily concerned with those ranks directly involved with passenger welfare, the conduct and performance of other crew members had important, though indirect, consequences. Indeed, the regular ratings scored the highest number of complaints. New hands were naturally afraid of going aloft, but any man who refused to go up or could not hold on was dubbed as a 'regular soldier'. An able seaman was expected to be a good helmsman, capable of taking a bearing and doing all the work connected with the rigging; if he failed through negligence or poor seamanship, he was disrated. On the *Sultana* in 1864 an able seaman 'had to be turned from the wheel, he not being able to steer the ship, he not even knowing the points of the compass' (Official Log, BT 99/252); another log entry (*Eme* 1873, BT 99/1033) made note of the sailor who 'did not know one end of the ship from the other'. Apart from sheer ignorance, liquor was perhaps the most common source of incompetence. Several instances are cited of a man being drunk at the wheel; one diarist recorded how the helmsman in his drunken stupor 'steered the ship the wrong way' (Ricou 1872). Captains occasionally issued a weekly 'grog' allowance, but when the men obtained illegal supplies by broaching the cargo, the saloon cellar or the medical comforts, the usual result was abusive behaviour, fighting and the refusal or inability to work. The lives of those in authority could also be endangered. One master described how an inebriated sailor was summoned aft, assaulted him, threatened to use his sheath knife and tried to kick him in the face (Official Log *Flying Cloud* 1864, NMML). The crew of the *Vernon*, a vessel chartered by the Commissioners in 1864, broached the cargo, became intoxicated and mutinied. The surgeon-superintendent directed that they put into Rio de Janeiro where the mutineers were brought before a naval court and the chief officer was given command of the vessel (see RHSQ Immigrant Ships).

Any number of other factors could spark off trouble. On the *Utopia* in 1862 fifteen of the crew refused to work because of a private quarrel among their watch; the captain, officers, four seamen and several passenger volunteers brought the ship into port (RHSQ Shipwrecks). Once pistols and knives were drawn when the surgeon exerted his authority 'to prevent familiarity with the single women' (COL/A19:61–2052); another doctor had difficulties with crew members who stole from the ship's stores, became 'helplessly drunk' and tried to break into the female compartment (COL/A627:90–9167). More than once, the master and his mates supported by the surgeon and his constabulary ranged forces against belligerent or uncontrolled sailors (see, for example, Log *Earl Russell* 1864, NMML). If the ring-leader could be identified and dealt with, the situation was usually resolved more quickly. Passengers were also known to supply the men with drink or incite a disturbance among them (see, for example, COL/A79:66–1494 and COL/A205:75–89). On the other hand, a mutinous crew always created unrest among the immigrants (see COL/A194:74–952). On the *Montmorency* in 1866, mutiny was avoided only by keeping loaded revolvers at the ready, both day and night (Davies 1935:314). It took judicious handling to deal with discontent or bring a volatile and potentially dangerous situation quickly under control.

Recorded offences ran the full gambit of possible violations. In particular, sailors interfered with the immigrants and tried to communicate with 'the girls'; vessels steered from the aft posed additional problems, and firemen accommodated on the after deck of steamships needed 'constant surveillance'. The surgeon on one voyage recommended two of them for the B.I. 'Black List' (COL/A660:91–6105). During the early years of the colony, the incidence of men 'jumping ship' on arrival was particularly high, but diminished with the introduction of steam and continuous crews. Some obviously signed on with the intention of emigrating (especially the passengers' cook and baker); others were desperate to escape despite the penalty of a three-month prison sentence if apprehended. A hard master or news of a gold strike were sufficient incentive. Water police, appointed at each colonial port, handled refractory crew, while en route, offenders were reprimanded by the master, disrated, warned of impending fines, deducted wages and imprisonment, or put into irons until they sobered up and agreed to behave. Punishments could be unduly severe; flogging was not unknown and one apprentice, given a twelve-month sentence for stealing, died in the Brisbane gaol (COL/A184:73–1474). A few masters and mates brutalized their men. Nevertheless, the safety record for Queensland ships suggests a creditable level of control and competence. Several surgeons reported a well-behaved crew, and passenger diaries revealed a sympathy with these hard-worked men and an admiration for their endurance and courage. But immigrant attitudes towards the sailors changed on steamships since conditions had improved and the ratings mostly worked behind the scenes.

Deck petty officers received no remuneration from the government, yet many a carpenter made life afloat more comfortable. He repaired broken berths and tables, constructed privies to replace those washed overboard, secured the ports and battened down the hatches in rough weather, made swings for the children and fixed wash-tubs. More than one surgeon noted the carpenter's invaluable service and recommended him for a gratuity. Although he might be asked to make a coffin, it was usually the sailmaker's task to prepare for a burial. On the *Scottish Bard* in 1883 the seventy-three-year-old sailmaker received a bonus for each shroud he made (Cook 1883). He and the boatswain (bosun), who was responsible for the deck machinery and rigging, played a vital role in maintaining a safe ship. Any incompetence or negligence on the latter's part could seriously endanger the crew; for this reason the bosun on the *Storm King* in 1871 was disrated to 'A.B.' (Official Log, BT 99/846). His position also gave him the power to influence the men for good or ill (see COL/A55:64–1599). Another person who helped set the tone on board was the chief steward; his efficiency or 'filthy habits' set the standard of living for the captain, officers, surgeon and saloon passengers. Moreover, he had access to the ship's stores and 'held the corkscrew'. Surgeons regularly complained that stewards, by holding themselves responsible to the captain alone, flouted the temperance clauses and were sometimes guilty of selling liquor to the immigrants (see QVP 1866:1041–042). The Queensland authorities certainly did not approve of the chief steward on steamships employing men who worked out their passage for 1/– a month and often became a burden on the colony (QVP 1900:V,658). The ship's cook could also make or mar the voyage for those who dined at the captain's table.

The immigrants' cook and baker, however, belonged to a quite different order. They received their instructions from the Agent-General, were responsible to the captain and the surgeon-superintendent, and were paid, in addition to the regular wage, a government gratuity of £5 for satisfactory service. An assistant was usually appointed from among the immigrants. The cook was expected to keep the fires alight, make the galley available to passengers at certain hours, prepare the food and serve it punctually. The baker had to produce bread each Monday, Wednesday and Friday and on the alternate days, bake pies and cakes prepared by the immigrants (see ISS 1875:13,17,54–6). It took more than a certain level of expertise to satisfy three to five hundred people every day. Reports describe the difficulties under which many of the men worked – a small galley, an inadequate range, poor ovens, insufficient utensils or a pitching vessel. In addition, they bore the brunt of grumbling about the quality of the provisions, the monotony of the diet or the cooking, and had to cope with petty thefts.

More than half the complaints relating to crew incompetence referred to the cook or baker, and the majority of these were justified. Surgeons frequently attributed the disharmony and digestive troubles on board to the poor quality cooking and baking. But the complaints registered more than incompetence; they covered every kind of misconduct – insubordination, rudeness, drunkenness, extortion, favouritism and immorality. 'The cooks was very uncivel disoblidging fellows', recorded a diarist (Good 1863). Immigrants feared one 'brutal and repulsive' man; scalds and injuries were not uncommon as the result of a cook's carelessness. Several were disrated, forfeited their gratuity or had to be confined for misconduct. Dismissal was the usual penalty for food 'proper spoiled' or bread which one passenger declared was 'not fit to give a pig' (Cook 1883). One baker, in addition to being dismissed and having his wages deducted, was charged for the food he ruined (Official Log *General Caulfield* 1864, NMML). But finding a replacement was easier said than done, particularly if there was no one willing or able to take over. In this event, and when the cook or baker fell ill, the other had to perform both functions (see, for example, Official Log *Sirocco* 1865, BT 99/301 and COL/A396:84–5342). On the other hand, some of them improved as the journey progressed or after the galley was enlarged; and others gave excellent service or earned an extra bonus for having performed well under trying circumstances.

The health of a ship very much depended on the crew member appointed to operate the water-distilling apparatus. Several appointees had no idea how the mechanism worked and caused its breakdown; one deliberately fouled the machinery (he also assaulted the surgeon and was imprisoned on arrival, COL/A291:80–1749); but sometimes the equipment itself was at fault. A serious predicament developed when no one could be found to effect repairs. If an operator's work met with the surgeon's approval, he received a £5 gratuity. While the provision of a good and constant water supply was considered essential, the task of serving out the water and rations, because it was so open to corruption, demanded the 'special oversight' of the surgeon. The purser's duties might be delegated to the third mate, to someone specifically appointed for the purpose, or be combined with those of the storekeeper or ship's clerk. The authorities frequently received recommendations that this officer should be selected by the Agent-General or the surgeon-superintendent rather than the port emigration officer, that he should not work his passage out, need any training or have to serve in a dual capacity (see, for example, COL/A510:87–5989).

The purser contracted to abide by the *Instructions*, serve out rations 'equitably, regularly, and punctually' according to the fixed scale, keep the storeroom and issuing book in order, and adhere to the temperance clauses in the regulations (see ISS 1875:45–8). He was provided with a 'well-balanced' pair of scales, and paid at the rate of 1/– for each statute adult (this amount had been raised from 6d to encourage a better performance). Occasionally the surgeon or one of his constables supervised the purser as he served out the rations. Even so, quite a few succumbed to temptation. One was described as 'a thoroughly practical thief', another sold liquor at 'enormous prices', and some proved totally inefficient. The purser of the *Renfrewshire* in 1875 was so intoxicated at embarkation that he was discharged immediately, his replacement fell off the gangplank and drowned, and the third mate refused to undertake the duties. Although the man finally appointed was totally inexperienced, he appeared to manage reasonably well during the voyage (COL/A216:75–3321). Despite controls, medical comforts were often misappropriated; the storeroom on one vessel became known as the 'tap-room'. If this area was too small, poorly secured, inconveniently located or placed too close to the single-women's compartment, the consequences were predictable. Any purser who violated the agreement could be disrated or dismissed and most certainly would have had all or part of the head-money mulcted. Yet there were those who dealt 'even handed justice to everyone' and were commended for their tact and good judgement (see COL/A61:64–3275).

Officers on any vessel – whether a fourth mate, the chief officer or a junior engineer – belonged to a class, separate and distinct from the remainder of the crew. Sometimes they took advantage of their position to ill-treat the men, ignore the contract and regulations, or subvert authority. Only the first mate and the purser received a government gratuity; but the behaviour and performance of all the officers materially affected shipboard life. Although the engineers' duties did not bring them into contact with the immigrants, some were guilty of associating 'too freely with the single women' (COL/A422:85–3143). On one British India vessel, so many charges of misconduct were levelled against the engineers and officers that the company held an inquiry as soon as the ship returned to London (COL/A527:87–9338). The fourth mate on steamers usually handled the passengers' luggage and issued the water rations; the third mate could be appointed as the purser; but the second mate who was responsible for one of the watches rarely had any involvement with the immigrants. The first officer, however, because he deputized for the master, received 6d head-money for every statute adult landed alive. If he or the captain proved unsatisfactory, the authorities had the right to demand that neither be employed again on a government ship (see ISS 1875:37). According to the contract, both had to remain with a vessel while immigrants were on board.

The captain dealt with incompetence, negligence or misconduct among the officers. Once when his ship was skimming along at ten-and-a-half knots with the studding sails set, a master heard snoring from the wheelhouse and found the second mate 'wrapt up in coats' fast asleep; he was reprimanded (Official Log *Bayswater* 1864, NMML). The chief officer whose 'error of judgement' resulted in the wreck of the SS *Dacca* in 1890, was dismissed (QVP 1891:IV,25). Those who treated their men harshly, indulged in drink or immorality, incited insubordination or encouraged the ratings to embezzle cargo and stores, were penalized. A chief officer was imprisoned for fourteen days after the cook reported he had been beaten several times during the voyage (Official Log *Castle Eden* 1864, NMML). If their misconduct affected the passengers, this demanded the surgeon's attention; some resisted his authority, and one second officer actually victimized the doctor, accusing him of murder, assaulting him and throwing muddy water in his cabin (COL/A83:66–2417). An adverse entry in the medical log or the surgeon's refusal to sign a gratuity voucher, meant that an officer might be denied his head-money or be black-listed. Occasionally, one of them received particular mention for his 'exemplary conduct' and support of the surgeon.

Traditionally, the master had supreme command over everything on board; but on British vessels carrying Queensland-government immigrants, his position was modified to allow for the exercise of the surgeon-superintendent's authority. Out at sea, however, the situation often changed. Of the complaints recorded against the master, almost 30 per cent referred to his failure or refusal to support the surgeon. Some allowed the crew access to the passengers, issued wines to the steerage, would not attend inspection rounds between decks and negated the surgeon's authority; others used the immigrants to 'fetch and carry' for the saloon (COL/A392:84–4132). On the whole captains and surgeons worked together with a reasonable degree of tolerance and cooperation, even to the point of 'perfect unanimity' between them. Less than 10 per cent of the complaints involved incompetence. The two masters who admitted to being off-course were dismissed; one, in fact, sailed past Moreton Bay (his destination) and finally dropped anchor in Keppel Bay, 400 miles up the coast (COL/A46:63–2709). Others were dismissed because they failed to control their men, or because they lacked the 'kindness and consideration' so necessary for emigrant vessels.

Captains, like every class on board, became intoxicated (they also received a daily liquor allowance of 2/6); and more than one was found blind drunk during a gale (see, for example, COL/A187:73–2064). Some could not resist the single women and were guilty of 'criminal proceedings' on board; others were discourteous and used offensive language. One master so insulted a married woman that she emptied a bowl of soup over him (Anon 1883). Another described their skipper as

> 'an uneducated man, who treated all passengers like dogs . . . He quarrelled perpetually with the doctor, who was the only gentleman on board . . . Even the medical orders given me by the doctor . . . were countermanded by the captain . . . He put us on half rations for the last week . . . and for several weeks stopped our usual supply of water.'   (QVP 1864:926)

The master held an unenviable position; he had to control a rough bunch of men, navigate a vessel through 12,000 miles of ocean, be responsible for the general oversight of the entire community and share his authority with someone he often did not, or could not, respect.

The ideal master was experienced, temperate, and a 'judicious disciplinarian'. These were the qualities appreciated by the authorities and the majority of passengers who might sign a testimonial expressing their gratitude or organize a party for 'the healths' of the master and his men (see Foote 1977–78:33–4 and Good 1863). Diaries and other accounts leave no doubt that the captain was regarded as the highest authority on board, despite the status accorded the surgeon-superintendent. Indeed, the doctors themselves acknowledged that 'the success of the voyage' depended on the master (COL/A566:88–9996). But if he over-reached his authority or failed in his duties and the charges against him were sustained, he was dismissed from the service, with all or part of his gratuity (1/– for each statute adult landed alive) deducted. The allowance of 1/6 head money for the captain of a German vessel was obviously meant, in view of the surgeon's position, to secure the satisfactory command of vessels chartered by the Queensland government. In four known instances a master was charged with violation of the 1855 passenger act;[4] three were fined or imprisoned. The decreasing incidence of complaints and allegations, particularly after 1881, reflects the general trend towards improvement and the trimming of the surgeon-superintendent's authority.

The necessity for strict discipline, complete segregation from the immigrants, especially the single women, and the careful selection of masters becomes even more apparent when we examine age patterns for the crews of Queensland vessels; half the men in an average crew were aged between 20 and 29 years.[5] Although they ranged from a deck boy of 13 to the sailmaker of 73 years, almost two-thirds of the total sample were less than 30 years old. This proportion was as high as 73.8 per cent in the 1860s; it fell to 68.5 per cent in the 1870s and showed a marked decrease for the last two decades (53.5 and 55.7 per cent). The introduction of steamships and the employment of continuous crews as well as rising standards in the merchant marine undoubtedly contributed to this increase in the age of seamen, a factor which would have helped reduce disciplinary problems.

The increase, however, was confined largely to the senior ranks. Some 95 per cent of the masters were 30 or more years old. This proportion increased from 88.7 per cent in the 1860s to 96.2 per cent in the 1880s and far exceeded that for any other rank. The mean age for masters was 37 years (for surgeons it was 34.5 years). Captains of Queensland vessels were not only more mature and better qualified as the period progressed, but they commanded a position of unrivalled seniority and authority. Officers and petty officers (deck and engine-room), able seamen and storekeepers also became older, but the pattern for the engineers, ordinary seamen (including deck boys), engine-room ratings, cooks, stewards and apprentices remained relatively unchanged. Mean ages for each of the ranks, with the exception of ordinary seamen (18 years), apprentices (16 years) and cooks (39 years), ranged between 26 and 36 years. Despite the age increase, the majority of sailors on Queensland ships were men in the prime of life; this certainly would have had a bearing on their health record.

Each man signed on to perform a specific function, and if he became disabled or died, the work load for others increased accordingly. This could have serious consequences, particularly on a smaller vessel; it was therefore in the master's interests to attend promptly to any reported sickness among his men. 'Capt. A. is rather careful as to how he listens to all their complaints . . . we can ill afford to have them laid up in the bad weather', commented a passenger on a short-ship in 1866 (Hume and Fowler 1975:136). We have already noted that, although medical examination was available for merchant sailors, the provision tended to remain a dead letter. Even when it was enforced, as on Queensland government ships, doubts can be raised concerning its efficacy, particularly when chronic conditions such as heart disease and diabetes mellitus terminated fatally during the voyage or men joined ship with untreated venereal disease. But diagnosis, generally, could be a problem. When the emigration officer for the port of London was questioned about a reported case of tuberculosis among the crew of the *Darling Downs* in 1874, he replied that it was well known that a person of 'consumptive habits', in fair health at departure, could sink rapidly with climatic changes (QVP 1875:II,641). On a voyage in 1884 the immigrants' cook became so ill with tuberculosis that the baker had to take over his duties (COL/A396:84–5342).

Only 158 cases of illness or injury among Queensland crews have been located for the whole period, and most of these were extracted from extant logs available up to 1875 (surgeons when listing morbidity rarely distinguished between the crew and passengers).[6] The sample is therefore limited and distorted, but it reveals certain patterns. In the first place, the average number of cases for voyages with a record of crew morbidity gradually decreased over the four decades, thus suggesting an improvement in crew health. Secondly, officers, petty officers and able seamen seem to have suffered more than the other ranks. These men, at least on sailing ships, were exposed to extreme hazards. The diseases themselves also highlight other trends. Surprisingly, not one case of scurvy has been found in records, even during the period that this problem was seen to be increasing at a disturbing rate; in fact, several logs noted the absence of scurvy on board. Although one crew demanded rum instead of lime juice and others complained that the anti-scorbutics were adulterated or insufficient, sailors on Queensland vessels apparently remained scurvy-free. This says something for their health at embarkation and their dietary at sea. The 'Dietic Diseases' category included only two cases, both of delirium tremens (see Table 11, p.355 for a classification of diseases).

Forty-one of the cases fell within the zymotic (contagious and preventable) diseases group – smallpox, measles, diarrhhoea, dysentery, scabies, malarial and other fevers, and venereal diseases which accounted for fifteen cases, almost 10 per cent of the whole. Such was the reputation of sailors, that many masters freely administered the 'blue pill' for any condition presenting with VD-like symptoms, and persisted with its use after 1867 when most other mercurial preparations were withdrawn from the 'List of Medicines'. Dr Harry Leach, the compiler of the *Captain's Guide*, explained that the scale had been revised 'on principle that, if little good could, little harm should, be done'; but he observed six years later that 'the active proclivities of captains in amateur doctoring' still existed (BMJ 1873:II,168). The few records after 1867 indicate that masters of Queensland ships generally prescribed treatment 'according to instructions', though one captain in 1873 dispensed the 'blue pill' for what he diagnosed as jaundice. He had earlier recorded in the log that one of his men was off-duty complaining of 'sore throte an pains ins his Leggs his Boddy was covered with pimples fro wich I treated him as Directed for venerial Desease gave him Ioded of potisum & gargle for is throte'. An entry a month later noted that the medicines were exhausted and the affected sailor was 'apariantly emproving' (Official Log *Abbey Holme* 1873, BT 99/1032).

Accurate diagnosis, however, presented particular difficulties for the non-professional, as the following log entry illustrates: 'AB off duty & apparently sick complaining of pains all over, & pain in the side, administered mustard poultice to his side, & castor oil to open his bowels, the sickness originated from bleeding of the nose' (Official Log *Pekina* 1873, BT 99/1017). Sometimes a sailor shammed sickness to avoid going aloft in bad weather or as a form of protest (see Official Log *General Caulfield* 1864, NMML). If the vessel carried a surgeon, the problem was usually referred to him; several entries simply stated the diagnosis together with the fact that the sick man was under the doctor's care. Indeed, a number of surgeons complained that the crew required as much attention as the immigrants (see COL/A94:67–2061). An experienced master often acquired considerable medical knowledge, and impressed passengers with his skill: '[he] is quite a doctor and has a huge medicine chest under the cabin table' observed one of them (Hume and Fowler 1975:136). On some voyages he assumed the medical duties when the surgeon was out of action, or threatened to take over if the doctor proved inefficient (see, for example, COL/A79:66–1498 and COL/A318:81–3324). Most masters had their favourite remedies – castor oil as a purgative, poultices for pain and inflammation, potassium iodide for respiratory infections, stimulants, special diets and, of course, the time-honoured Dover's powders (a mixture of opium and ipecacuanha) as an emetic. One captain treated crew and passengers alike with 'three remedies . . . First there was castor oil, then black draught and failing either of those to heal, he mixed them for the third remedy. If expostulated with, his answer was "What does it matter. It will all go down the lee scupper" ' (Hale n.d.) Many seafarers must have suffered as much from the treatment as they did from their illness. Certainly one can agree with Roddis (1941:105) that the reduced morbidity and mortality among crews was due, not to their medical care, but rather to the prevention of scurvy, vaccination for smallpox and the provision of distilled water. Improved living and working conditions may also be added.

Nevertheless, these conditions must have contributed to the fifteen cases of 'Constitutional Diseases' – rheumatic complaints and tuberculosis. Another thirty-seven cases were 'Local Diseases' – respiratory affections (bronchitis and pneumonia), nervous disorders, urinary problems and haemorrhoids. Only one man was recorded with bursitis of the knee, despite the scrapping and scrubbing of decks; but a significant number in this disease group related to the digestive system – gastro-enteric and liver disorders, with alcohol consumption doubtless being an important factor. Skin problems – ulcers, ringworm and especially suppurating fingers – also scored high. Because of his work, a sailor's hands were naturally prone to injury and infection; they became very hard and horny and were liable to crack and 'fester underneath and have to be lanced' (Hume and Fowler 1975:136). There were a few 'Ill-defined Diseases' – dropsy, debility and tobacco narcotism. An unrecorded number succumbed to sea-sickness; sailors had no special immunity. The remaining forty-four cases, almost 30 per cent of the total, were attributed to 'Violence', from falls, fights and other injuries. This proportion more than doubled in the mortality statistics to reach 62 per cent, a figure which is comparable to the 66 per cent for violent deaths in the merchant marine as a whole between 1861 and 1900.[7] In commenting on sickness and death among sailors, Roddis (1941:96) sees a clear relationship between venereal disease, alcohol consumption and accidents.

On sailing vessels falls from aloft were common. If a man hit the deck he would, very likely, be killed. One fortunate sailor crashed thirty feet on to a skylight and suffered only minor cuts and bruises (Hume and Fowler 1975:159). Another, an apprentice, was sent up the mizzen mast but could not hold on because of the cold; his fall was broken by a rope (Hume and Fowler 1975:145). When a man fell into the sea, there was the chance of rescue, except in the midst of a gale. The captain of the *Western Monarch* in 1882 sustained a fractured patella and lost three of his men overboard during a severe storm (COL/A343:82–4452); but on a voyage in 1866, the cook's assistant was washed into the sea with one wave and back on to the deck with the next, 'clean over the bulwarks' (Hume and Fowler 1975:151). Even under favourable conditions, a sailor might be taken by a shark. Reporting the death of one of his men, the captain of the SS *Duke of Sutherland* in 1887

(Crew List BT 99/1568) noted: 'It is believed that when the 3rd mate saw Wylie throw up his arms, that he was then pulled down by a shark for he was never seen to rise again.' Engine room explosions, being thrown against the deck structures or becoming entangled in the ropes and rigging, most commonly caused fatal injuries. One surgeon's ungarnished report described how the clew of the mizzen stay sail struck the second mate, 'scattering his brains over the starboard life boat' (COL/A213:75–2633). It seems the hazards of a sailor's life were limitless. A passenger practising with his pistol accidentally shot the helmsman through the chest; the surgeon extracted the bullet and hoped 'the case might progress' (Log *Elizabeth Ann Bright* 1864, BT 99/301).

Of the 153 crew deaths on Queensland voyages, 95 were the result of violence; 70 drowned, 13 died from injuries received while working or during fights, 8 suffered from heat apoplexy, 2 died of scalds and 2 committed suicide. Localized diseases such as brain disorders, apoplexy (stroke), paralysis and 'fits', cardiac complaints, pneumonia and asthma, peritonitis, gastro-enteric and liver diseases, account for twenty-four deaths; under the 'constitutional' category (fourteen deaths), all except two died of tuberculosis, one of the most devastating diseases among seafarers; the 'zymotic' group – smallpox, measles various fevers, dysenteric diarrhoea, venereal diseases and erysipelas – represented another thirteen deaths; the cause of death for the remaining seven included 'hard drinking', haemorrhage and debility.[8] As the period progressed and standards at sea continued to rise, mortality among seamen on the Queensland route gradually diminished, with the average number of deaths per voyage for the four decades registering at 0.17, 0.16, 0.11 and 0.03. These figures follow a similar trend in the British merchant marine between 1860 and 1900 when decadal means for the annual deaths per 1,000 seamen were 22.9, 21.4, 17.8 and 13.2. Certainly the change in mode of travel contributed to the decrease in Queensland crew deaths; steamships recorded 0.07 per voyage and halved the figure for sailing vessels.

Relative to the total crew mortality, the proportion of deaths for able and ordinary seamen and boys (57 per cent) and apprentices (6.5 per cent) exceeded their corresponding rank proportions (46 and 5 per cent respectively), while the death percentages for all the other ranks were less. The very nature of their work exposed these men to constant dangers, with apprentices being particularly vulnerable on account of their age and lack of experience. Indeed, almost 20 per cent of the deaths occurred in the under-20 year age group which represented only 12 per cent of the crew complement. The over-35 year group also suffered disproportionately, with this older category accounting for 35.7 per cent of the deaths compared to 21.6 per cent of the crews. These results support the claim that most of the crews on British ocean-going vessels in the 1860s, a period when much attention was being focused on their poor working conditions, were broken in health between the ages of 35 and 40, and that their life expectancy did not exceed 45 years (Course 1963:195). The records for Queensland crews clearly indicate that much of the morbidity and most of the deaths directly related to the sailors' living and working conditions. Moreover, there is no evidence to suggest that the men were subject to diseases prevailing among the passengers; the two communities appear to have been effectively segregated.

Since the crews on passenger vessels to Queensland were drawn from the vast pool of men serving in the British merchant navy, they shared the benefits of technological, social and legal developments which steadily raised the standard of the marine during the second half of the last century. The reputable shipping companies and the requirements of colonial governments largely set the pace for improvement. In time, better qualified, healthier, and more mature and disciplined sailors appeared on the Queensland route. But two particular factors had an important bearing on these men – the introduction of steamships to the route in 1881 and the level of seamanship demanded by the colonial authorities. By strict adherence to their regulations and contracts and through the payment of gratuities, the government sought to secure a sufficient, controlled and competent crew for each of their vessels. These crews were medically examined, had the services of a qualified doctor and were provisioned and accommodated as well as, if not better than, other sectors of the marine, both British and foreign. All crew members, especially those whose duties directly concerned the passengers, were expected to work for the good of everyone on board.

The unique social structuring on Queensland immigrant vessels involved a fine balance between duties and responsibilities, inducements, privileges and penalties for both passengers and crew. The purpose of the whole system was to promote health, good order and harmony at sea in order to provide the optimum conditions for a much needed, highly selected and largely subsidized population. Having examined and discussed the policy, procedure, and the personnel employed to achieve these ends, as well as the composition and nature of the immigration, we may now consider the results and assess the effectiveness of health care for immigrants in transit to the colony.

LIFE AT SEA

A seventeen-year-old, sailing alone to Queensland in 1885, kept a daily record of life at sea for his parents: 'It is doing me a great amount of good' he wrote, 'as it is getting me ready to rough it & manage for myself when I land' (Lumb 1885). He was the kind of person the colonial authorities wanted – young, healthy and willing to work. Moreover, he was making the most of the voyage arrangements. How well did these detailed arrangements translate into practice? Did they provide Queensland immigrants with healthy travelling conditions?

The outcome of a voyage primarily depended on the extent to which the health-care programme could be implemented, and on the nature and attitudes of those for whom it was designed. Although the volume of immigration fluctuated and the mode of transport changed, the principles undergirding both policy and procedure for securing suitable immigrants altered little throughout the colonial period. The insistent urge to develop Queensland sustained the policy, while the programme continued to operate on the premise that if young and robust people were selected and provided with a healthy environment in transit, they would be able to contribute to the progress of the colony. Modifications to the system were the result of changing labour demands, technological developments, and detected abuses and irregularities. Early administrators tackled the task with much enthusiasm but little expertise. Gradually, a more coordinated and efficient approach emerged as experience accumulated, transport and communications improved and the standard of living began to rise; every aspect of the heavily subsidized system was carefully regulated and supervised. Even so, the best-laid plans and arrangements could break down. The following chapters will attempt to analyse results and isolate factors responsible for the success, or otherwise, of the health-care programme by looking at the actual conditions under which immigrants travelled, morbidity, births and deaths at sea, and whether or not future colonists were the kind of people the government desired.

The several reports submitted at the voyage end provide one of the most fruitful sources for determining policy effectiveness, since they contain official observations and immigrant comments.[1] Reports are available for 87 per cent of the government voyages, 83 per cent of the Commissioners', 68 per cent of the private immigrant, 53 per cent of German, and 4 per cent of short-ship voyages. The average number of comments per voyage for the whole period is greatest for government ships and for those under sail. Clearly the authorities paid most attention to the voyages for which they were responsible, especially during the early years; better conditions on the steamships apparently reduced the need for comment. Some 4,339 statements relating to all aspects of immigration have been examined in order to isolate problem areas in the programme. However, only 43 per cent of the comments were listed as complaints; the remainder noted a particular situation or commended arrangements and personnel. The marked decrease in the proportion of complaints from 60 per cent in the 1860s to 27 per cent in the 1890s, speaks for itself.

Surgeons contributed 59 per cent of the statements, immigration officials (the Agent-General, immigration agent and health officer) 25 per cent, and passengers 8 per cent; sub-officers (matron, constables and others) and crew were responsible for the remainder. Passengers registered the highest proportion (92 per cent) of complaints for any one group, since they were questioned about the voyage during the arrival inspection. Nevertheless, some were 'loud in their praises'; and after 1880, the immigration agent frequently recorded 'no complaints'. Surgeons and their staff were responsible for the management of immigrants, and not surprisingly scored the lowest complaint rate (30 per cent). The comments not only indicate that conditions of travel improved, but that those responsible generally considered these conditions to be adequate. Even the Brisbane bureaucrats who were geared to detect problems noted dissatisfaction in only 53 per cent of their statements. The majority of complaints (61 per cent) had to do with the voyage arrangements – the state of the vessel and its fittings, the dietary and cooking, medical supplies and cleanliness, as well as activities for mental and moral enrichment. A further 27.5 per cent referred to the personnel – the surgeon, sub-officers and crew. Since government supervision continued after arrival, another 7 per cent mentioned that facilities at the immigration depot and quarantine station were less than adequate; a certain number (3.5 per cent) expressed concern with the selection and embarkation procedures; the remaining few were beyond human control.

Anyone embarking for the colony could expect extremes of climate, especially if he or she travelled under sail. The weather during some voyages was so stressful that, no matter how sound the ship or how competent the crew, the lives of all on board were endangered or their health suffered. Sometimes a captain sought refuge in a port, though often he had no option but to ride out the storm and hope to survive. The hatches would be battened down and immigrants were confined below 'in a continual uproar' for several days, even weeks (see Watson 1968:4–5 and QVP 1880:II,397–99). Difficult conditions soon after leaving the home port accounted for 22 per cent of the comments relating to the weather; passengers did not take long to discover that being rocked in the cradle of the deep proved 'the reverse of agreeable' (COL/A550:88–5791). A storm at sea, though 'something grand', was terrifying; the waves could 'swallow you up in double-quick time', observed one awe-struck traveller (Lumb 1885). They could also cause considerable damage.

The captain of the *Wansfell* entered the following in his log on 10 December, 1864 while easting at 42 degrees south:

'1 p.m. . . . strong gale and v. heavy sea. 4 p.m. gale increasing with severe squalls . . . 5 p.m. . . . sea growing very dangerous & squalls terrific, 6 p.m. . . . a tremendous sea struck the ship . . . washing away Quarter Boats, Bulwarks, Hatchways, Skylights on Poop, quarter part of the livestock & any moveable thing on deck, staveing in side lights on both sides & half filling the tween decks & cabin . . . by 1 a.m. we had the ship pumped out . . . A.B. severely injured in the leg by a cask of provisions.'

(NMML)

Battened in below, immigrants were thrown together in the dark, frightened and drenched as 'plates pans cups mugs pannecans' and loose boxes tossed from side to side with every lurch of the ship; children screamed and the wind howled through the rigging (see Ricou 1872 and Blasdall 1862). For several days before the wreck of the *Netherby* in 1866, 'the Captain could not obtain a sight of the sun to know his exact position', so he posted an extra watch and took other precautions, but a 'thick fog' descended and the ship hit a reef and stuck fast in Bass Strait. Throughout the night, as the water rose between decks, everyone prepared to go ashore. At first light the operation began and by 4 p.m. passengers and crew were safely landed on King Island; they watched the vessel being dashed to pieces and waited to be rescued (see COL/A82:66–2231).

In addition to the heavy seas in the Southern Ocean, the cold and continual rain, thick fog, sleet, hail and snow increased the discomfort. This weather came as a sharp contrast to the scorching sun and high temperatures of the tropical calms when the pitch between the deck boards ran 'like water', the vermin multiplied, and passengers suffered from heat apoplexy and exposure to the sun. Iron-hulled vessels tended to exacerbate the extremes of heat and cold. Although the steamship voyage produced fewer climatic contrasts, the difficulties could be as great as on sailing vessels; rough seas, heavy rains, hot and sultry days sometimes persisted throughout the passage. From all accounts, nothing could compare with the intense, 'insufferable' heat of the Red Sea, aggravated by dust storms and strong head winds. Indeed, most of the weather comments (26.5 per cent) referred to this stage of the journey; 'the heat makes it impossible to do anything' ran a diary comment, 'so there is little to do but lie on deck and melt' (Acton 1889). The Queensland coast also had a reputation for bad weather at certain times of the year; a few vessels were struck by lightning or ran onto a reef. Despite recommendations to avoid arriving during the hot, wet months, a large number of immigrants disembarked or spent the quarantine period under cyclonic, monsoonal conditions. However, some voyages experienced remarkably good weather throughout. Mellor Lumb's ship averaged 250 miles a day and sailed 'as steady . . . as a salloon carriage'; he believed it was his duty and that of 'everyone else on board to thank God for fair winds and the absence of storms' (Lumb 1885). The changing moods and colours of the sea, a beautiful sunset, a starlit night or a moon that gave light like 'one of Edison's Household Electric Burners' created a good atmosphere; so did the excitement of passing another ship that might take home mail or bring news.

The discomforts and dangers of the sea, so vividly described and illustrated in the nineteenth-century media, were risks that any immigrant had to face. Indeed, the whole process of uprooting and departure involved some trauma. This could be aggravated by hasty selection, inadequate preparation for the voyage, insufficient or incorrect information, misrepresentation, impersonation or a last-minute rush to make up the quota for a vessel. Immigrants sometimes arrived at the embarkation port to find their clothing supply was too meagre or they had to buy bedding and utensils. Once, three young men were given the wrong sailing date and missed their ship (COL/A227:76–2976). At the port, a breakdown in organization could heighten the confusion or prevent a thorough inspection of the passengers, provisions and fittings; lists and other documents might be incomplete or the instructions misunderstood. In the event of an epidemic or a sudden change for the worse in the weather, departure was delayed or hastily rescheduled. Pre-embarkation lodgings also presented problems, particularly if there was no emigrant depot.

A married man and his family arrived at the East India docks in London in 1863 and went directly on board the *Beejapore*. Here they found 'a very confused seeign' with tins, boxes, bedding and the paraphenalia of several hundred emigrants strewn everywhere. Men were pushing and shoving, women were shouting and children crying: 'such a meddley . . . could not have failed to amusused a painter' (Good 1863). If passengers availed themselves of the subsistence money and stayed in near-by lodgings, they could be fleeced by the landlord. Continental travellers passing through English ports were often the target of fraudulent agents. Early in the 1880s the Queensland government instituted a full-scale inquiry into the operations of one agency after immi-

Plate 9 Getting berth numbers

grants claimed they had been subject to 'downright imposture and extortion (QVP 1882:II,569). Plymouth, despite its limited facilities (these were upgraded in 1882), was certainly an improvement on London. Here the confusion and the cold, foggy weather compounded the difficulties of departure, until the opening of the Blackwall Emigrants' Home in 1884. By the following year, a near-perfect system was in operation. Passengers arrived at the depot in time to be examined; their luggage was forwarded to the vessel; and when all was in order, they were taken by rail to embark at Gravesend in the Thames estuary. Although immigration was beginning to taper off by this time, the records suggest that, throughout the period, every effort was made to facilitate embarkation formalities for Queensland immigrants (see Plate 9).

The initial chaos on board usually subsided once passengers found their sea-legs and the effects of seasickness, which might keep them in a state of 'apparent intoxication' for days, had worn off. Establishing the daily routine invariably ran into difficulties when members of the new community chose to ignore or resist the regulations; there were always a few who had problems adjusting to the changed life-style and unfamiliar 'laws'. The interplay of immigrant cooperation, vessel arrangements, and supervision by the surgeon and his staff determined the outcome of a voyage. Most surgeons organized the daily routine according to instructions, and immigrants knew when they were expected to rise and retire, carry out the cleaning duties, eat, air their bedding, do their washing and attend the weekly roll-call on the poop deck. Times were also fixed for the doctor's consultation hours, for dispensing medicines and medical comforts, and doing his rounds to visit the sick or inspect the sanitary state of the vessel (see Plate 10).

Although the pattern of life was similar, there was considerable variation between and within each voyage, depending on the number carried and their 'antecedents'. On some vessels the matron was responsible for upwards of 200 single women (see COL/A563:88–9568). Each consignment usually included a few troublesome and 'objectionable' girls, quite apart from the married women who resented the matron's control and whose children were noisy and disruptive. Sometimes a dividing bulkhead which allowed communication, an insecure lock, or the poor location of the female toilets demanded the matron's

The ladies on deck

The bachelors in the 'tween decks

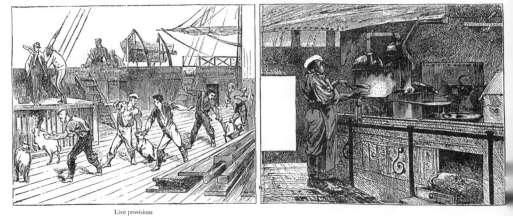

Live provisions

Plate 10 On board the *Indus*

persistent vigilance. So did the young rakes in the saloon. Her task could be further complicated by an untrustworthy assistant or inefficient nurse, and a replacement had to be found. The matron's authority within her domain continued until 1892, after which time the Queensland regulations no longer applied. When immigration resumed in the late 1890s, she had neither the power nor support to enforce discipline. Often a matron's work extended well beyond her job description, and several requested a bonus for 'the extra work of body and mind' during a trying voyage or weeks in quarantine. One of them pointed out that she had to attend serious cases of illness, including a confinement, because the doctor 'was incapable of performing his duties' (COL/A269:79–53). Sometimes the matron's accommodation was far from satisfactory; one threatened to resign if her cabin was not better lit and ventilated (COL/A333:82–1449). Another allowed her husband to share her cramped quarters, but the authorities did not approve (COL/A70:65–2115). Jane Chase, with thirty years' experience to her credit, dared to write to the Colonial Secretary in 1882 suggesting that the matron's duties be revised and her accommodation improved. She also noted with pleasure that the surgeon's power had been trimmed, adding that 'their tyrant importance of self' made it impossible to work with some of them (COL/A334:82–2108).

Before the establishment of a permanent staff of matrons in 1866, most were selected from among the immigrants and often proved unsuitable. Although problems with their selection and appointment continued after this time, the majority gave satisfactory service. Only 2.2 per cent of the complaints concerned the matron and referred to her negligence, incompetence, brutality or intemperance. Some could not handle the physical demands of the job; others, through inexperience or lack of training and tact, had no idea of control or cleanliness. There were those who were too strict, a few gave 'cause for scandal', and several were 'addicted to drink'. One or two managed to control their problem during the voyage, but had access to liquor coming up the river and arrived 'in anything but a creditable condition' (COL/A250:77–5868). The matron who, in a drunken rage, almost bit off a girl's finger, had to be restrained in irons (COL/A80:66–1544). Another thrashed a lass who accepted the doctor's invitation to sit on his knee during rounds (COL/A210:75–1154). Yet another was described as 'the most unchristian and tyrannical woman' (COL/A387:84–2820). Inevitably some clashed with the surgeon and even the captain. Any woman who could not cope with her duties was dismissed, but those who did well received the highest commendation: 'kind, considerate, and a good disciplinarian', 'very zealous', 'excellent', 'more of a mother than a matron' ran some of the reports. The frequency of such remarks increased during the latter years when only the most reliable were retained on the staff.

The standard of constables for each voyage directly related to the quality of the immigrants. Surgeons occasionally suggested that these men should not be 'drawn from the ranks', and that they should have an independent status and mess separately; answerability would therefore be enhanced and the tendency to favour their 'chums' be reduced. Nevertheless, their only mark of authority was the government badge, until the later British India steamers introduced a navy jacket trimmed with red braid (see Blake 1956:46–7). Surgeons looked for strong, dependable and respectable married men, and it would seem that they chose well, since surprisingly few constables proved unsatisfactory considering the numbers selected. Some had difficulty following instructions; several were insolent to the surgeon and matron or abused the passengers; others felt that the work involved was not worth the pittance they received. Having to supervise the segregation of the different compartments and the cleanliness of the immigrant areas, from six in the morning until ten at night, was a thankless task (COL/A69:65–2018). Certainly extra men were enlisted to cope with an epidemic or disruptive elements on board; but constables deserved every penny of their gratuity, particularly those with special duties. In addition to running to and fro with meals and rations in all conditions, removing rubbish and bringing up the girls' luggage from the hold, the men who served the single female section were exposed to moral pressures; most complaints referred to 'improper conduct'.

Some surgeons had the greatest difficulty finding a suitable person to conduct the schools or replace a teacher if he resigned, became ill or had to be dismissed. However, his role was considered so important that the matron, purser or even the surgeon might step in as a substitute. More than 200 schoolmasters' reports have survived. These and the surgeons' assessment of their performance together with the fact that only seven complaints related to teachers, indicate that the majority, whether professionals or amateurs, took their duties seriously. Many achieved 'gratifying' results, despite the difficult conditions under which they worked. A few showed little interest in their pupils, violated the regulations or had limited teaching skills. One report ran: 'their were 10 scolars but only 2 Books this cawsed us to advance the best readers' (COL/A349:82–5865). Another teacher dropped all his 'h's except for the final 'has'; but he had second thoughts and scored out the 'h' (COL/A206:75–596). While the success of the school largely depended on the superintendent's support, there were mutual advantages. Teachers ran the library, acted as interpreters, and sometimes assisted with the medical work (see COL/A345:82–4816). Indeed, one surgeon suggested that the schoolmaster be made second-in-command to the superintendent (COL/A221:76–1061). He worked seven days a week but could rest on Sundays if a clergyman or passenger of 'good moral and religious character' was invited, with the surgeon's approval and the parents' consent, to participate in the classes and services (see ISS 1875:52).

The evidence thus far suggests certain conclusions. First, the surgeon-superintendent was, in theory and practice, responsible for the well-being of immigrants as they travelled. Second, as the organization became more efficient, so the failure rate among the passenger personnel decreased; by the late 1880s little fault could be found with the conduct of vessels. Third, one of the basic strengths of this decidedly utilitarian and paternalistic system lay in the fact that, on the superintendent's recommendation, the government gratuity for any of his staff and the crew members involved with passengers could be withheld or deducted. Moreover, it was clearly understood that any deficiency he reported in the shipboard arrangements would be thoroughly investigated on arrival. Official correspondence and parliamentary inquiries leave no doubt that the colonial authorities were locked into an on-going crusade to correct abuses and improve conditions of travel.

By 1900, the situation seemed satisfactory. Sailing vessels had been withdrawn from the service, the smaller steamships were considered inadequate and the larger steamers were 'roomy, well ventilated and well arranged' (QVP 1901:IV,1050). Although emigration officers as early as 1874 claimed that no system was 'more complete' than Queensland's (QVP 1875:II,611), there was no cause for complacency then, or at any other time during the period. More than 70 per cent of the statements relating to shipping standards drew attention to some defect. A vessel might be in first-class condition, but could not be readily adapted for immigrants; those with ample deck space and lofty 'tween decks fitted the purpose admirably. A few were built with the needs of emigrants in mind, but others like the *Wansfell*, one of the smallest and oldest of the Black Ball fleet, did not meet the requirements. It was chartered by the Commissioners in 1866 and arrived in Queensland after an exceedingly uncomfortable voyage; the caulking gave way, the decks leaked and berths remained constantly wet (COL/A80:66–1753).

Leakage because of inadequate water-proofing was a persistent, though diminishing, problem and accounted for almost 30 per cent of the vessel-related complaints. There were many reasons for this – insufficient caulking, the effect of rough seas, temperature extremes and heavy cargo on the timbered decking of sailing ships, ill-fitting booby hatches, rotting rubber around the portholes, seepage through ventilation shafts, skylights and scuttles. A defective pumping mechanism or faulty plumbing accentuated the problem. Although iron-hulled sailing ships seldom required pumping out, there was always 'a soakage of offensive matter, dangerous to health . . . going on into the lower parts'; these had to be disinfected or regularly flushed with salt water (QVP 1876:II,1097). Poor drainage also allowed the accumulation of waste and filth in the scuppers, especially on washing days. Some of the steamships had wooden decks which were not underlaid with iron and leaked badly as the timbers opened in hot or heavy weather. Many a carpenter worked hard trying to keep a vessel water-tight, while swinging stoves and hot sand dealt with the damp between decks.

Another common complaint was space. The recreation area on the upper deck was sometimes 'much lumbered and very dirty', being cluttered with coals and cargo, livestock and machinery (see COL/A75:65–3369). Yet, other decks were 'magnificently spacious and clean', with room 'to walk and share' (COL/A88:67–519). Single women found they had very limited space for relaxation on vessels steered from the stern; if the single men were too cramped, they encroached on the family area and generally created trouble. Since fresh air and exercise were regarded as prerequisites for health, any problem that kept passengers cooped up between decks during the day was immediately investigated. After all, the space for the berthing area had been calculated on the assumption that people would spend two-thirds of each day on deck; illness and prolonged foul weather upset this calculation. The height between decks was also noted, for this regulated the ventilation, light, and degree of crowding in the berthing area. Apart from the *Wandrahm*,[2] it seems that all other immigrant vessels for the colony adhered to or improved on the legal requirements; but not all met with approval. For example, the SS *Nuddea*, a bounty vessel, was not only improperly ventilated, but carried a total of 770 souls – 'a number . . . far too great for wholesome and healthy conveyance' (see QVP 1883–84:1355– 356).

There were other lesser problems that created discomfort and concern. The lower decking on some vessels sloped or was not properly secured and produced an 'unpleasant' elasticity (COL/ A84:66–2795). Small or poorly fitted portholes were useless; there were none on the *Beausite*, another German vessel. Hatches, when unprotected by awnings, insecurely fixed or fitted with faulty booby-covers proved hazardous; sometimes they were so located that it was difficult to prevent communication with the female section. On several vessels, the single men and marrieds had to share the one opening, and frequently the single men's hatch was kept open around the clock to allow access to the crew's quarters or the hold. Injuries sustained by falling down a steep, narrow companionway, especially one without handrails, were common. On a voyage in 1866, a single, two-flight ladder provided the only means of access to the female compartment (COL/A77:66–867). Indeed, the sources of danger were countless – faulty ropes securing equipment, the breaking of a cable chain or the anchor coming loose, insufficient and unseaworthy lifeboats, naked lights in the hold. A passenger who fell overboard, drowned because 'Clifford's patent lowering apparatus' had been improper- ly fitted and valuable time was lost (COL/A84:66–2795). Life saving drill and lectures were introduced on some of the later vessels.

The greatest fear at sea was a fire. The few that broke out on

Queensland ships were traced to an open lamp, faulty lightning conductors, a galley or bakehouse oven placed too close to the bulkhead. All were quickly extinguished and caused minimal damage, except the fire that spread to the single men's quarters following an explosion in the coal bunker of a steamer in 1883; several were injured (COL/A376:83–6659). One or two false alarms caused the 'wildest confusion'; in one instance, after women and children were almost trampled to death in the stampede, the culprit was punished with solitary confinement for a week (COL/A349:82–5779). On most vessels a fire brigade was organized, but they were of little use if the engine was out of order or the force pump was defective. This indispensable machine, apart from its use during a fire, raised the daily water supply for drinking, cooking and sanitary purposes, and was constantly in demand during heavy weather.

Dangerous cargo was forbidden on passenger vessels, but the location and stowage as well as the type and quantity of what was permissible, could expose immigrants to considerable risk. Early ships carried several hundred tons of general merchandise and government stores, including anything from stationery to sheep, police uniforms to railway plant. If the cargo shifted during a gale, it had to be hastily restowed to prevent disaster. Some ships were so heavily laden that they leaked badly and sat so low in the water that the decks remained constantly awash and the ports had to be closed (see COL/A225:76–2040). On the other hand, insufficient ballast or cargo caused a vessel to 'pitch terribly'. Certain cargoes were believed to be inimical to health. During the 1860s, the New South Wales government would not allow salt to be carried on their immigrant ships, but the Queensland authorities agreed with the Commissioners that small quantities seemed harmless while large consignments were 'unquestionably highly objectionable' (COL/A32:62–2083); salt was believed to vitiate the air. On a voyage in 1865, the 'offensive odour' from a previous cargo of guano was held responsible for at least two deaths (COL/A69:65–1890).

Most of the difficulties with steamship cargoes related to their discharge at ports along the Queensland coast. The authorities strongly disapproved of immigrants assisting with the off-loading before the operation was fully mechanized. In fact, steamship travel produced its own set of problems; the engines and machinery were noisy and constantly vibrated, 'wild heat' generated by the boilers raised temperatures in their vicinity to abnormally high levels and heat absorbed in the tropics often made conditions intolerable. In port, immigrants were kept below for twelve to eighteen hours to avoid injury during cargo handling and to prevent them interfering with coaling – a filthy, rowdy and discomforting procedure; saloon passengers usually slept ashore to avoid the inconvenience and 'unsavoury surroundings'.

The voyage to Queensland, by sail or steam, was a fair test for any ship. Some captains tried to remedy problems as they arose, others chose to ignore them. On arrival every deficiency in the vessel and its arrangements was carefully investigated; if it could be shown that preparations had been effected without 'regard to comfort and convenience' and that the passengers had suffered as a result, the shippers were warned, asked to withdraw the vessel from the service or penalized. A considerable number of complaints in the early years involved German ships and the older Black Ball vessels; but dissatisfaction with arrangements extended beyond the organizational phase to reach new levels in the mid-1870s, just before the corruption in the London office was exposed, and again in the 1880s with bounty vessels not covered by the government regulations. Complaints relating to the out-fitting of vessels accounted for 27 per cent of the total registered; but the proportion gradually reduced over the four decades.

In 1877 a former Queensland surgeon-superintendent wrote to the *British Medical Journal* outlining the problems he encountered a few years earlier:

'Ships are often got ready so hurriedly for sea that the contract work for the emigrants' department is often very miserably executed. The plumbing is frequently very bad; leaky pipes are a cause of frequent complaints; and condensers, which break down shortly after leaving, are a source of much dissatisfaction and many growls . . . The store water is generally put in tanks, from which it almost always issues good and wholesome, though sometimes necessarily tinged with iron rust. It should never be stored in casks. The bathing on board is limited, as regards room accommodation. The single females are supplied with one bathroom, and the rest of the passengers are left without. Other fixtures, such as the baker's oven, ought to be used on board before leaving, as I recollect having to stow away one oven as useless. It is impossible, in the hurry of the last hour or two (and very often these fixtures are not placed until the last moment), for the surgeon to prove these things himself.'

(BMJ 1877:I, 574)

For the immigrants, their first contact with the vessel fittings was in the berthing area, their 'home' for the next two to four months. An assisted passenger in 1862 described his accommodation:

'we proceeded to look for our respective Births which I compare to so many Chests of drawers with the drawers out . . . There is just sufficient room for one to lay down all his length you must not try to pull up your knees or they will come in contact with the boards.'

(Blasdall 1862)

In the married compartment it was often 'uterly impossable to sit upright'; 'the very young children slept with their parents and the older children piled in together somehow in other double bunks' (quoted in Charlwood 1981:118). On the SS *Roma* in 1886 a couple and their 'large' eleven year-old daughter shared a thirty-six inch wide double bunk which, in the words of the immigration agent, 'must have been uncomfortably small' (COL/A467:86–4053). The need to remain on deck as much as possible would have been imperative, given the limited space, leakage, lack of ventilation and poor lighting on some vessels.

Complaints relating to accommodation were not confined to the steerage compartments. Four single men travelling intermediate on the *Young Australia* in 1868 claimed they had been berthed in a saloon water-closet and were 'showered with cold [water] day and night' (COL/A109:68–2496). On the same vessel six years earlier four ladies in the second cabin were huddled together in two berths, deprived of decent rations and facilities, and had to mingle with the immigrants: 'the noise, filth, drunkenness and swearing were altogether frightful' (ANL Letter Book I:35, M468). Other second-class travellers complained of cramped quarters, wet berths or a privy located unpleasantly close to their cabin. Such passengers referred to the shippers for compensation; the government was responsible only for the immigrants, the majority of whom seem to have accepted their situation without complaint unless it was particularly bad. 'We have good beds', recorded a young lad, 'our bunks are 6 ft 9 ins long and 22 inches wide 2 ft deep. there is no fear of our falling out' (Anon 1883). One can understand why many ignored the ruling that single men be berthed separately, and removed the dividing board or slept on deck. At one time hammocks were installed; these were preferred to the two-tiered swinging cots (COL/A75:66–152). The replacement of wooden by iron bunks in both the single compartments during the 1880s proved beneficial in every way, except that the latter tended to sag and reduce the limited space between the upper and lower berths (see COL/A500:87–3918). However, the suggestion to install iron bunks in the married section was not followed through since Johnson's patent berths (the family cabin arrangement), introduced a few years earlier, had proved satisfactory despite complaints from some surgeons that they harboured dirt and impeded ventilation. If bunks were hastily constructed or nails were used instead of screws, the inevitable happened and the upper sections collapsed, 'precipitating their occupants on to those in the lower berths' (COL/A297:80–4333).

Under the sardine-like conditions on some German vessels, parents and as many as three children shared a double bunk; even fourteen-year-olds slept with their parents. The *Wandrahm* was fitted with triple-decker double berths which allowed 2 feet 10 inches for the lower, and 3 feet 4 inches for the upper space between berths (QVP 1866:1019). Early German ships also made no provision for segregating the sexes, though conditions on several British ships before the system was properly organized left much to be desired, with only a 'flimsy' and useless partition separating the single men and married people. Apparently it was not feasible to keep the different nationalities on board apart, but recommendations for the better location of berths were generally implemented, with greater attention given to the effect of leakage and proximity to hatchways, privies and especially ventilators which could create 'cold air tunnels' (see COL/A72:65–2787). Surgeons regularly complained that the bottom bunks were either too close to the deck or the boards could not be removed to allow a thorough cleaning. Filth also tended to accumulate in the berthing area if there were insufficient tables and forms. Occasionally these were of such poor quality that they fell apart well before arrival; on one voyage the carpenter used the chicken and sheep pens to provide replacements (COL/A128:69–2736).

Ship-kits issued under the Queensland regulations were intended to equip immigrants with reasonable quality bedding, utensils and personal-care items, since bedding purchased privately was known to be stuffed with shavings, lumpy flocking and vermin-infested rags. Mark Blasdall moaned to his journal in 1862: 'My bones aches awful today in consequence of the softness of the shavings of which my bed is composed.' Although certain items in the kit were criticized – shoddy utensils and 'useless' soap – there were few complaints. One young man was so impressed with the quality of his that he decided not to throw it overboard on arrival (Lumb 1885). Sometimes immigrants were 'accidentally deprived' of their mattresses when they took them on deck to 'air and sweeten'. This created real distress in the cold weather, especially if they did not have sufficient warm clothing. It was not unusual for a navvy to embark with only one suit of dirty clothes, but many passengers found their wardrobe to be inadequate or unsuitable. Tweeds and corduroys, for example, were too hot for the tropics and difficult to dry if drenched by cold, salt water. One surgeon suggested that at least two lightweight suits be included (COL/A522:87–8404). During the hot weather the men improvised with sheets; one wished he had brought 'a whole Tailors shop in light clothes' (Lumb 1885). Straw hats, unless secured with a pugaree, were soon blown overboard, and immigrants with poor quality shoes and boots were most at risk on a wet deck.

Every little detail came under scrutiny, but arrangements for the single women were the focus of official concern. Seven vessels had no bulkhead dividing the girls from the married section; on others the partition was made of perforated wooden planking or needed constant repairs. The only access to the sail room on the *Zamora* in 1877 was through the female compartment, and the girls had to be turned out on deck, en masse, each time the room was needed (QVP 1877:II,1151). The forbidden territory stretched male ingenuity; two young fellows carefully crafted a duplicate key but were caught just in time (COL/A67:65–1307). In several instances the door to the married section was boarded over, or a constable was posted near the entrance to the female area. The most satisfactory arrangement proved to be a double louvred-partition incorporating the luggage room. Although the government failed in their attempt to charter vessels solely for single women, they refused, for the sake of 'morality and decency', to allow unaccompanied girls on ships carrying single men, and for a time refused saloon passages to single males wanting to travel on immigrant vessels (QVP 1865:662). Separate berthing continued throughout the period, but by the late 1890s, the strict segregation no longer applied.

Many young women suffered because of the 'complete isolation' ruling. Perhaps the worst example was on the notorious *Wandrahm* in 1866 when ten girls were housed in a cabin measuring 12 ft by 5 ft 7 in (QVP 1866:1021). That same year, the absence of portholes on a British ship made the female compartment 'almost insupportable' in the tropics, and even on the 'roomy' SS *Duke of Portland* in 1900, conditions were 'tryingly close' at times. The accommodation for thirty women on a bounty vessel in 1883 was described as 'scandalous'; ventilation, light and space were 'carefully disregarded' and there was only one toilet (COL/A371:83–5334). But they did well compared to the 362 immigrants and crew on the *Wandrahm* which provided a total of four privies, situated in the bow and virtually inaccessible to the single women; if the ship was on a wind, the two lee closets were unusable (QVP 1866:1017). On some British vessels the situation was not much better. One allowed only four privies for 355 immigrants, and on another, a three-seater toilet with a single soil pipe served the needs of 125 girls (COL/A75:65–3369 and COL/A297:80–4333). According to the surgeon, this latter arrangement was 'a great source of trouble' and decidedly 'indecent' since it was installed in the bathroom.

Inadequate toileting facilities for women and children remained a problem throughout the period. Privies on the later steamers accommodated only five or six at a time, there were no hand basins and, at most, two baths – one for the single women,[3] the other for the family section, many of whom added to the 'great unwashed'. It was impossible to maintain a 'pure atmosphere at night' or reduce the incidence of skin diseases and vermin unless married men and women had separate facilities. One surgeon noted with satisfaction that the family bath he organized was used by the mothers and children at least eighty times during the voyage (COL/A225:76–2040). Single men, both steerage and cabin, made their own arrangements, but objected to bathing in public (see Beaumont n.d.:10). However, the tropical heat usually forced them 'up on deck during the night in a state of utter nudity' to bathe (COL/A332:82–1154). German vessels, certainly the earlier ones, made no provision whatsover for bathing, except for immigrants with 'the itch' (scabies).

Few voyages were vermin-free, but some were more 'alive' than others; it seems, for example, that 'habits of cleanliness' were promoted more on the Commissioners' vessels than the Black Ball ships (QVP 1863:II,487). Passengers concerned for their personal hygiene took exception to those who embarked in a filthy state, wore lousey clothing or changed only once a month.'There has been a lot of lice found this week and I know they come from the Irish men' Mellor Lumb wrote home in 1885, adding that he would rather wash his clothes 'every day than be bothered with such Vermin one minute'. Although immigrants reported suspects to the doctor, they devised their own methods for protection and control. Several diaries describe the evident enjoyment of 'live stock hunting' when 'Fine Fat Bucks' were impaled on a pin and thrown overboard (Blasdall 1862). Even cabin passengers had their problems with infested bedding and cockroaches 'galloping' over them (see Hume and Fowler 1975:151, Taylor 1969:87 and Pownall 1975:139).

Apart from passenger indifference, baths could be rendered useless for any number of reasons. Some were too short or too narrow, others were put out of action when the vessel heeled over slightly. Both toilets and bathrooms suffered from faulty plumbing, fragile fittings and fixtures, or hasty construction; being built on deck, they were especially vulnerable in rough weather. 'Fortunately nobody was there' commented an immigrant after the privies were washed overboard in a storm (Ricou 1872). The authorities disapproved of the practice on some voyages of demolishing the deck structures a day or two before arrival. Occcasionally facilities were described as 'ample' or 'superior', but more often, attention was drawn to blocked pipes, foul seepage and odours, described as 'unpleasant' or 'abominable' depending on the direction of the wind or the temperature. On one vessel an outlet pipe had been inadvertently plugged from the outside (COL/A361:83–2693). Toilets required constant attention in order to regulate the ventilation, light, privacy and the non-stop flow of hot water from the condenser, and to prevent them becoming 'fever producing machines'. The use of lead sheeting instead of pipes frequently resulted in flooding, and the reverse occurred when the distilling apparatus broke down or was shut off. A flush system for the toilets and cold water for the baths were recommended, but these depended on continuous pumping.

Some privies had no fastenings or the doors fell off their hinges; others had no doors at all and 'looked disgusting when filled with occupants' (COL/A78:66–955). The needs of children seem to have been most neglected, and as a result they 'performed acts between decks which should have been done elsewhere' (COL/A316:81–2878). Smaller and lower seats were suggested since even little children were sent to the toilets unattended. One wonders how many immigrants were familiar with water closets. They generally used their slop pail at night and during bad weather, a factor that could scarcely have improved the atmosphere below. Many a night-stool or 'tween deck water-closet had to be removed because of the stench or its close proximity to the berths. However, the alternative of an open hatch for the single girls, it was feared, would promote indiscipline and immorality during the voyage, and prostitution on arrival (see COL/A227:76–2426). Facilities which allowed the girls to chat to sailors at the wheel were also regarded as 'highly objectionable'. A persistent underlying tension existed between functionality and economy on the one hand and the physical and moral needs of immigrants on the other.

Keeping immigrant areas clean proved a full-time job. Although the standard procedure altered little over the four decades, the difference between vessels was great; some were 'remarkably clean', others 'absolutely filthy'. But of all the comments relating to sanitation, only a quarter complained of a lack of cleanliness, and the incidence of such complaints decreased. In 1886 Dr Hickling was reported to have kept his ship so clean that not only the rats, but also the cats died (QVP 1886:III,760). A new colonial governor sailed to Queensland on the SS *Quetta* in 1889 and was so impressed whenever he inspected the vessel that he awarded £14 in prizes at the end of the voyage (COL/A579:84–4118). Perhaps the condition of other ships would have improved had a governor been on board. The single women's compartment maintained the best record for 'apple-pie order' and cleanliness;

here the matron was primarily responsible. A few surgeons (and captains) failed to carry out their sanitary duties satisfactorily, but most seem to have met the requirements, even under difficult circumstances. Dr Woodward claimed that the whole ship was cleaned and disinfected daily under his supervision (COL/A191:74–159).

An unclean vessel generally reflected immigrant attitudes; some were 'not cleanly in their habits' or were 'careless as to the accumulation of filth'; others resisted the duties or refused to clean. Such attitudes had to be dealt with promptly – offenders were put in irons or had their rations reduced. In 1880 a young man was charged under the passenger act and sent to prison for forty-eight hours on arrival (COL/A302:80–6137). Problems occurred most frequently with full-payers travelling steerage, and increased with the bounty system. Since several of the early bounty ships arrived in a very dirty state (second-class passengers were exempt from duties), the government allowed for paid sweepers. This scheme met with varying success, was condemned by more than one surgeon and, within twelve months, had been withdrawn (QVP 1889:III,175). Immigrants embarked knowing they were expected to be 'House keepers, Footmen, Cook and Charwomen all in one' (Lumb 1885).

Sometimes the fault lay with the cleaning materials – insufficient disinfectants, sand, lime or sawdust, poor quality soap or rock-like holystone; brushes and brooms were regularly 'lost' or appropriated by the crew. Although surgeons put in a request for wash tubs, passengers had to make do with dust bins and old flour casks. Washing day was quite an event: 'from 4 until 10 a.m. the Broadways being crowded with Males and Females and their washing Utensils sloshing the soap suds about' (Blasdall 1862). On a fine day clothes dried well, but remained dirty during cold, wet weather; one surgeon suggested a drying closet – connected to the condenser! Other obstacles to cleanliness included leaky decks, seepage from faulty plumbing, 'muck and sludge' from the farmyard (particularly the pigsty) and poor stowage of coals. On steamships coaling was a most filthy and discomforting operation, yet there is no mention of any steps being taken to protect the berthing areas from coal dust. The suggestion of canvas screens seems sensible when we read one passenger's experience: 'Everything about the ship has been miserable to-day . . . inches deep in coal dust, bunks, one's clothes, food, water & everything . . . I was like a sweep' (Acton 1889). Dirt tended to accumulate if berths were too close to the floor or the sides of the vessel, and also in poorly lit areas.

'Exceedingly dark' places needed artificial light even when portholes and hatches were open. Lighting became a real problem during the long winter evenings, in bad weather and when the candle supply ran low; the level of discontent and the number of petty thefts increased. There were repeated requests for longer burning candles, better locks for the lamps and more secure light fittings in the hospitals and toilets. On the whole, sperm-oil lamps were preferred to the 'very dangerous and smelly' paraffin lamps. Needless to say, electricity was the answer. Poor lighting and inadequate ventilation frequently went hand in hand. Since air flow depended on a range of mechanical and physical factors, it proved almost impossible, as Dr Russell pointed out, to produce a clean, odour-free environment in a confined space, with few openings, defective ventilating equipment and the bedding of seventy-nine children (COL/A365:83–3624). Although constant experimenting met with some success, ventilation problems were never fully resolved. We read of surgeons trying to 'clean the air' and reduce the temperature between decks; they adjusted the wind sails and scoops, dealt with partitions that obstructed air flow and tried to prevent draughts. On one German vessel 'ozoniferous fluid' was used to 'sweeten the atmosphere' (COL/A196:74–1433). Edmond's apparatus worked so efficiently on the *Charlie Palmer* in 1866 that the surgeon required very few disinfectants, but the same equipment completely failed on another vessel; it was not connected to the condenser and there were no side-scuttles to create a through draught (COL/A77:66–807 and COL/A84:66–2795). It seems that the most effective arrangement on sailing ships were side openings communicating with mushroom ventilators in the bulwarks, while on steamships hydraulic fans achieved the best results, unless they permitted leakage (COL/A87:67–234 and COL/A356:83–1462).

All too often the sanitary programme aborted because facilities fell short of the demand or illness and foul weather intervened. Most sick passengers, apart from maternity cases and those with contagious diseases, were cared for in their berths. This usually meant that cleaning in their immediate area was interrupted, a

Plate 11 The breakfast bell

situation that could easily get out of hand during protracted seasickness or in the event of a severe epidemic. Efforts to spruce up the vessel in order to impress the authorities on arrival were often negated as heavy rains reduced between decks to 'a perfect state of slush' (see COL/A192:74–470). Despite the careful planning, surveillance and evident improvements, immigrants, by and large, had to cope with less than ideal conditions while at sea. But no two voyages were alike; each had to be individually assessed according to official standards. This evaluation also applied to the dietary and water supply.

Twenty per cent of the total complaints focused on food and water (see Plate 11). After all, the daily routine revolved around ration distribution, cooking and meal times: 'the greatest proportion of our time is spent in eating' observed a young fellow who had to learn to cook to survive (Blasdall 1862). Another was moved to describe the situation in verse: 'Some made up things to boil while others made up things to bake. But what most of us did want Twas a real good beef steak' (Parrington 1869–70). It did not take long for immigrants to detect and deal with any discrepancy between the rations they received and the quantities stated in the purser's list or the contract ticket. On the *Scottish Admiral* in 1883 the men began complaining:

> 'we fancied [the food] was not enough so we managed to get a pair of scales and weighed it & found every thing that was allowed us short weight. Then all the Captains of the Messes went to the doctor & told him that if we did not have more to eat we should starve so he called the third Mate up and then had the Capt down to us has well so they well overhauled the mate for not giving us our weight.'   (Anon 1883)

If the problem lay with the purser alone it could be rectified; but in several instances inquiries revealed a fraudulent collusion between the suppliers, the shippers and the servants. In 1875 the *Star Queen* reached the colony in a shocking state, having been poorly outfitted and short-rationed; immigrants referred to her as the 'Star-ving Queen'; the captain was fined £200 for leaving England with short supplies (QVP 1876:II, 1137–183). About this time inaccurate scales were placed on the Queensland vessels. While the London office was being cleaned up and reorganized, officials were gradually tightening the procedure for examining provisions both at embarkation and on arrival. By the late 1870s the possibility of fraud had virtually been eliminated. The immigration agent investigated all passenger complaints; some were justified, but others he dismissed because the immigrants looked 'so healthy'. There was one man who reported that he had been deprived of his jam allowance, but his appearance indicated that he must have had 'a large supply of animal foods instead' (COL/A393:84–4346). No one had to starve, even under the worst conditions, since vessels put into port en route if supplies were running low. In fact, on occasions such as Christmas, extra rations were issued.

Difficulties with the supply of fresh water created real hardship on several German vessels. The surgeon of the *Wandrahm* wrote in his report:

> 'the water . . . was of the worst quality possible, some of it having been kept in casks which formerly had contained petroleum. Of this fluid the people . . . received sixteen and a half ounces per diem . . . [their] sufferings . . . especially in the tropics, can be better imagined than described . . . I will not here speak of the parents I have seen running the greatest risk of being severely punished with a rope's end for attempting to fetch a drop of water to their sick or dying children . . .'
>
> (QVP 1866:1020)

This was not an isolated incident; until well into the 1870s German ships did not carry water-distilling equipment. By comparison, all British ships for the colony installed a condenser which was expected to produce a minimum of 500 gallons a day, though the output actually ranged from 200 to 700 gallons. Reports of a faulty mechanism, insufficient coals or an incompetent operator were frequent, but vessels kept a back-up supply of tank water. Occasionally this also failed. In 1863 the immigration agent requested that the second moiety payment for the *Wanata* be withheld since 'a due supply of water for the voyage' had not been put on board (COL/A38:63–568). On another voyage passengers were put on short rations when the condenser failed and it was found that twelve casks had leaked and the tank water was sour (COL/A109:68–2452).

Although there were very few instances of acute shortage, the quality of the water supply was regularly questioned. In 1881 immigrants on the SS *Almora*, one of the first steamers to enter the trade, complained that the condensed water was contaminated, caused much sickness and was not 'a very seductive beverage' (COL/A325:81–4803). Sometimes water from the evaporator bubbled into the condenser and carried with it unkilled pathogenic bacteria (see Roddis 1941:108). Although the source might be doubtful, steamers took on water as well as provisions at each port. Problems with the quality therefore persisted. In the latter years passengers had the benefit of cooled drinking water – a welcome change from tea and coffee in the tropics. Dr Taylor in 1884 advised against drinking warm water since it caused 'a depressed condition of the great sympathetic nerve centres' thus rendering a person 'liable to gastric disturbance and heat affection' (COL/A381:84–1331). Loaf sugar added to the lime juice was said to make 'a nice drink', but chilled beer was out of the question, except in the saloon or second cabin. The privileged few on sailing ships also had fresh milk from the farmyard cow, while nursing mothers and weaned children in the steerage received a ration of reconstituted (tinned or powdered) milk. This was sometimes shared with others in the mess; but mothers had to drink their daily issue of stout or porter at the dispensary. A hopeful father once took his baby and joined the queue: 'You see, Sir, unless I have some stout I shall be obliged to wean this child' he explained to the surgeon (Cook 1883).

Despite claims from time to time that Queensland vessels were better provisioned than other emigrant ships, three-quarters of the dietary-related complaints referred to poor quality rations and food. If supplies were 'huddled together at the last minute', poorly secured or stored 'in a disorderly manner' in the hold or an overheated part of the ship, they were spoiled or ruined (see, for example, COL/A195:74–1153). Damaged provisions and food-stuffs rejected by dissatisfied immigrants amounted at times to what could only be described as 'shameful waste'. One surgeon failed to understand why people 'accustomed to hardship' should grumble (COL/A187:73–2064); but it required a certain level of adjustment to appreciate salt or tinned meat, hard biscuit and doughy bread. Nevertheless, immigrants generally recognized the difficulty of provisioning '400 souls on the wide ocean', and decided to 'put up with' the fare and supplement it from their private supply.

The meat and bread caused most of the grumbling, and this was not restricted to any one class. Second-cabin passengers on one voyage were refunded £5 for the fresh meat they did not receive (COL/A101:68–374). But who was to blame if some of the animals were lost overboard or died prematurely? Surgeons' reports clearly indicate why so many passengers were 'prejudiced against preserved meat': it was 'little better than carion', had 'a sodden appearance', was 'tainted', 'overdone, stringy and taste-less', and was 'not fit for pigs'. At one stage inquiries revealed that a defective curing process was at fault (COL/A76:66–510). Salt pork and compressed beef, on the whole, proved acceptable; and until refrigerated meat became a regular item of the dietary, fresh fish was the luxury. Apparently porpoise tasted like 'good beef', but dolphin tail soup was *the* delicacy. The bread could fail for any number of reasons – the baker, the ovens, lack of equipment, the flour or insufficient malt and hops. Occasionally salt water was inadvertently used instead of fresh. 'We are having our worst bread now the dough not rising, which caused it to bake sad; the loaves being half their usual size and as heavy as lead', Mellor Lumb recorded as he neared the journey's end (Lumb 1885). Sometimes the quality of the bread improved, but seldom was it 'wholesome and sweet' throughout. Inferior flour could affect all the baking. 'I think there is Plaster of Paris in it' a passenger complained to the surgeon (Blasdall 1862). Biscuit had to be used as a substitute unless it was 'mushy' or 'mildewed and maggoty' or the grinder refused to function. Criticism of other items was also not uncommon – rotten eggs and potatoes, poor quality cheese and rancid butter. The bully soup was once described as 'bad water made worse' (Blasdall 1862).

The dietary had to be adjusted if supplies ran low, were 'inedible' or unsuitable. By drawing on the substitute provisions and medical comforts, surgeons were able to accommodate the needs of children and the different religious and racial groups on board, or change the rations according to the weather and currently held views on energy requirements. At each port along the steamship route they supervised the purchase of meat, rice, fruit and vegetables. Rather than risk the 'fresh' meat at one port, the surgeon bought live sheep and had them slaughtered; the passengers enjoyed several dinners of Irish stew (COL/A566:88–9996). German vessels were frequently criticized for the scanty and often 'objectionable' rations issued to children. Even on the British ships it was felt that the older children needed more food, and that the little ones should not be given hard biscuit and other adult items. Some doctors therefore allowed more soups, milk and farinaceous foods for the younger children, while others insisted that adults, whose physical activity was so restricted, required fewer animal products (see COL/A358:83–1992). After 1881 increasing interest in this topic and the wider range of foodstuffs available meant that the scale was regularly modified and complaints were fewer.

Well-prepared rations could be tasty and 'nurishing', but mass production, monotony, substandard equipment, inefficient cooks and rough weather spoiled many a meal. Because of a shortage of baking pans on the *Scottish Hero* in 1880, immigrants had to use their dinner plates and wash basins (QVP 1880:II,397). If the cook was at fault, the surgeon or master might be able to encourage him to do better. On one voyage the quality of the 'Oat meel porrage' so improved that 'you would not think the same man cooked it' (Lumb 1885). However, problems persisted as long as the mess system remained and immigrants were partly responsible for the cooking. Although family and friends shared the duties whenever possible, very often total strangers had to work together. Some messes 'fell out' and regrouped, other functioned amicably; several elected and agreed to pay one of their members to take charge and cook for the duration of the voyage (see Anon 1883). Disagreements chiefly arose over the division of labour, ruined food and laziness, especially among the young men. Following the suicide in 1891 of a married woman who was travelling alone with her children to the colony and could not cope with shipboard life, particularly the mess duties and dietary, surgeons were instructed to check at each hatchway during mealtimes (COL/A669:91–9678). Despite individual tastes and the several difficulties, many immigrants were apparently satisfied and found minimal cause for complaint, except an expanding waistline. According to one of them, no one on board had 'gone any thinner, but nearly all . . . had to let their belts and waistcoats out an inch or two' (Lumb 1885).

'Purposeful' activity contributed as much to health and 'good order' as a dry berth, a full belly and agreeable companions. Apart from eating and cleaning, Queensland immigrants had every opportunity to turn their spare hours to good account. For mothers, at least, the days were fully occupied:

> 'We rise before six, get the children bathed and ready for school, and our bed folded up on hinges by half past seven; breakfast at eight. We wash our dishes, while the husbands sweep our floors, and we are all expected on deck by nine o'clock for the day. We have a free library, and read and chat till one – dinner time. Tea about five, then comes time for getting ready for bed our little ones.'

> (Hinshelwood 1963–64)

Only 13.6 per cent of the hundreds of comments relating to the various activities on board expressed dissatisfaction, and most of these involved the school. Without exception, teachers complained of a lack of 'educational space', equipment or books: 'I have had to move to about *six* different parts of the ship. It has been a mere system of make shifs [sic] from first to last during the voyage' bemoaned one of them (COL/A42:63–1629). Yet the school reports show that the children seemed to make satisfactory progress, despite distractions, disruptions (sickness, rough weather and ports of call), parental indifference and even opposition; children were taught in an open area, and parents sometimes kept back their older offspring to look after the little ones. Several teachers maintained that the shorter, punctuated steamer voyage made the effort a waste of time. Nevertheless, most schools reported a 90 per cent attendance rate, and the progress of some pupils was said to be 'amazing'. Ages ranged from three to fourteen years and classes from less than ten to more than sixty. The claim by one teacher that his school 'laid a good foundation for future learning' no doubt pleased officialdom (COL/A223:76–1572).

The long sea voyage was also intended to 'improve' the single women. Books were available from the school and library and the matron might provide instruction; but there is no mention of organized lectures and entertainment, apart from the occasional dance on deck during a tropical evening. Imagine the daily life in this compartment with upwards of a hundred single women, most of whom were aged 15–35 years, living in strict isolation, the young and innocent mixed with those who had 'seen life'. They cleaned, prepared meals, exercised on deck for a few hours, did needlework and chatted; once a week some of them looked forward to a visit from their relatives. The less regulated life for the single men often gave rise to boredom and mischief: 'Spent the evening nocking about the ship in search of some fun' ran a diary entry (Blasdall 1862). Many a schoolmaster abandoned the evening class for lack of interest, though Continental immigrants sometimes appreciated the opportunity to learn English. According to surgeons who had difficulties organizing lectures, 'it would have been but labour lost' (COL/A197:74–1558). Yet the response varied greatly. There was nothing more gratifying, reported Dr Scott, than 'to watch the grave, upturned, bronzed faces eagerly drinking in every syllable' (COL/A67:65–1307). In addition to the lectures – the topics ranged from first-aid to phrenology – debates, readings, discussions and sometimes a ship's newspaper added variety. The library seems to have been well used, despite some unsuitable volumes. Books attacking the Papacy had to be removed and several surgeons recommended that 'lighter works' and more pamphlets on the colony be included. As the period progressed, 'intellectual' activities became increasingly popular.

Each section of the vessel made arrangements for their own entertainment – with the surgeon-superintendent's approval. 'Innocent amusements' that had 'no demoralizing tendency' and were 'calculated to improve the moral tone and promote happiness' were encouraged (see COL/A360:83–2005). Diaries and reports describe how much immigrants enjoyed concerts, theatricals and dances, a brass band, a minstrel show or a choir. Athletics and games (even cricket) worked off excess energy and kept passengers warm in the southern latitudes (see Plate 12). There was something for everyone: 'We have had a jolly night tonight, there being songs, Dancing, Boxing & a Welsh Religious meeting and a Bible Class, all at once', Mellor Lumb (1885) recorded. He willingly obliged with his fiddle for either dances or hymns. Religious services frequently had to be cancelled because of the weather, sectarian rivalry or indifference. Several surgeons' reports complained of 'poor Sabbath observance', while others noted that the day was spent 'in the strictest manner' (COL/A79:66–1209; 241:77–3559). Passengers with little interest in religion but having nothing else to do joined in the services 'more from curiosity than the hope of gaining anything good for their Souls' (Blasdall 1862). Sometimes the only services held on a

Plate 12   Cricket match

voyage were during a storm or for a burial; informal Bible classes and meetings attracted more interest. This all points to a strong dissenter element and a resistance to organized religion, except among cabin passengers and the Irish Catholics. Since the colonial authorities saw no necessity for appointing a 'Religious Instructor', they did not hesitate to inform Father O'Grady when he requested remuneration for acting as chaplain on the *Rockhampton* in 1866, that 'no state aid' was available.[4] But at least one medical-superintendent believed that 'a clergyman's presence on board every ship carrying emigrants would be a great improvement' since 'morality and cleanliness – therefore health – go frequently hand in hand' (BMJ 1877:I, 574). One wonders how many surgeons felt comfortable in their role as moral guardian.

Much of the leisure time was absorbed with story-telling or gossiping, writing, mending, fishing, watching the changing moods of the sea or the sailors at work. The children, when not at school, had 'everything possible to amuse them' (Cook 1883). Some surgeons reported a trouble-free, 'pleasant voyage', with 'a feeling throughout the ship of contentment and cheerfulness' (COL/A376:83–6687); but most had their share of problems since the various activities, however beneficial, failed to eliminate gambling, thefts, intemperance and fighting. Thus the adult male passengers, while not welcoming the duty, recognized the need for keeping the night-watches. With all its limitations the voyage was, for many immigrants, 'the only long holiday . . . in their lives' (Blainey 1968:158). Some had been given 'flattering reports' of life at sea and were frankly disappointed; but others clearly enjoyed the experience though they grew tired of their confinement, the rules and duties, the same faces and the everlasting sky and water. As they neared the 'Promised Land', excitement mounted; the ship was scrubbed 'spic and span' and new arrivals donned their best clothes.

The frustration and sense of anticlimax can be imagined when the vessel had to be quarantined. If pratique was merely delayed to observe the development of symptoms, immigrants remained with the ship and went ashore daily 'for a run on the sand' (COL/A213:75–2453). Almost 60 per cent of the quarantine complaints related to deficiencies in the accommodation and provisions. Problems chiefly arose over who was responsible for the supplies – the government or the shippers. Facilities at each site along the coast remained less than adequate, with reports regularly reaching Brisbane of dilapidated buildings infested with white ants and damaged by cyclones, of over-grown, unfenced lands, and of the need for better tents, bedding and utensils. A few improvements were effected, but most northern stations had no caretaker, no jetty access and not even a small boat for ferrying supplies and equipment from the mainland. Moreover, poor communication with Brisbane left officials at northern ports in doubt concerning the law or how to act in specific circumstances. Should only the sick be landed and quarantined while the ship continued? Vessels were often delayed while awaiting instructions.

Conditions, though slightly better in Moreton Bay, were strained beyond capacity if more than one infected ship arrived at the same time. Problems with the anchorage slowed the process and passengers complained that they had to wade through mud and water to reach the station since the jetty was useless at low tide and constantly needed repairs. Each quarantine period produced a catalogue of complaints – make-shift housing and tents that afforded little protection, insufficient beds and bedding, primitive sanitation and polluted water, irregular supplies of food, medicines and disinfectants, hopeless cooking arrangements and difficulties isolating the sick. If the sheep (the next day's meal) went missing in the scrub, communication broke down with the mainland, aborigines attacked or a cyclone blew in, the situation could become critical. Mosquitoes and sandflies, and the destruction of infected clothing and bedding increased the hardships. Apart from having to cut grass to stuff their mattresses, the single men on one occasion had to remain in bed while their clothes dried (COL/A78:66–916). Understandably, the threat of quarantine was seen as an effective inducement for strict sanitation during the voyage.

The situation got so bad that even before the permanent station on Peel Island was complete, it had to be pressed into service. In 1878 a ship-surgeon submitted an urgent appeal for alterations and additions; the site was one 'huge water closet', with a single privy for each 'compartment', the kitchen could cope with no more than one family at a time, and improved hospitals, a luggage shed and an extension for the jetty were needed immediately (QVP 1877:I,980–81). Ten years later another surgeon complained of the filthy state of the station, a drunken caretaker and unfinished buildings. At least by then a disinfecting chamber had been installed, the cemetery had been relocated away from the water-holes and the single women's quarters had been enclosed with a six-foot high fence. For immigrants, the novelty of being on land again soon wore thin with the 'idleness and hope deferred'; as the weeks passed, tensions mounted. All too often as the epidemic was brought under control, new diseases appeared (see QVP 1876:II,1131). Nevertheless, every effort was made to keep to a routine, maintain order, isolate the sick and release the healthy.

Disembarkation produced its own problems if immigrants had to be mustered by lamplight or there was not sufficient police supervision. However, the final stage of the voyage, from the bay upriver to the town, was filled with excitement and relief. Townsfolk turned out to greet the new arrivals. An enthusiastic response to the new land provided a fitting conclusion to many diaries: 'Of all the paradises in the World, this is the Capital' declared one admirer of Brisbane (Cook 1883). The immigration depot with its spartan, sordid accommodation, tarnished the reception. Soon after the land-order system began, Jordan suggested that better facilities on arrival would improve the initial impression, but it seems his advice was ignored for, within a few years, the imperial government was investigating the situation (CO 386/76:383). Even as late as 1884, arrangements were 'beggarly in the extreme' (COL/A419:84–2304). Some 80 per cent of the comments relating to arrival in the colony complained of the reception facilities. A river punt, a rickety wharf or a long walk brought immigrants to wooden barracks, a converted warehouse or tents. Arrangements were similar for each port; so was the confusion over provisions and the lack of protection from intruders.

Abijou Good arrived with his family in 1863 and spent the first night at the Rockhampton 'depot' cooking over a bush fire and sleeping under the stars. They fared better than immigrants sent to the 'new' building twenty years later; this was 'the dirtiest place' with everyone 'huddled in . . . like so many cattle' (Anon 1883). For a time Maryborough's barracks had no privy and when one was installed, local residents complained of the 'offensive smell' (COL/A265:78–3776); water was not laid on until 1882. The following year, according to a newspaper report, 400 immigrants landed in Maryborough from the *Shenir* and were 'marched up to the depot two miles off in a drenching rain . . . the place was filthy and all alive too. Dirty mattresses were laid on the floor' (COL/A387:84–2686). Even in Brisbane, which received the majority of immigrants, the depot was far from adequate until the late 1880s. Two brothers in 1883 took one look at the building, found it 'worse than the ship', and went in search of lodgings (Anon 1883). One can readily imagine the state of affairs if several vessels arrived at the same time, or if there were sick and weakly passengers and pregnant women on board. Given the circumstances, it is remarkable that so few complaints were lodged against the depot wardsmen and matrons. If the labour demand was reasonable, new arrivals usually remained only a few days in the depot. Within twenty-four hours of the arrival of the *Beejapore* in 1863, 'the depot was visited by . . . people . . . who were in want of servants & by the time it was dark about fifty . . . had been ingaged. this was considered very good especialy as it was sunday' (Good 1863). It was only as immigration tailed off that facilities improved; the provision of a luggage shed at the new Brisbane depot was one such improvement. Throughout the period immigrants had suffered hardship and inconvenience because of lost or damaged baggage. Broaching and poor stowage en route was common, and problems increased when steamers began calling at ports down the coast. Compensation claims amounted to considerable sums, and in one instance the government withheld the second moiety payment (see COL/A380:84–891). Employment opportunities frequently had to be forfeited if luggage was overcarried or the unloading delayed.

New arrivals might also be delayed if they were called as witnesses in the official investigation of a voyage. The proceedings of 106 Immigration Board inquiries have been located; almost a half of these were held in the 1860s and dealt with a little less than one third of all immigrant voyages for that period; the proportion fell sharply in the following decades. Very few of the inquiries in the 1860s and 1870s involved voyages out of Hamburg, but the German records are far from complete. Moreover, the government probably recognized the limitations of this immigration and the problems with interpretation. However, they were determined to improve standards on British ships; the careful investigation of the first Black Ball vessels led to the introduction of the Queensland regulations, the enforcement of which formed the basis of evaluation for subsequent voyages with government-assisted passengers. In addition to the board inquiries and select committee investigations, specific arrangements and the system in general were debated in parliament. Such action reassured immigrants that they were protected and had a means of redress in the event of ill-treatment and substandard travelling conditions. Despite the occasional criticism levelled against them, immigration boards seem to have faithfully carried out their mandate. As a result personnel were dismissed or penalized and the Agent-General regularly received instructions to exercise greater control of the operation at his end; abuses were dealt with and shipping contracts were modified. The authorities believed, like Henry Jordan, that 'irregularities and imperfections' in the system could be remedied (QVP 1866:1045). A perusal of the British medical journals in the latter part of the nineteenth century leaves the impression that conditions on Queensland vessels were definitely superior to those for the transatlantic run.

Many of the complaints relating to voyage arrangements were clearly justified, some were ill-founded or over-stated, others revealed persistent problems; but their decreasing incidence together with the growing number of positive statements demonstrates that the management of vessels on the Queensland route gradually improved. This improvement, despite repeated discrepancies between the ideal and the actual, was fundamentally due to the government's unrelenting efforts to provide colonists in transit with the healthiest possible environment.

MORBIDITY

During the first Australasian Sanitary Conference in 1884 attention was focused on problems relating to morbidity and mortality on immigrant ships. Delegates agreed that 'every life lost upon the voyage and every person landed with a constitution damaged by disease entails a loss upon the community not easily appraised' (QVP 1885:III,487). The Queensland authorities shared this concern, for they were disturbed when a vessel arrived from overseas reporting unsatisfactory conditions, sickness and death. Where and why had the programme failed? Were the diseases and deaths preventable? What control measures had been applied and how effective were they? Answers to these questions stimulated continuing efforts to provide the best available health care on Queensland passenger ships. We have seen that conditions on these gradually improved during the colonial period, but was this improvement reflected in a healthier immigration?

Apart from the annual immigration returns and evidence submitted for select committee inquiries, the authorities made no attempt to collate and classify other relevant information contained in the official voyage reports. The immigration agent in his yearly report summarized and commented on details relating to new arrivals; the English Registrar-General issued gross emigration statistics for Great Britian; the Commissioners reported on voyages conducted by them, discussed the working of the passenger acts and noted developments in the colonies. But none of the statements on emigration from Britain or immigration to Queensland contained the detailed data available for landed populations. No official publication documented the age or cause of maritime deaths. Yet the vital statistics for Queensland's immigration were all there – in the voyage reports, the passenger lists and in the shipping records. The health officer noted crew and passengers who were ill at the time of arrival and the reasons for morbidity en route, and listed births, deaths and causes of death; the surgeon's report, a much fuller document, commented on the voyage arrangements and gave an account of passenger behaviour, sickness, births and deaths; the immigration agent was primarily concerned with the state of the vessel, but he often included valuable medical data; in addition, there were the quarantine reports. All this information could have provided a systematic, continuous assessment of immigrant health in transit. Apparently it was used solely to determine whether the regulations had been satisfactorily enforced. Any modifications therefore tended to be made on the basis of individual voyage reports rather than on a coordinated, quantitative overview of available data. The gradual improvement in conditions at sea and the quality of immigrants undoubtedly provided sufficient evidence for the viability of the system. Incidentally, passenger diaries mentioned various ailments and injuries, many of a minor nature that were never treated by the surgeon.

A fundamental difficulty lay in the fact that the morbidity and mortality lists did not conform to a consistent format. Furthermore, nineteenth-century nosological systems were based on symptomology related to the environment, constitutional defects, and disorders in a localized part of the body rather than aetiology; diseases were categorized in terms of descriptive evidence rather than a critical, objective analysis of their underlying pathology. For a greater part of the century, only a handful of diseases were recognized as having a specific causative agent; and the fact that diseases themselves were 'subject to . . . perpetual change' added a further complication (see Peter 1975:81–124). Classification schemes therefore reflected the divergence and confusion of current medical thought; but they provided a framework for examining the health of a community. The Farr system which was used for the registration of deaths in Britain was adopted by the new colony and retained until 1885 when a revised classification was introduced.[1] Although the change was considered necessary in the light of recent developments in medical science, it interrupted the continuous, comparative analysis of certain disease categories. Apart from this major revision, the system had been modified over the years and the list of diseases extended. For example, in 1869 typhus and typhoid fevers were officially differentiated. Yet as late as 1880 Queensland's Registrar-General noted that, in some of the returns, typhus, typhoid and infantile fevers were included under the 'typhus' heading (QVP 1880:II,149); changes took time to percolate through to the ranks. The problems associated with determining and applying a satisfactory nosological scheme were enormous.

Although the Farr system had been modified, its basic structure of five major categories remained unchanged. Zymotic diseases – those associated with an external cause or influence and therefore regarded as preventable – constituted Class I which distinguished four orders. The first, miasmatic diseases, included fevers and diseases such as measles, smallpox, dysentery and malaria which could reach epidemic proportions; they were thought to be caused by a specific contagion, a polluted environment (air, food and water) or both. The second order, venereal diseases, were acquired through contact with a known source of infection; the third, dietic diseases, represented disorders associated with a dietary imbalance such as scurvy and alcoholism; and the fourth contained diseases of parasitic origin, scabies and worms for example. Class II – constitutional diseases – had to do with internal factors or a 'predisposition' within the body. This class was something of a catch-all. Conditions such as gout, dropsy, cancer and mortification (gangrene) were contained in the first order, diathetic diseases; the second order included the tubercular diseases – scrofula in which the bones and lymphatic glands were affected, tabes mesenterica which involved the abdominal and peritoneal glands and was one of the most common disorders of early childhood, phthisis or consumption, and hydrocephalus ('water on the brain') which was seen as a consequence of tubercular meningitis. Class III represented diseases localized in the nervous, circulatory, respiratory, digestive, urinary and integumentary (skin) systems, in the joints and bones, and in the 'organs of generation' (these included only female disorders). Class IV listed developmental diseases under four categories relating to children, adults, 'old age' and nutrition; the latter included the convenient labels of 'atrophy' (wasting diseases) and 'debility'. Class V was divided into two sections; the first ('violence') had five orders – accidents or negligence, battle wounds, homicide, suicide and execution, and the second included conditions for which the cause was not specified or could not be defined – inflammation, 'natural causes' and 'visitation of God'.

The revised classification, by expanding and refining the old system, demonstrated the changing perceptions of certain disease entities and their aetiology. Class I, for example, became three separate classes – zymotic, parasitic and dietic. Although much of the old terminology was retained, this change together with the restructuring of the new Class I reflected a growing acknowledgement of the germ theory of disease causation. Zymotic diseases were grouped into six orders (miasmatic, diarrhoeal, malarial, zoogenous, venereal, and septic) according to their symptoms or the source of infection. A specific causative agent – disease-carrying 'miasms', 'seeds', 'germs' or 'microorganisms' which invaded the body from without – was recognized for each. Thus puerperal fever, formerly listed under 'childbirth' (developmental diseases), was transferred to the septic diseases category in the new scheme. Apart from ascribing a distinct aetiology to the parasitic and dietic classes, their content remained essentially unchanged.

By contrast, constitutional diseases presented no such clarity of definition. The absence of categorization and substantial revisions to this group suggest not only confusion, but a regression in medical thinking. Rheumatic diseases (gout, rheumatism, rheumatic fever, 'rheumatism of the heart', but not arthritis), tubercular diseases and other conditions such as rickets, cancer, diabetes mellitus and blood disorders, all thought to be generated by some 'bias' in the body, were included in the new Class IV, while dropsy (generalized oedema), tumours and gangrene were relegated to the class containing diseases with 'ill-defined and not specified causes'. Hydrocephalus, however, was grouped with disorders of the nervous system. Another factor which could have contributed to the uncertainty reflected in the new Class IV was an increasing awareness of the communicable nature of consumption. An article in the *British Medical Journal* of 1879 (II, 704–05), for instance, noted 'an alarming fatality' from phthisis among the aboriginal population of Australia since the arrival of the white man. Gradually, medical and lay opinion acknowledged that tuberculosis in all its forms was not only 'highly infectious' but could be transmitted from animals to humans (see, for example, QVP 1896:III, 1001). By the end of the century, its constitutional origin had been ruled out, and it was no longer fashionable to refer to persons of 'consumptive habits'.

Changing concepts of what constituted developmental diseases (the new Class V) produced a much shorter list containing only congenital and old-age disorders. Those associated with childbirth were transferred to a new order (diseases of parturition) created within Class VI – Local Diseases; and dentition (teething), the time-honoured diagnosis for many childhood ailments (see Maddick 1973 and QVP 1896:III, 1002–003), was reclassified under diseases of the digestive system. Conditions such as atrophy, debility and inanition (cessation of breathing or 'want of vital powers') were removed to the ill-defined diseases class; but paediatric disorders were not given a specific category. The list of local diseases was greatly expanded to include new orders relating to the special sense organs (ear, eye and nose), the lymphatic system, parturition and locomotion. Incidentally, diseases of the male generative organs were added to this section. The inclusion under digestive diseases, of sore throat and quinsy, formerly listed in the miasmatic category, may be regarded as a retrograde step. All forms of mental illness remained as diseases of the nervous system. Nevertheless, the generally improved definition and localization of disease highlighted the growing specialization within medicine. The new Class VII ('Violence') retained the original orders except for 'battle wounds' (the Queensland classification distinguished murder by whites, aborigines and other coloured persons). Finally, Class VIII included all conditions defying classification, but omitted the ill-defined causes of the old scheme such as 'visitation of God': aetiology had become more objective.

The new system, however, demonstrated persistent problems in medical theory and practice. Both the microscope and stethoscope had come into wider use, but the absence of diagnostic techniques regarded today as essential, meant that nineteenth-century nosological systems, of necessity, continued to rely on the observation of symptoms, the parts of the body affected or current theories. This subjective approach gave rise to considerable diversity of medical opinion. A germ theory of disease might seem plausible, but without actual evidence of the causative agent, the emphasis on the role of environmental factors remained; it was not until the 1880s that pathogenic bacteria were regularly isolated and demonstrated. Moreover, the success of sanitary science and public health programmes in the prevention and control of disease, particularly epidemic and contagious diseases, reinforced the environmentalist position. While it was generally believed that infectious diseases were the result of 'the contagion or seed, which is the external or exciting cause; and such a state of the body as renders it a fit ground for that seed to grow in, which is the predisposing or internal cause' (QVP 1885:III,486), effective public health reform was seen as the means to eliminate such 'seeds'. This view provided a rationale for the health-care programme on Queensland immigrant vessels. But there is no evidence that those responsible for the programme ever considered, for example, submitting the water supply on board to microscopic examination. The surgeons' reports indicate that, despite a growing awareness of the germ theory, they were almost all convinced miasmatists and sanitarians.

Although the officially accepted classification of the causes of death was subject to obvious limitations, the first colonial Registrar–General urged Queensland doctors to use the scheme, for 'to depart from it to suit the ideas of individual medical gentlemen, would be to sacrifice the . . . advantage of an unity . . . to the vain hope of drawing up a form that would please all, the subject being one in which perfect unanimity is impossible' (QVP 1861:873). The plea was repeated during the next twenty-five years until the introduction of the revised system which it was hoped would, in the 'new light of science', prove more acceptable to medical men (QVP 1885:II,560). Queensland ship-surgeons, however, were not required to follow a particular scheme when completing the Classified Summary Form or in their report of 'the number of cases of each disease' for the voyage. As a result, morbidity lists varied greatly. A few surgeons simply stated the total treatments and gave no further details; those familiar with the classification listed numbers for each category; some described the incidence of certain diseases, especially diarrhoea, in relative terms ('few', 'average' and 'numerous'), while others painstakingly recorded precise figures for each disorder.

For the purpose of this study, disease lists have been submitted to a scheme based on the revised classification but modified to accommodate the earlier system, both morbidity and the cause of death, and variations in the terminology used by the surgeons (see Table 11, p.355). This scheme outlines seven classes (parasitic diseases have been included in the zymotic class), divides constitutional diseases into three categories (rheumatic, tubercular and other) and does not allow a separate order for diseases of the special sense organs. Immigration morbidity lists rarely distinguished between crew and passengers, or cabin and steerage, though some reports noted the compartment or group among whom sickness most prevailed. Some 472 lists have survived. These, together with the twenty-one voyages for which the number of cases only has been recorded, cover 77.5 per cent of the immigrant ships, both British and German. Over the four decades 27,516 cases of specific illness were reported while another 6,613 were not given a diagnosis. In addition, 89 diseases were listed with a 'few' cases, 71 had an 'average' number, and 87 had 'numerous' cases. Although these descriptive cases cannot be included in the analysis of morbidity patterns, some attempt has been made to take them into account in the discussion.

The average number of treatments per voyage for each decade (85, 65, 35 and 3) must be viewed with caution since less than one-tenth of the voyages in the 1890s submitted a morbidity list.[2] Nevertheless, the figures suggest an improvement in health which accelerated after 1880. Dr Byrne saw 852 different cases during the voyage of the *Eastern Empire* in 1866, an average of 502 passengers and 5 crew members treated each week. He attended those confined to their berths once, sometimes twice, a day, paid two visits to the hospitals during the night, and not surprisingly suffered a breakdown in health. Yet there is a certain satisfaction in his remark that 'deaths were not in proportion to illness' (COL/A83:66–2611). In his report Dr Byrne noted 'the 93 cases of malignant measles' which produced 'venomous boils and eruptions' and isolated cases of smallpox and cholera. The health officer completed the list: 'Diarrhoea about 100 Dysentery 2 Hooping cough about 50 . . . Rheumatism 100 Typhus 2 . . . 1 Scurvy & cutaneous Diseases about 100. None infectious – Catarrh and Debility a large number [of] Emigrants having embarked in a weakly condition'; he also reported a woman suffering from acute mania after childbirth (COL/A83:66–2586).

Over the whole period, sailing ships registered 57 and steam 23 cases per voyage. The fact that steamers almost halved the passage time for sailing vessels would largely account for the difference. Nevertheless, the figures reflect a decline in morbidity, improved conditions of travel and rising standards among the immigrants. Contrary to expectations, German morbidity rates are less than those for British immigrant vessels during the first two decades; but there are relatively fewer lists for the German ships and it is possible that many cases of illness did not come to the surgeons' attention. Although a comparison of passenger and short ships is not feasible because of the very limited sample for the latter (a total of twenty voyages with thirty-six cases in all), the relative numbers involved indicate that there was much less sickness on short-ships.

Approximately 60 per cent of the cases with a diagnosis were zymotic diseases; the majority of these belonged to the diarrhoeal (51 per cent) and miasmatic (44 per cent) orders. Decadal variation for this class (69, 48, 55 and 64 per cent) reciprocally fluctuated with proportions for the localized diseases (19, 37, 32 and 24 per cent) which represented 28 per cent of the total morbidity. It must be noted that digestive system disorders accounted for half the localized diseases. Despite the potential hazards on board, only 3 per cent of the cases were due to violence, a similar proportion to that for constitutional diseases. Most of the remaining cases (6 per cent of the total) came under the 'ill-defined' category. Each of the different voyage types – sail and steam, British and German – show proportions similar to those for the several classes of disease listed above. Interestingly, only 9 per cent of the short-ship morbidity were localized diseases, while the constitutional class represented 8 per cent. Does this suggest firstly, that short-ship passengers were better fed than regular immigrants, and second, that tubercular patients set out on the longer sailing ship voyages hopeful of improving their health? However, the over-all morbidity pattern indicates that infection introduced at embarkation and the change in life-style and dietary were responsible for much of the sickness at sea. This becomes more apparent when disease frequencies are compared (see Table 10, p. 354).

Diarrhoea was the most common ailment. Apart from the 'numerous' cases, this disease represented 28 per cent of the specified morbidity, and was no respecter of persons, although little children seemed to suffer most. Nevertheless, the mean number of cases per voyage decreased over time – 19.5 in the first, 13 in the second, and 9 in the third decade; there was only one recorded case for the 1890s. In 1891, after his twenty-fifth voyage to the colony, Dr Hickling reported that it had been 'remarkable for the absence of diarrhoea of all forms' (COL/A660:91–6105). Measles held second place in the list of most commonly occurring diseases, accounted for 11 per cent of the morbidity, and also played havoc among the juvenile sector. Although measles was not as prevalent as diarrhoea, it persisted with little improvement, as the decadal means (5.1, 4.1, 4.2 and 1.0) indicate. The relative incidence for both diseases was higher on steam than sailing ships. Since a large part of the steamer route lay in the tropics, this favoured 'summer diarrhoea' and the spread of measles. Moreover, epidemics of the latter were common and particularly virulent throughout the nineteenth century.

Colic, constipation and 'derangements of the digestive apparatus', taken together, occupy third place in the list, but make up less than 5 per cent of the morbidity. They are followed by bronchitis and in fifth place, 'debility' which could have been the result of any number of ailments. Next in order are catarrhal affections, 'ship sore throat' (quinsy was often included under this label), whooping cough and the common cold, which was usually accompanied by 'chills' and coughs. If trauma such as fractures, dislocations, burns and scalds are added to 'wounds and injuries', they replace skin eruptions (herpes, impetigo, psoriasis and pemphigus) in the tenth position. Rheumatism and scarlet fever are next in sequence. However, attention must be drawn to menstrual disorders in fourteenth place since these relate to slightly less than 30 per cent of the total immigration. Typhoid (enteric) fever, abscesses, dysentery, phthisis (consumption), 'simple' fevers and remittent fever (one of the malarial category) complete the listing of the twenty most frequently occurring diseases. This list therefore allows us to consider a range of possible causative and 'predisposing' factors for sickness at sea – undetected infection at embarkation, climatic variation, close living, lack of bathing and toilet facilities, a questionable water supply, food preparation and restricted physical activity. If passenger and crew morbidity frequencies are compared, the differences are immediately obvious; 30 per cent of crew disability was due to trauma, with venereal diseases (9.7 per cent) next in order. The mode and sphere of operation for these two communities were separate and distinct.

Decadal and voyage-type variations reveal other patterns and hint at changing attitudes towards disease and diagnosis. For example, the omission of sore throats and injuries from the 1860s' list and of sore throats from the German list suggests that, in view of more serious complaints, these were not considered sufficiently important to warrant mention in official reports. On the other hand, skin eruptions are listed only for the 1860s and 1880s, and for immigrant vessels and steamships. These disorders undoubtedly related to poorer quality immigrants and their more cramped accommodation in the first decade, and to the higher temperatures for steamer travel in the 1880s. Seasickness, however, is included only in the 1860s' list. Could its effects have been exacerbated by the inferior shipboard conditions for this period? Passenger diaries and doctors' reports indicate that this malady inevitably accompanied every voyage; cases were usually so numerous that, unless complications developed, they were not recorded. Graphic accounts abound of the agonies of adjusting to the ship's movement, especially in bad weather. An immigrant in 1863 recorded how 'the wind increased & the sea boiled & foamed, the ship rolled & it became imposable to sit or stand on deck i became very sick & went below where i found every thing in the greatest uproar every one was fearfully sick . . . i may hear mention that the Dockter & several men who had been at sea several times before were sick' (Good 1863). Another wrote, 'it is not the being seasick, but the after effects of it, when you dont feel to care wether the ship goes to the journey's end or goes down' (Lumb 1885). A writer to the *British Medical Journal* in 1872 (I:328) aptly observed that, 'If a channel ferry scheme had occurred to Dante, he would doubtless have added another depth to his *Inferno.*' Some passengers looked the 'picture of misery' for the entire voyage; others remained unaffected. One young man who enjoyed watching his fellow travellers 'casting up accounts at the end of the day', noted that one of the pigs died 'through sea sickness' (Ricou 1872).

An assessment of the prevalence of 'fevers' on Queensland vessels highlights nineteenth-century problems with diagnosis and suggests further disease trends. For example, remittent fever was relatively common on German vessels whereas simple and non-defined fevers figured on British immigrant sailing ships, especially in the 1860s. Most surgeons seem to have differentiated between typhus and typhoid fevers though it is possible that a proportion of the non-defined fevers could have been classed as either one of these diseases. Typhoid fever and severe gastric disorders were particularly prevalent on German vessels; but digestive disturbances (colic and constipation) were more common on British ships. The reason for this clearly lies in the difference in water supply since typhoid fever is a water-borne disease. The government's insistence that immigrant vessels be supplied with 'pure and sufficient' water meant that the incidence of severe intestinal diseases was reduced on British ships. Thus the problems of adjusting to the shipboard dietary became more apparent. Menstrual disorders were also the result of altered circumstances. It was recognized last century that 'the more considerable changes in habits of life alter the methods of menstruation', especially in the case of a sea voyage (BMJ 1885:I,1212); but why these disorders should show a sudden increase from twentieth place in the frequency listing for the 1860s to ninth place in the 1870s is difficult to explain. Perhaps there was a link with the relatively greater number of cases of hysteria reported during the second decade. Also, menstrual problems do not appear in the lists for the last two decades or for German vessels. Possibly other more serious conditions demanded attention on ships out of Hamburg; and could it be that the steamer voyage was not as disruptive or distressing as the long haul under sail? There is a further anomaly in the morbidity pattern for the 1870s; this is the only decade in which phthisis (pulmonary tuberculosis) figures in the list (thirteenth place). However, the disease occupies eighteenth place in the steamship list. Complaints relating to selection and the embarkation inspection during the difficulties of the mid-1870s point to one explanation; the greater number of cabin passengers after the introduction of steamers suggests the other. Not only were cabin travellers exempt from inspection, but during the second half of the century, the long voyage, and emigration to the Antipodes were increasingly recommended as a 'cure' for consumption.

An article in the *Lancet* in 1863 (L I,163) asserted that sufferers from chronic lung complaints were often 'marvellously restored' by the voyage and a year or two of residence in Australia. The following year an immigrant to the colony described one of his companions:

'A convalescent consumptive patient
Four years he's been in hospital despairing of his life
Till all the Doctors told him emigration
To Queensland's more favoured Clime
Might prolong his life sometime'

(Bushby 1865)

Thomas Beaumont set out in 1870 on a 'constitutional' voyage to Australia after 'a severe attack of spitting of blood'; his physician believed that sea travel would be the only means of restoring him to health (Beaumont n.d.:1). In the mid-1870s, an 89 per cent improvement rate was claimed for patients availing themselves of such treatment; in the opinion of one medical man, it would be 'superlatively dangerous' to delay the voyage once destructive lung disease was suspected (BMJ 1876:II,360). While both the advantages and disadvantages of sea travel for chest diseases and chronic ill-health were frequently debated in medical journals of the day, no consensus for this fashionable prescription was reached, apart from the recognized benefits of a 'change' and the fresh air.

Minor surgical cases appear in two lists, for the 1870s and German ships, but they are not connected. In fact, only three surgeons mention such cases; others obviously recorded the complaint rather than the treatment. Dr Weddell on a voyage in 1877 performed sixty minor operations, and a German surgeon in 1870 reported that he extracted twenty-five teeth in addition to a number of catheter applications (COL/A233:77–373 and COL/A150:70–3133). Another disorder which occurs only in the 1870s' list is 'dentition'; but after this time, the marked decline in the reported cases probably reflects growing doubts concerning the morbid effects of this complaint. From Hippocrates to the middle of the nineteenth century, teething was associated with many early childhood disorders and, indeed, was retained until 1920 as a cause of death in the official classification (see Maddick 1973). The 1880s' list includes several diseases which require comment. For example, no cases of chicken-pox were registered in the 1860s, there were only twenty-seven in the second, but 127 cases in the third decade. Did the hotter voyage account for this? Eye diseases also occur only in the 1880s' list, though the average number of cases per voyage was slightly higher in the 1870s and 'severe opthalmia' was known to be prevalent along the Rhine during the 1860s (see COL/A70:65–2380). Mouth complaints – gum boils, stomatitis, ulceration – were another feature of the 1880s, but the incidence for these was relatively higher on German ships. Although the pattern for the 1890s is completely atypical, the cases which have been recorded show that infectious diseases (measles, smallpox, mumps, whooping cough) rather than shipboard-related ailments were the primary problem. This is the only decade in which mental illness appears in the list, but cases were noted throughout the period. Headaches sometimes received a mention, and given conditions at sea, must have been a common complaint.

Morbidity patterns for the first three decades reflect changing conditions of travel, but the relative incidence of two diseases in particular demonstrates the impact of introducing steamships to the Queensland route. While sporadic cases of cholera had appeared on sailing ships during epidemic times, it was not until December 1885 that a severe outbreak occurred. At the height of the 1866 pandemic, three cases were found on the *Queen of the Colonies* as passengers embarked in London; two died before they left the Thames, the third recovered, and there was no further evidence of the disease for the remainder of the voyage (ECR 1867:6). Almost twenty years later, the SS *Dorunda* coaled at Batavia (Djakarta) and within ten days the first cholera victim was reported. The disease spread rapidly and scores of passengers succumbed. This was a unique event in the history of the colony's immigration; it generated international publicity and became the subject of protracted parliamentary inquiry. Although the source of infection was never conclusively pinpointed, all Queensland-bound steamers for the next few years had to observe quarantine while coaling at Batavia (see QVP 1886:III,747–808). The fact that no other vessel was affected bears testimony to the effectiveness of protective measures adopted for colonial ships.

The other condition was heat apoplexy (sunstroke) and its sequlae. Reference has already been made to the intensity of the equatorial sun, the heat-absorbing potential of iron-hulled vessels, high temperatures near the boiler rooms of steamships, and climatic problems on the Suez–Torres Straits route. Although most diaries and journals describe the discomfort and distress experienced in the tropics, none can compare with Dr Cunningham's account of the passage through the Red Sea on the SS *Dacca* in June, 1886. As the temperature rose above 100 degrees between decks, he prepared for several cases of heat apoplexy, but conditions far exceeded his worst expectations. 'People . . . swooned away one after the other in all directions' and the decks were strewn with

> 'prostrate forms who with pale faces, naked bodies & out-stretched arms presented a spectacle of a collection of corpses . . . Any words of mine are simply inadequate to describe the sufferings both mental and physical of those 2 days & 3 nights . . . Scarcely *two* hours elapsed from the time of the seizure before the patients were corpses. The surface of their bodies was intensely hot to the touch. Power of deglution entirely suspended from the onset. The Pulse rising in a few minutes to 150 beats per minute, and sinking as rapidly as it rose. Whilst the clinical Thermometer registering 111 to 112 degrees of heat with evacuation by the patients of copious, black grumous motions . . . clearly indicated the fact that the lesion of some large blood vessel . . . had probably taken place sealing the patient's doom from the onset . . . No disease, is so sudden in its assault, or so brief in duration before fatal in its effects. It gives no premonitory warning whatever beyond . . . a feeling of lassitude, and a "queer sensation in the head".'
>
> (COL/A475:86–5780)

Dr Cunningham, despite his tough constitution and years spent in the tropics, suffered most severely with symptoms like those of 'fish poisoning – violent pumping of the carotid arteries whilst one's brain felt as if squeezed in an iron vice'. He was left with a 'general depression', unable to eat, sleep or take an interest in anything. Many immigrants over the years went through a similar experience in the very hot weather. Some died, others fully recovered, and a few were left with permanent 'mental impairment'.

The morbidity lists covered a wide range of conditions, and although only the most prevalent have been discussed, it has been possible to illustrate patterns of sickness at sea; the reports also contained information beyond a mere catalogue of ailments. Surgeons' comments relating to morbidity were as vague and limited or as specific and detailed as the lists. The format for their reports included sections for recording the stage of the voyage and the part of the vessel in which most of the sickness occurred; but the majority ignored these, assuming perhaps that the nature of the illness would provide the needed information. Hence, only 14 per cent of the specified diseases referred to a particular group of passengers. Of this number, slightly more than half involved children, 40 per cent were common to all compartments, 4 per cent related to the single women, and the remainder equally affected the married people and single men. This pattern at least suggests that children were the most vulnerable group afloat. Almost all (98.1 per cent) of the diseases developed at sea, a handful (1.6 per cent) of them were present on arrival, and only fifty-four cases were recorded in the quarantine reports. While a proportion of the latter were carried over from the voyage, much of the quarantine morbidity – bronchitis, pneumonia, diarrhoea, dysentery, sunstroke and injuries – may be attributed to conditions at the station. A centipede bite was definitely a new problem.

A total of seventy-eight vessels were quarantined. These were distributed over the four decades as follows:

	1860s	*1870s*	*1880s*	*1890s*	*total*
No. of vessels	20	24	31	3	78
% total voyages	9.1	7.4	5.7	1.3	5.9
% immigrant voyages	12.3	15.0	11.5	15.0	12.8

Almost a quarter of the vessels arrived with more than one contagious disease on board. Three ships in the 1860s and seven in the 1870s were German; this meant that the proportions (13 and 24 per cent) for German voyages exceeded the immigrant percentages. All three in the 1860s arrived with typhus, known as ship or jail fever, a lice- or flea-borne infection which thrives in overcrowded and famine conditions. Six British ships were detained for the same reason that decade; only four typhus-infected vessels were recorded for the 1870s, but the number may have been higher since the cause of quarantine is unknown for three of the German ships. After 1880 typhus fever does not appear in either the quarantine or morbidity lists – further evidence of improved conditions at sea and on land (see Cumpston and McCallum 1927:333–45).

By contrast, the number of vessels arriving with typhoid or enteric fever increased over the period – three in the 1860s, twelve in the 1870s, nine in the 1880s and one in the 1890s. It is possible, given the problems with classification, that some of the typhus vessels of the 1860s also carried typhoid fever. Since this disease is transmitted through contaminated food and water supplies, its continuing prevalence after 1880 was probably due to taking on fresh food and water at the various ports of call. In 1877 the *Windsor Castle* reported an isolated case of suspected enteric fever involving a fifty-four-year-old woman. The health officer insisted on quarantine, but the surgeon pointed out that her condition had been brought on 'by nervous anxiety & not by any hygienic defect or neglect' (apparently the problem was a colitis of psychosomatic origin). Moreover, because of his 'lively recollection' of living under canvas on Peel Island on a previous occasion, he believed it would be foolish to jeopardize the health of 400 passengers for the sake of this one doubtful case (see COL/A245:77–4536). The Central Board of Health was convened and overruled the health officer's decision; the vessel was admitted to pratique. This was yet another insult for the health officer, for only a few months earlier his decision had been countermanded when the *Western Monarch* was released before completing the prescribed period of detention; it seems that certain Board members had a vested interest in the ship's release (QVP 1877:I,969–94). At every level quarantine was fraught with difficulties (see Wilburd 1945).

Virulent measles, alone or in association with another disease, detained nineteen ships; all except two arrived during the 1860s and 1880s. Interestingly, only one of the vessels was German. Since the difference in voyage time from Hamburg and the British ports was insignificant, it is reasonable to assume that the disease which affected the Continental immigrants was less virulent. Measles, typhoid (enteric) and typhus fevers accounted for two-thirds (fifty-two) of the quarantined ships. Another thirteen arrived with scarlet fever, two with whooping cough and six with smallpox. The *Hannah More* reached the colony in 1865 in a healthy state; the smallpox cases this ship carried had been 'mild' and all had recovered. The four-day detention was a precautionary measure. On two other ships, only the crew had smallpox;

apparently it was not obligatory for seamen to be vaccinated (see BMJ 1871:I,289). Neither, it seems, was this required of Continental immigrants; in 1871 the *Shakespeare* arrived from Hamburg with sixty-six cases of smallpox (AMJ 1871:224). Diphtheria and chickenpox were also present on several vessels, four were detained with 'fever', and only the SS *Dorunda* was quarantined for cholera. Pratique was refused for two others in the 1880s, one because of malarial fever among the lascar crew and the second owing to a recent, severe outbreak of whooping cough. Although a number of ships were affected with this disease in the 1860s, the colonial authorities decided that quarantine was not necessary (see COL/A65:65–632); but in this one instance, it was deemed advisable that the passengers be kept on board for a week to bring the situation under control. During the last two years of the century, quarantine regulations and precautions were strictly enforced at all Queensland ports since the bubonic plague had reached the colony. However, none of the immigrant vessels was affected.

Officials responsible for recording immigrant health investigated possible reasons for illness, injury and the outbreak of disease at sea (see Plate 13). The fact that a 'cause' has been assigned to only a quarter of the cases suggests that the aetiology was unknown, self-evident, inferred or ignored. But the source of this information is limited, being largely dependent on a single statement by the health officer and an indefinite heading in the surgeon's report. Until 1886 the health officer, on the arrival of a vessel, put the following question to the captain or surgeon: 'was there any unusual state of the weather, which might lead you to suppose [the] existence [of disease] to depend rather upon atmospherical causes than upon specific contagion?' (QGG 1879:24,846). This was a somewhat leading question; its omission after 1886 reflected current developments in medical theory. The surgeon, in his report, simply had to state what he considered the 'supposed cause' of a particularly prevalent disease. Despite these limitations, aetiological patterns for immigrant illnesses are discernible.

The reported 'causes' for the whole period fall roughly into the following categories: the state of the weather (heat, cold, damp, climatic changes) and 'atmospherical' causes, 49.5 per cent; specific contagion, 8.6 per cent; diseases introduced at embarkation or during the voyage, 15.6 per cent; 'poor health' or the 'feeble' state of immigrants at departure, 5.3 per cent; polluted water and problems with the dietary, 12.2 per cent; poor sanitation and 'filth', 4.1 per cent; voyage conditions, clothing, neglect and other sundry causes, 4.7 per cent. This breakdown indicates that, although a specific causative agent was recognized for certain diseases and the germ theory was gaining ground, aetiology remained firmly tied to the environment. Since all the listed causes were external factors, most of them could be prevented or remedied. It is therefore not difficult to appreciate the colonial authorities' unrelenting insistence on better selection, careful inspection and strict sanitation, as well as their efforts to improve voyage arrangements.

A random selection of the 'supposed' causes of maritime morbidity reveals an interaction between observed facts, tenuous theories and insufficient diagnostic evidence. The health officer's report for the *Naval Reserve* in 1865 is fairly typical for the first decade. Sickness during this voyage was due to the introduction of measles and typhus at embarkation, wet beds, deficient ventilation, noxious fumes from a previous cargo of guano, the sudden change to cold weather after the tropics, and the great number of children on board (COL/A69:65–1890). That same year, the outbreak of typhus on a British vessel was attributed to personal uncleanliness ('bad habits of body') among the immigrants, their poor health and salt in the cargo (COL/A68:65–1771); yet a few weeks later, a German surgeon was at a loss to explain the great mortality on his ship since the cargo consisted mostly of bricks (COL/A69:65–2036). In the 1870s the cargo no longer featured as a cause of disease, but other 'predisposing' factors remained. For instance, an Immigration Board inquiry maintained that sickness on board the *Countess Russell* in 1873 could be traced to overcrowding the vessel with children, immigrants who were not 'cleanly' in their habits, defective ventilation, bad weather throughout the voyage, and an inefficient surgeon (COL/A186:73–2107). Occasionally a specific cause-effect relationship was noted: the deliberate short-supply of provisions on the *Kapunda* in 1875 was held responsible for the appearance of scurvy towards the end of the long voyage (COL/A215:75–3040).

Sometimes reasons for a healthy voyage were listed. Dr Rendle believed that freedom from disease on the *Queen of Nations* in 1876

HEALTH OFFICER'S REPORT. *"Charlie Palmer"*

QUESTIONS to be put by the Health Officer to the Surgeon and Master, or other Person in command of any Ship or Vessel arriving in MORETON BAY.

QUESTIONS.	REPLIES.
1. What is the name of the Vessel, and Tonnage?	Charlie Palmer
2. What is the Master's name?	C. Smith
3. Have you any, and what Bill of Health?	none
4. From whence did you come, and when did you sail?	Plymouth 2 Decr 65. arrived Moreton Bay anchorage March 18th ff. at 2 p.m.
5. At what Ports have you touched on your passage?	none
6. Did you receive any Cargo or Passengers at the intermediate Ports?	————
7. What is the nature of the Cargo, and the number of Officers, Mariners, and Passengers?	General Cargo 27 all told. —
8. What Vessels have you had intercourse or communication with on your passage, and from whence did they come?	none
9. What is the Surgeon's name?	Dr John North
10. Are you aware that any Epidemical, Contagious, or Infectious Disease prevailed at the place from which you sailed, or at any of the places which you have touched, or on board of any Vessel with which you had communication? If so, state where and when.	I am not

Plate 13 Health officer's report

QUESTIONS.	REPLIES.
11. In the course of your voyage have any Persons on board suffered from sickness of any kind, and what was the nature of such sickness, and when did it prevail? How many persons were affected by it, and have any of them died in the course of the voyage?	Monomania 1 Diarrhœa about 50 Dysentery ... 4 Bronchitis 1 Catarrh 16 Scald 1 Diarrhœa 2
12. What is the date of the last death, and the cause of it?	March 1st — Scald
13. How many sick have you now on board, and from what Disease?	1. Dysentery. Convalescent
14. If any of the Crew or Passengers have died during the voyage, state the nature of the Disease of which they died, and the date?	20 Feby Ellen Mahon Œt 43 probably 63 of Dysentery 1st March C. Wallace Œt 4y. Scald
15. Upon the appearance and prevalence of any Disease, was there any unusual state of the weather which might lead you to suppose its existence to depend rather upon atmospherical causes than upon specific contagion?	The Diarrhœa commenced as we approached the tropics The Catarrh as we got into the Southern Latitudes
16. Are you aware of any circumstances, during the passage, or at present, which would render it expedient to place the Ship and People in Quarantine?	I am not
17. How many Births have occurred during the voyage?	Males. — Females. None
18. To the correctness of the foregoing statements, are you ready to make declaration, if required?	I am

On Board the Charlie Palmer
Moreton Bay, March 19th 1866
11.15 am.

J H ___ M.D.

H.S. —

was due to a liberal dietary, good cooking, favourable weather, attention to his instructions and cooperation from the master and other officers (COL/A226:76–2300). He attributed the various 'trifling' ailments to a change in the 'mode of life', lack of exercise, want of cleanliness, a poor knowledge of food preparation and the bad bread. Dr Rendle also claimed that tonsilitis and sore throat resulted from breathing contaminated air, neuralgia arose from indigestion and foul odours, and inadequate care and attention by parents was responsible for 'wasting' among the children. Indeed, mothers were frequently accused of being 'bad nurses' and having no idea of 'the benefit of . . . pure air, cleanliness and warmth' (COL/A194:74–952). Others fed their sick offspring with anything from salt pork to plum pudding and dosed them with brandy and wine 'until the poor little things were drunk' (QVP 1883–84:1360). One surgeon had a difficult time 'preventing (parents) killing their children by exposure to sun, and wet Decks' (COL/A 449:85–9738). Particular problems were reported with Continental parents who, it seems, had little understanding of the basics of child-rearing and could not be persuaded or compelled to act appropriately (see COL/A324:81–4635). One Swedish mother allowed her new-born baby to become so filthy that the sub-matron had to wash and dress him each day (COL/A442:85–8098). Illegitimate children were sometimes smuggled on board; the surgeon of a German vessel found one such baby in a 'state of semi-starvation' hidden behind a berth (COL/A227:76–2426).

The detailed information in some surgeons' reports is as interesting as it is revealing. Dr Young in his carefully itemized account of morbidity on the *Glamorganshire* in 1874 outlined the problems he encountered and possible reasons for them (see COL/A195:74–1022). The 80 cases of diarrhoea, mostly among children, were traced to a change of water and food; the 12 cases of dysentery in adults arose from a similar cause; 28 children developed whooping cough associated with diarrhoea; a case of rheumatic fever was attributed to the damp atmosphere during heavy rains which caused the blood to 'deteriorate'; 14 cases of tonsilitis were due to 'quick changes in the climate' and two children became ill with simple continued fever for the same reason; 15 women, 13 of whom were single, complained of amenorrhea brought on by a change of habits and diet which 'unavoidably takes place in every ship'; an infant suffered from 'blood impregnated with syphilitic poison'; the one passenger with venereal disease was a person of 'dirty habits' and a case of psoriasis was described as a 'constitutional skin complaint'. There were four serious accidents, all resulting from falls, in addition to minor cuts, burns and bruises. Dr Young managed to 'replace the gut' of a baby with an umbilical hernia, but she died of 'debilitation' two months later. He clearly regarded disease in terms of the current miasmatic and constitutional theories.

A decade later, in 1882, Mr Paddle FRCS submitted a similarly detailed description of morbidity on board the *Southesk* (see COL/A337:82–2960). Measles and typhoid fever broke out almost simultaneously after a month at sea. He believed the former had been introduced at embarkation. Although he had refused a passage to a family with 'two measly children', they had mingled with other immigrants and the disease first appeared five days after passengers had access to their luggage for the first time. But he had no positive clue about the origin of the typhoid. According to the germ theory, it could have been brought on in the same way as measles; yet he had no doubt that defective ventilation between decks and the smell of fomenting beer from casks which had burst in the hold were 'precipating causes'. These factors were also said to be responsible for the many cases of sore throat. Mr Paddle maintained that the great amount of sickness among the children was due to germs passed on from unwashed napkins and bedding; whooping cough 'originated . . . from the children sitting immediately under the ventilators . . . and from their . . . running about on deck in wet boots'. Most cases of diarrhoea occurred in the tropics and were the result of the passengers 'sleeping at night without any protection to their trunks, and being thus chilled by the lower temperature of early morning'.[3] In other instances, it 'could be traced to excessive drinking of water or their food' which was often improperly cooked. The 'closeness of the 'tween decks . . . and the exposure of the patients to draughts while perspiring' caused tonsilitis, and 'damp and cold' brought on bronchitis; two cases of Bright's disease (a kidney complaint) were seen as a complication of measles; a case of haematemesis (vomiting of blood) was 'vicarious to menstruation'. Mr Paddle treated patients with tuberculosis, venereal disease, hysteria, ophthalmia, skin eruptions, 'numerous boils', scabies, scalds and abscesses as well as extracting thirty to forty teeth. He accommodated the germ theory within the traditional paradigm of disease causation.

Their reports indicate that surgeons, by and large, followed a similar approach; they recognized a specific contagion for certain diseases, but related most of the sickness to shipboard arrangements, climatic conditions, the number of children, the passengers' health at embarkation, their lack of commonsense, ignorance and 'uncleanly habits'. Immigrants also recorded their ailments, most of which they associated with their living conditions. In fact, there is a remarkable similarity between the professional and lay attitudes to disease. Apart from seasickness, injuries and accidents, immigrants listed 'heartburn', colic and 'inflammation of the bowels', 'liver complaints', fevers, sunstroke, measles, toothache, 'violent colds' and sore throats. One blamed the 'unpalatable' water; another ate 'too freely' of pickled cabbage; and the lad who left off his 'drawers and flannels' trying to rid them of lice, believed this resulted in his 'bad cold' (Anon 1883). Sickness was seen as an abnormal condition requiring some kind of intervention. The young man who tried several remedies to stop his vomiting declared that he was 'proper sick of being sick' (Lumb 1885).

A breakdown of the suggested causes for the twenty most prevalent diseases sheds further light on medical opinion and immigrant attitudes. Seventy per cent of the cases of diarrhoea were attributed to adverse climatic and atmospheric conditions, and 25 per cent to bad food and water. Dr Taylor saw a connection between the two; he believed that frequent changes in the drinking water on steamships had 'a tendency to render one more susceptible to climatic influences' (COL/A432:85–5686). However, Dr Barry, one of the Commissioners' surgeons, was an exception; as early as 1864 he maintained that both diarrhoea and typhoid fever were due to 'a specific contagion taken on board' (COL/A59:64–2605). Most of those who noted a cause for typhoid fever placed the blame with 'germs' and filth. On the other hand, dysentery was regarded largely as a dietary problem. Surprisingly, more than half the 'digestive derangements' (colic, nausea, etc.) were related, not to the diet, but to the climate; several surgeons observed that colic and constipation increased during rough weather (see, for example, COL/A582:89–5824). Another was convinced that the 'colicky and diarrhoeal symptoms' which broke out after leaving Batavia were the result of 'malarial atmospheric conditions'; there could be no other explanation since he had purchased no fresh fruits and the food and water on board were 'quite good' (COL/A396:84–5342). Throughout the period attention was directed to the quality and quantity, rather than the nutritional value, of the rations. The water supply must surely have contributed to enteric disorders far more than was suspected. On the *Scottish Hero* in 1880, the condenser broke down, the privies began to smell and 'diarrhoea then prevailed to an alarming extent' (QVP 1880:II,397); the smell, not the contaminated water, was held responsible.

No one doubted that measles was an infectious disease, yet climate and poor health at embarkation were listed as the cause in 20 per cent of the cases. It usually broke out soon after departure, but on at least two voyages did not appear until the vessel had been at sea for more than a month. Both these episodes were related to the immigrants having access to their luggage for the first time; some admitted they had come from a measles-infected area (see COL/A338:82–3192 and COL/A337:82–2960). Apparently the disease was endemic around the London docks; in 1876 it proved singularly fatal to seamen owing to 'complications with intense catarrhal inflammation of larynx and trachea, broncho-pneumonia, and albuminuria' (BMJ 1876:I,452). Similar complications were reported on several Queensland voyages. Apart from a few whooping-cough cases associated with poor ventilation, both this disease and scarlet fever were acquired through contagion or 'introduced at embarkation'. Most cases of consumption were established before the voyage; bronchitis, catarrh, coughs and colds were wholly attributed to the weather, and so were most of the sore throats, although defective ventilation was recognized as a contributory factor. Climate was also linked with the majority of debility and rheumatism cases, atmospheric influences gave rise to simple fevers, and many of the passengers with remittent fever had the disease or were in poor health at departure. While menstrual disorders were related to a changed life-style, some of the cases of menorrhagia (excessive flow) were definitely the result of induced or spontaneous abortion. Abscesses and a small proportion of skin eruptions were generally connected with indifferent health, but a lack of personal hygiene accounted for 90 per cent of the latter. The major shipboard diseases therefore resolved into three major aetiological categories – infection, 'constitutional' problems and the maritime environment.

Almost all injuries sustained at sea came under the last category. Potential hazards were legion, even in calm weather – an open, unprotected hatch during coaling or bringing up provisions from the hold; narrow companionway ladders, sometimes without handrails; poorly secured bunks; unguarded machinery or a slippery patch on deck. A child lured into the rigging, fell; another caught her foot in the rudder wheel and sustained a compound fracture; a woman tripped on some loose-lying ropes, suffered a severe head injury and lost the sight of an eye; many slipped down ladders and steps; a passenger was hit by the main top-mast stay-sail sheet, thrown against the bulwarks and remained unconscious for 'several days'. On a voyage in 1865, one of the lifeboats came adrift, killing one immigrant and disabling two others. An Immigration Board inquiry found that the accident was due to 'wilful neglect'. The Black Ball Line compensated both the injured, the captain was prosecuted and imprisoned under the passenger act, but there was no acknowledgement for the family of the deceased (COL/A69:65–2247). Fights, pranks and 'incidents', especially among the single men, frequently resulted in injury. The sleepwalker who tried to climb into another's bunk and rout its occupant had his head gashed open (Anon 1883); the lad whose hammock was cut down as he slept was badly bruised (Blasdall 1862).

The number of accidents multiplied quickly during a heavy swell or stormy weather. One of the single men listed those who were injured in his compartment as the vessel tossed about – the first fell and hurt his back, the second had both eyes blackened, a third had his finger amputated when a door slammed shut on his hand, and a fourth was knocked down and 'nearly had his eye cut out' (Anon 1883). J.P. Ricou described the 26 June, 1872 on the *Indus*: 'just before six this evening a tremendous sea came over damaging the ship's hospital making a severe wreck among the physic', a patient was 'carried right out of his berth by the water', the cook was thrown about, his assistant had his head cut open, and an old lady was twirled around the deck 'like a cork'; a broken skylight admitted 'tons of water' and the falling glass inflicted serious wounds (Ricou 1872). On another voyage an immigrant wrote home: 'several have been very badly scalded when the ship is rolling they slip down sometimes with boiling Soup or Tea, two or three have fallen down the Hatchway. there is scarcely a day passes without some slight accidents' (Cook 1883). Scalds and burns, sprains and strains, cuts and bruises were so common they rarely reached the surgeon's report, but fractures of the skull, back and limbs as well as dislocations and head injuries required prolonged medical attention. Much of the trauma involved upper extremity fractures, many sustained, no doubt, as the hand extended to break a fall.

It is possible that seasickness, despite its agonies, prevented further accidents; at least the sufferer was rendered immobile. Because of the vast numbers afloat last century, this complaint received regular coverage in the medical and popular press. Journal articles posited a range of aetiological theories from the purely mechanical to the esoteric. Some medical men held that either hyperaemia or anaemia (an excessive or reduced blood supply) of the brain and spinal cord was responsible; others related the malady to the sympathetic (involuntary) nervous system or 'a certain impression on the senses'; and there were those who accepted a 'constitutional' or even psychological explanation, having observed that men of 'good physical development' and people with 'strong heads' were rarely affected. The role of the imagination was fully explored. One Queensland passenger maintained that the smell of paint between decks aggravated the problem (Acton 1889). Whatever the cause, few would dispute the observation that the 'focus of discomfort [appeared] to be not the brain but the solar plexus' (BMJ 1872:I,328). The 'unpleasant circular movement' as the vessel pitched and rolled reminded one suffering immigrant of 'the merry-go-rounds at the fairs' (Hume and Fowler 1975:140). Try as they might, no one produced a fool-proof explanation or remedy for seasickness.

Fortunately, other ailments responded to measures for controll-ing sickness at sea. Having discussed morbidity on Queensland ships and the possible reasons for it, we may now assess the preventive and remedial action taken to keep immigrants alive and healthy during the voyage. In the first place, there was selective screening. This applied only to assisted immigrants; but the second measure, medical inspection at embarkation, was intended to check the health of all steerage passengers. From time to time, both procedures fell short; not only did immigrants arrive for departure ill-clad, diseased or with obvious physical defects, but the examination was often described as a 'farce'. The medical officer of a vessel taking navvies to Queensland in 1866 described them as physically inferior, 'loafing scamps'; at least thirty had syphilis (COL/A79:66–1494). Sometimes a local practitioner signed the medical certificate knowing the candidate was unfit, though not infrequently he was pressurized into this by the patient who wanted to emigrate to improve his health or by a family who was determined to be relieved of an unwanted member. Several surgeons at embarkation detected passengers with infectious disease or other defects and refused them a passage, but the outbreak of epidemics at sea indicated how many cases had been missed and how impossible it was, with the limited time for inspection, to ascertain whether immigrants were carrying the 'seeds of disease'. On a bounty vessel in 1883 the surgeon was allowed only four and a half hours to examine 618 people (QVP1884:II,632). Even by the end of the century, the time allotted was 'hardly sufficient' (QVP1900:V,653).

Delegates to the 1884 Sanitary Conference recommended a procedure that would not only determine if passengers came from an infected area, but would also provide for their complete isolation (QVP 1885:III,495). The scheme, however, was not feasible since it required time and improved facilities. When ship-surgeons were questioned about immigrants who should never have been passed, they invariably pointed out that the inspection was public and cursory and allowed opportunity for little more than checking a person's tongue and vaccination mark. Although a florid rash, a high temperature or an obvious physical disability could be detected, single women even in the late stages of pregnancy managed to conceal their condition. As the *Young Australia* was about to sail in 1866, Dr Syme noticed that one of the emigrants was in a 'maniacal state' but was too busy to deal with him (COL/A83:66–2524). A similar situation occurred on another voyage when an assisted passenger was allowed to embark with terminal consumption; he died en route (COL/A168:72–964).

In 1876 an article which called into question the whole system of medical inspection at embarkation and made particular reference to the Queensland emigration, appeared in the *British Medical*

Journal (1876:II,636–37). Two ex-surgeons of the colonial service responded. The first maintained that the system was satisfactory; although there had been no depot when he took charge of a vessel in 1866, he had been allowed sufficient time for inspection (BMJ 1876:II,844). The other surgeon, who incidentally had been dismissed from the service for criticizing the quarantine arrangements, agreed with the original article. Only a few months earlier he had superintended a ship from London where there was no depot and immigrants had to fend for themselves in the cold and snow; they were mustered and examined on the poop deck shortly before departure. Under such circumstances, Dr Harricks asserted, few questions would, or could be asked. He therefore regarded the provision of a 'properly fitted' building with an isolation area as an urgent necessity; here emigrants could be housed and inspected, together with their outfits, and take a compulsory bath (BMJ 1877:I,574). Although departure facilities improved, neither the Plymouth depot nor the Blackwall Home made arrangements for bathing or isolation. In fact, the inspection procedure changed little over the period, possibly because upgrading it would be too costly; moreover, the standard of emigrants was rising. An additional precautionary measure was introduced for steamships: immigrants were prohibited from going ashore or purchasing goods from bum-boats at the coaling ports.

Dr Harricks had also been a ship-surgeon with the transatlantic emigration, and despite his criticism of the embarkation arrangements, he conceded that 'the regulations on board Queensland ships regrading morals, discipline, and dietary, [were] almost perfect'; he recognized the government's determination to provide a healthy environment during the voyage (BMJ 1877:I,574). Such provision extended beyond prevention to the control and treatment of disease. The lime-juice was checked at embarkation and issued to passengers as soon as they entered the tropics; several surgeons recommended a daily allowance for the entire steamship passage. According to the records only twelve cases of scurvy or 'scorbutic affections' were reported for the whole period. Most of these occurred in the 1860s and possibly related to poor health at departure rather than any deficiency in the supplies (the only exception was the *Kapunda* in 1875). Dr James Gardner who worked for the Commissioners, the Queensland government and the coolie emigration during the 1860s and 1870s claimed he 'never saw a single case of scurvy' among the passengers in his care. But on a coolie ship when symptoms (swollen and bleeding gums, feverishness and a measles-like eruption) appeared, he immediately distributed lime-juice and within seven to eight days, the symptoms 'had all abated' (BMJ 1878:II,844). This evidence was intended to defend the use of lime-juice as an antiscorbutic, since a number of medical men continued to doubt its efficacy and recommend alternatives (see, for example, BMJ 1878:I,177). For years the theory persisted that an excess of salt in the blood from a salt-meat diet, rather than a lack of fresh fruit and vegetables, gave rise to scurvy (see BMJ 1867:II,413) – hence the concern with a salt cargo. Queensland surgeons apparently never questioned the provision of lime-juice and faithfully administered it during the 'hot' stage of the voyage.

The medical comforts were essential for both the prevention and treatment of disease, but these supplies generated considerable complaint. Doctors were occasionally guilty of misappropriating the 'stimulants', despite the precautions of a dual control of the storeroom key and a written counter-check for each issue; and there was always the problem of broaching by passengers and crew. On one vessel the medical comforts were kept in a poorly partitioned section of the hold and it was all too easy to bring up the wine with the coals (COL/A210:75–1662). Sometimes they were stored with the regular rations or were inconveniently located. Surgeons often reported unsuitable items. Apart from the medicinal alcohol (porter, stout, sherry, gin and brandy), the special supplies included oatmeal, arrowroot, barley, sago and tapioca, dried soups, meat extract and preserved chicken, mutton and beef, condensed milk, loaf sugar and vinegar, as well as methylated spirits, hops, marine and regular soap, and 'quick lime'.

More than 60 per cent of the comments relating to the medical comforts were critical of one or more of the items, though a small proportion (9 per cent) remarked on their excellent quality. Complaints of a shortage became less frequent and usually followed a protracted voyage or an epidemic; sometimes captains made good the deficiency from the ship's stores. Surgeons were known to distribute the supplies 'injudiciously' or use them as a substitute for spoiled food, despite their intended use as a dietary supplement, a preventive and a remedy, or to accommodate climatic changes. Beef tea, soups and rice were issued in the tropics or salt meat was replaced with preserved mutton and chicken. Dr E. Goodridge maintained that the absence of diarrhoea among the children was entirely due to the special diet of boiled rice, milk and arrowroot he prescribed for them (COL/A412:85–377); while another surgeon attributed the passengers' health to his careful administration of the medical comforts 'when anyone showed any symptoms of weakness' (COL/A61:64–3275).

Poor quality or a limited supply of stimulants featured regularly in the complaints. According to one doctor, if the alcohol was to be used for 'medicinal purposes only', then it ought to be the best quality. 'Peculation', leaky casks, burst bottles, and an unusually high demand, but rarely under-rationing, accounted for any shortage. Milk was also a problem, often being bad, inferior or insufficient. Some surgeons asked that a cow be included with the medical comforts; others reported that good quality, un-sweetened, preserved milk, mixed with water, tasted like the 'real thing' and was often preferred to stout. The cereal products, soups and meat extracts apparently gave satisfaction, but 'condensed eggs', issued in lieu of fresh ones which quickly went rotten, had a mixed response. Several reports suggested that the medical supplies be adjusted for each voyage according to the number of children, pregnant women and nursing mothers on board, or increased for steamers because of the longer periods in the tropics; a few recommended a complete revision of the list. In 1870 Mr Wigg noted that 719 of the 800 lb of loaf sugar remained at the end of the voyage. Would it not be better, he urged, to replace this item with tea and double the quantity of milk which was 'of great value during and after seasickness, and for children', and in most cases, was of more use than malt liquor or wine? (COL/A140:70–1255). Other suggestions included the substitution of flour and fresh meat for rice and oatmeal, the addition of preserved turnips and an increase in the amount of meat extracts and soups. However, one doctor reported that lying-in women grew very tired of the 'everlasting beef tea' (COL/A157:71–1944). Several surgeons strongly recommended additional facilities for carrying ice on steamers, once its 'paramount importance' in the tropics was recognized.

The medicines also came under constant review, with requests for improvements in the scale, quality, and conditions under which they were prepared and dispensed. Although shipping contracts stipulated that a 'proper dispensary' to house the medicine chest be fitted up for the surgeon's use, the practice on many vessels was to appropriate a portion of the male hospital or the doctor's cabin for the purpose. Sometimes the area allocated proved useless because of its inconvenient location, limited space or poor lighting and ventilation. Trying to compound remedies and attend to out-patients in a cramped hospital ruled out private consultations; female passengers had to be examined in their berths. A dispensary wedged between the bathroom and a privy remained dark and damp; if it was situated over the boiler room and steam pipes, it understandably became 'very hot'. A few were flooded with the slightest sea, or the porthole could not be opened. During heavy weather one surgeon had to work in six inches of water; another described conditions in the 'hole' provided for him as 'unbearable'. Access to the dispensary on steamers was often crowded with saloon servants. On the SS *India* in 1892 the 'surgery' was located 'in the middle of the deck space for cooks, sailors, and firemen', with the galley on one side, a large steam pipe at the door and the condensing machine underneath; 'The ordinary temperature in warm weather ranged from 98 degrees – 110 degrees making it impossible to remain in it without great discomfort' (COL/A718:92–14666).

The effect of such conditions on the medicine supply can be imagined. Occasionally, the chest was insecurely fixed and the jars were fitted with corks instead of glass stoppers or contained rancid ointments and adulterated drugs. Complaints reached a peak in the late 1870s when it was discovered that the medicines had not been obtained, as directed, from the Apothecaries' Hall in London. But, unlike German surgeons who were supplied according to the Hamburg law, British doctors rarely had to resort to the captain's medicines or provide their own. Nevertheless, they submitted suggestions for improvement. The Queensland government had adopted the 1855 scale recommended for emigrant vessels and continued its use even after the new *Pharmacopoeia* of 1866 rendered certain drugs obsolete; other drugs were considered entirely unsuitable. Mr Wigg FRCS was sufficiently concerned with the deficiencies to send the Colonial

Secretary a seven-page revision, pointing out, for example, that 2 oz of chloroform for every 100 adults was insufficient for even one operation (COL/A141:70–1255). That same year Dr Doudney reported (COL/A145:70–1993) that, although the chest contained enough croton oil (a powerful laxative) to supply the colony for five years and the equivalent of 172,800 doses of hydrochlorate of morphia, there was 'not one drop' of chlorodyne (a gastric sedative). Other surgeons registered the need for increased quantities of specific items to deal with colds, constipation and diarrhoea, bruises, tapeworms and 'lousiness'; many regarded the new scale for passenger ships issued by the Board of Trade in 1875 as totally inadequate in the event of an epidemic. Ten years later, two of the permanent surgeons felt compelled, in the light of their experince and recent developments in medical practice, to present the government with an updated and 'suitable' list of drugs (COL/A422:85–3355).

All British emigrant vessels had to be supplied with medical stores – bandages and bed pans, sponges, phials and syringes, splints and water-proof sheeting – and a case of surgical instruments to supplement those provided by the surgeon (see ISS 1875:70–1). As usual, there were complaints and requests for more bandages, a small stove for boiling water and preparing invalid foods, or water cushions for patients with bed sores. One surgeon listed the following omissions – bottles, corks and test-tubes, belladonna plaster and cotton wool, small tooth combs, carbolic soap, an infant's feeding bottle and a fine mesh strainer; he also asked for adhesive cement to repair broken articles (COL/A226:76–2300). It was, however, impossible to anticipate all the medical needs of 400 people, so the government, guided by current practice, allowed a reasonable range of essential supplies, leaving it to individual surgeons to adapt and improvise. Yet many of them had to work under trying conditions, often with facilities stretched beyond their limits during a severe outbreak of disease.

Hospitals were intended to isolate infectious cases and accommodate lying-in women, but frequently fell short of requirements; they accounted for the largest proportion (20 per cent) of the complaints relating to the outfitting of vessels. Since immigrant ships, in theory, carried only healthy people, provision for the sick was kept to a minimum. The consequences of this were summed up by the adviser to the New South Wales government in 1883:

> 'Even under the most favourable conditions as regards accommodation and dietary, and the most skilful medical supervision, there can be no doubt that a large number of people crowded together within the narrow limits of an immigrant ship are especially liable to suffer severely when disease of an infectious nature breaks out amongst them; and this liability is increased tenfold when, the provision for the isolation of the sick being inadequate, it is necessary to treat such cases in their ordinary bunks amongst the healthy passengers.'

(QVP 1885:III,551)

Many Queensland surgeons would have heartily agreed with this statement. For the same reason they condemned the 'pernicious practice' of placing the hospitals between decks, contrary to the regulations, especially if deck-houses were available. This was a perpetual problem in the 1860s, and although the situation improved in the next decade, the practice was reintroduced on many of the steamers. Dr Dunkley suggested fitting out a lifeboat in which isolation cases could be nursed (COL/A494:87–1041). There were no sick-bays on some of the early German vessels, but this was probably better than what passed for a hospital on the *La Rochelle* in 1862. The space allocated for this purpose was not divided from the general compartment and had no light or air: 'A more wretched place . . . to consign a person to even in health cannot be imagined' commented the immigration agent (COL/A32:62–2065).

Even when hospitals were on deck, they might be so located that the surgeon was exposed to all conditions reaching them; hot water pipes passed through some; others adjoined the bakehouse or were built above the boiler-room. On the SS *Roma* in 1883, deck hospitals were situated over wells which had to be sounded at regular intervals (COL/A369:83–4939). To gain access, one might have to pass through the second-cabin compartment, a berthing area or, in one instance, an 'extremely offensive' water-closet (COL/A207:75–807). On steamships, there were problems with noise from the steering apparatus and coaling; patients were covered with coal dust, stifled behind closed doors and ports, or had to be moved. Doctors also objected to the practice of placing the lying-in section near the single women, often with little or no screening; they certainly did not approve of adjoining male and female hospitals, especially if the dividing bulkhead had to remain incomplete to allow ventilation. The most suitable arrangement, at least for sailing ships, seems to have been a well-constructed deck-house which accommodated both hospitals separated by the dispensary. No such consensus was reached for steamships, though most agreed that infectious disease should be isolated on deck. Cases of smallpox and typhoid fever were usually sent ashore at ports en route and picked up by a later vessel (see, for example, COL/A711:92–11747).

Poor ventilation and lighting or lack of protection from the elements meant that some hospitals were virtually useless. On one ship, children with measles had to be nursed on the open deck because of leakage from the condenser. On another, the floor of the maternity ward was constantly awash with 'contaminated material' from a defective privy; the surgeon was amazed that none of the new mothers developed puerperal fever (COL/A361:83–2693). Some hospitals were unbelievably cramped, totally inadequate or lacked the most basic amenities. A 'disgraceful' six-foot cube served as one lying-in ward, while another with three beds (one was occupied by the nurse) had to accommodate five women, all delivered about the same. On one occasion when the despatching officer was questioned about the facilities, he pointed out that a 7 ft 6 ins by 10 ft cabin containing four bunks in the single women's compartment was almost double the legal requirements (COL/A494:87–1041). Presumably the male sick-bay on the *Corlic* in 1875 (see diagram) was also within legal limits. It had no porthole, housed two infectious patients and functioned as a pharmacy and an out-patients' department (see

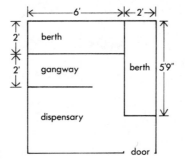

COL/A207:75–807). The four-bed male hospital could not cope with the needs of the 376 men on the SS *Nuddea* in 1883, so the captain organized another four beds in a temporary structure on deck (QVP 1883–84:1356,1359). Bunks were usually two feet wide and varied in length from four to six feet. After one vessel set sail, it was found that the swinging cots provided for the hospital were too large. Sometimes the portable privy was not supplied or the toilets were inaccessible. One surgeon suggested each hospital should have a hip bath, but it is difficult to imagine where such an item would be kept or used.

With this limited accommodation for the sick, medical officers were well advised to concentrate on preventive measures and establish a satisfactory health regime from the outset. Many had to work hard to enforce strict sanitation, encourage passengers to make the most of the fresh air, and regulate the dietary to suit all classes and conditions on board. On earlier vessels the disinfecting and antiseptic agents – Condy's fluid, carbolic, chlorinated lime and 'sulphur bombs' – were reserved for controlling an outbreak of disease. When scarlet fever appeared on the *Gauntlet* in 1877 shortly after leaving London, the surgeon decided to put into Plymouth where the two affected children and their families were landed and the emigrants removed to a hulk in the harbour while the vessel was thoroughly fumigated (BMJ 1877:II,598). As the period progressed, disinfectants were applied more and more as a preventive, and by the 1880s were used daily on some vessels. Extra precautions were taken following the cholera episode in 1885; Dr Woodward described, how on the SS Dorunda's next voyage, he brought every passenger on deck after leaving Batavia and had the vessel 'fumigated throughout with chlorine gas and sulphur fumes and afterwards limewashed the between decks' (COL/A468:86–4384).

Whatever their specific effect, the smell of the chlorine, sulphur and carbolic would have emphasized the need for cleanliness and forced immigrants up on deck. As the *Scottish Hero* neared the colony in 1883, Mrs Cook was impressed with efforts to keep the ship healthy:

'they are expecting two more deaths . . . but one thing I do hope . . . we shall not be kept in quarantine. Every morning the doctor and two constables come round and examine all the bunks, and scatter disinfecting powder, and fluid all over the place, for they say there is every sign of sickness especially as we are going to the two extremes from cold to heat. Our diet has been changed a little every day there is boild tapioca served out, and about three times a week the children have boiled rice, with eggs & milk in it . . . in the place of salt beef we get fresh meat . . . Yesterday we were all marched up on deck at 11 o clock, and the whole place was covered with brimstone & sulphur, the hatchways were closed as soon as the fire was put to it . . . it was opened about an hour after and the smoke came out like a chimney. today it smells so sweet I cant believe any sickness can come now.'

Disinfection was also an integral part of the treatment for infectious disease. The usual procedure with measles, for example, was to isolate the patient in hospital, throw his bedding overboard, fumigate the berth and thoroughly wash and disinfect or destroy his clothing. When scarlatina and diphtheria broke out on the SS *Taroba* in 1889, the surgeon immediately isolated those affected, destroyed their beds, linen and clothes, fumigated with sulphur between decks and 'hung cloths saturated with carbolic' around the sick bay (COL/A569:89–238). The demands on the medical officer during an epidemic could be very great indeed. On certain voyages 'parasitic troubles' and 'lousiness' required constant attention. A passenger on the *Scottish Admiral* in 1883 described the treatment meted out to some of his fellow travellers:

'There is several Irish men lousey so we told the doctor & he had their beds thrown away & they put in the hospital by themselves & all their hair cut has close to their heads has possible . . . they look just like monkeys they have took away their clothes so that they cannot come out.'   (Anon 1883)

The single men's compartment was then sprinkled with chloroform which may have killed the 'live stock' or made them easier to catch. All immigrant fittings on a quarantined vessel were either thrown overboard or burned, and the ship, luggage and cargo were fumigated. Passengers and their effects at the station underwent a rigorous routine of washing, airing and disinfection. Methods ranged from 'simple exposure to the sun and air' to the use of elaborate disinfecting chambers which required a degree of competence to operate. In one instance, when instructed to fumigate a man's clothing, 'attendants popped the gentleman himself into the chamber' (QVP 1885:III,527). The records suggest that controlled heat was the most effective method, and that over the years, clothing and bedding were often unnecessarily destroyed.

Despite sanitary progress, 'the art of therapeutics' in the second half of the nineteenth century remained 'almost stationary' (quoted in Villiers 1962:131) and offered a very limited range of specific preventives and remedies – vaccination for smallpox, lime juice for scurvy, quinine for malaria and mercury for venereal disease. Yet sickness demanded a 'cure' and doctors, unsure of the aetiology, could only treat symptoms. Unfortunately, medical logs have not survived, but the list of medicines (see ISS 1875:68–70), a few surgeons' reports and immigrant memoirs provide a general picture of the curative phase of health care at sea. The shippers tried to comply with a surgeon's request for additions or changes to the medicine chest which was stocked with a basic selection of drugs to deal with common shipboard ailments – astringents for diarrhoeal complaints, laxatives for constipation, purgatives and emetics for a 'good cleaning out' and a variety of remedies for sore throats and respiratory affections. There were poultices and plasters for use as counter-irritants, anti-inflammatory and anti-spasmodic drugs, analgesics to relieve pain, sedatives, antiseptics, ointments for skin diseases and linaments for bruises and sprains. Chloroform was widely used as an anaesthetic. With the instruments and equipment available, a surgeon could perform minor and major surgery and handle difficult obstetrical cases. They carried out procedures ranging from a tooth extraction to the removal of a uterine tumour; but lacerations, fractures and amputations usually exercised their surgical skills.

Doctors seem to have followed a conventional, conservative and commonsense approach. Mr Paddle detailed some of the remedies he used on the *Southesk* in 1882 (COL/A337:82–2960): measles responded to a diaphoretic mixture (induces perspiration) plus a diet of milk and beef tea, but in cases complicated with bronchitis, Dover's powders (opium and ipecacuanha) proved most effective; astringent powders, a mixture of sulphuric acid and opium or, in certain cases, Dover's powders seemed to be the answer for diarrhoea, although the substitution of preserved meat for pork apparently reduced the number of cases at the height of an outbreak; 'small doses of stimulants, with arrow-root or beef tea soon restored the worst cases [of seasickness] to health' and when all other remedies failed, he found 'a mixture of acid Hydrocyanic dil, sp. ammoniae arom. and Bismuthe carb. was useful'. However, the patient with typhoid fever and an abscess at the base of his tongue died, despite attempts to save his life with a laryngotomy.

There seemed no limit to the combination of drugs and remedies. Apart from Dover's powders, a variety of other opium-based treatments were administered for diarrhoea and dysentery. One surgeon applied hot fomentations and alternated castor oil with a mixture of powdered chalk and opium to alleviate colic associated with diarrhoea and vomiting (COL/A462:86–2742). A young lad in 1862 described how a dose of the doctor's 'favourite Salts which he would give for each and every complaint' relieved his vomiting and constipation (Blasdall 1862). An immigrant arrived in 1892 in a 'very weak state' suffering from 'dyspepsia' which had failed to respond to treatment – 'an alkali mixture of soda and emetin' and a light slop diet (COL/A718:92–14712). The invalid diet was prescribed for most illnesses, but could be carried to extremes. A poor lass with a sore throat complained bitterly after nine days on a regimen of tapioca pudding and beef tea (COL/A384:84–1831). The remedy for a case of scurvy in 1883 did not fall into the 'slop diet' category: 'the fellows teeth are all loose' recorded a passenger, 'and he is to eat raw potatoes to get them firm' (Anon 1883). Potatoes, incidentally, are a source of vitamin C.

Stimulants and external massage were administered to cholera victims during the 1885 epidemic since the disease was characterized by severe cramps and a 'collapse' of bodily functions. Cases of mental illness – delusions, mania, melancholia and imbecility – were regularly reported throughout the period; doctors drew attention to the need for a lock-up or some other means of restraint. Remedies for trauma were also recorded. A sprained ankle was sensibly treated with a wet bandage and elevation of the foot; a severely lacerated forearm which the surgeon considered amputating responded to 'Wine Quinine and Porter' (COL/A88:67–532). Was the treatment imbibed or applied? Prescriptions for seasickness were legion, ranging from champagne to Worcester sauce, though the profession seemed to favour bromide of sodium (a mild depressant) and rest in the recumbent position. Nevertheless, the only 'real remedy' was 'to remain on land' (BMJ 1883:II,270). Self-medication was common; passengers took with them their favourite or recommended nostrums – mustard plasters to alleviate 'inflammation of the bowels' and nausea, magnesia to relieve seasickness and peppermint to aid digestion. A married woman who had a 'fit' was soon 'put right' with vinegar (Ricou 1872); another immigrant, after several days of professional treatment, took some of his own 'composition' and found this did 'more good than all the doctor's stuff' (Lumb 1885); but the outcome is unknown for the man who, in one dose, swallowed twenty Beecham's pills as a preventive for cholera (QVP 1886:III,757). Clearly the body's defences played a major role in recovery from disease and injury; and medication, from whatever source, had as much a palliative as a curative effect.

Morbidity patterns and efforts to deal with disease and injury on Queensland immigrant vessels not only shed light on difficulties with medical theory and practice in the second half of the nineteenth century, but demonstrate why the colonial authorities persisted with their programme of prevention. Much of the sickness related directly to specific infection and the maritime environment rather than constitutional disorders, and therefore points to the relative effectiveness of selective screening and the embarkation inspection, despite complaints about both. Moreover, the decreasing incidence of disease as the period progressed, reassured the government and those involved with health care that, although there was always room for improvement, the underlying principles needed no change and should, at all times, be strictly enforced.

PATTERNS OF BIRTH AND DEATH

Queensland's immigration service developed in response to better organization and communication, tighter controls, a faster and more spacious means of travel with increased amenities, the establishment of a permanent and reliable staff of surgeons and matrons, and rising standards in the merchant marine. Immigrant health also improved. Were officials aware of the impact of these developments? The record they kept of how many survived the voyage and the numbers born en route would have been one indicator of how the system was functioning; but there is little evidence that any attempt was made to analyse these vital statistics. If births and deaths and causes of death at sea are examined with reference to the several facets of immigration – age, sex and nationality, vessels, voyage arrangements and passage times – certain patterns emerge which provide a definitive evaluation of immigrant health and further demonstrate that a complex of factors rather than a direct cause-effect relationship determined the outcome of the health-care programme.

In addition to those listed in official returns, some 214 births and 190 deaths have been located.[1] Many of these were infants who were born and died at sea. Such births did not affect the numbers embarked or the final payment and were apparently disregarded; yet they are an integral part of the health status of immigrants and must be included. On the other hand, the 257 lives lost in the wreck of the *Wilhlemsburg* in 1863 have been excluded since only five of the survivors finally reached Queensland by an indirect route (see COL/A51:64–652), and their inclusion would distort overall patterns. However, the fact that no other lives were lost through shipwreck certainly contributed to the satisfactory survival rate for Queensland vessels. According to the final totals (see Table 5, p. 349) 1,643 infants were delivered live at sea or in quarantine between 1860 and 1900, and 3,299 souls died. This means that 99.3 per cent of the numbers embarked in the United Kingdom and Hamburg landed in the colony; the proportion increased from 98.6 in the first to 99.9 per cent in the last decade.

Although vital statistics for any population include marriages, it is not surprising, given the shipboard arrangements, that only a few took place en route to Queensland. Apart from the surgeon whose marriage to one of the single girls during the voyage created a stir among Brisbane officials, the other nine all involved cabin passengers. However, the age distribution of the immigrants and the length of the voyage were such that a relatively high birth rate could be expected. During the 1860s and 1870s, births represented 1.09 and 0.95 per cent of all who embarked compared with the 0.40 and 0.03 per cent for the last two decades. The dramatic decline between the first and second half of the period clearly related to the shorter steamship passage; but the number of births varied greatly from one voyage to another. The record goes to a German vessel, the *Lammershagen*, in 1873; seventeen babies (eight male and nine female) were added to the 382 souls who embarked – 4.45 per cent of the passenger complement. Only nine were born during the ninety-four days at sea; the remainder arrived while the ship was in quarantine for another forty-three days. Births outnumbered deaths and 386 new colonists finally landed; the voyage as a whole registered a birth rate equivalent to 179.9 per 1,000 of the population per annum.[2] This is a remarkable record compared with the Prussian birth rate of 39.6 for 1873 (see BPP 1901:xv,135). The closest contender among the British vessels was the *Naval Reserve* in 1865; her birth rate of 101.8 was almost three times that for England and Wales for the same year (see BPP 1901:xv,125). Thirteen infants were delivered at sea and a fourteenth, born in quarantine, did not survive.

Apart from the 1,643 live births, 36 still births have been located in surgeons' reports, shipping logs and immigrant diaries. This number represented 2.1 per cent of all births, and was probably much higher. The proportion fell from 3.1 per cent in the first decade to 1.1 per cent in the next and rose to 1.9 per cent in the 1880s when reporting was more complete; there were none in the 1890s. The sex of a third of them has not been specified, but of the remainder, 13 were males and 11 females. Still births were apparently of little consequence: 'a married woman gave birth to a child still born it was thrown overboard the same night' recorded a passenger on the *Indus* in 1872, sixteen days out at sea (Ricou 1872). Two more still births occurred during the same voyage, both to single girls. Other records hint at similar trends. Surprisingly, the authorities did not require further details of these or illegitimate live births. Perhaps the frequent reports of 'doubtful' and 'objectionable' characters among the single women sufficed. Doubtless, a percentage of the abortions, 'flooding' and menstrual problems recorded in the morbidity lists related to illegitimate pregnancies.

Immigrant birth rates, despite fluctuations, show an overall decrease for the four decades. This trend is also evident, but to a lesser extent, for the populations of the sending and receiving countries (see BPP 1901:xv,125,135 and QVP 1901:II,1265). Between 1860 and 1900 the annual rate for England and Wales per 1,000 of the population dropped from 34.5 to 28.7 with a high of 36.3 in 1873. Similarly, Prussia fell from 38.6 to 36.1, reaching a peak in the mid-1870s. For Queensland the decrease was more marked, from 47.9 in the first year of the colony to 30.2 in 1900. The falling birth rate was common to all the Australian colonies and had been 'regular and persistent since 1885' (see Coghlan 1904:179). In Queensland it was attributed to the depression of the 1890s and the cessation of state-aided immigration which aimed at introducing women of child-bearing age. In fact, the situation was seen as critical by the mid-1890s; officials deplored the tendency among European and American parents 'to avoid the trouble and responsibility attending the rearing of offspring' and hoped that such notions would not gain a 'substantial hold' in the colonies (QVP 1895:III,304). Apart from the decline, the birth rate pattern for Queensland immigrant vessels bore little resemblance to the landed populations; differences between each shipment – numbers, length of voyage, and regulations – produced marked variations in the crude annual birth rate.[3] Indeed, the contrast between vessels subject to the passenger acts and short-ships is so great that it needs no further elaboration. Rates for German ships, by and large, far exceeded those for British immigrant vessels of the same period and reflected the greater fecundity in Prussia.

By determining annual percentages for births at sea relative to the numbers embarked it is possible to compare the British emigration and the Queensland immigration for the period under consideration. Emigration rates also show a decline, but they remain considerably lower than those for the colonial immigration (see Table 6, p.350). The discrepancy must be largely attributed to the British records which were often incomplete and did not include quarantine births and deaths. Moreover, calculations were based on the annual outflow rather than individual voyages and ignored such variables as the passage time. Thus a comparison of the two patterns is virtually meaningless.[4] The only similarity between the immigration, the British emigration and the landed populations was the gradual decline in the birth rate. However, a more useful comparison emerges from the immigration itself when births are related to the number of married and single women of child-bearing age, 15 to 44 years inclusive (see Table 6). The adjusted rates for the 1865–67 period seem excessively high, but may reflect the relaxation of regulations at this time in order to induce as many people as possible to sail for the colony. Incidentally, the increased colonial birth rate immediately following the boom periods of immigration in the mid-1860s and the early 1880s would have assured the authorities that the expenditure had, to some extent, been justified.

Details of the infants born on Queensland vessels reveal further patterns which appear unique to the immigrant population.[5] Of the 98 per cent for whom their sex is known, 49.2 per cent were males and 50.8 per cent were females. The proportion of females was 50.7 per cent in the 1860s and 51.4 per cent in the 1870s; numbers equalized in the 1880s, and the three births in the 1890s were all girls. By contrast, the sending and receiving countries as well as the British emigration consistently recorded more male than female births. The male percentages for Queensland fluctuated around the 51 per cent mark and were slightly higher than those for England and Wales, but were more in line with the emigration figures. In his 1891 report, Queensland's Registrar-General noted that it was 'an acknowledged fact in all parts of the world' that a 'much larger' proportion of male than female children were born (QVP 1892:II,687). This peculiar excess of female births for the Queensland immigration is difficult to explain; at least it was a step in reducing the male–female imbalance in the colony. However, the majority of multiple births were males. Of the ten sets of twins, one (a male and female) was still-born; for those that survived, six were males, one was female, another was bisexual, while the sex of the last is not known.

Some attempt has also been made to distinguish first births. In view of the government's preference for young married couples without children and the interval between application and departure, one would expect a number of young wives to be advanced primigravidae at the time of embarkation. Records for the 1860s are limited and there are only three births in the 1890s, but figures for the intervening decades show the relatively high incidence of such births and the effect of the passage time. More than a quarter of the infants born live during the 1870s were first children, while the proportion dropped to approximately one-tenth in the 1880s. On sailing voyages, expectant mothers usually had to accept the vessel they were offered; but with the regular, more frequent schedule and shorter voyage time for steamships, women in the advanced stage of pregnancy were strongly advised not to travel until after their confinement (COL/A563:88–9303). This would have also contributed to the lower birth rates after 1880.

A small fraction of the births (2.6 per cent for live and 5.6 per cent for still) took place not at sea, but during quarantine. The latter environment, though more stable, was perhaps more questionable. Infants born on sailing ships represent 85 per cent of all births (live and still) and 0.99 per cent of the total number embarked on these vessels. The proportion for steamships (0.26 per cent) illustrates the effect of a shorter voyage on an already declining birth rate. The decrease was more gradual on sailing ships, from 1.11 per cent to 0.78 per cent between 1860 and 1890, compared with a drop from 1.18 to 0.03 per cent for steamships over the four decades (there were only seventeen births on steamers in the 1860s and 1870s). An analysis of live births relative to the voyage types highlights the effect not only of steam travel, but also of the regulations under which vessels sailed, as Table 9.1 demonstrates.

Table 9.1   Birth rates: percentage of totals embarked

vessels	1860s		1870s		1880s		1890s	
	sail	steam	sail	steam	sail	steam	sail	steam
British immigrant	1.1	1.2	0.9	0.4	0.8	0.3	–	0.0
German	1.5	–	1.5	–	–	–	–	–
short-ship	0.4	–	0.1	–	0.3	–	–	0.0

The birth rates for ships covered by the Queensland regulations and the Commissioners were similar, but exceeded those for privately-organized vessels; this pattern maintained for the first three decades. The fact that the colonial government preferred to assist young married couples would contribute to the higher rates; private ships, not bound by this consideration, usually carried a larger proportion of single men.

There can be no doubt that fertility patterns and the relatively greater number of married people (see Chapter 2) account for the high birth rates on German ships. This situation would have added to the degree of crowding and discomfort during the voyage. As far as can be determined, all infants born on German vessels drew their first breath in a steerage or 'hospital' bed. Birth percentages for the total immigration indicate that the steerage rate was almost four times that for cabin passengers; fewer and older married couples and women whose husbands had gone ahead to the colony travelled in the better class. At least sixteen British babies were delivered in the less cramped conditions of a cabin while the remainder, like their Continental counterparts, often had to battle for survival under decidedly difficult circumstances. More than 10 per cent (188) of them did not reach the colony.

The new-born infants who died open a window on the health of Queensland immigrants. Male babies had the lower survival rate; 88 per cent of the male births lived, compared to the 89.5 per cent for female babies. Although these proportions gradually improved from 87 to 88.9 per cent for males and from 88 to 91.1 per cent for females during the first three decades (all three in the 1890s survived), the figures suggest that in transit, both the male foetus and new-born were most at risk. Five per cent of the deaths occurred in quarantine. These were confined to the first half of the period; but the proportion rose to almost 10 per cent in the 1870s when the greatest number of vessels were detained. Babies born on steamers seem to have fared better, with a survival rate of 92.6 per cent compared to 87.8 per cent for those delivered under sail. In fact, the percentage of new-born deaths on sailing ships in the 1880s was not only twice that for steamers, but reached its highest level for the period. This apparent reversal of the over-all pattern relates primarily to better documentation for this decade. It is meaningless to compare immigrant and short-ships since only two new-born deaths have been recorded for the latter. Most short-ships registering a birth carried a surgeon, an arrangement which seems to have been made with the anticipated delivery in mind. The survival rate for live births on passenger sailing ships leaving the United Kingdom during the first two decades was 87.5 per cent, while the corresponding figure for German vessels was approximately 90 per cent (88 per cent in the 1860s and 91.5 per cent in the 1870s). This is somewhat surprising given the conditions under which Continental babies were born. Perhaps they were more lusty than British infants; yet the more likely explanation lies in the recording of such deaths. The survival rate for cabin (81.2 per cent) compared to steerage (89.3 per cent) births is also unexpected; but this comparison is distorted by a very small cabin sample (three of the sixteen babies died). On the other hand, the results may suggest 'constitutional' differences between classes and nationalities.

Considering the less-than-ideal environment to which new-born infants were introduced, it is a wonder so many lived; the instinct for survival was strong. The first baby born on the *Selkirkshire* in 1882 was 'a very tiny mite', but he lived and thrived (Thomson 1882). The following year Dr Ford-Webb reported, with understandable satisfaction, that the two-and-a-half month premature baby he delivered and which weighed only 2 lb at birth was still alive and well when they reached the colony (COL/A403:84–7126). A healthy birth, especially the first on a voyage, was usually a cause for rejoicing and celebration. The first for the *Erin-go-Bragh* occurred appropriately on St Patrick's day and the baby was baptized 'Patrick' before it was announced she was a girl; but everyone seemed happy with the compromise of 'Mary Patrick' (Blaikie 1980:11). Many babies carried evidence of their birthplace through life; all nine, male and female, born on the *Beausite* in 1863 were given the name of the ship.

Records which reveal the other side of the picture also suggest why more than 10 per cent died. Mrs Cook, writing to her mother in 1883, was aware of the problems: 'The first baby that was born gets on very well, the next one died in three weeks, and now there are five waiting, daily expecting to be carried off into the Women's Hospital. It is laughable, for there are only 3 beds, & one of them is for the nurse. They are kept there a fortnight, so that is not bad' (Cook 1883). Official reports detailed the unsatisfactory conditions for parturient women – leakage from an adjoining bathroom, the smell of a nearby privy, insufficient accommodation, and on steamers, the disturbance of the steering mechanism and the discomforts of coaling. After inspecting the *Renfrewshire* (a bounty vessel) in 1884, the immigration agent declared that the lying-in hospital was totally unsuitable and that the two occupants of this dark, ill-ventilated cubicle between decks were 'to be pitied' (COL/A380:84–774). On a voyage in 1863, the female hospital could not be used because of the 'offensive odour' from a syphilitic patient (COL/A45:63–2372). For one reason or another, women were often confined in their berths. Apart from the restricted space, limited ventilation and lack of hygiene, there might be noisy children and sick passengers in the vicinity; a difficult delivery or a storm at sea would make the situation intolerable. Several women went into labour while suffering from seasickness and births were frequently recorded just prior to landing; one mother had to be confined as immigrants were trans-shipping in Moreton Bay. The most dramatic birth occurred within twenty-four hours of the wreck of the *Netherby* in 1866. As soon as passengers were safely landed on King Island, a shelter of branches and canvas was hastily erected to serve as a maternity ward; a healthy little girl arrived and both mother and baby did well (COL/A82:66–2231).

The outcome was not always as favourable. A total of thirty-two maternal deaths (1.95 per cent of the live births) have been recorded, with the proportion falling from 2.6 per cent in the first to 1.8 per cent in the third decade. Disorders associated with childbirth – post-partum haemorrhage, undilated os uteri, etc. – accounted for 53 per cent of the deaths and puerperal fever for the remainder. Two of the mothers were single women; in one instance the baby was immediately adopted by a married couple on board. But the chances of survival for any neonate whose mother died were slim, especially if a wet nurse was not available. Pressures on pregnant women and new mothers were often very heavy; in addition to difficult conditions of travel, inadequate lying-in facilities or indifferent health, they often had to cope with other children, some of whom fell ill and died during the voyage. One family lost their two children, and it was only after the birth of the third that the father became 'more cheerful' (Cook 1883). A particularly sad incident in 1863 involved the death of a mother and her new-born infant shortly before arrival. While at anchor off Moreton Island, a burial party went ashore, the boat was caught in squally weather and the husband drowned (see Foote 1977–78:45). The situation could be critical for a father left with the responsibility of a young family, including a new baby.

The highest proportion (34.6 per cent) of new-born deaths was attributed to prematurity. This figure reached 43.5 per cent during the 1880s when it represented 2.14 per cent of the total immigrant deaths for that decade. The problem was not unique to the maritime population; both England and Wales and Queensland reported a similar increase.[6] It was believed that mothers did not take sufficient care of themselves during pregnancy (see Weedon 1898:122). At sea, it was more likely that adjustments to shipboard life, the effect of the ship's movement and particularly seasickness contributed to early labour (see BMJ 1885:I,1212). The constant vibration of steamship engines may have been an additional factor after 1880. The remainder of the deaths, apart from the 6.4 per cent with no specified cause, cover a wide range of disorders. Inanition ('want of vital powers') accounted for 15.4 per cent of the deaths. This label seems to have been a convenient diagnosis for infants who simply ceased breathing, often within a few hours of birth. Also included were 'wasting' diseases like debility, atrophy, exhaustion and malnutrition (15.5 per cent); bronchitis and pulmonary affections, especially collapse of the lung (9.1 per cent); convulsions and spasms (7.4 per cent) and enteric problems – diarrhoea, dysentery, enteritis, 'inflammation of the bowels' and colic – 5.3 per cent. Since married couples shared a 6 ft by 3 ft berth, it is surprising that only three babies died as a result of over-laying or asphyxiation; another three succumbed to measles and the final seven presented with problems ranging from an ear abscess to haemorrhage. These infant deaths meant that 1,455 instead of 1,643 extra souls reached the colony; the gains were further depleted by 3,111 deaths among the total number who embarked.

Any discussion of mortality rates last century focused on the influence of the climate, public health measures, and the occupations, sex and ages of landed populations; a younger community, for instance, could be expected to have a lower death rate (see Coghlan 1904:183). Maritime mortality was also determined by such factors; but those relating specifically to the voyage seem to have had a greater impact. The year 1861 has the highest immigrant death rate for the colonial period.[7] Only three British immigrant ships sailed to Queensland that year, but their recorded mortality was equivalent to death rates of 87.2, 83.9 and 170.2 per 1,000 of the population per annum. The latter vessel carried 454 immigrants, 21 of whom died; there were 4 births and the voyage lasted 102 days. These figures suggest that mortality rates at sea were determined as much by the numbers embarked and the passage time as by any other factor. Indeed, the only apparent similarity between the maritime and landed populations is a decline in the death rate between 1860 and 1900, though this was more gradual and subject to less variation for the sending and receiving countries than it was for the immigration (see Figure 9.1). In England and Wales the death rate fell from 21.6 in 1861 to 18.2 in 1900 and remained consistently lower than the Prussian rate which dropped from 25.4 to 21.8 over the same period. The decrease reflected the falling birth rate (a large proportion of deaths were children under one year) and a rise in the standard of living. Fluctuations within the decline for both countries usually indicated the presence of epidemic disease or the effect of war. For Queensland, there was not only a more marked overall reduction in the death rate from 18.6 in 1860 to 11.7 in 1900, but also a greater variation which corresponded to peaks in the immigration and the immigrant mortality (compare Figures 2.1 and 9.1).

If annual immigrant death rates are distinguished according to voyage-type, the resulting patterns show that, although passenger act and short ships defy comparison, rates on German vessels are considerably higher than those for the British ships, and that all three exceed landed deaths rates. Annual maritime mortality seems to reflect the volume of flow while individual voyage death rates suggest the influence of more intrinsic factors. The greatest number of deaths (77) occurred on the *Sultana* which left

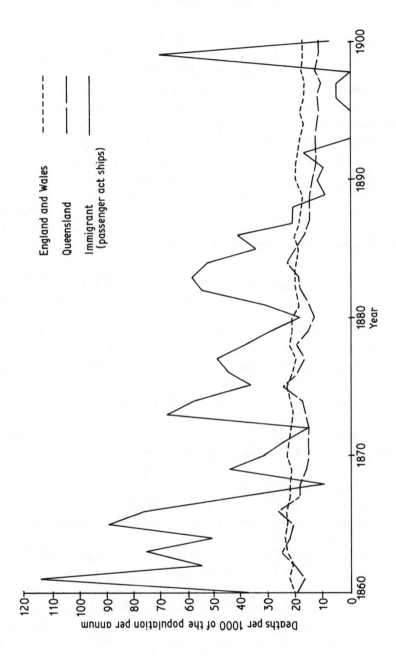

Figure 9.1 Immigrant and landed populations: death rates 1860–1900

Liverpool in November 1865, called at Queenstown, sailed with 567 passengers and reached Hervey's Bay (Maryborough) after 115 days at sea. The death toll, although offset by eleven births, represented 13.6 per cent of the number embarked and a death rate of 471.4, more than five times the mean rate for passenger act vessels arriving in 1866. All except of two of those who died were children of 'tender age'. The Immigration Board concluded that children required 'as much pure air as adults' and that far too many had been crowded on board (QVP 1866:1014). Three years earlier the *Lancet* (L 1863:I,160) had drawn attention to the 'great disparity' in the proportion of deaths on four Queensland immigrant vessels in 1862 and suggested that a more thorough inspection at embarkation would avoid future 'lamentable visitations' of epidemic and infectious disease.

Yet the colonial ships never reached the proportion of deaths recorded on some of the transatlantic voyages during the Irish famine years of the 1840s and 1850s when a 10 per cent mortality was common and sometimes rose to 40 per cent for a passage which took a third of the time (see MacDonagh 1961:51). According to Robson (1965:4–5), convict transports to Australia recorded a loss of only 1.8 per cent between 1787 and 1852; but it must be remembered that few, if any, children made the voyage and the majority of convicts were males with an average age of 26 years. By comparison, immigrant vessels to Port Jackson (Sydney) in 1837 and 1838 registered a 5.7 per cent loss (Fitzpatrick 1969:65). The high mortality on earlier Australian ships was said to be due to constant seepage between decks, poor ventilation, the chartering of three-decked vessels and 'fear and superstition' among the peasant classes regarding medical treatment (Welch 1969:17–18).

The record death rate (as distinct from the number of deaths) for the Queensland immigration is held by a German vessel, the *Peter Godeffroy*, in 1865. Fifty-nine deaths, five births, a voyage time of 121 days and a passenger complement of 284 resulted in a mortality rate (712.1 per 1,000 per annum) thirty times that for Prussia in 1865; one-fifth of the number embarked did not reach the colony. That same year, another seventy-three souls, representing a death rate of 433.3 (15.4 per cent of the shipment), perished on the *La Rochelle*. She also sailed from Hamburg as cholera and disease were raging across Europe, and on arrival in

Brisbane was sent to the quarantine station. This was in a filthy state, typhus fever continued unabated, dysentery broke out and a growing tension between the Hungarian surgeon and German passengers finally erupted in a 'revolution' (see COL/A77:66–706). Then the disease-ridden *Wandrahm*, also from Hamburg, dropped anchor in Moreton Bay; there had been sixty-six deaths en route (15.8 per cent of the passengers and a death rate of 496.7). Facilities, despite extra tent accommodation, were stretched beyond their limits, but the quarantine procedure got under way; immigrants were told to bathe more privately since few of them had a change of clothes; many suffered with the cold. A total of twenty-two deaths were reported during quarantine, yet not all these were due to disease; six young men, wanting entertainment, went floating off on a log and four drowned (COL/A78:66–706).

Immigration mortality rates not only exceeded those for the landed populations, but also those for the total British emigration (see Table 7, p. 351).[8] However, for reasons noted earlier in relation to birth rates, such a comparison is unreliable and certainly contradicts qualitative evidence. By 1860 it was commonly acknowledged that the Australian migration was 'better conducted than any other in the world' (L 1863:I,160). Queensland, on the whole, maintained this reputation. In 1875, for example, the Agent-General claimed that mortality on the colonial ships was lower than that for the New Zealand immigrant vessels (QVP 1875:II,611). Even during the early trial-and-error period, those reports which deplored the high death toll for isolated voyages remarked on the comparatively low immigration mortality. Jordan particularly stressed this point when questioned about the conduct of his system. According to him, any increase had been due to the indiscriminate shipping of navvies – an 'irregularly selected class' with dirty habits and few clothes; he maintained that his 'very careful arrangements for cleanliness and good order' kept disease and death within acceptable limits on navvy vessels (QVP 1864:1022; 1866:1085; 1867:222). But one wonders how he reached the conclusion that mortality on the eleven ships he despatched between 1862 and 1863 was no greater than could be expected among a similar number of people for the same period on land (QVP 1863:II,495). Nevertheless, Jordan admitted that a large number of children on board adversely affected the death rate (QVP 1867–68:II,88).

Mortality at sea dropped sharply after 1866 and remained at a steady level until 1873. The sharp increase for that year must be attributed to the German influx since the death rate of 1.4 per cent for vessels leaving the United Kingdom was considered 'favourable' (QVP 1875:II,732). The rates throughout the 1870s usually reflected the state of German vessels, while peak mortality in the 1880s (particularly 1882 and 1883) was a response to the rapid increase in the volume of immigration and conditions on the bounty vessels. Despite fluctuations, the decline which began in 1867 continued, and the colonial officials in their annual reports commented on the 'gratifying' improvement. This, they claimed, was almost entirely due to a reduction in the number of children travelling on immigrant vessels (QVP 1889:III,175). Periodic family-size restrictions had been enforced (see QVP 1875:II,631), and although these were lifted in boom times, their reintroduction after 1885 must have contributed to the reduced death rate in the late 1880s and 1890s. However, a much wider range of factors was involved.

Some 53.8 per cent of the immigrant deaths for which the sex is known were males and 46.2 per cent were females. These proportions remained constant for the first three decades, but reversed in the 1890s, with a male–female ratio of one to three (there were only seventeen deaths in the last decade). By comparison, almost two-thirds of the deaths for the total British emigration between 1860 and 1900 were males, with this proportion rising to 72.4 per cent for the last decade. Is it a coincidence that these ratios, except for the 1890s, are similar to those for the colony; or do they suggest that the Queensland population reflected the British emigration as a whole rather than the controlled immigration? In England and Wales between 1860 and 1900, the mean death rates for males and females were 21.5 and 19.2 per 1,000 per annum respectively, and for Queensland were 18.0 and 14.5, thus indicating that males were more at risk than females. But if immigrant deaths are related to the embarkation totals for each sex, we find that the female rate of 1.47 per cent slightly exceeds the male rate of 1.27 per cent. The differences between the British and Queensland migrations and the landed and maritime populations point to two conclusions: first, because of the assistance given to young married couples and single women, the Queensland immigration had a proportionately greater number of females and therefore female deaths than the British emigration; and second, that females in transit, unlike their counterparts on land, were apparently more susceptible than males to conditions at sea.

Since the maritime environment largely determined morbidity patterns, it may also be expected to have had a demonstrable effect on mortality rates. Almost 95 per cent of the total deaths occurred at sea, and as the incidence of quarantined vessels decreased, so the proportion of quarantine deaths was reduced from 7.5 per cent in the 1860s to 0.0 per cent in the last decade. Deaths on sailing ships accounted for more than 80 per cent of the total mortality. This means that 1.9 per cent of passengers under sail died compared with 0.6 per cent on steamships. Although conditions were more favourable on the latter, the figures must be qualified: mortality on sailing vessels over the four decades was 2.5, 1.6, 1.3 and 0.0 per cent while the corresponding proportions for steamers were 2.2, 0.4, 0.7 and 0.2 per cent of the numbers embarked. Since less than one per cent of the immigration departed for the colony under steam before 1880 and an insignificant number travelled in sailing ships after 1890, the only comparable period is the third decade. In the 1880s, steamships registered a mean death rate equivalent to 39.4 per 1,000 per annum; for sailing ships it was 44.1. This difference is not as great as might be expected if we consider that steamships provided more amenities and space, a reduced passage time and a route which allowed cases of infectious disease to be sent ashore at ports of call; it also reflects improved conditions on sailing ships. Although the government admitted that steamer mortality included 'accidents of a preventable nature' and ought to have been lower, they recognized the advantages of this mode of travel and decided not to renew the sailing ship contract after 1888 (see QVP 1883:II,419–20).

The effect of voyage regulations further illustrates the difference between sail and steam. During the 1860s mortality on short ships (0.3 per cent) was insignificant; but losses on the Commissioner's vessels (1.5 per cent) were decidedly less than on ships chartered by the Queensland government (2.2 per cent). The lower rate demonstrates the benefit of years of experience and of carrying only one class of immigrants. According to the Commissioners, the 'satisfactory' death rate of 0.8 per cent for all vessels despatched by them between 1860 and 1869 was due to reliable medical men and freedom from shipwreck (ECR 1870:13). Similar mortality rates for privately organized (2.3 per cent) and government ships suggests that those responsible had to contend with comparable organizational problems and conditions at sea. However, the most glaring discrepancy for the 1860s exists between passenger act and German vessels with their respective death rates of 63.4 and 148.3 per 1,000 per annum (2.1 and 5.2 per cent of the number embarked). The fact that the Continental immigration was largely left in the hands of the shippers and that Prussian law rather than the more stringent British regulations applied to voyage arrangements are obvious reasons for the discrepancy; but other factors were also investigated. During the inquiry following the arrival of the *La Rochelle* and the *Wandrahm* it was found that immigrants had embarked in a 'weak and sickly state of body . . . arising from bad living, poverty, old age, and . . . the presence of actual disease'; their clothing supply did not allow for either cleanliness or health; medical comforts, food and water, especially the quality of the latter, were inadequate; and the vessels were overcrowded, poorly ventilated and carried 'too large a proportion of children and aged persons' (QVP 1866:1015–016). But these vessels in no way compared with the mortality for a Hamburg ship which sailed to New York in 1867. Of the total complement of 465 crew and passengers, 105 died from typhus fever and cholera; there was no doctor on board and the ship's officers had to attend to the patients (see BMJ 1868:I, 161).

Fortunately, with better organization and a more rigid adherence to the regulations, the situation improved for both British and German ships during the next decade, yet the difference (1.2 and 3.2 per cent) remained. In the early 1870s the German agent continued to send large families believing they made the 'best colonists' (QVP 1872:1438–39). When difficulties developed, it was decided to forward Continental passengers via England; but this decision was reversed at the end of 1875, partly because the authorities did not want emigrants from areas where cholera was endemic travelling on British ships (QVP 1875:II, 733). Although the death rate for short ships increased in the 1870s and continued to rise in the 1880s when greater numbers travelled by this means, they maintained a lower mortality (0.6 per cent) than on immigrant vessels, despite the lack of medical supervision. Reasons for this have already been alluded to – more space, better dietary, and the fact that they mostly carried adult, cabin-class passengers.

Immigrant steamers in the 1880s may have had a better record than sailing ships, but this applied only to vessels subject to the Queensland regulations. While the percentage of deaths on privately-organized bounty steamers (1.2 per cent) was lower than that for bounty sailing ships (1.6 per cent), the death rate was actually higher (56.4 compared with 48 per 1,000 per annum). Moreover, the bounty rates exceeded mortality on government vessels, both steam (38.9) and sail (43.5). Evidence from official reports, and particularly from the SS *Nuddea* inquiry, indicates that less attention was given to space, ventilation, dietary, and 'good order' on the private ships. The death rates alone provided a sufficient reason for bringing these vessels under the Queensland regulations. Again in the 1890s, because of the mortality and arrangements for private ships, the authorities questioned the wisdom of entrusting the conveyance of immigrants to the shippers (QVP 1900:V,649–74). If the Queensland delegate to the Australasian Sanitary Conference in 1884 had gone armed with the relevant statistics, he could have demonstrated the benefits of a health-care policy at sea directly supervised by the government.

Maritime deaths were consistently linked with the degree of crowding on a vessel; no one doubted that health depended on sufficient 'breathing space' and 'pure air'; the incidence of infectious disease and the lack of specific remedies supported this claim. But was there any substantive evidence? When the mean decadal death rates are compared with the average tonnage and superficial area of vessels, we find there exists a direct inverse relationship between mortality and both tonnage and deck space for passenger act ships: the death rate decreased as vessel size increased. For example, the superficial area for British immigrant ships increased from 6,818 sq ft in the 1860s to 7,557 sq ft in the 1880s, while the death rate fell from 63.3 to 44.1 per 1,000 per annum over the same period. Likewise, the tonnage for immigrant steamers increased from 2,006 to 2,770 tons in the last two decades and the death rate was reduced from 39.4 to 16.9. A similar correspondence held, though to a lesser extent, for German vessels; short ships defy comparison.

Since surgeons were required to record the most unhealthy phase of the voyage, we must also ask if the route and time of travel influenced death rates. Apart from the few early steamers and those belonging to the Gulf Line in the late 1890s, the southern route was used exclusively by sailing vessels and the northern by the British India steamships. Mortality patterns for the route would therefore be almost indentical to those for sail and steam. However, a comparison of the percentage of deaths for the numbers embarked at the various ports shows an intriguing pattern. In line with previous results, the highest mortality was on vessels out of Hamburg. For immigrants departing from Great Britain, those most at risk travelled on ships which sailed from Liverpool and called at Cork (Queenstown) before proceeding to the colony. The death rate for these voyages reached 3.8 per cent, and for those out of Liverpool alone was 3 per cent. Most of the northern sailings took place in the 1860s; their mortality was considerably higher than for ships leaving London (1.6 per cent) during the same decade. Could this partly explain why so few immigrant departures were organized from Liverpool and Cork in the 1870s? Were these emigrees less healthy than those from the south? No Queensland ships left from Cork after 1880.

The overall picture sharpens even further when the combined death rate of 0.9 per cent for the southern ports (London, Southampton and Plymouth) is compared to the 2.2 per cent for Liverpool, Glasgow and Cork. The difference was greatest in the 1860s, but reversed in the 1870s when most of the immigrants were despatched from London. As the number of departures from Glasgow increased in the 1880s, the south reclaimed the healthier record. It would seem that future colonists sailing from the south of England were more robust than the Irish, Scots and northern English who embarked at the 'northern' ports. Yet there was another and more likely explanation: Queensland's emigration was administered from London, and it was therefore possible to keep a closer check on the selection procedure, medical inspection and voyage arrangements in the south. Thus the relatively high death rates for the southern sailings during the 1870s could be partly the result of difficulties in the London office, for it was during this time that reports of poorly selected immigrants and unsatisfactory conditions at sea became more frequent.

Morbidity patterns have shown the effect of the weather on the health of immigrants; but is there any evidence that the time of departure influenced the mortality? Death rates for the whole period were slightly more elevated during the summer (April to September) sailings, with April registering the highest rate; yet this pattern is not reflected in a quarterly analysis for each decade. The period with the greatest proportion of deaths shifted from the first quarter in the 1860s, to the second in the 1870s, and to the third in the 1880s. In fact, no predictable trend emerges such as that for England and Wales where mortality was highest in the winter and dropped during the summer. The only tentative conclusion that can be drawn from the immigrant mortality is that voyages which experienced marked temperature extremes tended to be the most unhealthy. For instance, a sailing ship leaving England in April's variable weather at the end of the winter would travel into the heat of the tropics before heading towards the cold of the southern latitudes. A steamer departing in the summer months, especially between July and September, would be subject to high temperatures and possibly monsoons for most of the voyage.

Mortality rates for arrival times show less variation than the departure pattern; and the two peak months of July and October seem to correspond with the greater numbers leaving by sailing ship in April and by steamer in August. The quarterly pattern indicates that vessels arriving during the last three months (the first half of Queensland's summer) had the highest death rates. Colonial mortality also increased in the summer months, and the authorities advised that immigrants should avoid arriving and having to acclimatize during this time (QVP 1863:I,371). Since great importance was attached to climatic influences, seasonal and diurnal changes on land and at sea were carefully documented; the surgeon was required to keep a record of the temperature in the several compartments of the ship. On the whole, the maritime death rates suggest that, although there was some relationship with seasonal trends on land, mortality at sea was more influenced by the climate en route, particularly rapid changes, temperature extremes and periods of protracted heat.

If the many facets of the voyage environment affected immigrant death rates, so too did variations in the passenger complement. We have already noted the marked discrepancy between British and German voyages; 4 per cent of the Continental embarkees died compared with the 1.7 per cent for British immigrants. What better proof did the authorities need to show that the regulations should be strictly enforced whenever possible? But the regulations covered only steerage passengers; cabin travellers were exempt. According to the records, there were thirty-three cabin deaths, 0.4 per cent of all who sailed by this class. The proportion remained the same (0.5 per cent) for the first two decades and fell to 0.3 per cent in the third; there were no cabin deaths in the 1890s. Overall mortality for the steerage (1.3 per cent) was more than three times the cabin rate. Clearly, the better accommodation and dietary available to a generally more healthy and 'respectable' class of people contributed to the difference.

Almost half the cabin deaths were single men; but their death rate, although much higher than the rates for single and married women, was similar to that for the married men, as the following table illustrates. Even in this better class, children and infants, especially the girls, seem to have been most at risk.

Table 9.2   Statute-adult deaths: percentage of totals embarked

	married		single		1–11 years		infants	
	M	F	M	F	M	F	M	F
cabin (1860–1900)	0.4	0.1	0.4	0.1	0.3	0.6	1.8	2.7
total (1860–1900)	0.5	0.8	0.3	0.2	3.6	3.4	12.2	10.2

Differences between the cabin pattern and that for the total deaths, 99 per cent of which were steerage, are immediately obvious; they also indicate that the two classes remained well segregated during the voyage (see Table 8, p. 352, for the detailed statute-adult classification of deaths). The mortality rate for steerage married women was higher than that for their husbands and four times the rate for the single women who had the lowest mortality of any group afloat. The death rate for the latter fell from 0.5 per cent in the 1860s to 0.2 per cent in the 1870s, and continued this trend in the last two decades. As immigration became more organized, controls tightened on the single female sector and by the 1870s, few loop-holes in their protection remained; their carefully prescribed programme allowed minimal risks, both physical and moral. Were the authorities aware that their policy had the greatest benefit where it was most effectively applied, and that the survival rate was highest among the group most urgently needed in the colony? However, the death rate for the single men compared favourably, despite their greater freedom and exposure to physical danger.

The fact that mortality was greatest among children and infants comes as no surprise. Death rates were similar for boys and girls (1–11 years), and rose steeply for infants, with male babies registering the higher rate. Since the total deaths do not include babies who were born and died at sea, this result adds support to earlier evidence relating to male infant vulnerability. In general, the results suggest that exposing babies and small children to voyage conditions was likely to reduce their chance of survival. Male infant mortality reached a peak (15 per cent) in the 1870s, but this was due to an exceptionally high death rate on German vessels; 27 per cent of the male babies who sailed from Hamburg that decade, died. An explanation for this does not readily present itself; and to complicate the picture, the death rate for German baby girls (21.2 per cent) exceeded the male rate (16.1 per cent) during the 1860s. Apart from these anomalies, a similar trend maintained for both nationalities, with one exception; on German vessels the single-male mortality (1.6 per cent) was double that for the single women, compared with the minimal difference on British ships for the same period (0.4 and 0.3 per cent). The high masculinity for Continental deaths is puzzling. Did the effects of war and upheaval in Europe during the 1860s and 1870s lower their resistance to disease?

An analysis of the specific age of death elaborates the statute-adult pattern. Eight per cent of all the children under 5 years did not survive the voyage, a rate well in excess of that for any other age category. The proportion reached 14.5 per cent in the first decade, but steadily declined to 1.1 per cent in the 1890s (see Figure 9.2). There was a dramatic difference between the under-fives and the 5–9 year group (0.8 per cent). The percentage rate fell to 0.3 per cent for the 10–14 year-olds and reached its lowest level for the 15–19 year category (0.2 per cent). Thereafter, the rate gradually increased to 4.1 per cent for immigrants 65 years and over. Patterns for the age-specific death rates for England and Wales and Queensland were similar – high in the first five years of life, falling to the lowest point for the 10–14 year group and rising to the highest level for those seventy-five years and over. Soon

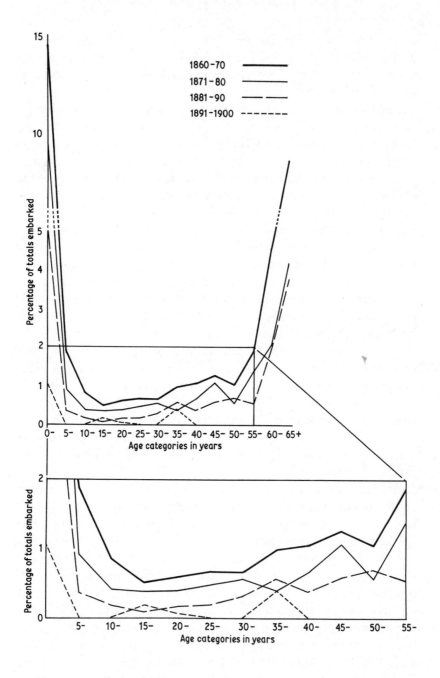

Figure 9.2 Immigrant age at death

after immigration began, colonial officials made note of its impact on Queensland's mortality; in 1865 the high death rate for the under-fives was attributed to the large number of deaths among new arrivals (QVP 1866:1102). Although patterns for the landed and immigrant populations are similar, there are two particular differences. In the first instance, the proportion of elderly deaths is much higher on land than at sea since the number of old people (sixty years and over) who sailed for the colony represented only 0.3 per cent of the total immigration. Also, irrespective of their age, most of those who set out were determined to arrive. Nevertheless, the mortality rates show that shipboard arrangements were not designed for the aged or the very young. The other difference relates to the groups with the lowest mortality – 15–19 years at sea and 10–14 years on land. Since all unmarried immigrants over the age of fourteen were berthed in the single compartments, children under this age remained with their parents and were therefore exposed to the greater amount of sickness in the married section.

Variations within the adult group (fifteen years and over) are of interest. For each of the three compartments, the gradual rise in mortality between 15 and 49 years gives way to a more marked and erratic increase over the age of fifty. Single women, however, proved the exception; for some unaccountable reason, their death rate fell in the 30–34 year category, rose sharply for the next five-year period, then fell dramatically again and remained low until the over-fifty increase. The higher percentage of deaths for older women, both married and single, suggests that they coped less satisfactorily than older men with the rigours of life at sea. Death rates for married and single men in the successive age categories were similar; but married women under the age of sixty suffered more than their single counterparts and had consistently higher mortality rates than the married men. Doubtless, the pressures of pregnancy, child-bearing, nursing and child-care, in addition to the ordinary adjustments to maritime conditions took their toll on married women, particularly in the 25–44 year group. These pressures were reflected in the high mortality among the little children and infants. Consequently the mean age for all deaths was 7.4 years compared to 21 years for the total immigration.

Attention must also be drawn to two particular features of the juvenile mortality. First, the survival rates for both male and female babies were higher than those for the one-year-olds. This may be explained by the fact that breast-feeding afforded immunity and that the shipboard dietary did not readily adapt to the needs of recently weaned children. Moreover, little children beginning to investigate their environment were much more at risk on a ship than the less mobile babies. Added to these factors were the frequent complaints by surgeons that mothers had little or no idea of child-rearing. There is no record of a nursery ever being organized, only comments that older children were kept away from school to look after the younger ones. The fact that the school was open to children over the age of three or four may have contributed to the decrease in mortality rates between three and fourteen years. The second point of interest lies in the death rates for two- and three-year-olds. Although the survival rate was higher for female babies and one-year-olds, this trend reversed for the next two years; then, for the remainder of the age span up to sixty years, the percentage of male deaths was greater than the female. There is no clear explanation why girls of two and three years were more at risk than boys of that age, but a similar situation is hinted at in the colonial population.

When details of juvenile deaths for the British and Continental immigrations (1860 to 1880) are compared, the lack of planned health care for the latter is even more apparent. Infant mortality (20.3 per cent) on ships out of Hamburg was almost double that for British vessels (11.9 per cent); 30 per cent of the German one-year-olds (22 per cent of the British) did not survive the voyage; and for two-, three- and four-year-olds, the German rates were almost three times those for the British, a pattern which continued for the 5–9 age group (3.2 and 0.9 per cent) and the 10–14-year-olds (1.9 and 0.3 per cent). Medical inspection for German vessels was a farce; no provision whatever was made for babies and little children, many of whom embarked in a debilitated, diseased state and suffered greatly in transit. The contrast is less marked for the adult sectors of the two populations. Both followed the general pattern of increasing mortality with increasing age, but differences are discernible. In each age category, the death percentages for German men, married and single, are consistently higher than those for the corresponding British groups. Again, this may be partly attributable to war-time conditions in Europe and the fact that the healthiest were conscripted. The much greater mortality among German married women compared to the British, also points to 'indifferent antecedents', poorer health and inferior conditions at sea. It is impossible to compare the single women since the age at death is known for only four of the German girls. A relatively high proportion of the older German passengers (60 years and over) did not reach the colony.

In order to complete the picture relating to the physical status of immigrants as they travelled, we must examine the causes of death (these have been recorded for 83 per cent of the cases).[9] Of the total deaths with a specified cause, 41.4 per cent were the result of zymotic diseases, 31.7 per cent had a local origin, 10.8 per cent were attributable to constitutional diseases, 7.2 per cent were ill-defined, 5.6 per cent were due to violence, 2.6 per cent were developmental disorders, and 0.7 per cent were classified as dietic diseases (see Table 9, p.353). A breakdown of the classes into their several orders shows that miasmatic diseases were responsible for 20 per cent of all deaths, with this proportion decreasing from 27 per cent in the 1860s to 12 per cent in the 1880s; by the last decade not one death was due to an infectious disease or fever. This satisfactory trend reflected a number of developments – a gradual decline in the major epidemic diseases such as typhus, typhoid and cholera, public health reform, improved selection, embarkation inspection and voyage arrangements, and healthier emigrants.

These factors did not have the same impact on diarrhoeal diseases which accounted for 19, 16, 22 and 15 per cent of the deaths over the four decades, and seemed to relate to specific voyage conditions such as the water supply, the level of sanitation, the degree of crowding, the dietary, and in particular, protracted hot weather and the presence of other diseases on board. Diarrhoea was commonly associated with measles. Malarial and septic diseases each caused one per cent of the deaths, a handful (six) were of parasitic origin (mostly due to worms), and only one died from venereal disease. Mortality for the dietic class was attributed to malnutrition, scurvy (three deaths) and alcoholism. Under constitutional diseases, those of tubercular origin, particularly phthisis and tabes mesenterica, accounted for 9 per cent of the total deaths and were doubtless present, but undetected or ignored, at the time of departure. Rheumatic fever, variously labelled as pericarditis or 'acute rheumatism', was responsible for seven deaths. Prematurity (previously discussed) and congenital problems such as a 'malformed heart' accounted for 3 per cent of the deaths, while at the other end of the developmental scale, three died of 'old age' or had 'worn out'. Marasmus, a wasting disease of uncertain aetiology usually affecting babies, caused the majority of deaths listed under 'other constitutional diseases' (2 per cent of the total); the remaining cases in this order included cancer, rickets, anaemia, and 'scorbutic haemorrhagic diathesis', a complaint unrelated to scurvy.

The largest proportion of deaths with a localized cause involved diseases of the respiratory system (croup, bronchitis, pneumonia, and other pulmonary disorders) which represented 12 per cent of the total. These deaths were said to be due to conditions in transit, especially sudden climatic changes; but the immigrants' health at embarkation was definitely a contributory factor. According to the annual mortality lists, respiratory diseases were the primary cause of death in England and Wales during the second half of last century. Passengers with a 'lowered resistance' or susceptible to 'chest affections' were more at risk during the voyage, despite claims for the curative properties of sea air. Most fatal diseases of the nervous system (9 per cent of the deaths) were the result of infection or 'constitutional defects'. However, a disorder such as 'brain fever' which seemed to have been associated with meningitis, encephalitis or heat apoplexy, was difficult to classify. This was also a problem with a number of deaths relating to the digestive system (7 per cent of the total). For example, were stomach cancer and dentition, constitutional or digestive diseases? 'Liver disease' was usually a chronic problem; gastritis and quinsy could have been attributed to shipboard pathogens. Disorders of the circulatory system – cardiac disease or cardiac 'debility', syncope or 'sudden heart stoppage', endocarditis, and hypertrophy of the heart (a 'fattened' heart) – claimed another 2 per cent of the deaths. It is likely that most of these complaints as well as the urinary diseases (1 per cent) – nephritis, Bright's disease (a catch-all term for a range of kidney disorders), haematuria and bladder diseases – were long-standing ailments. Difficulties with pregnancy and parturition (1 per cent) contributed to the high mortality among married women. Only five deaths were related to the generative, locomotion and integumentary (skin) systems.

All deaths due to accidents or negligence (5 per cent of the total) obviously involved the immediate environment. The inclusion of heat apoplexy (sunstroke) in this category produced a sharp increase in the proportion of 'violent' deaths during the second half of the period. As might be expected, drowning was common; passengers were washed or fell overboard. Sometimes, contrary to the regulations, they climbed into the rigging and fell or went swimming and were taken by sharks. One tropical night, a somnambulist bunked down on the roof of a privy and in his sleep, walked off his perch, climbed over the bulwark and was drowned (COL/A128:69–2734). Only seven suicides were recorded for the whole period. Of the four who jumped overboard, three were mentally unbalanced at the time and the fourth was the married woman who could not cope with life between decks. One man poisoned himself, another took his life while suffering from delirium tremens, and suicide was suspected in the case of the man who 'disappeared'. The final class, ill-defined disorders (7 per cent of the deaths), suggests any number of possible causes. Were debility and atrophy due to a 'weakened constitution' at the time of sailing, the result of illness during the voyage or an inability to adjust biologically to conditions at sea? Often, only a single diagnosis was recorded, and this referred to the terminal symptom rather than a specific disease. The label 'inanition' provides no clue as to the aetiology. Also, tumours and abscesses may have had a shipboard or previous origin.

An analysis of the causes of death according to the statute-adult classification reveals significant contrasts in the mortality patterns (see Table 9, p.353). Twenty-two per cent of the deaths among married men and 23 per cent of the single-male deaths were due to miasmatic diseases, chiefly typhus and typhoid fevers. Predictably, the miasmatic category claimed the greatest number of children (28 per cent of the 1–11 year-old deaths) and, together with diarrhoeal diseases, was responsible for more than half their deaths and almost 40 per cent of the infant mortality. Diarrhoeal diseases took the heaviest toll among babies but proved less fatal for the adult sector, resulting for example, in only 5 per cent of the single-male deaths. On the other hand, single men had the highest incidence (20 per cent) of tubercular diseases, while the proportion (17 per cent) for married men was not much less. Most of these deaths were due to phthisis, and possibly related to their previous occupation since many were industrial labourers and miners. Incidentally, consumption accounted for only 8 per cent of the crew deaths, compared to the 62 per cent due to violence (drowning, injuries, etc.), a proportion three times that for the adult male passengers.

In view of the protection for single women, it is surprising that accidental deaths accounted for 24 per cent of their mortality; but many of these were the result of heat apoplexy following the introduction of steamships. Although married women registered only 12 per cent for 'violent' deaths, this was offset by deaths associated with child-bearing. Both female adult categories suffered relatively less than adult males from miasmatic and tubercular diseases, while the latter took a heavier toll among adults as a whole compared to the younger members afloat. Children and infants recorded higher proportions than the adults for deaths due to diseases of the nervous, respiratory and digestive systems, but adults fell victim to circulatory disorders. These and digestive complaints affected women more than men, though the reverse held for respiratory diseases. Again this could be related to male occupations. Although the proportion of children's deaths involving the nervous system exceeded those for adults, they were different, resulting mainly from convulsions or encephalitis rather than apoplexy (strokes). Children's, and especially infant deaths, also registered higher percentages than adults for ill-defined causes such as debility, atrophy and 'inanition'.

According to the diagnostic patterns for the different age categories, miasmatic diseases (primarily measles, scarlet fever and whooping cough) accounted for 33 per cent of all deaths in the 5–14 year group. The proportion was considerably lower (19 per cent) for the under-fives, but rose to 23 per cent for the 15–29 year group where typhus, typhoid and other fevers took their heaviest toll, and then fell to 11 per cent for the older group (30 years and over). Accidents caused the highest proportion of deaths (19 per cent) in the older category. Diarrhoeal diseases played havoc among the under-fives and represented 23 per cent of their deaths. This proportion gradually declined between 5 and 29 years, but thereafter increased. Apparently those in the prime of life (15–29 years) had the greatest resistance to such disorders, although the reverse was the case for tubercular diseases which were responsible for one fifth of the deaths in this age group. Complaints about

Australia being the dumping ground for consumptives seem to have been justified. Indeed the practice of sending 'desperate cases' to the colony was held responsible for the high incidence of phthisis in Queensland (see QVP 1871–72:429). Taking the immigration as a whole, the juvenile sector were largely victims of epidemic and diarrhoeal diseases with supervening complications such as bronchitis and convulsions, while the adult categories succumbed to 'filth-related' fevers, tuberculosis and accidents. The mortality patterns demonstrate that, apart from deaths due to violence, it is almost impossible to differentiate between an aetiology of shipboard or passenger origin. Since selection and medical inspection could not be guaranteed to eliminate disease, strict sanitary measures afforded primary protection in transit.

A list of the causes of death in order of incidence (see Table 10, p.354) allows comparison with landed mortality and immigrant morbidity. Diarrhoea heads the list and was responsible for 16.3 per cent of all deaths at sea; measles (9 per cent) occupies second place. This order corresponds to the morbidity pattern. In England and Wales during the same period, respiratory diseases and phthisis claimed the greatest number of lives, whereas in colonial Queensland the pattern varied, with the most common causes being phthisis, diarrhoea and dysentery, convulsions, and pneumonia. A pioneer environment, a warmer climate and the presence of aliens (the Chinese and Kanakas were particularly susceptible to tuberculosis) largely determined the differences between the two landed populations. The Queensland Registrar-General's reports suggest that, as a result of immigration, deaths due to diarrhoea and respiratory diseases increased in the colony. Interestingly, measles does not figure in the list of the fifteen most frequently occurring causes of death for England and Wales; shipboard life seems to have favoured its spread. However, the incidence of phthisis was lower at sea (fifth place) than on land, despite the fact that 59 per cent of the immigration was aged 15–29 years, the age group most prone to pulmonary tuberculosis. In the mother country just over a quarter of the population fell within this age category, yet phthisis ranked second highest as the cause of death; in the colony it was a number-one killer. Does this indicate that immigrant screening was relatively effective?

Bronchitis, a serious affection at sea, ranked third – a place that is occupied by 'digestive derangements' in the morbidity list.

Although the latter ailments caused much discomfort and distress, they were not generally fatal. The same may be said for catarrh, coughs and colds, skin eruptions and minor injuries, rheumatism, menstrual problems, abscesses and seasickness. To some extent whooping cough falls into this category since the high morbidity resulted in relatively few deaths. On the other hand, several disorders appear in the mortality list that are not included with the most common diseases. One such, convulsions, ranks fourth for marine deaths and was a symptom that usually signified the fatal termination of a 'great majority of infantile diseases . . . of the digestive and nervous systems' (QVP 1880:I, 148). Although this diagnosis was listed in the official classification, medical practitioners were urged to record the specific disorder. After 1880 the incidence of convulsions declined for the landed populations, but there was no appreciable change in the maritime returns. Dentition, another 'vague and indefinite' cause of death, reached as high as ninth place in the immigrant and seventh in the Queensland mortality lists for the 1880s. However, by that time 'medical men with fresh ideas' had begun to associate the symptoms with 'errors of dieting' (Weedon 1898:123). Two other poorly defined causes, marasmus and inanition, both of which related to infants and little children, appeared only in the marine mortality list. By comparison, the 'somewhat indefinite' debility figured in all lists. Its relative incidence increased for immigrant morbidity and decreased for the mortality; in Queensland, debility disappeared after 1880 from the list of the most common causes of death, but the reverse occurred in the English list. Problems with diagnosis and classification plagued the records.

At sea the relative frequency of deaths due to tabes mesenterica (tuberculosis of the abdominal glands in children) and hydrocephalus (associated with tubercular meningitis) decreased. Did this indicate an improvement in child health or a shift or refinement in diagnosis? Scarlet fever and measles also diminished as fatal maritime diseases, a trend which was evident in England; more effective isolation could have contributed to the decrease at sea. Both these diseases did not even rank in the Queensland list; it would seem, therefore, that the voyage and quarantine reduced their mortality in the colony (scarlet fever epidemics were common in England but not in Queensland). The disturbing increase in prematurity as a cause of death on land was not matched by a like increase at sea, possibly because of the marked decline in marine births after 1880. One encouraging feature of the immigrant listing was the diminishing mortality due to typhus and typhoid fevers and enteritis in the second half of the period; however, this reflected the English pattern. Although Queensland's Registrar-General deplored the growing prevalence of typhoid in the colony, he reported in 1880 that some physicians believed that 'no real case of typhus [had] . . . presented itself' (QVP 1880:I,149); quarantine had effectively checked the disease.

Heat apoplexy (sudden collapse from exposure to the sun or high temperatures) was one cause of death at sea which showed an alarming increase after 1881. 'Brain fever' may have been another variant, since this disease first appeared (in tenth place) in the immigrant mortality list for the third decade. The provision of deck awnings in the tropics had been mandatory from the early years of immigration, and passengers were advised to sit no longer than five minutes in the sun since its rays, though similar to those in England, had 'a very different effect on the brain' (Taylor 1969:69). A few deaths from sunstroke were reported during the first two decades, but the number rapidly multiplied following the change to steamships and the equatorial route (see Plate 14). Steaming through the Red Sea, temperatures frequently remained in excess of 100 degrees between decks, both day and night (see COL/A435:85–6370). The authorities soon registered the problem, and after seeking medical advice, decided that the route could be safely used throughout the year provided due attention was given to ventilation and overcrowding (QVP 1884:II,668); all that was needed was a slight modification in the health-care arrangements. Yet the problem persisted. In 1887 the colonial Central Board of Health recommended that a better ventilation system be installed on steamers, that double awnings be fitted, and that the deck space be increased to twelve superficial feet. They also suggested that the maximum passenger complement be reduced to 250 and that children under the age of three should not be carried between June and October (see COL/A486:87–490). Even in the warm Queensland climate, relatively few deaths from this cause were reported. The influence of the marine environment is further illustrated by comparing mortality frequencies for sailing and steamships. Apart from diarrhoea, the three most fatal diseases on sailing vessels were measles, phthisis and bronchitis; on steamers,

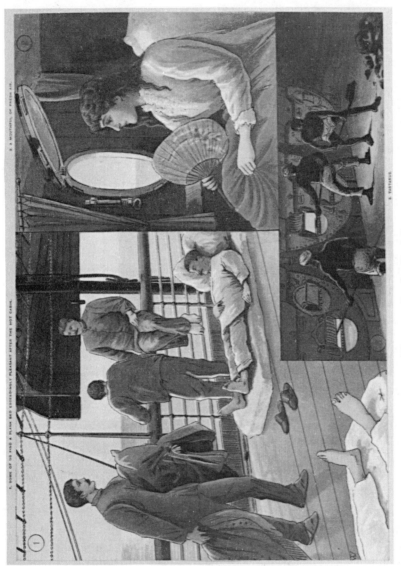

Plate 14   In the Red Sea

the order of incidence was heat apoplexy, convulsions (also possibly related to the heat) and measles, followed by intestinal infections (enteritis, dysentery and cholera). These differences reflect the mode of travel and the relative increase in the proportion of adult immigrants.

The following table of the primary cause of death for each group afloat reveals significant variations in the overall pattern.

Table 9.3   Statute-adult classification: most common cause of death

		1860–70	1871–80	1881–90	1891–1900
married	M	typhus fever	phthisis	heat apoplexy	
	F	phthisis	puerperal fever	heat apoplexy	heat apoplexy
single	M	phthisis	phthisis	phthisis	alcoholism
	F	phthisis	heart disease	heat apoplexy	heat apoplexy
1–11 years	M	diarrhoea measles	diarrhoea measles	diarrhoea measles	
	F	diarrhoea measles	diarrhoea measles	diarrhoea measles	croup
infants*	M	diarrhoea measles	diarrhoea bronchitis	diarrhoea bronchitis	diarrhoea
	F	diarrhoea convulsions	diarrhoea bronchitis	diarrhoea convulsions	

* Exclusive of infants who were born and died at sea

The isolated occurrence of typhus fever in the 1860s supports previous evidence relating to a rising standard of living among emigrants as the period progressed. It may also point to the fact that typhus and typhoid fevers were not distinguished in the classification until 1869. Puerperal fever possibly reflects difficulties with both the British and German immigrants in the 1870s; but was cardiac disease in any way related to the high incidence of menstrual problems among single women during that decade? The predominance of phthisis deaths during the first half of the period could indicate inadequate selection, or the fact that this disease was superseded by heat apoplexy after 1880. In England and Wales the prevalence of tuberculosis began to diminish after 1850. However, the continuing frequency of heat-stroke deaths demonstrates deficiencies in the health-care arrangements. If the authorities had taken more positive steps to deal with the problem, a greater number of the much-needed female population would have reached the colony alive and well.

Diarrhoea, the number-one killer among children and infants at sea, was generally attributed in the colony to the summer heat and 'carelessness on the part of the mothers combined with improper food' (Weedon 1898:121). Reports for several German vessels claimed that children actually died of starvation because of 'unwholesome food' which caused 'catarrhus intestinalis infantum' (diarrhoea) followed by general atrophy and death (QVP 1866:1021). Closer attention to the needs of little children and better facilities for isolating infectious disease would doubtless have saved lives. But juvenile mortality was inevitable; if it exceeded 'normal' limits, the authorities tended to restrict family size rather than substantially modify the health-care procedure. The aim, after all, was to introduce a healthy workforce. If we consider this statement in relation to the primary cause of death for the major age groups – diarrhoea for the under-fifteen category, phthisis for the young adults (15–29 years) and heat apoplexy for those 30 years and over – we must ask why officials did not wage a more vigorous campaign against tuberculosis. Perhaps they recognized the limitations of the screening process and were relieved when sufferers did not survive the voyage. Also, the failure to deal effectively with heat apoplexy could have stemmed from an awareness that this problem mainly affected the older age group.

The final mortality patterns involve a comparison of the most common causes of death on British and German vessels during the first two decades, and quarantine deaths between 1860 and 1890. Except for diarrhoea, the main killer diseases on British ships were measles, phthisis and bronchitis while the corresponding German pattern listed scarlet fever, typhus and pneumonia. Passenger health at departure and the degree of supervision en route contributed to these results which, with the foregoing aetiological patterns, also suggest that curative measures had little effect on the outcome of the most prevalent diseases at sea. More than half (54 per cent) of the quarantine mortality (the cause is known for 139 of the 192 deaths) were due to diseases other than those for which the vessels were detained; this proportion reached 65 per cent in the first decade. Typhoid (enteric) fever claimed the greatest number of lives (13 per cent of the deaths with a specified cause);

two-thirds of these occurred during the 1870s, a time when growing concern with the unhealthy state of the colony's towns and the increasing prevalence of typhoid fever, forced through the first public health act and quarantine regulations (see Barclay 1971). Although more could, and should have been done to improve conditions at the stations, a number of quarantine deaths were unavoidable.

Mortality and birth patterns at sea not only reveal a complex of interrelated causative factors, but demonstrate that the immigration and landed population patterns, bore little resemblance, despite the impact of passenger health at embarkation. Shipboard conditions largely determined maritime mortality. But in the final analysis, government intervention was the most influential factor; it regulated the selection of immigrants, the type of vessel, the degree of crowding, arrangements on board, as well as measures for preventing disease. Although the authorities apparently made little attempt to adapt the policy to different and changing needs, results amply confirm the fact that mortality was lowest when the health-care programme was most effectively enforced. Moreover, 99 per cent of the number who embarked reached the colony, and the gradual decline in the mortality rate over the four decades indicated an increasingly healthy immigration. If the Queensland government at the close of the nineteenth century had drawn together all the evidence relating to births and deaths on vessels carrying immigrants to the colony, they would have had good reason, despite limitations in the system, to be pleased with the record.

HEALTHY IMMIGRANTS?

New colonists were expected to be physically fit and morally respectable; 'suitability' implied much more than arriving alive and well. Following his visit to Queensland in 1875, Anthony Trollope advised would-be emigrants that 'the old, the idle, the reckless, and the soft-handed will only come to worse grief in [the] colony than the grief which they will leave behind them' (Trollope 1875:I,187). All who sought to promote Queensland never deflected from this approach; they saw the potential of the land and the need for suitable people to exploit it. At the close of the period Charles Dicken, the acting Agent-General, wrote:

> 'It is a country blessed with the natural advantages of good soil and climate and varied temperature . . . waiting solely for a healthy increase in her population to enable her to take a very prominent place among the exporting countries of the world. It must not, however, be supposed . . . that persons of a lazy, dissolute, and immoral temperament – although possessing capital – will do any better there than here . . . what Queensland wants are men of character, with integrity of purpose and energy, to develop her resources . . . and shape its destiny with such conscientious care as to make its people truly great and prosperous.'
>
> (Dicken 1900:95)

Musgrove (1963:126) concurs with Huntington (1927) that 'migratory movements have tended to select the resourceful and resilient, whose survival value was high'; results for the Queensland immigration support this observation, and the high survival rate at sea at least suggests a degree of physical 'resiliency'. Yet the response of immigrants to the voyage and their presentation on arrival, in addition to their physical status, were all taken into consideration by the authorities as they determined whether a particular shipment measured up to colonial standards. When the *Renfrewshire* arrived in 1875, the immigration agent reported that the passengers were a 'respectable and desirable class'; some married couples had capital, the single women would make good servants, and the single men were 'strong [and] healthy'. There had been three deaths, two of them infants, and seven births en route; the surgeon had few complaints with arrangements on board, and none with the ship's officers and the passenger personnel; immigrant health and conduct were generally good (see COL/A216:75–3321). The previous year, a shipment who had been selected for 'their muscular work more than their moral character', did not meet with official approval (QVP 1875:II,624–25). Each consignment of new colonists was assessed at several levels – how they had been provided for in transit, their general state of health, behaviour, appearance and 'respectability', and whether or not they settled satisfactorily after arrival.

Evaluating voyage arrangements and the 'vital statistics' of passengers was relatively straightforward and objective; character assessment involved more subjective evidence, and an appreciation of nineteenth-century middle-class morality. Honesty, integrity, thrift, diligence and hard work were as much hallmarks of health and of a progressive, 'civilized' people as physical well-being. Extant reports and records have been thoroughly searched for details of immigrant behaviour and attitudes. These, together with descriptions of their physical status and efforts by the authorities to deal with situations that frequently fell short of the ideal, have made it possible to determine, in the fullest sense, if immigrants were 'healthy'. Apart from the screening procedure and voyage arrangements, guidelines were drawn up for creating a disciplined, harmonious environment at sea. Immigrants had to be prepared for colonial life, and this preparation included measures for correcting, even penalizing, undesirable tendencies. It was a known fact that well-ordered vessels generally had a satisfactory health record and that well-disciplined passengers exhibited certain moral and physical strengths.

Some 1,216 statements relating to immigrant potential have been extracted from the reports of 428 voyages; these represent 71, 48 and 1.5 per cent respectively of passenger act, German and short ships and fall into the following categories: behaviour (46.5 per cent), health (28.5 per cent), general suitability (16 per cent), follow-up information (9 per cent).[1] 'Normal' voyages received relatively few comments. A decrease in the average number of comments per voyage (with a report) – 3.5, 3.0 and 2.5 between 1860 and 1890 – suggests an improvement in immigrant standards. Surgeons were required to assess 'the general state of health on board during the passage, and on arrival' (ISS 1875:34) and note behaviour; colonial officials registered their observations; some of the passengers and personnel added further statements, and if the Agent-General was present at departure, he usually forwarded his remarks to the colony.

More than 40 per cent of the health-related statements recorded satisfactory or improved health during the voyage; this proportion increased by 15 per cent between the first and last decades, a trend which was in line with the declining morbidity and death rates. The remaining comments all referred to poor health brought on by chronic illness or disease and injury sustained at sea (41 per cent), a 'weakly', 'delicate' or 'starved' condition (20 per cent), too many children or large families (13 per cent), 'slovenly' habits or a lack of personal hygiene (13 per cent), a disturbed mental state or deficient intellect (8.5 per cent), old age, poor selection or problems with inspection (4.5 per cent); health assessment clearly related to the immigrants' capacity for work. Despite adverse comments, the impression remains that officials were, on the whole, satisfied with the physical potential of new arrivals, and that this satisfaction increased over time; most immigrants were in the prime of life and had apparently thrived during the voyage.

Since health care was an integral feature of the immigration system, any defects in the design or administration of one materially affected the outcome of the other. For instance, the presence of constitutional health problems among passengers suggested a fault in the selection procedure. More often than not, however, investigation showed that such cases involved cabin-class travellers who were exempt from screening or steerage full-payers who had slipped through the departure inspection. In these situations, the government was caught in a cleft stick; if they applied rigid selection to full-paying and bounty passengers, this might deter the class of capitalists needed in the colony. As a compromise, they tightened controls whenever possible. It was a serious matter when unsuitable immigrants reached the colony at the government's expense, having suppressed information, used bogus referees or made application through a dishonest agent. Also, doctors, in their ignorance of Queensland or unable to offer their patients an alternative treatment, encouraged emigration; even approved practitioners were known to sign the medical certificate for persons with 'weak chests and a tendency to rheumatism' (QVP 1884:II,632).

Age and family-size restrictions sometimes meant that 'the most desirable persons' were denied a passage, but lifting these restrictions also had unfortunate consequences, particularly for the very young and the elderly. No such limits applied to remittance passengers (the government introduced controls through an increased nomination fee), and as a result 'undesirable' emigrees, mainly among the Irish and Germans, sailed for the colony. Although several Hamburg vessels carried 'a superior class' of colonists, many arrived with 'old, feeble and worn out immigrants' (COL/A185:73–1157). Sometimes it was difficult to square official reports. Heussler, for example, stated that passengers embarking by the *Cesar Godeffroy* in 1862 were in 'good health . . . of good moral character' and included 'strong labourers'; but on arrival, the immigration agent reported the 'extreme inferiority' of some, adding that the surgeon assured him that many were 'in a half starved and filthy condition' at departure (COL/A25:62–234,351).

Much of the criticism levelled at selection focused on the cotton operatives, despite Jordan's claim that he observed 'much strictness' in screening them, and on the navvies and bounty passengers. Cases of misrepresentation multiplied greatly under the pressure of a high labour demand in the colony or a rise in the volume of emigration from the home countries. Navvies were frequently described as men who 'lived by their wits' rather than the sweat of their brow (QVP 1866:1037), as Rev. Father Dunne, who accompanied several Irish contingents to Queensland, knew well. He condemned the shippers' practice of sending 'confidential' agents into 'the highways and byways' offering free passages to make up the complement for a half-filled vessel (COL/A81:66–

2049). When a similar situation arose in the mid-1870s, the Agent-General was instructed to stop filling up ships at the last minute with the 'floating population' of seaport towns (QVP 1875:II,645–46). Many bounty passengers who poured into the colony the following decade, were 'badly clad', too old for work, and fell 'below the standard' of regular government immigrants. On one vessel, unduly large families and several passengers with obvious physical defects, displeased officials; one old man was 'helpless with rheumatism and other infirmities', another had a lame leg, and two had the sight of only one eye (COL/A379:84–281). In 1884 the immigration agent, alarmed by the number of new arrivals admitted to the Brisbane hospital during the previous twelve months, sent the Colonial Secretary a list of these patients with the comment that bounty passengers were often poor returns for the £10 invested in them. Many were sickly, aged or frail; 'how they are to earn a living here, where the first requisite is robust bodily health, I am at a loss to conceive' he concluded (COL/A387:84–2983).

Despite the shortcomings of the embarkation inspection and the facilities under which it was conducted, a sufficient number of problems were detected and penalized to serve as a warning to others who might try to circumvent the system. Legally, immigrants holding a contract ticket could not be refused a passage unless they were suffering from infectious disease. Several surgeons reported sending home 'measley' passengers and their families; and one young man who exhibited feverish symptoms after embarking in Greenock was relanded when the vessel called at Queenstown (COL/A84:66–2795). But certain conditions required sensitive handling. The Agent-General in 1870 refused to apply 'inquisitorial tests' to determine whether or not immigrants had venereal disease. He pointed out that 'respectable males or modest females' would decline the Queensland subsidy if 'subjected to such gross indignities' (QVP 1871–72:710). As a rule financial assistance was withdrawn from government passengers found to be 'unsound' in body or mind at the time of departure. In 1864 a remittance immigrant for Queensland arrived in Plymouth intending to sail in one of the Commissioners' vessels, but was refused; the surgeon decided that her 'withered hand' would 'incapacitate her for employment'. Eventually, the colonial authorities refunded the deposit on the grounds that 'the nominee was decidedly ineligible' (COL/A62:64–3446). The following year the Commissioners allowed a one-armed man to proceed only after he paid the full fare (COL/A69:65–1817). Similarly, a nominated family with a blind fifteen-year-old daughter were passed when the father agreed to pay the balance of the girl's fare on arrival in the colony (COL/A74:65–3455). But in 1871 the German authorities insisted, in the face of protests, that a Swiss 'hunchback' be accepted as a free passenger since he was technically 'sound in body and mind and free from disease'. The colonial emigration agent promptly added another clause to the certificate for Continental immigrants, stating that applicants should in no way be 'deformed, disfigured or crippled' (COL/A158:71–1971).

As corruption increased in the London office, complaints relating to inadequate screening reached a peak. In 1875 the immigration agent reported that a growing number of 'idiots and cripples', certified as fit by local doctors in England, were not only being sent to the colony at government expense, but had to be maintained in public institutions until they could be returned (COL/A216:75–3321); families with as many as nine children and 'totally destitute' of clothing were allowed to travel (COL/A215:75–3165).[2] Brisbane officials demanded 'quality not quantity' and called the Agent-General to account for such 'undesirables'. In response to a stream of complaints from the colony, he pointed out that, while each shipment of Irishmen included 'certain defects inherent to poverty and want of education', these were offset by 'muscle and the capacity for hard work' (QVP 1875:II,573). The Agent-General was apparently unaware of the abuses in his office, and although remedial measures were introduced, unsuitable immigrants continued to arrive. A surgeon in 1877 felt obliged to accept as a free passenger a young women with advanced consumption who was travelling with her family; she had been passed by a *bona fide* medical practitioner, though her condition was 'obvious even to the untrained eye'. At least the government had to pay only half her subsidy; she died during the voyage (COL/A246:77–4840).

The situation temporarily improved following the complete overhaul of the immigration system and the London office in 1879; a medical certificate was introduced for steerage full-payers in order to prevent the colony becoming 'the resort of invalid indigent patients' (QVP 1879:II,171). Then came the 1883–84 influx; selection controls were again haphazardly applied. The surgeon of the *Earl Granville*, a bounty vessel in 1883, listed four passengers who, in his opinion, should never have been accepted – two married men, one with chronic dyspepsia and the other suffering from leg ulcers, and two single women, a 'confirmed epileptic' and a lady who was not only 'deficient in intellect' but exceeded the age limit (COL/A358:83–1992). A few months later two domestics, who had both been through the screening process, arrived in the colony but proved totally unfit for work; one was 'eccentric' and the second was so 'dreadfully disfigured' with cancer and her 'stench' so great that she had to be isolated (COL/A372:83–5523). Yet that same year a young man with a glass eye presented for embarkation on a government ship and was refused; he signed on as one of the crew and worked his way out to Queensland (IMM/117:803–16). As immigration tapered off, officials were able to control the process more effectively. In 1886 the Scottish agent reported that he could not recommend the emigration of crofter communities since they lacked the 'needful stamina . . . and fertility of resources' for such a venture (QVP 1887:II,575). Several subsidized immigrants who were detected with a deformity during inspection, were not allowed to proceed until they paid the full fare; one or two over-aged and disabled steerage full-payers were denied a passage on government vessels. But, as the Agent-General pointed out in 1885, it was 'an invidious task to reject persons' who had broken up their homes and were often penniless, and also expensive to return them; for him, the 'final approval' at departure proved 'a task of great care and anxiety' (QVP 1886:II,898; 1888:III,146).

Out at sea, problems which had been deliberately or unconsciously overlooked came to light. However, without an adequate knowledge of an immigrant's medical background, it was often impossible to detect mental illness, epilepsy or tuberculosis until symptoms became apparent. Inquiries revealed that several cases had previously been in an asylum or had a family history of insanity. Voyage reports are dotted with references to the 'feeble minded', 'imbeciles', the suicidal and those suffering from delusions and mania, or simply described as 'mad'. A few required constant supervision; others disturbed the immigrants and had to be restrained. The dangers for epileptics and those 'subject to fits' can be imagined; one wonders how many consumptives spread the disease to healthy passengers. Immigrants who were over-aged, feeble, ill-clad or 'lousey' required special attention.

On steamship voyages, the sick and the insane could be left at the next port of call. The brief comment, 'lunatic left at Aden', appears on the passenger list for the SS *Duke of Argyll* in 1885 against the name of a twenty-two-year-old single man who was travelling alone to the colony as a bounty immigrant (IMM/120:115–125). Such a provision was one of the advantages of steamer travel, yet there existed a divergence of opinion among surgeons regarding the relative merits of sail and steam. Dr Young superintended five voyages under sail before transferring to steam in 1881; he was immediately convinced that the health of passengers on steamers was 'infinitely better' (COL/A330:82–433). But Dr W. Goodridge who made six voyages in the 1880s, five of which were on sailing ships and death-free, firmly believed that people were 'healthier and better in the sailing ships than in steam' (COL/A564:88–9997). Comparative mortality rates for that decade might be used to support both conclusions.

The response of passengers to the complex of factors affecting their health as they travelled, varied greatly. Some did not survive, others arrived in a far from satisfactory condition, while many improved or remained in 'excellent health and spirits throughout'. Voyage accounts illustrate this wide spectrum. On the *Royal Dane* in 1865, cabin passengers became ill, new mothers had a difficult time because of the shocking lying-in facilities, and the children, through 'want of proper nutriment', arrived in a 'very emaciated' state (COL/A70:65–2115). Later that year, Dr Scott submitted a glowing report of the improved health of immigrants on the auxiliary steamer *Great Victoria*; it was 'most gratifying' to see them acquire 'a ruddy hue and a firm step', and to watch their children whose lives had previously been 'one long, sickly wail . . . dancing above the deck and singing lustily' (COL/A75:66–48). Although a relatively high proportion of the younger members were adversely affected by shipboard condi-tions, many were not, as descriptions of 'fat and well' youngsters and others 'as happy as the day is long' indicate. By and large, voyage reports drew attention to immigrants who fell short of the desired standard – isolated cases of physical and mental disability, and the small number who, in an otherwise healthy shipment, 'could have been rejected' or were 'not fit for hard work'. But the growing frequency of such comments as 'young, healthy, and of a robust build', 'well selected' and 'of a class well suited for land work', supports earlier evidence of an increasingly healthy immigration.

On arrival, all reports, together with the names of any who had left the colony or were incapable of work, were carefully assessed. If the general tone of a vessel suggested that immigrants had been poorly selected, the responsible party was instructed to upgrade the quality of future shipments. Detailed particulars of all passengers, whether government or full-paying, who were over-age or had embarked in an unfit condition were forwarded to the Agent-General requesting him to check each case with the certifying doctor, and, if necessary, dismiss the selecting agent. Full-payers found to be blind, consumptive, of 'weak intellect' or deformed were denied a land order. These measures and the constant reiteration of colonial standards also contributed to the improved health of immigrants over the years. But there was another, a singularly pragmatic factor. The following lines do not exaggerate what lay ahead for new arrivals, especially those who went 'up bush':

'Three years I landed here,
  a healthy active fellow,
But now my bones all ache,
  and my skin is nearly yellow;
There is no rest by night or day,
  from the evils here that plague you –
Mosquitoes, snakes, sandflies,
  and the cursed fever and ague.'
(quoted in Clark 1957:387)

In 1889 a young man concluded his account of the pleasant steamer voyage with a vivid description of the agonies he endured reaching an inland mining camp (Acton 1889:80). New colonists had to be physically healthy.

The detection of physical and mental disabilities was relatively straightforward, but how were undesirable moral characteristics determined? The application form for government immigrants which included clauses testifying to the candidate's respectability (see Chapter 2) was one method; observing passenger conduct, attitudes and reactions between the time of departure and arrival was another. Statements relating to immigrant behaviour have been categorized under several obvious headings and divide almost equally between 'good' and 'bad' conduct. The 'good' proportion increased from 38 per cent in the first decade to 62.5 per cent in the last – another indication of an improvement in the quality of the immigration. Surgeons contributed 78 per cent of the statements and the immigration agent, 13 per cent; the remaining few were extracted from shipping logs and illustrate how some captains endeavoured to maintain 'good order and harmony' on board. Almost two-thirds of the comments did not specify a particular category of immigrants, but of those that did, 41 per cent related to the single women, 34 per cent to the single men, 15 per cent to married people and 10 per cent to cabin travellers. Apart from the cabin group, this pattern was the reverse of that for health-related comments. Predictably, most of the statements which referred to a specific group were 'bad', and many of these involved the navvies – a class who failed to reach 'the colonial standard of morality and good behaviour' (QVP 1876:II,1054). The majority (61.5 per cent) of the 'bad' reports had to do with disorderly or insubordinate conduct, 25 per cent with drunkenness, theft and misrepresentation, and 13.5 per cent with immorality.

Emigration touched the whole person, throwing into bold relief his or her 'antecedents' and expectations. The decision to uproot and replant was rarely made on the spur of the moment, and though voluntary, was almost as irrevocable as transportation for life. Apart from the small percentage dredged up at the last minute from the 'highways and byways', government and full-paying passengers alike planned and prepared. Affairs at home had to be settled and personal arrangements for the long voyage and new life had to be made. There was also the emotional trauma of breaking ties with family, friends and community. All this required a certain stamina and resourcefulness; but undergirding the whole process was an element of hope and the anticipation of a better life. As the nineteenth century progressed, emigration ceased to be 'the last resort of the hopeless, but became the means of achievement to the hopeful' (Carrothers 1969:244). This transition is reflected in 'emigration iconography' (see Edelstein

1981) and literature; paintings and etchings contrasted the present
and the future by depicting those left behind bidding farewell
from grey shores while the departing group look towards the
distant horizon where the sun's rays are breaking through the
clouds. Hope, a fundamental immigrant characteristic, was
essential to health; it derived from and was moulded by the old
society, but had not yet conformed to colonial ideals and reality
(see Rickard 1981:10–13). Sometimes hope was founded on false
expectations which, if shattered, resulted in discontent.

The immediate and practical details of packing, travelling to the
port, and coping with embarkation formalities muted the trauma
of farewell. However, departure could be a chaotic, confusing and
even distressing experience. London before 1884, Glasgow and
Cork offered few amenities to facilitate the process; conditions at
Plymouth and Liverpool were often little better. To complicate
matters, there might be difficulties outfitting the vessel or delays
because of the weather or an epidemic. Not all immigrants were as
organized as the cabin passenger who, as she prepared to the last
detail for 'a safe and agreeable' journey, determined to 'keep up a
brave heart' and leave the outcome 'in the hands of Him who rules
the sea & land' (Hume and Fowler 1975:97,104). The situation
between decks allowed no such reflection, perhaps only regrets, as
everyone struggled to settle in. One young man summed up his
experience in verse:

> 'We were punched and pulled and trailled about
> Getting our boxes safe on board
> Trying mid darkness noise and shout
> To get them below and safely stored.'
>
> (Bushby 1865)

Official inspections, last-minute purchases, collecting the ship's
kit, organizing luggage and the final drinking spree obliterated
other considerations. According to one surgeon, 'The bustle
attending the departure of the Emigrants . . . was calculated to
subdue those deeply painful sensations to which so few refuse to
yield in the immediate prospect of a long and distant separation'
(COL/A334:82–2136).

As conditions improved, so did descriptions of the departure. A
party of young men arrived at the Blackwall Home on the

afternoon of 7 October, 1885, had tea and 'got nicely settled down'. At 7 p.m. there was a religious meeting with singing and 'very earnest addresses' and at 10 p.m. they turned in. Single men, women and married folk were accommodated separately. The next day, after passengers and their luggage passed inspection, the remainder of the time was free. At night, another speaker delivered 'sound spiritual and moral advice'. On the morning of the 9th, immigrants were taken to Gravesend where they boarded the *Silhet*. At 3 p.m. the Agent-General and other officials, satisfied that all was in order, left the ship. Two hours later, the tug was attached, the anchor raised, and off they sailed (Lumb 1885). Under these circumstances it was possible to keep a close watch on intending travellers, curb misbehaviour and, if necessary, reject any 'bad' or 'doubtful' characters. For most of the voyages, such streamlined organization was out of the question.

Apprehension and anticipation, resignation and regret, bewilderment and excitement come through in diaries and other accounts of the final farewell. To one observer the parting seemed like a 'premature death' on the one hand, and on the other, it created a larger-than-life hero's image of those who were prepared to sever established links and venture forth 'in search of fortune and a name' (RHSQ *Mainstay* 1863:5). 'We seek a stranger's land to win What Britain us denied', wrote Mr Randall as he departed for the colony (Randall 1868); he was later to return to England as one of the Queensland lecturers. Most emigrant ships were given a 'rousing farewell'. When the *Selkirkshire* left Glasgow in 1882, young people in small boats surrounded the ship and sang Scottish songs all night (Thomson 1882). Reactions to departure were as varied as the individuals setting out; 'some shed tears, others shouted & laughed others did neither but waved their hats or handkerchiefs' (Good 1863). Abijou Good remained on deck as the *Beejapore* set sail in 1863 and pondered 'the cruel destiny' which compelled him and his family to leave home and kindred to 'face we know not what in a foreign land'; had he been able to obtain the 'common nessasarys' in life, he would never have emigrated. He finally went below with 'a heavy heart'.

Immigrants with families seemed to find the parting more difficult than the single men and women. One young man captured their sense of adventure and confident expectation as he wrote:

'Tho' we leave proud England's shore,
    Tho' we leave our homes of old,
Tho' we may return no more,
    There's a dwelling for the bold.'

(RHSQ *Mainstay* 1863:5)

The following lines, however, came closer to the Queensland ideal:

'To another clime, to another land,
Where the high and low together stand,
And all alike go hand in hand
To work right hard and willingly.'

(RHSQ *Mainstay* 1863:7)

When the SS *Dacca* sailed in May 1890 with 223 domestic servants, a newspaper reporter observed that 'the most striking feature' among them was 'the entire absence of any indication of that sentiment commonly supposed to be appropriate to the hour of leaving the land of one's birth and kith and kin'. He asked several girls their reason for emigrating; most admitted it was marriage (see ANL *Daily News* M 468). From the beginning the colony had established its reputation as a excellent marriage market as reports regularly reached home of young women marrying soon after arrival (see, for example, QVP 1864:1049). Whether work, husbands or fresh opportunities attracted, the future for the majority who embarked looked good, or at least better than what they could expect if they stayed at home. Most immigrants were highly motivated to survive and remain healthy.

The first few days at sea demanded constant adjustment; preparation for pioneer life had begun. How would they adapt? If a vessel embarked passengers at two home ports, this initial phase was considerably extended. After the *Beejapore* left London, she called six days later at Cork for the Irish contingent. They came on board crying, drinking whiskey, praying, swearing and 'chattering in a gibberage that the divel himself could not understand'. The surgeon tried, but failed to prevent London embarkees going ashore. That evening a Lancashire man did not return; one of the Irish said he purchased the man's ticket and box, but as he also had his private papers, 'fould play' was suspected. Two women came back 'three parts drunk', three men missed the ship and had to reach it by rowing boat, and a fourth failed to appear altogether. He left a wife and child to proceed to the colony without him. Once under way, fighting soon broke out between 'a dandy irishman' from Dublin and 'a rough uncouth irishman from the mountains'. Other peasants stunned their fellow travellers by drinking tea from their chamber pots and eating directly from the saucepan (Good 1863).

Not all accounts are as colourful as this, but it illustrates some of the moral and disciplinary problems associated with immigration; the system was open to abuse at every level. In the early years the different methods of operation encouraged irregularities such as the sale by nominees of their passage warrant. Although the system was better coordinated after 1869, frequent cases of misrepresentation and impersonation were reported. There were 'single' women who had husbands among the passengers and crew; others took advantage of a free passage to join their husbands in one of the southern colonies. Couples who were not married travelled as man and wife; emigration provided the perfect opportunity for deserting a spouse. The Colonial Secretary maintained in 1865 that cases such as the man who left his wife and six children to emigrate with another woman were common and indicated that the system for issuing certificates needed to be far more stringent (QVP 1865:663). Some immigrants sailed under an alias, old colonists changed their names with the intention of returning to Queensland at government expense, and in one instance, an invalid who had been sent back to England paid £1 for a free ticket and tried to reach the colony a second time (COL/A158:71–1992). Applicants were known to alter their occupation or age in order to qualify for a subsidized passage. During the problem period of the mid-1870s, the name of a fictitious clergyman appeared on many certificates (QVP 1875:II,581). A few passengers emigrated to evade the law; one man arrived to find that detectives had taken the overland route and reached the colony before him; he was arrested for 'breach of the Bankruptcy Laws of England' (COL/A148:70–2504). Although others must have escaped detection, the incidence of all such cases seems relatively low compared to the numbers who embarked. Nevertheless, their occurrence disturbed the authorities for they revealed weaknesses in the system and undesirable traits in the immigrants.

Passengers faced three major areas of adjustment during the voyage – the physical environment, the routine and the regulations, and their fellow travellers. Any of the arrangements on board could give rise to discontent, but the weather, perhaps more than any other circumstance, affected behaviour. Many diaries record flared tempers as the temperature rose, and the frustration and impatience with unfavourable winds or a seemingly endless passage. Also, it was a new experience being 'governed' by a medical officer; yet immigrants were expected to acknowledge his authority, submit to his discipline and be supervised by those appointed to work under him; their lives had rarely been so structured. Some recognized the necessity and good sense of such organization; others found it difficult to accept. If the surgeon did not command respect or tension developed between him and the master, ill-will and a lowered morale generally prevailed. The third area involved relationships. Many immigrants would have been accustomed to cramped living conditions and minimal sanitary facilities at home, but it was another matter having to share a closely confined, rude and spartan environment with strangers and foreigners for two to four months. No wonder, as Rachel Henning observed (1963:60), 'There was a good deal of stiffness and party feeling on board.' On the whole, passengers were genuinely interested in their fellow travellers, noting and often reacting strongly to their different attitudes, customs and conduct.

A smooth routine and discipline, good weather, food and health, as well as sufficient diversion greatly helped in allaying fears, preventing discord and controlling misbehaviour. Yet any system, however perfect, could not eliminate these problems. 'Human nature is human nature', Henry Jordan pointed out early in the period, 'four hundred people . . . cannot all be expected to observe such a strict rule of life as altogether to escape the lynx-eyed scrutiny of officials in Brisbane'. And, he added, no-one could demand 'unquestioning obedience' except from the 'lowest class' who saw their passage as 'a kind of charity' (QVP 1864:1019, 1866:1051). Dr Maclean who supervised several voyages in the 1860s and 1870s also took a realistic approach; he accepted that, with four or five hundred people of mixed classes and 'difficult antecedents . . . cooped up in narrow limits' for four months, there were bound to be some grumblers (COL/A79:66–1210).

Discontent – the symptom of anxiety, poor health, boredom or a 'peevish' personality – usually resulted in disruptive behaviour. Many a surgeon found that unless it was nipped in the bud, conditions on board quickly deteriorated.

Anxiety levels could rise for any number of reasons and at any time – while discussing reports of the colony, during stormy weather, if the crew threatened mutiny or when it was rumoured that supplies were running low. One afternoon in mid-ocean on board the *Light Brigade* in 1863, 'the appalling cry of "Fire!" burst upon us' wrote one of the passengers. 'There was an immediate shriek from the women; but alarm was unnecessary, as the flames were already extinguished.' This event served as a warning for 'continued carefulness' and a reminder that everyone held 'in his hands the lives of upwards of 400 souls' (RHSQ *Mainstay* 1863:12–13). Although communal concern was the ideal, self-interest often surfaced under stress. An outbreak of infectious disease was also disturbing. Immigrants knew there was no certain escape; who would be the next victim? Yet the confident handling of such an outbreak helped keep the situation under control. Dr Scott described how, in 1866 when 'cholera was raging about the East India docks', they took on passengers with 'choleraic symptoms', left immediately, coasted along the spithead and observed developments. Only one died and the others recovered, so they proceeded to the colony; he was most impressed with the immigrants' behaviour. Apparently, the control he established initially produced the desired results since there was no need, throughout the voyage, to issue 'the slightest rebuke' for misconduct (COL/A84:66–2914). By contrast, when cholera broke out on the SS *Dorunda* in 1885, panic spread despite attempts to conceal the diagnosis, and the healthy refused to assist with the sick and dying (QVP 1886:III,781).

On the *Beejapore's* voyage in 1863, as measles made 'sad havoc' among the children, and little bodies were quickly bundled over the ship's side, Abijou Good confided to his diary that it was 'a fearfull thing to have to record the deaths of so many human beings'. None of his family was affected, but he registered his anxiety, grief and anger while the epidemic lasted. Reactions to death not only expressed an individual's sensitivity and involvement but also a corporate concern. One can sense the empathy of a married woman for the young bride of six months whose husband died suddenly during a voyage in 1885; she wrote, 'few of us shall forget her cry of anguish which followed the dull splash of the heavy body into the twilight sea' (Hinshelwood 1963–64). Then there was the carefree eighteen-year-old travelling first class in 1865; he noted each steerage death as it occurred and against one made the brief, almost brutal comment, 'Another child buried, no wonder there were sharks about' (Hurle 1967:31). A succession of deaths at sea usually had a depressing and demoralizing effect, but the isolated funeral could be impressive. This is how one young man described a burial during his voyage:

'a fine breeze [was] blowing from the stern; the ship rocking . . . and shipping seas every 5 minutes or so. The sailors stopped work at 2 p.m. . . . six of them being dressed in their best clothes for carriers. The Union Jack was hoisted a few minutes before the ceremony took place, the corpse was sewn up in canvas, and a bag full of old iron placed at her feet; then put on a board and carried to the lee side, where the Captain read the burial service . . . when he came to a certain part, the sailors heaved the board slightly and the body slid off into the sea, feet first at 4.7 p.m.'

(Lumb 1885)

While every event provided some diversion from the daily routine, many passengers, especially the single men, found the hours of idleness difficult to fill. The majority, being labourers and artisans, were unaccustomed to the comparative inactivity; if they could not read or write or had no interest in self-improvement, they frequently stirred up trouble to relieve the boredom. Failing that, they might take 'a little nap to pass away the monotonious time which presses very heavily' (Blasdall 1862). Even saloon passengers soon discovered what 'a new sensation' it was 'so busily to do *nothing* all day long' (Hume and Fowler 1975:112). On the shorter steamship voyages immigrants also found that being shut up together for weeks with no outside contact was 'enough to make anyone, however interesting, get "stale" ' (Acton 1889). Petty irritations and personality conflicts were inevitable; 'everyone was agreeable except the women in the next berth to me . . . I can get on with every one else very well', Mrs Cook wrote to her mother in 1883. A passenger with time to spare mused on these problems:

'Within the limits of our little kingdom ample scope might indeed be found for the social economist to collect a vast amount of useful information . . . The necessary confinement in which a large body of people is kept tends . . . to force to the surface the peculiarities of their different temperaments . . . The mind here has little to fall back upon but itself; if, therefore, it has not that innate strength . . . to support itself, its weakness will grow . . . Look at the parties into which our little society is soon divided; we have our exclusive set, our jolly set, our quiet set, our noisy set, our sporting set, our grumblers, and our contented set . . . most of these unfortunate quarrels and bickerings arise out of mutual misconceptions, heightened by a disordered mental state.'

(RHSQ *Mainstay* 1863:43,44)

Life at sea dislocated previous behaviour patterns and introduced a new set of demands. Healthy adjustment required more than keeping physically fit.

Behaviour-related comments indicate that many immigrants adapted to their new circumstances and turned the experience to good account. An ordinary scene between decks presented 'a very business like appearance men tailoring sailors engaged with getting ships provisions . . . women nitting stockings some of us writing' (Blasdall 1862). One young fellow who kept himself happily occupied throughout the voyage described a typical day:

'Up at 6 a.m. Finished dough and cake making, then breakfast after which came the order for boxes to come up . . . Boxes put back by 12 at noon. Had dinner and then commenced to wash . . . finished just in time for tea. At 7 p.m. we had a Bible Class.

(Lumb 1885)

Once passengers found their 'sea legs', settled into a routine and learned to get along with their travelling companions, the voyage could be most tolerable. The 'better classes', having no cleaning or cooking chores, seemed to find it more difficult keeping themselves occupied and frequently interfered in steerage affairs. On a voyage in 1887, they created so much strife that the surgeon recommended all future vessels be fitted with 'proper dividers' to keep each class 'completely separate' (COL/A500:87–3953).

Varying degrees of 'good' behaviour were reported. Some

To be filled in, and delivered to the Immigr

back by first mail to the Queensl

Ship "_Fly_

Port at which the Passengers were Embarked.			Ports put into after Leaving.			
Port.	Date of Passengers' Embarkation.	Date of Sailing.	Port.	Cause.	When.	When left
London	1869. 21st Jany	1869. 24th Jany				

| | ADULTS. | | | | CHILDREN. | |
| | MARRIED. | | SINGLE. | | 1 to 12 | |
	Male.	Female.	Male.	Female.	Male.	Female.
No. of Passengers Embarked . . .	23	30	107	58	16	11
No. of Deaths on the Voyage . .					1	2
No. of Births on the Voyage . . .						
No. of Passengers landed	23	30	107	58	15	9

Equal to _230_ Statute Adults.

G. C. Paynter

Plate 15

on Agent in the Colony, and a Duplicate Copy sent

l Government Emigration Office, London.

"Cloud"

	LIST OF BIRTHS			
	On board the _Ship "Flying Cloud"_			
	Mother's Name.	Child's Name.	Sex.	Date of Birth.
	Susannah Comport	John Comport	Male	1st February /69
	Susannah Comport	William Comport	Male	1st February 1869
	Mary Ann Hutton	Hutton	Female	8th April 1869
	Sarah Thorn	Thorn	Female	9th April 1869
	Harriet Edward Millward	Millward	Male	11th April 1869

Arrival.

rt of Destination.	Date of Arrival.
Brisbone	1869 April

INFANTS.

	Female.	TOTAL.
	4	250
		6
	2	5
	6	249

Under 1.

	LIST OF DEATHS					
	On board the _Ship "Flying Cloud"_					
	Place of Residence before leaving Britain.	Parent's Name.	Sex.	Age.	Date of Decease.	Disease.
	Maidstone	George & Susannah Comport	Male	10 hours	1st February 1869	Premature Birth
	Maidstone	George & Susannah Comport	Male	almost	1st February 1869	Premature Birth
	Portadown Co Armagh	Samuel & Isabella Fisher	Male	2 weeks	16th February	Convulsions Teething
	Sevenoaks Kent	Richard & Susan Bowden	Female	20 months	16th April 1869	Hooping Cough
	Brinley Hill Stafford	Joseph & Harriet Millward	Male	infant	21st April 1869	Hooping Cough
	Leamington Warwick	William & Maria Ward	Female	2 months	23rd April 1869	Hooping Cough

urgeon-Superintendent.

vessels carried 'a carefully selected . . . quiet and orderly people', everyone seemed content and the surgeon and immigrants alike were commended; but more often, 'elements of discord' disturbed the peace in an otherwise well-behaved shipment. On the *Charlie Palmer* in 1866 the single men gave no trouble, while some of the single women were insubordinate, though no more than might be expected from their 'previous habit' (COL/A77:66–867). If a surgeon was able to identify trouble-makers, he usually lost no time applying the necessary discipline. Even before the *Southern Ocean* set sail from Plymouth in 1866, a group of 'rioters' were put off the ship for inciting a sailor to assault the chief officer. One superintendent found from experience that 'a little severity at first' produced good and lasting results (COL/A80:66–1605). Some voyages began badly, but after a few weeks at sea, behaviour showed signs of improvement. According to the health officer, the order, discipline and cheerfulness on board the *Young England* in 1865 was to 'the great credit' of the surgeon and the captain. Although, initially, there had been 'a great tendency to mutiny and wife beating' (one woman sustained several fractured ribs), the situation was so transformed by the time of arrival that the immigrants put on a concert to demonstrate their newly acquired skills. His report concluded that singing was 'of great advantage to health' (COL/A70:65–2218). Indeed, music was an important feature of life at sea; passengers organized a band, joined a choir or performed individually. 'We have 2 Melodians, 1 Accordian, 1 Concertina, 2 Flutes, 1 Tambourine and 1 Violin . . . so you will see we are not short of music – such as it is', Mellor Lumb (the violinist) told his family. Another wrote, 'The reader as no idea what a pleasant effect music and singing has at sea' (Ricou 1872). After all, entertainment was intended 'to improve the moral tone and promote happiness' (COL/A376:83–6687).

A deterioration in behaviour was usually attributed to relaxed discipline by the surgeon, master or both. On the SS *Nowshera* in 1883, after the doctor and captain disagreed, the latter became obstructive and allowed his crew to take liberties with the single women; this led to 'a pooh-poohing of the rules' and 'corruption among the emigrants' (COL/A370:83–5145). Disorderly and insubordinate behaviour ran the gamut from rough play and petty thefts to drunken fights and blatant immorality. Gambling and obscene language were often deliberately overlooked, despite the regulations, abstracts of which were posted in 'conspicuous places' on board; sometimes these were torn down or defaced to the extent that it was recommended they should be printed on calico (COL/A302:80–6137). In many instances the problem lay not so much with the captain or surgeon but in the selection of 'undesirable' immigrants. Dr McLean found his consignment in 1865 'rough and very turbulent and difficult to manage . . . a great proportion were navvies' (COL/A69:65–1850). Other surgeons' comments were more expressive – 'extremely insubordinate and riotous', 'have most certainly left the country for their country's good', 'outrageous', 'expected regular handouts of grog and tobacco', 'a mob of rowdies', 'very dirty and coarse'. Some had been drawn from the 'loafer' class and 'the lowest back slums of London' or were 'running away military and striking working men'. Many a matron had trouble with 'impudent' and 'impertinent' girls, or married women who were 'coarse and dirty' and refused to control their children. Little wonder that schoolmasters reported that some of their pupils were 'boisterous', disruptive and unmanageable. In general, the 'rowdy' elements on British ships tended to be the navvies or 'Irish of the lowest class', while among the Continental immigrants, the Danes had the worst reputation. On the *Reichstag* in 1876, for example, the Germans and Italians gave no trouble, but the Danish men behaved abominably and the girls were extremely foul-mouthed (COL/A227:76–2426).

Frequently personal uncleanliness and unacceptable behaviour went hand in hand. Dr Wilkinson had a difficult voyage in 1882 coping with a measles epidemic and unruly immigrants; he found the married people, in particular, 'a most peevish, jealous, dirty, quarrelsome set, careless as to the accumulation of filth, permitting their children to deposit their excrement on the lower deck'; others emptied their urine cans in the gutter ways (COL/A345:82–4816). Theft was another common form of aberrant behaviour; 'one should think from the quantity of articles stolen that we had a few london Sharpers on board', Mark Blasdall noted in 1862. Immigrants mostly 'borrowed' or pilfered food rations, mess utensils, bedding, clothing and small personal items, though occasionally large sums of money and valuable articles were involved. In the early years, the 'loss' of purses containing money, contract ticket and land-order warrants was a 'common occurrence' (COL/A42:63–1726). The vigilante groups must surely have reduced the incidence of theft and reassured passengers, yet the adult male immigrants were often 'much averse to keeping watch at night' (COL/A67:65–1386). One group who refused to do the 10 p.m. to 2 a.m. watch, were finally talked into it by the surgeon; 'They wanted both the Toffy and the half penny' observed a fellow traveller (Lumb 1885).

Following the introduction of steamers, the control of immigrants at the coaling ports presented a major disciplinary problem. Several men so disrupted proceedings at one port during a voyage in 1883 that the shipping company claimed compensation for the twelve-hour delay (COL/A354:83–498). The ship's constables remained on duty, but it was impossible, without cooperation from the shore police, to prevent passengers going ashore or to stop them buying fresh fruit, liquor and local goods from the bumboats. Many soon paid the price with 'digestive problems', one young man contracted malaria, and another was left behind. The desire for alcohol as much as curiousity and adventure resulted in the breaking of port rules and lay at the root of a good deal of misconduct. Some immigrants managed to smuggle a supply on board, others broached the cargo or ship's stores, and on a few voyages liquor was sold openly and indiscriminately. The captain and officers of a German vessel in 1873 organized the sale of more than 1,200 bottles of brandy and gin (COL/A185:73–1157). Intoxication among saloon travellers was also relatively common; did the prescription of a sea voyage to cure 'a craving for alcohol' (see BMJ 1889:I,983) aggravate the problem? Certainly, if the steerage passengers and crew had access to drink, 'good order' disappeared; 'there as been rows all day by some drunken fellows', ran a diary entry on the *Indus* (Ricou 1872), 'the sailors having taken a drop too much they assist in making more row'.

When the complement of single men numbered more than one hundred, it was 'usual to see a fight every day'. Fists, mops, brushes, knives or any available implement might be used. Women resorted to slapping and lashing out with their tongues. Two married ladies once looked as though they would come to blows, but 'gave over after an hours clicker clacker'; the fascinated observer supposed they 'got short of steam' (Blasdall 1862). 'Pugallistic encounters' and squabbles flared up more quickly as the days became hotter or during a run of cold, foul weather.

Occasionally, passengers were victimized on account of some physical or personality defect; one young man arrived in 1863 in a state of 'complete mental derangement', allegedly brought on by the ill-treatment he received from his fellow travellers (COL/A45:63–1066). The 'betting mania' became so prevalent on most voyages that the surgeon turned a blind eye unless it disturbed other passengers; four young men who played cards all night and kept others awake were 'brought up before a court martial' the next day (Ricou 1872). It was also impossible to prevent 'beastly and insulting' language; one immigrant found 'the cursing and swearing enough to disgust a pig' (Anon 1883), while another recorded it was so 'thoroughly detestable' that he looked to the Bible class for relief (Lumb 1885). Surgeons regularly reported foul-mouthed passengers, but on one voyage the immigrants reported the doctor for not curbing the bad language (COL/A117:69–304).

As the period progressed, immorality increasingly became the focus of concern. Preventive measures operated at two levels – the selection of 'good' and suitable girls and the protection of their character and morals during the voyage. Although several emigration societies screened and sponsored middle-class women,[3] investigating the background and work potential of free immigrants often proved a more difficult and sensitive issue. The primary test of a girl's respectability, it seems, was whether or not she had 'fallen'. The Emigration Commissioners refused to accept single women with illegitimate children, but these women could sail on a government vessel if they paid the full fare. Eight single girls embarking as assisted immigrants on the *Queen of the Colonies* in 1866 seemed doubtful; their tickets were withheld while inquiries were made, and when it was found they had been sent from a home for 'fallen women', the selecting agent was immediately dismissed. Although four of them subsequently sailed for the colony (one was delivered of a baby en route), they were denied a land order on arrival (COL/A91:67–1426). Practical as well as moral considerations prompted such actions; pregnant single women not only made it difficult for others in their compartment, but frequently became a burden on the colony or added to the prostitute population.

Despite precautions and a tightening of the selection procedure, vessels regularly arrived with one or more of 'these objectionable cases'; emigration conveniently relieved a family of embarrassment or cleared the parish of any responsibility. But, asked the Brisbane bureaucrats, how did these women manage to escape detection? Investigations revealed that the doctor or character referee rarely knew of their condition. However, as late as 1891, an immigrant rejected by a clergyman, was passed by the selecting agent who was aware she had an illegitimate child, was six months pregnant with another and had come from an institution (COL/A654:91–4024). This was exceptional, since agents knew they would lose their appointments if they sent girls from 'refuges and reformatories'. Even at the departure inspection, such cases slipped through. If the surgeon was suspicious he normally asked the matron or a married women to check; at one stage, it was suggested that a 'jury of matrons' be set up to assist with the examination (QVP 1900:V,654). But opinions varied; one doctor pointed out that they could not be too cautious in expressing an opinion, while another believed they should be given authority to reject any single women of 'doubtful morality' (COL/A523:87–8516; 599:89–10522). After years of sustained pressure to improve the quality of the female immigration, the Agent-General assured the colonial authorities in 1889 that 'no trouble [was] spared to secure girls of the very best character' (QVP 1889:III,174).

Out at sea, it soon became apparent if girls with a 'good' certificate were not 'good characters'. In the early years there was also the possibility that some who were not in the 'family way' before departure, might well be by the time of arrival. Immigrants sailing on the *City of Brisbane* in 1862, prior to the introduction of the Queensland regulations, reported promiscuity, rape and venereal disease; for five months, single women were exposed to 'unbridled licentiousness, [and] an uninterrupted course of demoralization' without a matron or a 'properly constituted' surgeon to protect or check them (COL/A31:62–1994). However, one of the young men on board seems to have been oblivious to the dangers; 'The moon came out with her cheerful smile showing many couples engaged in the art of courting', he wrote in his diary, 'they lie along the spars . . . & upon the Hay Market as the deck house is called' (Blasdall 1862). With the circulation of such reports and rumours of increasing prostitution in the colony, the government began enforcing a rigid system of protection, despite resistance to measures like the weekly visiting session; this was eventually extended to friends as well as relatives of the single women (COL/A358:83–1992). Continuing isolated instances of 'improper intercourse' were invariably the result of defective structural fittings, lack of discipline, intoxication and, not least, the 'bad' nature of some of the girls. When immigration resumed in the late 1890s, the regulations no longer applied and the single women, although berthed separately under the care of a matron, were allowed to mix freely with other passengers and the crew. The authorities could not intervene, but continued to be concerned for their welfare and considered reintroducing the 'old' system (QVP 1900:V,649ff.).

Unsuitability was not only confined to immorality; 'troublesome' girls included the 'rough and vulgar', the 'insubordinate' and those who embarked in 'a filthy and vermin-ridden' condition. One such became most indignant when the doctor ordered her to bathe and cut her hair (COL/A158:71–1992). Yet, at the other end of the scale, surgeons reported a 'respectable' group, 'a superior class', and those who were 'industrious and amenable to discipline'. More than once the Irish girls were singled out for commendation. But the voyage itself was expected to have a salutary effect on behaviour. Dr Scott hoped that women who emigrated with the intention of becoming prostitutes might, surrounded by 'the wonders of creation, be weaned from the error of their ways' (COL/A67:65–1307). A more down-to-earth suggestion recommended lessons in 'ordinary household duties' to improve discipline at sea and enhance their performance in the colony (COL/A497:87–3075). On arrival the girls were taken to 'well-conducted depots', carefully supervised, and given 'the best advice a paternal Government can provide' (QVP 1900:V,625). By 1900 the authorities believed they had achieved the desired results: 'Queensland as a whole [was] . . . as free from public or secret immorality as any part of the Empire' (QVP 1900:V,625). This concern for the single women had deeper roots than the desire to protect them; the colony had a reputation to improve (many female convicts were prostitutes), an image to create and a future to shape. Defective morality would impede progress.

Although misbehaviour, by and large, stemmed from a disregard of the regulations or an inability to conform to middle-class standards, a small proportion related to differences of class, creed and nationality. The level of interaction on vessels out of Hamburg varied considerably; there was 'good intermixing' on some, while on others, 'international rivalry' prevailed, a situation often aggravated by a lack of interpreters. On the *Alardus* in 1873, Scandinavians had to communicate with the surgeon in English, a language foreign to both; and the Danish girls, by flirting with the crew, set a bad example for the German girls (COL/A185:73–1157). Surgeons were careful to note nationality differences. For example, Dr Thon, a German who superintended the *Charles Dickens* in 1879, reported that the Danish, Swedish and Norwegian single men were a dirty lot and had to be driven from their bunks to prevent disease; they were also lazy, indulged in petty thieving, refused to attend English classes and 'pressed aft' for the single women; the German and Swiss behaved better. In the married compartment, the Danes 'had a great aversion to fresh air', gave their children inappropriate food, and resented the Germans; this undermined his position (COL/A272:79–943). In fact, Scandinavians complained so often of favouritism towards the Germans, that the authorities considered alternating vessels from Copenhagen and Hamburg (COL/A227:76–2560). Friction also developed on British ships carrying a Continental contingent. Special arrangements were made for the *Arthurstone* in 1881 to accommodate the large numbers of Germans on board; but for most voyages it was simply not possible to segregate the various groups. Italians suffered on the *Indus* in 1877 because of 'their ignorance of English customs' (COL/A240:77–3267); fighting was reported on the SS *Jumna* in 1891 when a particularly provocative Scotsman used insulting gestures and attacked several Italians (COL/A680:91–14025).

Strained Anglo-Irish relations, however, were responsible for much of the strife on British vessels. Out at sea in 1863, one of the immigrants recorded the growing tension: 'the weather is dreadfully hot & it seems to have heated the blood of a great many of the passengers particularly the irish. they are beginning to be very quarrelsome'. First squabbles, then sporadic fighting broke out, and finally 'the irish gathered in groups all over the deck threatening the English' (Good 1863). According to an Englishman on the *Indus* in 1872, the Irish wanted 'to make themselves too officious', but being in the minority, were 'obliged to be very quiet' (Ricou 1872). Following a concert on the *Silhet* in 1885, as the audience rose to sing the national anthem, 'All the Irishmen went walking away in a body there was no hissing or bad behaviour . . . . After it was all over the Irish came back and made a very feeble attempt at God save Ireland' (Lumb 1885). The young man who described this incident, also recorded that he had been unaware of the marked difference, both in appearance and attitudes, between the Orangemen and the southern Irish. Shipboard life broadened horizons and reinforced prejudices. Surprisingly, religious services were rarely disturbed by either sectarian rivalry or mischief makers. A priest usually accompanied Irish shipments in the early years and maintained a measure of control, though they were known to disrupt the school, visit the single women's quarters 'in a covert manner' and conduct the Mass while drunk (see COL/A72;65–3060).

Class differentiation remained a persistent problem throughout the period. As we have seen, the Commissioners' ships carried only steerage passengers, short-ships mostly catered for saloon travellers, but the government vessels had to accommodate three, sometimes four, classes. On the latter, the landed social structure maintained: 'The masses below deck represented the masses at home . . . the captain's table was the seaborne equivalent of a manor house' (Charlwood 1981:105). Yet there were exceptions like the publican who was returning to the colony; he beat his wife, used offensive language and clearly belonged to 'the masses', but he was able to afford the 'better' class. Although a levelling process was at work, differences were frequently emphasized as a defence against the changes, uncertainties and the unfamiliarity of their present situation. Dr Scott spoke for a good many surgeons when he outlined two fundamental reasons why Queensland government vessels should not carry a mixture of classes. First, there was the matter of space. Not only did the cabin passengers occupy an area far out of proportion to their numbers, but dividing between decks into three or more compartments effectively reduced the space and did not allow adequate exercise for the release of pent-up energy. Second, a proportion of the cabin passengers were lively young men with 'rampant passions' and, loosed from parental constraint, they roamed the vessel, disturbing the peace and devising ways of gaining access to the single-female section; their arrogance was 'destructive of good feeling' (COL/A67:65–1307). Each group jealously guarded their deck space, but regularly encroached on another compartment's territory. Those in the saloon assumed they had the 'run of the ship', while insisting on exclusive rights to their area. Steerage travellers resented these 'scions of Nobility' and 'aristocratic Fops' using their status and freedom to 'exercise authority over the poorer classes' (Blasdall 1862).

Some surgeons managed to keep 'above' and 'below' deck completely separate, but others continually met with resistance from those 'not accustomed to control of any kind'. Dr Underhay claimed that carrying cabin passengers turned emigrant ships into 'floating brothels and seminaries of vice' (COL/A72:65–2787). The fact that single women were usually berthed directly below the cabin area did not make the situation any easier; Dr Webb, on the SS *Tara* in 1890, overheard some 'disgraceful conversations' (COL/A610:90–3198). Twenty years earlier on the *Indus*, a few of the saloon men were found smuggling notes through to the girls offering them work as prostitutes on arrival (COL/A143:70–1993). Although the experiment to send one-class vessels seemed to succeed, it proved commercially non-viable; again the ideal was at variance with reality. Colonists who joined steamers as first-class passengers to travel between the Queensland ports proved particularly troublesome. When those at the cabin table played off the captain and officers against the surgeon, they subverted his authority and usually disturbed the whole ship. Occasionally, saloon passengers and immigrants worked off their tensions and surplus energy through an 'approved' wrestling or sporting tournament.

Apart from the friction with the upper classes, the steerage compartment, representing as it did a range of social levels from the lower-working to the middle classes, produced its own internal conflicts. Sometimes parents objected to their children being indiscriminately mixed in the school (see COL/A128:69–2736); but much of the ill feeling was initiated by the full-paying immigrants who 'fancied themselves' and created 'a constant source of grumbling' (COL/A216:75–3321). Those returning to the colony after a visit 'back home', 'had the edge' on 'new chums' and lost no opportunity to let this be known, even though many of the subsidized immigrants were of a similar or higher social status. Full-payers felt they should not be subject to the same rules and regulations. There was some basis for this attitude since shipping agents often gave them to understand there would be no restrictions during the voyage, and according to the *Queensland Guide*, they could expect 'cabin comforts' and 'table indulgences' (see COL/A421:85–3250; 576:89–3340). They therefore refused to do cleaning duties or paid others to do them, were insolent and insisted on going ashore at ports along the route. 'This constant trouble with full payers takes up most of my time', Dr Collins complained in 1888 (COL/A567:88–10818). Several surgeons recommended that the regulations be stamped on the contract tickets; and in 1884 the immigration agent advocated that the full-paying steerage class be excluded on government ships since they were 'a great source of annoyance', a number immediately went south, and others proved 'unsuitable colonists' (COL/A404:84–7454). Following the wreck of the SS *Dacca* in 1890, some of the steerage passengers reckoned they had been unjustly compensated, but the authorities dismissed their claims as unreasonable; men professing to be 'agricultural labourers' had lost valuable sets of carpenter's tools and 'ball dresses trimmed with lace' were regarded as unnecessary 'to the outfit of a domestic servant' (COL/A624:90–8229).

Anyone connected with emigration knew that, for the sake of discipline and health during a voyage, misconduct of any description had to be 'promptly and severely checked'. As Rev. Father Dunne pointed out in 1863, 'if order be not established and maintained an emigrant ship is no better than a floating hell' (quoted in Crowley 1951:245). Surgeons could appoint extra constables if a situation proved difficult to control; but corporal punishment was forbidden, so they regularly sought advice concerning appropriate disciplinary measures. Although a few recommended that a lock-up be provided, this was seen as impolitic since Queensland would be the only emigration service having to resort to such an expedient (QVP 1866:1054). Others believed that physical punishment of any sort was useless, and that miscreant immigrants ought to be threatened with prosecution on arrival (see, for example, COL/A226:76–2300). The type of correction was left to the discretion of the surgeon and captain; and cabin passengers were not exempt. One of them consumed too much brandy, was found by the captain 'apparently insane' and bleeding from dagger wounds, and was securely restrained (Log *Pekina* 1873, BT 99/1017); a married woman in the second cabin fell out with her husband and used such 'disgraceful language' she had to be put in irons (Log *Sirocco* 1865, BT 99/301); a 'reverend gentleman' who stirred up much trouble among the immigrants was finally placed in solitary confinement on biscuit and water for eight days after assaulting a constable (COL/ A190:73–2517).

The use of irons or handcuffs was the most common form of punishment, with periods of detention ranging from an hour to a week (cases of particularly violent behaviour might be given the strait-jacket treatment). Offenders were confined below deck, in an empty hospital or on deck, as a public example. An immigrant on the *Flying Cloud* in 1865, 'having several stolen articles found in his possession . . . was handcuffed round an upright stanchion on the main deck from 10 am to 1 pm as a thief' (Log, NMML). The tempers of two fighting Irishmen quickly cooled when they were restrained on the poop in freezing weather (Ricou 1872). A married woman who refused to remove 'a tub of dirty clothes and soap suds' from her berth was placed in irons in the hospital, but after twenty-four hours was released 'on her promising to behave better for the future' (Log *Wansfell* 1861, NMML). Cancelling or reducing the rations for a time was another common corrective. Dr Russell's list of 'breaches of discipline' and how he handled them is fairly typical – spilling water, one day off rations; dirty bathroom and refusing to clean, off bread three days; taking bread from the issuing room by force, three days in irons; sharing the bread, three days on biscuit and water; striking a constable on the head, twenty-four hours in irons (COL/A365:83–3624). Some surgeons tried to make the punishment fit the crime; two young men caught forcing an entrance to the single female compartment were put to 'hard labour' to work off their ardour (COL/A370:83– 5250); an immigrant found asleep on the night watch had to do extra duty (COL/A477:86–6347). One foul-mouthed woman was placed in irons on deck and gagged, but the torrent of colourful language continued, so a constable sat opposite her and shot a pannikin of salt water in her face each time she opened her mouth. According to the surgeon, this had the 'desired effect' (COL/ A145:70–1993). A list of 'bad' characters was usually included with the official documents; and more than once, immigrants on arrival received a short prison sentence, under the passenger act, for refusing cleaning duties. A single man spent forty-eight hours in jail because he would not scrape and holystone the deck

(COL/A302:80–6137); but the navvy who abused the magistrate with 'blasphemous and obscene language' was given a three-month term (COL/A8:60–1985).

As the voyage neared its end, most of the strains and tensions relaxed. 'It is wonderful what a soothing influence the smell of land has on the tempers of crabbed three-months' voyagers', commented a ship's newspaper, and hastened to add that, 'considering the great number . . . packed in this man-coop we have pecked one another very little indeed. We have had our disagreeables, but we have also had lots of fun' (RHSQ *Mainstay* 1863:48). Impressions of the time at sea revealed a range of responses from the man who complained that they 'had a long and often rough passage . . . [and] were treated more like convicts than free people' (COL/A387:84–2686), to the one who declared he 'never enjoyed anything so well' (Lumb 1885). While the sick, the bereaved and the disgruntled might feel apprehensive, those in good health and spirits confidently faced the future. The doctor who noted 'the painful sensations' of farewell when leaving the mother country, also observed how, on reaching 'the land of their adoption, hope appeared to predominate over sadness' (COL/A334:82–2136). Evidence of this hope lies in the fact that, of the thousands who sailed, only seven committed suicide.

A great sense of relief accompanied the safe arrival of a vessel, but the sudden release from the physical and emotional constraints of shipboard life or the prospect of coping with an unfamiliar land sometimes intensified behavioural problems. The quarantine reports were peppered with instances of gross misconduct sparked off by disappointment and impatience, continued discipline and poor conditions. Even the few hours' steamer trip from the bay could get out of hand, especially if liquor was available. Apparently, a 'welcome drink' was usual (see Randall 1868), and immigrants sometimes arrived in 'a disgusting state of intoxication' (COL/A32:62–2065). Irregularities at the immigration depot differed little from those for the voyage except that some refused to leave or would not accept the employment offered to them; the wages might be too low, the work unsuitable or it was 'up country'. New arrivals from the United Kingdom, particularly those with an urban background, tended to remain in settled communities (see Morrison 1966:26). Continental immigrants, on the other hand, were generally prepared 'to carve for themselves permanent homes out of the scrub' (Schindler 1916:70).

Adverse reports were most frequent during the first half of the period. Coghlan (1918:II,937) records that, as navvies poured into the colony in 1865, 'the arrival of an immigrant ship was invariably followed by such disgraceful scenes of fighting and drunkenness that the very name of immigrant became a reproach'. A decade later, as the quality of new colonists began to deteriorate once again, the Agent-General was advised that if 'a more orderly and respectable' class could not be procured, it was 'better to be without them' (QVP 1875:II,620), and the immigration agent requested a high protective fence for the depot to keep out idlers and restrain immigrants (COL/A217:76–230). Local publicans did a roaring trade. Although most shipments included a number of 'quarrelsome' or 'dirty and untidy' people, the majority were seemingly well-behaved and, apart from times of recession, quickly found work or agreed to transfer to an area of high demand. Refractory immigrants, if apprehended, were punished. Three single men who arrived by the *Montmorency* in 1860 were charged with 'disorderly conduct' in the depot. One of them, having found a job, 'cooly and illegally' entered the ladies' section to select a wife; the police magistrate admonished and discharged him (COL/A8:60–1985). The three who assaulted the depot wardsman in 1888 were each imprisoned for forty-eight hours (COL/A550:88–5973).

Apart from specific comments relating to immigrant health and behaviour, a respectable appearance was immensely important. As Fitzgerald (1982:317) points out, policy makers held to the 'simplistic equation' between moral and material progress. Statements describing the impression created by new arrivals are widely divergent and have been difficult to summarize. The single women on one vessel were regarded as 'the sweepings of the streets' and totally unsuited as domestic servants, while on another, they were recorded as 'young, neat and cleanly, and . . . remarkably good looking' (COL/A326:81–5216; 80:66–1743). Moreover, the worst descriptions were not confined to any one type of vessel or the best to another; British and German, sail and steam, government and private all carried 'a few black sheep' and one or two 'downright bad characters'. Some 68 per cent of the comments expressed satisfaction (this proportion increased from 47 to100 per cent over the four decades); 10.5 per cent indicated a fair selection; only the remaining 21.5 per cent referred to new arrivals who fell short of the desired standard.

The immigration agent's report for the SS *Duke of Argyll* in November 1884 illustrates those qualities approved by the authorities: the married people were a 'fair average'; the single men were healthy and robust, though at least a quarter of the 'labourers' had, 'judging by their feminine looking hands, never done much hard work'; the single women were 'very respectable' (COL/A407:84–8021). At the lower end of the scale, we find descriptions such as 'dirty, lazy and . . . lousey', 'rough and ignorant', 'not an intellectual lot', 'indifferent . . . and inferior'. Other immigrants 'like the ship . . . [were] deficient in order and cleanliness' (COL/A75:66–247). The navvies of the 1860s were 'a rough class . . . rude and dissolute in their habits' (QVP 1866:1073); local employers in Maryborough complained that new arrivals during 1875 were 'an extremely undesirable type, morally and physically' (COL/A215:75–3199). However, the sorriest-looking shipments seemed to be those from Hamburg. In 1866, the *Wandrahm's* surgeon claimed that 'the scum of the population' had been collected (QVP 1866:1020), and as late as 1885, the Agent-General was loathe to pass the free-nominated passengers; but by 1891 a 'superior' class had begun to arrive (QVP 1886:II,898; 1892:II,810). As the period progressed, statements of approval – 'fine, robust people', 'eligible', 'a desirable acquisition to the colony' – became increasingly common. Yet it was a 'sturdy, hardy, and thoroughly agricultural appearance' that most impressed officials (QVP 1901:IV,1050). One of 'Jordan's lambs' from the early years of immigration recalled that Jordan did his work 'so well' that in a short time, 'many hundreds of sturdy farmers and their families, young farm labourers, and many others . . . [were] all bent upon going on the land . . . A magnificent lot of hardy pioneers they were, no wasters, no drunkards, no unemployable were to be found amongst them' (RHSQ Immigration). Colonial leaders never lost their vision of the small settler – young, healthy and respectable, financially independent and prepared to work hard on the land (see Plate 16).

Although follow-up reports represent only a fraction of the total comments, they shed further light on the suitability of immigrants. Thirty per cent referred to difficulties with employment, while 10 per cent readily found work; but the infrequency

Plate 16 Arrival – an address by the immigration agent

of such statements suggests that most new arrivals were absorbed into the workforce. However, a small proportion, apart from those who died at sea, failed completely to contribute to the life of the colony. Many of them were physically or mentally ill. Exact numbers are not known for those who were admitted to hospital or an institution soon after landing; but in the twelve-month peak period of immigration (1883–84), 177 cases were sent to the Brisbane Hospital. The immigration agent, while acknowledging that the unhealthy state of Brisbane at the time may have accounted for some of the admissions, was sufficiently disturbed by the high costs and death rate to demand an inquiry (COL/A387:84–2983). Twenty years earlier, eighteen fever patients from the *Flying Cloud* were hospitalized, each for an average of 53.5 days (COL/A57:64–2054). Some who were unwell on arrival would have been cared for by family or friends, others received medical attention during their time in the depot, and those suffering from physical disability, allegedly sustained as the result of negligence at sea, were brought before the Immigration Board. Most immigrants after recovering from acute illnesses were able to look for work, but chronic cases, without support, had to turn to the government for relief.

Assistance was requested for those incapacitated by insanity, imbecility, injury and organic disease, chronic heart complaints and consumption being the most common. Some cases were refused; but others, likely to become 'a permanent burden' on public funds, were shipped back to England at government expense. Certain others, such as widows whose husbands had died at sea or soon after arrival and left them to support a young family, were also given a return passage. Alternatively, charitable concerns raised the fare or the children were taken into custody while the mother went to work. Orphans without relatives in the colony were committed to care until old enough to earn a living. Destitute cases who could work were usually sent where labour was most needed, or were organized into public works programmes, collected government relief or drifted south. In times of recession, the colony saw a great wastage of healthy immigrants, and throughout the period, men with large families were particularly disadvantaged. Occasionally, new colonists were imprisoned for theft and other breaches of the law soon after arrival. The story is told of a middle-aged man, a kleptomaniac, who 'had been put on board by his loving family with a ticket to Brisbane'; the last heard of him was that he had not been allowed to land and 'was sent back' (Watson 1968:2–3). Lastly, there were those who used the system as a cheap route to the southern colonies; but improved detection, law enforcement and heavier penalties gradually reduced the incidence of such cases.

Given official expectations, it is not surprising that half the unfavourable follow-up comments relating to a particular group referred to single women. There were regular complaints of girls who passed as governesses, yet proved useless in that capacity or as servants; employers demanded 'more workers and fewer drones' (COL/A341:82–3901). Many young women emigrated to join male friends and a few clearly intended working as prostitutes. Cabin passengers and single girls who 'came to an agreement' as soon as they landed in 1870 were prosecuted under the immigration act (COL/A145:70–1994). Frequently, the oldest profession was the only alternative for those who did not adapt to colonial domestic service. In 1882, the immigration agent listed fifty girls who had 'resorted to prostitution' and the vessels on which they arrived during the previous year (COL/A334:82–2129). Although this number represented only 3.8 per cent of the single female complement for that period, all had sailed as free passengers. The authorities, concerned that public funds were being squandered, tightened the selection procedure. Nevertheless, the over-all performance of this sector of the immigration seems satisfactory. Morally, they caused the greatest concern, but single women were healthier and better behaved than any other group afloat.

The voyage health-care policy not only aimed at maintaining a healthy shipboard environment, but was, because of its emphasis on good order and discipline, instrumental in weeding out 'undesirable' immigrants and, where possible, correcting 'the error of their ways'. Many, in addition to physically benefiting from the time at sea, must have absorbed colonial values. There were defects in the system and problems with administration, some immigrants unfortunately died in transit and others were unsuitable, but the majority of new arrivals apparently satisfied the authorities; they were healthy, respectable, ready to work and determined to succeed. In short, they were able to contribute to Queensland's development.

CONCLUSION

In 1909, Queensland celebrated her jubilee. The official government publication, *Our First Half-Century. A Review of Queensland Progress*, furnished citizens with the 'salient facts' of the State's development and reminded them that, in the brief period since her founding, the country had been

> 'reclaimed from the wilderness, and made the home of a happy, progressive, and enlightened people. Bearing in mind what Queensland was fifty years ago, and what it is today . . . its jubilee was eminently worth celebrating . . . in the spirit of a people conscious of what had been done, and full of enthusiasm for continued development.'
>
> (1909:239)

Despite the teething problems, policy makers and the population in general retained a sense of optimism. No one, it seems, doubted that Queensland had progressed and would continue to do so.

From the time of separation, her leaders assumed that colonial viability largely depended on a land-related immigration policy. They were convinced that if suitable people were attracted to the country, then progress would follow as day follows night. Just as natural selection assured the survival of a species, selected immigrants would secure the successful development of the colony. The whole thrust of immigration, including the health-care policy in transit, was to swell the workforce and stimulate population growth. Successive governments, irrespective of their platform, maintained this approach and were prepared to subsidize and supervise closely the whole operation, but only under certain conditions; future colonists must be young, physically fit and morally responsible; a large proportion had to be single women. The evidence indicates that the majority of the quarter of a million souls who sailed from Great Britain and Europe for Queensland between 1860 and 1900 met these conditions. Careful screening had seen to that.

Each shipment was intended to reflect the ideal colonial society. Immigrants should be a sturdy, healthy people who conformed to the middle-class norms of industry, resourcefulness, integrity and respectability. Indeed, each floating community became an experiment in social policy, the fundamental principles of which remained unaltered throughout the forty years – selection of desirable immigrants, maintenance of health during the voyage and preparation for colonial life. Policy makers not only worked on the premise that if healthy people sailed under healthy conditions, this would diminish the need for curative measures, but they extended the health-care programme beyond disease prevention and treatment to provide for mental and moral fitness. This programme was based on rules for health and discipline embodied in the passenger legislation and the more stringent regulations enforced on government-chartered vessels and written into each shipping contract. Under these the company, the captain and his crew were expected to promote passenger welfare and bring the ship safely into port. The surgeon-superintendent, appointed as the policy's chief executive officer at sea, was one of a network of personnel responsible to the colonial authorities for coordinating each phase of the programme from embarkation to employment.

Some 80 per cent of the Queensland immigrants sailed under government auspices, knowing that compliance with the regulations would be in their best interests. The majority of them were in the prime of life; they travelled under conditions that had no counterpart on land and therefore generated patterns of sickness, birth and death which mostly derived from the maritime environment. Consequently, there are few similarities between the immigration and the populations of either the home or receiving countries. Although the programme was designed to meet every contingency during the voyage, the ideal did not always square with reality; physical and moral needs had to be balanced against functionality and economy. The results indicate that health care was, by and large, effectively applied on Queensland vessels; only 1 per cent of the numbers embarked did not survive the voyage and many of these deaths were under the age of five. Most of the remaining 99 per cent seem to have fulfilled the criteria required by the colonial authorities; those who did not were appropriately dealt with. And the data show conclusively that the survival rate and the quality of immigrants improved over time.

Many factors contributed to this satisfactory record – better organization and increasingly experienced personnel, rigid segregation of the passengers and crew, shipping developments (particularly the introduction of steamships to the Queensland route after 1881), the rising living standards and improved public health in the sending countries, and the motivation of immigrants to reach the new land and secure a better life. Yet one factor, more than any other, determined the outcome of a voyage – the extent to which the Queensland regulations were enforced. Vessels with the poorest performance were those on which the regulations did not apply, or were impeded or relaxed. The early Black Ball voyages, German ships and bounty vessels provide ample illustration of this. Single women, that group most controlled by the regulations, had the lowest mortality at sea.

The health-care policy for British and Continental immigrants sailing to colonial Queensland bore the clear imprint of rigid regulation, paternalism and the government's commitment to progress. But did the system pay off? A ninety-nine per cent passenger survival rate, a twenty-fold population increase between 1860 and 1900, and evidence of continuing expansion and material progress suggest that the fundamental tenents of the policy were viable and that the investment had been worthwhile.

NOTES

Chapter 1: Government policy (pp. 1–22)

1 Ross Fitzgerald (1982) in his exposé of the belief in progress and its impact on Queensland's development counterbalances earlier accounts of the country such as *The History of Queensland . . . An Epitome of Progress* (1921) and *Triumph in the Tropics* (Cilento and Lack 1959).

2 The Rt Hon. W. Monsell in 1870, for example, claimed that 'There could not be both State-aided and private emigration. Persons would never contribute money if they knew they could get it from the State' (PD Eng. 1870, cxcix 1022). For a full discussion of imperial policy see Crowley 1951:18 ff.

3 In June 1831 the British government appointed Commissioners to promote emigration to Australia. The Commission resigned at the end of 1832 and the work was taken over by the Colonial Office until the formation of the Colonial Land and Emigration Commission in 1840.

4 Sir George Ferguson Bowen (1821–99), a Classics graduate from Oxford and formerly Chief Secretary for the Ionian Islands, was Queensland's first governor, an office he held for eight years (Pike 1966). Sir Robert George Wyndham Herbert (1831–1905), also an Oxford graduate, became Gladstone's private secretary in 1855 and was called to the Bar in 1858. He went to Queensland as the private secretary to Sir George Bowen, was appointed as Colonial Secretary and became premier after the first elections in 1860. Following the troubles of 1866, Herbert resigned and returned to England. In 1871 he was appointed as permanent under-secretary for the Colonies (Serle 1949).

5 Only 15 per cent of all convicts transported to Australia were women, a large proportion of whom were 'prostitutes and petty

criminals'. Not all of them married and those who did were relatively old (see Robson 1965:4,9,141).

6 Since only one shipment arrived in 1860, the numbers involved have been included with statistics for the first decade of the colonial period.

7 See Lewis (1973:31ff.) for an elaboration of this facet of the colony's economic policy.

8 A transferable land order to the value of £18 was made available to anyone who paid the full fare for himself or another.

9 In 1857 the Victorian government sent an Agent-General to London to control emigration; other colonies soon followed their example. Henry Jordan (1818–90) was born in England, studied medicine and dentistry and went to Australia in the early 1850s as a missionary to the aborigines. He settled in Brisbane in 1856 and was elected to represent the town in the colony's first Legislative Assembly. In 1861 he took up the post of Emigration Commissioner for Queensland in London. Following his return to Brisbane in 1866, Jordan remained active in colonial affairs as a parliamentarian and public servant (Pike 1966).

10 Heussler was a prominent colonial figure, well known for his entrepreneurial ventures; he strongly advocated German immigration.

11 For an account of the Queensland Immigration Society conducted by Bishop Quinn, see Boland (1963–4:307–21). The whole point of the operation was that it should become self-perpetuating, with contributions from one shipment defraying the cost of the next. Jordan pointed out that, under these private schemes, immigrants not only forfeited their land orders, but were required to pay a considerable portion of the passage money to the sponsoring parties (QVP 1863:II,444).

12 The inhabitants of Brisbane petitioned the government to withdraw this scheme in 1862 (QVP 1862:235) about the time the British India Labourers Act was passed. This was never enforced and was finally repealed in 1886. In 1863 it was proposed that Chinese and freed negroes from the United States should be brought in to work on the plantations. But there were always those who believed Europeans could cope with manual labour in the tropics (see Mayne 1860–61,3:343).

13 Assisted passengers were selected and paid a nominal amount for their passage which helped defray the running expenses of the Queensland Office in London. The shippers received a land order for each statute adult who sailed under this arrangement.

14 Miss Maria Rye who conducted an emigration scheme on behalf of middle-class women and children was one of the most vociferous

complainants (see CO 386/76:382). By the time the whole issue was raised in the colonial Lower House, Jordan had assumed responsibility for the entire emigration to Queensland and the last vessel despatched for the colony by the Commissioners had arrived.

15 When the Agent-General took office in 1870, communication by telegram had reduced the time delay to six weeks. In 1872 London and Adelaide were linked by cable, and by 1875 the link between London and Brisbane was fully operational; a telegram took approximately three days. By the 1880s news could be relayed in two hours.

16 The Agent-General in 1874 refused to accept applications for free passages from families with children under six years of age. See QVP 1875:2,580.

17 Some years earlier an Italian contingent, the remnant of an abortive colonizing scheme in New Britain, settled in north Queensland and were among the first cane growers. Southern Queenslanders continued to oppose the importation of coloured labour, and in 1890 plans were made to attract British workers to the plantations (QVP 1891:IV,11). But these, like the Italian arrangements, had to be abandoned as the economy deteriorated.

18 The other Australian colonies were similarly affected with the rate of immigration dropping from one for every eighty Australians before 1890 to one for every 1,000 after 1890 (Koutsoukis 1966:57). To make matters worse, Japanese began pouring into north Queensland in 1894 (QVP 1894:I,102).

19 These arrivals are not included in the study since they did not travel direct from Europe. See Borrie (1954) and Lyng (1939) for an account of the Continental immigration.

Chapter 2: Emigration and immigration (pp. 23–49)

1 Data relating to Queensland's population and organized immigration (see Woolcock 1983:525–27 for tables) have been compiled from the annual statistical reports for the colony, the Agent-General's returns and summaries and the immigration agent's returns (QVP 1861–1901; QVP 1901:II,1333,1369) and the 'Census of Queensland – Synopsis' (QVP 1902:II,943). Estimates for the immigration vary considerably; official returns show that 240,210 entered the colony from overseas, while Chisholm's *Australian Encyclopaedia* (1958:s.v. Immigration) estimates 256,000. It was impossible to assess accurately the total inward and outward movements for the colony. Borrie (1958:1) points out that the migration record for each colony

'becomes increasingly complicated as facilities are improved for travel between the colonies – both sea and land – with colonial statisticians making no satisfactory attempt to isolate passenger traffic from genuine migration'.

2 The Agent-General advertised the colony through international exhibitions, the Imperial Institute, lectures and the publication of official handbooks. The popular pamphlet, *Queensland, The Colony for Working Men*, received wide distribution; placards were displayed in post offices around the United Kingdom and, towards the end of the century, lantern slides brought the colony to life.

3 See Carrier and Jeffrey (1953:95–6) and Carrothers (1929:306–09) for annual tabulations of the United Kingdom emigration between 1860 and 1900.

4 An attempt has been made to extract the United Kingdom component of the Queensland immigration in order to compare it to the total outflow from Britain and Ireland (see Woolcock 1983:527).

5 The Continental agent in his 1873 report stated that, of the 132,419 emigrants sailing from Hamburg and Bremen, only 2,245 embarked for Queensland; of these 315 were Germans, the remainder being Scandinavians, Swiss and Italians (QVP 1875:II,734–35). Some 17,949 Continental immigrants (6,362 in the first and 11,587 in the second decade) sailed for the colony between 1861 and 1879, compared to 8,050 for the remainder of the period; but the nature of the data is such that it has only been possible to use the numbers for the first two decades for the purposes of comparison.

6 For a detailed comparative coverage of the components of the United Kingdom emigration, the colonial immigration, and the populations of England and Wales and Queensland between 1860 and 1900 see Woolcock (1983:530–34). The tables are based on sources listed in notes 1 and 3 above as well as the *Census Report* for England and Wales (1861 to 1901).

7 In 1862 when the Society began, the Irish represented 38 per cent of the immigration for that year; in all, 8,949 statute adults were introduced under its auspices (see QVP 1863:II,401–501). More than 60 per cent of the remittance passengers forwarded by the Commissioners in 1863 were Irish (QVP 1864:411). Apparently the nomination system was popular among them, whatever their destination (see Crowley 1951:43–4).

8 According to the Agent-General's returns (QVP 1872–1901), an estimated 35,016 immigrants were full-payers and 200,055 were government subsidized.

9 Agents working for the Commissioners during the 1860s received a fee of 15/- for each single woman selected (CO 386/179:141–42). The

commission given to Queensland agents for full-paying passengers was usually double the fee for free and assisted immigrants (see QVP 1875:II,629).

10 The occupations of the Continental and United Kingdom immigrants are not distinguished in the records. Only those categories corresponding to the immigrant occupations have been extracted from the Queensland census figures. However, direct comparison between the immigration and colonial population is not possible after 1881.

11 The statistical analysis of these features (see Woolcock 1983:536–46 for tables) is based on the revised numbers for the immigration and derived from sources listed in Note 6 above and Cumpston (1927:571–77).

12 Such husbands were usually listed as single men, and their wives and children when they emigrated were accommodated in the single female compartment. These mothers, where possible, have been included with the married figures, but married men travelling alone could not be distinguished. This, therefore, produces certain distortions in the relative numbers for single and married immigrants. In the last years of the century, a married woman who applied for a subsidized passage was not allowed to travel alone without her husband's consent (QVP 1900:V,654).

Chapter 3: Shipping organization (pp. 50–81)

1 Although immigrants reached the colony via ships to the southern colonies, only direct sailings from British and German ports to Queensland have been included. For statistical tables relating to vessels and voyages see Woolcock 1983:547–62. Vessel data (tonnage, dimensions, year built, construction material and owners) have been derived from *Lloyd's Register* (1860–1900), *The Mercantile Navy List* (1865–1900), Stammers (1978) and Fairburn (1945–55). Supplementary information was located in the passenger lists (see notes on Table 1), Davies (n.d.), Crew Lists and Logs (NMML and BT27 and 99) and immigration returns (QVP 1860–1901). There is considerable discrepancy between the various sources; but, where possible, the net tonnage figures have been extracted and differences which occurred after the 1872 act transferred tonnage measurement to the Board of Trade reconciled. Voyage details (passage time, ports and quarantine) have been collated from *Lloyd's List, Shipping Gazette and Lloyd's List, Lloyd's Weekly Shipping Index* and the surgeons', health officers' and immigration agents' reports and other relevant sources.

2 The steerage rate for the Black Ball Line passengers was £13 with a surcharge of £2.18.0 to Brisbane and £3.17.0 to the northern ports, compared to £16 for British India steamers twenty years later.

3 The internal volume of the hull became the basis for calculating the 'under deck tonnage'. This, in addition to deck structures, poop and forecastle, provided a gross tonnage measurement. The former measurement, when known, has been used throughout this study.

4 The *Indus*, 1,139 tons, had been built on the Thames in 1847 and was an old P & O steamer converted to a sailing ship. The *Royal Dane* was a former American wooden ship, built in 1854 and acquired by the Black Ball Line in 1863. Both vessels were sold when the Line went into liquidation in 1866, but continued under charter with the reorganized firm until 1871 when they passed to the London Line operated by Taylor, Bethell and Roberts. See Stammers (1978) for a full description of the Black Ball ships.

5 Towson (1854:101). The first fleet to Australia in 1788 took almost thirty-six weeks and as late as 1850 the London–Sydney voyage averaged 120 days (Dunlop and Pike 1960:122); but between 1850 and 1855 the passage time was reduced from eighteen to fourteen weeks (Blainey 1968:192). The passage time in this study has been calculated from (and including) the day of departure from the first port at which immigrants embarked to (and including) the day anchor was dropped in a Queensland port. It does not include embarkation and trans-shipment days.

6 King Island, the scene of some fifty-seven wrecks, was known as the 'Marine Graveyard of Bass Strait' (Halls 1978:24), until measures were introduced to improve navigation. A Queensland immigrant sailing through the Strait in 1870 recorded that there 'lighthouses everywhere' (Ricou 1872).

7 See Hitchins (1931) for a history of the Commission. My summary of emigration reforms is based largely on MacDonagh's (1961) discussion of the development of imperial passenger legislation between 1803 and 1872.

8 Under the 1855 act all sailing vessels carrying more than one statute adult for every fifty registered tons, or steamships with more than one for every twenty-five tons were also subject to the legislation. Details of the provisions of this act are discussed in Chapter 4; in addition, it allowed for such emergencies as a passenger being sent to hospital, a delayed sailing and shipwreck.

9 Anderson and Anderson as well as McIlwraith, McEacharn and Company were London-based firms, while Thomas Law operated out of Glasgow. The last two firms continued to despatch vessels to the colony well after the commencement of the steamship service.

McIlwraith, McEacharn and Co. retained the contract, first signed in 1875, for sailing vessels to the northern ports until 1889. They amalgamated with BISN Co. in 1887 (see Lewis 1973).

10 The BISN Company, founded in 1862, developed from the Burmah Steam Navigation Company which had been formed in Calcutta in 1857 by two Scots, Mackinnon and Mackenzie (Saunders 1948:17–18).

11 Because of Godeffroy's links with the Prussian government, it was recognized that the contract was open to corruption (QVP 1866:1019). Indeed, the firm's political and economic ramifications would put them on a par with any twentieth century multinational company. Apart from their European connections, they were well established in the Australian trade and had strong interests in the Pacific.

12 Despite the government's original intention that the immigration be equally divided between Brisbane and the northern ports, this did not work out in practice. Unless immigrants had friends or relatives living in the vicinity of a particular port, they had no real concept of their destination and had to rely on the advice of officials in the United Kingdom to direct them where the labour need was greatest. It seems that in the early years, subsidized immigrants had little option but to go where they were sent, while full-payers could rarely be persuaded to accept anywhere other than Brisbane (QVP 1866:1052).

13 The time in quarantine has been calculated from (and including) the day after the vessel arrived in port to (and including) the day on which 90 per cent or more of the passengers were released. Voyages with delayed pratique or embedded quarantine have been excluded from the calculations.

Chapter 4: Passenger arrangements (pp. 82–113)

1 *Instructions to Surgeon-Superintendents of Queensland Ships Sailing Under the Direction of H.M. Government of Queensland* (London) were first published in 1864 and revised at regular intervals – 1866, 1872, 1875, 1879 and 1882. The Preface to the 1875 edition explains that many of the instructions were 'in substance the same as those contained in the Instructions to the Medical Officers, published by HM Emigration Commissioners', but were adapted to the needs of Queensland passenger ships.

2 In this study the total passenger complement (cabin and steerage, adult, child and infant), rather than the steerage statute numbers, has

been used since the statute-adult classification is not available for each voyage. Furthermore, current medical opinion held that a child required as much 'breathing space' as an adult (see QVP 1866:1019). Information for the German vessels in the 1860s is very limited, but the contract with Knorr and Co. in 1871 required 18 superficial feet for each statute adult (see COL/A185:73–1157). For tonnage and space tables see Woolcock 1983:563–64.

3 The Passengers' Act, 1855, s.26. The Commissioners continually experimented with various types of ventilating apparatus, requesting returns and running control studies on the vessels on which they were installed (see CO 386/179:36 and MacDonagh 1961:247). The ventilation of ships was a matter of concern for both the royal and merchant marines (see BMJ 1874:I,555 for an account of the various systems in use).

4 After a satisfactory trial period with water-distilling equipment, an order-in-council in 1859 sanctioned its use on all passenger ships (see ECR 1859). James Lind of the Royal Navy had successfully experimented with such equipment in the mid-eighteenth century (see Watt 1979:147).

5 The 140 days included full rations for 112 days and a four-week reserve supply. At one stage it was suggested that sailing ships for the northern ports be provisioned for 150 days (QVP 1876:II,1024–025). Since the Orient Line steamers to Sydney carried only seventy-five days' supply, requirements for the British India ships were reduced accordingly.

6 See ISS 1875:59 for details. I am indebted to Dr Margaret Crawford for providing a nutritional analysis of the dietary scale (see Woolcock 1983:565–66). The following is a summary of the composition of the items based on their cooked weight, according to McCannee and Widdowson (1960), and compared to current recommended daily amounts (see *Recommended Daily Amounts of Food Energy and Nutrients for Groups of People in the United Kingdom*, DHSS Report). These, however, serve only as a guide and must be applied cautiously in the historical context.

	protein	energy* value	calcium	iron
	g	k cal	mg	mg
ship's dietary – per diem	85.1	3296	212.7	25.03
recommended daily amounts				
men 18–34 years: sedentary	63	2510	500	10
moderately active	72	2900	500	10
very active	84	3350	500	10

	protein	energy* value	calcium	iron
	g	k cal	mg	mg
women 18–34 years: most occupations	54	2150	500	12
very active	62	2500	500	12

*Net energy value for protein, fat and carbohydrate

Vitamin levels have not been calculated since they are delicate, unstable substances and vulnerable to change. Lime juice was a valuable source of vitamin C. No salt meat was issued to little children, and eggs and preserved milk were added to their rations. For the German dietary see QGG 1861,2:93 and QVP 1871:926.

7 The 'Directions' were incorporated in schedules appended to the immigration acts and regulations. The minimum clothing supply was as follows:

	adult	child
shifts/shirts	6	9
flannel shirts/petticoats	2	4
stockings	6 pairs	6 pairs
boots/shoes	2 pairs	2 pairs
strong exterior suits/gowns	2	2
cloak/coat	–	1

The government supplied the later steamships with large straw hats, complete with pugaree to prevent them blowing overboard. Men were advised to purchase broad-brimmed felt hats.

8 Crowley (1951:143) maintains that the system of medical inspection remained unsatisfactory until the introduction of the Commonwealth medical examination in 1912. However, at least two medical men and a government official checked immigrants for the colony at the time of departure; subsidized passengers had been seen previously by a referring doctor.

9 The accuracy of many of the ages are doubtful. One matron, for example, remained at thirty-five years during voyages covering a five-year period; when matrons were first selected by the British Ladies Female Emigrant Society, the maximum age limit was set at thirty-five years (QVP 1864:920).

10 The health officer's report – a series of questions relating to the vessel, voyage and health of the passengers and crew – required written replies by either the master or surgeon. Some 347 such reports between 1860 and 1900 have survived.

Chapter 5: Surgeons (pp. 114–145)

1 Historically, surgeons rather than physicians joined the Navy and merchant marine; but by the nineteenth century the term 'surgeon' applied to any qualified medical practitioner in maritime service.

2 It has been possible to extract from the records (passenger lists, health officers' reports and crew lists) a complete listing of all those appointed by the Commissioners between 1860 and 1865 and the Queensland government between 1863 and 1892. Some names were incorrectly spelt and one surgeon changed his by deed-poll between his first and last voyage.

3 For full statistical details relating to the surgeons see Woolcock 1983:568–81. Data for their socio-professional profile have been compiled from the *Medical Directory*, *Medical Register*, crew lists and CO 386/186. Many of those listed in the 'Overseas Section' of the *Directory* gave only minimal details. The few who were Fellows of the Royal College of Surgeons (England) are documented in *Plarr's Lives*. Follow-up information is somewhat fragmentary, but for those who registered in Queensland, the *Government Gazette* is a useful source. The surgeons are discussed as a whole rather than distinguishing those appointed by the Agent-General.

4 Stammers 1978:256 and Crew List SS *Duke of Argyll* January, 1895 NMML. On bounty vessels, British India allowed 2/6 head money for each adult passenger (COL/A384:84–1589); an assistant surgeon received a flat rate of £8 per month.

5 Although surgeons were given a first-class return passage, this did not necessarily include a single cabin, and he was expected to contribute his services free of charge. The shippers paid the £50 gratuity and the return fare. During the 1870s, in place of the return voyage, the surgeon could claim £50 if he presented a first-class certificate within five months of arrival. A surgeon appointed to a British India vessel had to remain with the ship as a regular employee of the company for the return trip. This was a source of continual complaint since conditions were often unsatifactory and some doctors did not want to return by steamer.

6 Registration in Great Britain was introduced under the Medical Act of 1858 (21 & 22 Vict. c.90).

Chapter 6: Crews (pp. 146–178)

1 Seventy per cent of the British Crew Lists and Agreements for the 1860–1900 period are held in the Maritime History Archives, St

Johns, Newfoundland, Canada, 10 per cent at the NMML and 10 per cent at the PRO, England; the remaining 10 per cent are located in various archives in Great Britain and the Commonwealth. Official Logs are similarly distributed, but very few are available after 1875. Copies of certain crew lists are also included with the voyage reports in the COL/A series. Crew numbers or lists are available for 73 per cent of the sailing and 51 per cent of the steam voyages. Statistical details have been tabulated from these sources (see Woolcock 1983:582–94).

2 'Hoisting the dead horse' marked the end of one month at sea when advance notes expired and the crew began earning; the master issued a 'grog' allowance and sometimes the passengers took up a collection for the sailors (Randall 1868). Because of previous disasters during the Crossing the Line ceremony, any interference with the passengers was strictly forbidden (ISS 1875:20).

3 See QGG 1866,7:1281 for a reprint of the circular. Lime juice had to be obtained from a bonded warehouse and be officially certified to contain 15 per cent proof spirits; the one-gallon jars were sealed with oil. *Starving Sailors* (Watt, Freeman and Bynum 1981) deals at length with the question of scurvy, its prevention and treatment.

4 The master of the *Rockhampton* (1863) was charged with overcrowding; on the *Flying Cloud* (1865) the boats came loose causing a fatal accident; and on the *Star Queen* (1875) and the *Kapunda* (1877) there was a shortage of rations and water.

5 The ranks and ages of almost 10,000 seamen on Queensland-bound passenger vessels between 1860 and 1900 are known, with the greatest number available for the 1860s. German crews do not list their ages.

6 Apart from the Logs, a few references to crew health were located in the health officers' and surgeons' reports and immigrant diaries.

7 See BPP 1901 xv 115 (Table 36). In this study the Queensland crew deaths are related to the total voyages rather than the total crews since an estimate for the latter has not been possible. Information relating to crew deaths has been extracted from sources listed in note 1, the health officers' and surgeons' reports and 'Registers of Deaths of British Nationals at Sea' (BT 159). The latter do not cover all the Queensland voyages and suffer from transcription errors. The registers of deaths of British seamen (BT 153, 156, 157) are difficult to research unless names are known; they also cover a limited period. However, the 153 deaths may be taken as a reliable estimate of crew mortality on Queensland vessels.

8 Many sailing vessels were rigged with safety nets to 'strain' the men out of a wave in heavy seas (Knox-Robinson 1978:19). Heat apoplexy

usually resulted from sunstroke or the extremely high temperatures in the boiler room. Measles was a common and fatal disease not only among passengers, but also among sailors of the nineteenth century (BMJ 1876:I,452). Overcrowded conditions and constant exposure to cold and wet encouraged tuberculosis which was 'one of the most important causes of death and invalidism among seafarers' (Roddis 1941:51).

Chapter 7: Life at sea (pp. 179–215)

1 In addition to the surgeons', health officers' and immigration agents' reports, other comments were located in the Agent-Generals' and immigration agents' annual reports (QVP 1861–1901), Immigration Board proceedings, Logs and immigrant diaries. For a statistical analysis of the comments relating to voyage arrangements see Woolcock 1983:595–99.
2 This German sailing vessel in 1866 carried 240 immigrants on the upper and 112 on the lower passenger deck, 123 more than the number allowed on a British vessel of similar dimensions (QVP 1866:1017).
3 The single-female bath had to meet the personal cleanliness require-ments of fifty to two hundred girls for two to four months; a minimum of two baths was suggested in 1877 (QVP 1877:II,1152). Later it was recommended that a covered area on deck be provided for bathing and dressing (COL/A544:88–4195); but none of these suggestions seems to have been implemented.
4 COL/A84:66–2754. The Irish inhabitants of Brisbane petitioned the government to appoint a 'spiritual advisor' for their fellow country-men during the voyage since their 'reverence' for such a person would promote good order on board (COL/A61:64–3013). Although the Emigration Commissioners allowed for a 'Religious Instructor', clergymen were appointed only if they were of the 'same commun-ion' as the majority of immigrants; but this arrangement was not 'very satisfactory' since it was difficult to determine the religion of the majority until departure (CO 386/120:245–47).

Chapter 8: Morbidity (pp. 216–254)

1 In 1840 William Farr, an English doctor and vital statistician, was appointed to the Registrar General's Office which had been created under the 1836 Registration Act for England and Wales. Dr William

Ogle directed a committee of the Royal College of Physicians (London) which began revising the classification in October, 1880 and completed it in 1884. The English Registrar-General first adopted the revised classification in his 1881 report. For a comparison of the two schemes used in Queensland see QVP 1882:365 and QVP 1886:II,375. The 1856 New South Wales Act (19 Vic. no 34) which required that all deaths and their cause be registered remained in force in Queensland after separation. See Cumpston and McCallum (1927:6,16–19), for a discussion of both systems and their adoption by the Australian colonies.

2 The average number of treatments per voyage has been calculated on the basis of only those voyages for which the morbidity numbers are known. For a statistical analysis of morbidity at sea and during quarantine see Woolcock 1983:602–07. In addition to the surgeons' lists information contained in health officers', immigration agents', Immigration Board and quarantine reports, and scattered through passenger diaries has been submitted to classification and analysis.

3 The 'cholera belt', a wide flannel waistband, was recommended in nineteenth-century medical guides for anyone who intended visiting or living in the tropics. Ship's captains were advised to use 'a thick flannel belt or bandage around the stomach or loins [as] a great defence for sailors' against cholera (see, for example, *Mercantile Navy List* 1860:xxix).

Chapter 9: Patterns of birth and death (pp. 255–289)

1 Births, deaths and causes of death have been extracted from Immigration Returns (QVP 1861–1901), passenger lists (see sources for Table 1), health officers', immigration agents' and surgeons' reports, and the individual voyage returns (COL/A1–807), and immigrant diaries. These sources have been checked against 'Registers' (BT 158, 159, 160) which record births, deaths and marriages of British nationals at sea between 1854 and 1883, births and deaths from 1883 to 1887, and deaths only after 1888, and were compiled from official Logs (see Cox 1972, for an outline of the records of the Registrar-General of Shipping and Seamen), as well as Agreements and Crew Lists (BT 99 and NMML). Copying errors were detected in the 'Registers'; surgeons' reports provided the most valuable and reliable source of information. Births and deaths on the Commissioners' vessels are listed in 'Register of Deaths' (CO 386/171, 172). Vital statistics for the populations of England and Wales, Prussia and Queensland as well as the British emigration have been extracted

and/or compiled from the Registrar-General's reports for England and Wales (BPP 1861–1905) and Queensland (QVP 1861–1901) and Mitchell and Deane (1962).

2 The crude birth and death rates for landed populations relate to the number of live births and deaths per 1,000 of the population per annum. For the immigrant population the birth and death rates for each voyage have been calculated as follows, assuming that births and deaths occur at the same rate during the voyage:

$$\text{birth/death rate} = \frac{\text{no. of births/deaths} \times 365 \times 1000}{(\text{no. embarked} - \frac{1}{2}\text{deaths} + \frac{1}{2}\text{births}) \times \text{days of voyage}}$$

The number of voyage days includes quarantine, where applicable. Annual birth and death rates are the mean of the voyage birth/death rates for a given year. Decadal and total period birth/death rates have also been computed on the basis of individual voyages.

3 Such differences highlight the problems of attempting to compare landed and maritime birth and death rates since the latter are derived from individual voyage calculations. More than half the British voyages were exempt from the law, carried an insignificant fraction of the immigration and registered only eleven births; the inclusion of a large number of voyages with zero births and the high German rates tend to distort the overall results (see Woolcock 1983:609). If, for example, the birth rates for sailing and steamships are compared, the fact that the majority of short-ships were sailing vessels would clearly affect the mean rate for each category. Thus, any discussion involving voyage types and passenger characteristics not distinguished according to the legislation, refers to the percentage of the totals embarked. Moreover, all nineteenth-century records of births and deaths at sea related them to the total outflow. Annual percentage birth and death rates for the immigration represent the mean of percentages for the numbers embarked on each voyage. Decadal and total period percentages are also calculated relative to the means for individual voyages.

4 According to the English Registrar-General's reports, the mean crude annual birth rate for the total British emigration between 1860 and 1900 was 1.09, while that for England and Wales was 33.5; for the Queensland immigration it was 14.6. The mean annual percentage birth rate for the period was 0.11 for the emigration and 0.57 for the immigration.

5 For statistical details of the immigrant births, see Woolcock 1983:612–14.

6 In 1860 premature births accounted for 1.8 per cent of all deaths in England and Wales; by 1890 this proportion had risen to 2.7 per cent.

Corresponding figures for Queensland were 1.5 per cent and 3.8 per cent.

7 For statistical details of immigrant deaths, see Woolcock 1983:617–27. Death rate analyses exclude infants who were born and died at sea.

8 The annual crude death rate for the total British emigration recorded in the Registrar-General's reports yields a mean of 2.7 for the years 1860 to 1898, compared to 20.4 for England and Wales and 31.8 for the Queensland immigration during the colonial period. This pattern is similar to that for the corresponding birth rates. See p. 258 and Note 4 above.

9 Tables relating to causes of death at sea and during quarantine (see Woolcock 1983:629–24) also exclude infants who were born and died at sea.

Chapter 10: Healthy immigrants? (pp. 290–326)

1 For the statistical analysis of passenger-related comments, see Woolcock 1983:635–37.

2 In 1875 the Agent-General claimed that he knew of instances where nominated families were found in a workhouse and had to be sent to the ship with parish funds (QVP 1875:II,573).

3 Miss Maria Rye, for example, sent out 141 single women on the *Conway* in 1862; there were 96 governesses and the remainder were servants 'of a superior class' (COL/A35:62–2798).

APPENDIX

Note: For more detailed statistics of immigration to the colony of Queensland, see Woolcock 1983: 525–637.

Table 1 Emigration to Queensland 1860–1900

	embarked			landed
	Agent-General[1]	*immigration agent[2]*	*revised[3] numbers*	*immigration agent[2]*
1860–1870[4]	42,121	59,340	59,208	57,257
1871–1880	50,141	55,689	56,410	56,006
1881–1890	112,087	114,447	114,673	114,244
1891–1900	9,689	12,385	11,449	12,703
1860–1900	214,038	241,861	241,740	240,210

1 Compiled from the Agent-General's annual reports and summaries of passengers despatched through the London Office (QVP 1872–1901).

2 These figures have been compiled from the annual Immigration Returns (QVP 1861–1900), are adjusted according to the year of departure and arrival, and take account of births and deaths en route.

3 The revised figures have been compiled from the above sources in addition to passenger lists held at

    (a) the Queensland State Archives, Brisbane
    – Registers IMM/112–27
    – COL/A98:67–3308; 111:68–2855
    – Microfilms 231–33. These were filmed by the Geneological Society of Utah, USA, from lists held at the Queensland Branch of the Commonwealth of Australia Archives, Brisbane, and cover the years 1860–81.

    (b) the Public Record Office, Kew, England – BT 27.

4 The decadal breakdown used throughout this study corresponds to the

intercensal periods from 1861 to 1901, except the first immigration decade which includes 1860 when only one vessel sailed direct to the colony.

Notes on Table 1:

The annual reports of the Agent-General between 1870 and 1900 include details of numbers despatched and an updated summary of the emigration to Queensland conducted by the London Office from 1861. Discrepancies occur between the summary and annual figures, and the Agent-General's and immigration agent's returns.

The revised figures have been thoroughly checked against the above returns and are in part derived from them, but their primary source has been the passenger lists (IMM/112–27) which were used at the arrival muster; the original lists were destroyed once they were copied into the immigrant registers.

By comparing the various sources, every attempt has been made to compile as accurate a figure as possible for the number embarked on each vessel which sailed direct to the colony from Britain and the Continent between 1860 and 1900. The revised statistics for the Queensland immigration may therefore be used with confidence when comparing similar populations. Subsequent analyses involving passenger numbers in this study are based on these statistics.

Table 2   Passengers embarked for Queensland 1860–1900, statute-adult classification

	married		single		1–11 yrs		infant		non	
	M	F	M	F	M	F	M	F	spec.	total
1860	49	49	88	68	14	21	3	8	–	300
1	166	169	334	247	105	82	24	21	87	1,235
2	1,143	1,169	2,601	1,364	859	780	186	138	40	8,280
3	1,580	1,601	4,432	1,770	1,254	1,085	226	200	18	12,166
4	870	894	2,804	1,240	500	451	117	102	542	7,520
5	1,853	1,914	4,469	1,760	1,116	1,019	219	215	14	12,579
6	1,676	1,709	3,298	1,437	1,142	1,042	191	209	–	10,704
7	117	142	388	199	119	90	11	17	–	1,083
8	58	69	257	94	32	45	6	6	2	569
9	230	238	709	444	140	121	15	24	3	1,924
1870	383	392	1,032	555	213	184	48	41	–	2,848
1	404	439	1,318	682	312	277	57	47	4	3,540
2	378	396	839	623	228	211	36	43	–	2,754
3	1,099	1,136	2,331	1,340	774	746	161	141	–	7,728
4	1,349	1,379	3,134	1,537	998	936	163	178	–	9,674
5	636	654	2,178	1,356	459	465	78	65	–	5,891
6	671	711	2,267	1,070	489	466	100	71	–	5,845
7	768	806	2,249	1,179	551	511	87	85	–	6,236
8	913	944	2,654	1,278	601	602	116	112	–	7,220
9	421	442	1,695	895	243	276	45	51	58	4,126
1880	280	293	1,079	1,251	205	208	48	32	–	3,396
1	385	392	1,447	1,316	312	306	46	49	104	4,357
2	1,502	1,513	4,298	2,742	1,188	1,047	238	200	–	12,728
3	3,556	3,577	8,561	4,230	2,846	2,704	504	473	60	26,511
4	2,160	2,197	5,721	2,908	1,748	1,682	300	281	–	16,997
5	1,053	1,094	4,392	2,287	894	792	151	124	–	10,787
6	1,275	1,313	4,650	2,606	1,056	1,022	196	143	5	12,266
7	1,086	1,105	3,134	2,755	1,083	1,011	186	190	–	10,550
8	785	784	3,721	2,504	747	701	130	100	–	9,472
9	470	480	3,010	2,339	437	375	63	74	–	7,248
1890	193	195	1,455	1,462	214	189	21	28	–	3,757
1	169	181	1,317	1,236	141	134	21	23	–	3,222
2	81	105	463	474	59	70	14	11	–	1,277
3	32	61	140	110	17	24	6	8	–	398
4	19	42	94	63	29	31	5	2	–	285
5	25	61	133	83	15	17	3	8	–	345
6	37	78	186	152	37	27	3	15	–	535
7	64	97	222	191	49	54	5	11	–	693
8	65	117	337	217	56	55	15	7	–	869
9	91	141	593	404	97	85	16	13	–	1,440
1900	128	180	839	984	115	103	19	17	–	2,385
	28,220	29,259	84,869	49,452	21,494	20,047	3,879	3,583	937	241,740

Sources for Tables 2–4: see Table 1.

Appendix

Table 3 Voyages, Queensland immigration 1860–1900

	1860–70		1871–80		1881–90		1891–1900		1860–1900	
	Sail	Steam	Sail	Steam	Sail	Steam	Sail	Steam	Sail	Steam
Govt.	84	2	128	1	66	188	–	13	278	204
EC	29	–	–	–	–	–	–	–	29	–
Private	24	–	–	–	11	5	–	7	35	12
German	23	–	29	–	–	–	–	–	52	–
Short	56	2	167	–	226	27	56	173	505	202
Total	220		325		523		249		1,317	

Table 4 Passengers embarked, Queensland immigration 1860–1900

	1860–70		1871–80		1881–90		1891–1900		1860–1900	
	Sail	Steam	Sail	Steam	Sail	Steam	Sail	Steam	Sail	Steam
Govt	31,543	1,277	44,112	247	22,869	83,264	–	3,928	98,524	88,716
EC	9,064	–	–	–	–	–	–	–	9,064	–
Private	9,739	–	–	–	3,946	2,609	–	2,420	13,685	5,029
German	7,120	–	10,404	–	–	–	–	–	17,524	–
Short	390	75	1,647	–	1,616	369	108	4,993	3,761	5,437
Total	59,208		56,410		114,673		11,449		241,740	

Table Births and deaths★

	voyages	passengers embarked	births	deaths	passengers landed
1860–70	219	58,926	647	1,459	58,114
1871–80	325	56,410	539	889	56,060
1881–90	523	114,673	454	934	114,193
1891–1900	249	11,449	3	17	11,435
1860–1900	1,316	241,458	1,643	3,299	239,802

★The *Wilhelmsburg*, wrecked in 1863, has been excluded from all totals.
Sources for Tables 5–10: see Chapter 9, Note 1, on page 343.

Table 6 Births, British emigration and Queensland immigration 1860–1900

	British emigration % of total embarked	Queensland immigration					
		Live births				% of total embarked	% of females 15–44 years embarked
		M	F	U	total		
1860	0.19	–	I	–	I	0.33	0.90
I	0.24	6	4	I	11	0.89	3.08
2	0.24	34	37	7	78	0.94	3.90
3	0.16	62	62	13	137	1.15	5.05
4	0.18	32	40	–	72	0.96	4.65
5	0.20	73	87	–	160	1.27	8.67
6	0.20	67	57	3	127	1.19	10.86
7	0.17	8	3	–	11	1.02	8.03
8	0.14	4	I	–	5	0.88	3.55
9	0.10	8	13	–	21	1.09	3.36
1870	0.12	13	11	–	24	0.84	2.77
I	0.08	15	13	–	28	0.79	2.78
2	0.10	12	14	–	26	0.94	2.78
3	0.10	46	57	–	103	1.33	4.67
4	0.21	44	42	–	86	0.89	3.30
5	0.20	19	29	2	50	0.85	2.73
6	0.26	24	25	–	49	0.84	2.98
7	0.24	41	31	3	75	1.20	4.08
8	0.20	36	31	I	68	0.94	3.30
9	0.16	11	16	–	27	0.65	2.14
1880	0.06	11	16	–	27	0.80	1.88
I	0.04	12	8	–	20	0.46	1.38
2	0.06	38	39	–	77	0.60	1.97
3	0.11	90	72	2	164	0.62	0.29
4	0.09	37	31	–	68	0.40	1.50
5	0.05	6	20	–	26	0.24	0.85
6	0.05	18	16	–	34	0.28	0.95
7	0.04	8	19	–	27	0.26	0.78
8	0.03	9	11	–	20	0.21	0.66
9	0.04	6	4	–	10	0.14	0.39
1890	0.03	2	6	–	8	0.21	0.53
I	0.03	–	–	–	–	–	–
2	0.02	–	–	–	–	–	–
3	0.03	–	–	–	–	–	–
4	0.02	–	–	–	–	–	–
5	0.02	–	–	–	–	–	–
6	0.02	–	–	–	–	–	–
7	0.02	–	–	–	–	–	–
8	0.02	–	–	I	I	0.12	0.39
9	★	–	I	–	I	0.07	0.20
1900	★	–	I	–	–	0.04	0.09

★Emigrant births were not tabled after 1898.

Table 7 Deaths, British emigration and Queensland immigration 1860–1900

	British emigration % of total embarked	Queensland immigration					
		M	F	U	total	% of total embarked	% embarked + births
1860	0.31	1	2	–	3	1.00	1.00
1	0.36	20	18	–	38	3.08	3.05
2	0.30	87	84	–	171	2.07	2.05
3	0.27	147	99	24	270	2.27	2.25
4	0.28	64	46	10	120	1.60	1.58
5	0.38	189	199	–	388	3.08	3.05
6	0.51	221	179	5	405	3.78	3.74
7	0.33	10	1	1	12	1.11	1.10
8	0.30	–	1	–	1	0.18	0.17
9	0.19	13	8	–	21	1.09	1.08
1870	0.30	14	16	–	30	1.05	1.04
1	0.17	26	13	–	39	1.10	1.09
2	0.19	17	16	–	33	1.20	1.19
3	0.39	116	105	–	221	2.86	2.82
4	0.72	88	78	–	166	1.71	1.70
5	0.45	36	24	–	60	1.02	1.01
6	0.53	36	31	–	67	1.15	1.14
7	0.54	56	47	3	106	1.70	1.68
8	0.42	57	51	–	108	1.50	1.48
9	0.36	35	35	–	70	1.70	1.69
1880	0.13	8	11	–	19	0.56	0.56
1	0.16	9	19	–	28	0.64	0.64
2	0.16	85	67	–	152	1.19	1.19
3	0.24	193	156	1	350	1.32	1.31
4	0.26	88	83	–	171	1.01	1.00
5	0.23	29	31	–	60	0.56	0.55
6	0.16	53	29	–	82	0.67	0.67
7	0.22	22	15	–	37	0.35	0.35
8	0.08	16	18	–	34	0.34	0.34
9	0.14	6	6	–	12	0.17	0.17
1890	0.16	5	3	–	8	0.21	0.21
1	0.12	1	4	–	5	0.16	0.16
2	0.13	–	2	–	2	0.16	0.16
3	0.14	–	–	–	–	–	–
4	0.15	–	–	–	–	–	–
5	0.13	–	–	–	–	–	–
6	0.19	1	–	–	1	0.19	0.19
7	0.15	1	–	–	1	0.14	0.14
8	0.20	–	–	1	1	0.12	0.11
9	★	–	4	–	4	0.28	0.28
1900	★	1	2	–	3	0.13	0.13

★ Emigrant deaths were not tabled after 1898.

Table 8 Queensland immigrant deaths 1860–1900, statute–adult classification

	married		single		1–11 yrs		infants*			
	M	F	M	F	M	F	M	F	U	total
1860	1	1	–	1	–	–	–	–	–	3
1	2	2	4	3	10	8	4	3	–	36
2	2	8	10	6	50	44	22	20	–	162
3	9	8	10	3	84	64	36	21	24	259
4	7	8	20	4	23	22	11	8	7	110
5	12	31	30	13	107	100	33	42	–	368
6	32	31	33	14	111	93	32	34	5	385
7	1	–	5	–	1	1	–	–	1	9
8	–	–	–	–	–	1	–	–	–	1
9	3	1	2	–	4	5	2	2	–	19
1870	1	1	3	–	8	9	1	3	–	26
1	1	3	9	1	11	5	5	4	–	39
2	3	2	4	1	5	9	5	3	–	32
3	5	12	21	2	43	58	42	29	–	212
4	5	5	7	3	41	44	30	19	–	154
5	5	9	8	3	13	6	7	4	–	55
6	1	8	12	2	9	10	12	8	–	62
7	3	7	11	4	22	25	13	7	–	92
8	4	8	6	6	27	27	13	8	–	99
9	4	5	11	1	14	19	5	6	–	65
1880	2	1	3	2	1	4	2	3	–	18
1	–	2	3	5	2	8	3	4	–	27
2	2	4	5	5	39	34	36	22	–	147
3	13	24	24	10	69	64	72	50	–	326
4	5	11	11	3	35	35	35	30	–	165
5	1	6	8	7	11	8	8	7	–	56
6	9	12	12	3	12	3	18	10	–	79
7	–	3	5	2	5	4	12	6	–	37
8	–	5	2	1	5	5	8	5	–	31
9	3	–	–	1	2	2	1	3	–	12
1890	2	–	1	1	–	1	2	1	–	8
1	–	1	–	–	–	2	1	1	–	5
2	–	–	–	–	–	1	–	1	–	2
3	–	–	–	–	–	–	–	–	–	–
4	–	–	–	–	–	–	–	–	–	–
5	–	–	–	–	–	–	–	–	–	–
6	–	–	1	–	–	–	–	–	–	1
7	–	–	1	–	–	–	–	–	–	1
8	–	–	–	–	–	–	–	–	1	1
9	–	–	–	4	–	–	–	–	–	4
1900	–	1	–	1	–	–	1	–	–	3
1860–1900	138	220	282	112	764	721	472	364	38	3,111

*Exclusive of infants who were born and died at sea.

Table 9 Classified deaths 1860–1900

	percentages								total cases+	
	married		single		1–11 yrs		infants*			
	M	F	M	F	M	F	M	F	number	%
Class I										
Order 1	22	16	23	14	28	28	11	13	554	20
2	12	11	5	13	23	24	25	27	529	19
3	–	1	0	2	1	2	1	2	23	1
4	–	–	–	–	–	–	–	–	–	0
5	–	–	–	–	0	–	–	–	1	0
6	–	8	1	–	0	–	–	1	22	1
7	–	–	–	–	0	0	–	–	6	0
Class II	2	1	1	–	–	–	1	–	18	1
Class III										
Order 1	1	–	2	1	0	–	–	–	7	0
2	17	11	20	13	8	7	6	4	236	9
3	1	1	1	–	2	2	4	3	53	2
Class IV										
Order 1	–	–	–	–	–	–	0	–	68	3
2	1	–	–	1	–	–	–	–	3	0
Class V										
Order 1	3	2	3	5	10	10	12	14	250	9
2	5	7	5	6	–	1	0	–	43	2
3	8	4	9	8	13	11	21	15	338	12
4	4	8	5	9	7	8	9	7	190	7
5	–	–	–	–	–	–	–	–	–	0
6	3	1	2	–	1	1	0	–	20	1
7	–	1	–	–	–	–	–	–	2	0
8	–	11	–	1	–	–	–	–	22	1
9	–	–	–	–	–	–	0	0	2	0
10	–	–	–	–	–	–	0	–	1	0
Class VI										
Order 1	18	12	19	24	3	1	2	2	147	5
2	–	1	2	1	–	–	–	–	7	0
Class VII										
Order 1	3	4	2	2	4	5	8	12	197	7

+ Including infants who were born and died at sea.

* Exclusive of infants born and died at sea.

Table 10   Morbidity and mortality, Queensland immigration 1860–1900: order of incidence

	morbidity	*mortality*
1	diarrhoea	diarrhoea
2	measles	measles
3	colic, constipation	bronchitis
4	bronchitis	convulsions
5	debility	phthisis
6	catarrh	pneumonia
7	whooping-cough	debility
8	sore throat	tabes mesenterica
9	coughs and colds	scarlet fever
10	skin eruptions	heat apoplexy
11	injuries	premature birth
12	rheumatism	dysentery
13	scarlet fever	dentition
14	menorrhagia	enteritis
15	typhoid (enteric) fever	typhus fever
16	abscesses	typhoid fever
17	dysentery	marasmus
18	phthisis	brain fever
19	fever	hydrocephalus
20	remittent fever	inanition

Table 11   Classification for Queensland immigrant morbidity and cause
of death

Class I	*Zymotic diseases*	
Order		
1	Miasmatic:	measles, scarlet fever, typhus and typhoid fevers, catarrh, colds, mumps, diphtheria, acute meningitis, fevers
2	Diarrhoeal:	cholera, diarrhoea, dysentery
3	Malarial:	remittent and intermittent fevers, ague
4	Zoogenous:	anthrax, swinepox
5	Venereal:	syphilis, gonorrhoea
6	Septic:	erysipelas, septicaemia, puerperal fever
7	Parasitic:	aphthae, worms, scabies

Class II	*Dietic diseases*	
		malnutrition, scurvy, alcoholism

Class III	*Constitutional diseases*	
Order		
1	Rheumatic:	rheumatic fever, rheumatism, gout
2	Tubercular:	tabes mesenterica, tubercular meningitis, phthisis, scrofula
3	Other:	cancer, rickets, marasmus, anaemia

Class IV	*Developmental diseases*	
Order		
1	Birth and congenital:	premature birth, cyanosis
2	Old age:	senile decay, old age oedema

Class V	*Local diseases*	
Order		
1	Nervous system:	ear, eye, nose, encephalitis, apoplexy, hemiplegia, epilepsy, convulsions, spasms, hysteria, mania, melancholia, deficient intellect
2	Circulatory system:	cardiac disease, angina, syncope, phlebitis, haemorrhoids
3	Respiratory system:	laryngitis, croup, asthma, bronchitis, pneumonia
4	Digestive system:	stomatitis, dentition, sore throat, dyspepsia, gastritis, enteritis, hernia, peritonitis, ascites, hepatitis, colic, constipation, vomiting

---

Table 11 Classification for Queensland immigrant morbidity and cause of death (*cont.*)

Class V	Local diseases	
Order		
5	Lymphatic system:	adenitis, struma, spleenic disease
6	Urinary system:	nephritis, Bright's disease, anuria, gravel, cystitis
7	Generative system:	ovaritis, metritis, dysmenorrhoea, testitis
8	Parturition:	abortion, pregnancy dropsy, child-birth, puerperal mania, mammary abscess
9	Locomotion:	caries of spine, necrosis of bone, synovitis
10	Integumentary system:	boils, eczema, ulcers, herpes, ringworm, inflammation
Class VI	*Violence*	
Order		
1	Accident or negligence:	fractures, sprains, injuries, burns, sunstroke, poisoning, drowning, asphyxia, exposure
2	Suicide	
Class VII	*Ill-defined and not specified diseases*	
Order		
1	Ill-defined:	dropsy, debility, atrophy, inanition, tumour, abscess, seasickness, pains, 'surgical cases'
2	Not specified	

Note: The specific disease entities listed under each order represent only a selection of the diseases.

REFERENCES

Note: The following is a list of the references and sources used by the author:

Abbreviations

ANL   The National Library, Australia.
ANU   The Australian National University.
JHSQ   *Journal of the Historical Society of Queensland.*
JRHSQ   *Journal of the Royal Historical Society of Queensland.*
NMML   National Maritime Museum Library, Greenwich, England.
PRO   Public Record Office, Kew, England.
QSA   Queensland State Archives, Brisbane, Australia.

Acton, H.W. (1889) Diary containing letters written during a voyage from England to Georgetown, Queensland in 1889. MS 6157, ANL.
AMJ *The Australian Medical Journal.*
    M 468 Womens' Migration and Overseas Appointment Society Records, 1862–1901: Letter Book No. 1
                     Press Cuttings *Daily News* (2 May 1890) London.
                     —— *The Queen* (November 1890) London.
    MS 2569 Official Logs.
Anon. (1883) Voyage to Brisbane, *Scottish Admiral*, 1883. MS 4100, ANL.
Appleyard, RT. (1964) *British Emigration to Australia.* London: Weidenfeld & Nicolson.
Armstrong, W. (1964) *Square-Rigger Days.* London: Heinemann.

Austin, C.G. (1949) Early History of Somerset and Thursday Island. JHSQ 4(2): 216–30.

Barclay, E. (May 1971) Fevers and Stinks. Some Problems of Public Health in the 1870s and 1880s. *Queensland Heritage* 2(4): 3–12.

Bateson, C. (1974) *The Convict Ships 1787–1868*. Sydney: A.H. & A.W. Reed.

Beaumont, T.E. (n.d.) *Pencillings by the Way. A 'Constitutional' Voyage Round the World, 1870–1871*. Geoffrey Godden (ed.). London: Barrie & Jenkins.

Bird, J. (1968) *Seaport Gateways of Australia*. London: Oxford University Press.

Blaikie, G. (1 June, 1980) Our Strange Past. The Irish All At Sea. *The Sunday Mail* (Colour Supplement): 11.

Blainey, G. (1968) *The Tyranny of Distance. How Distance Shaped Australia's History*. Melbourne: Macmillan.

Blake, G. (1956) *B.I. Centenary 1856–1956*. London: Collins.

Blasdall, M. (1862) Journal of a voyage to Queensland in the *City of Brisbane*, sailing from London, 1862. MS 957, ANL.

BMJ *The British Medical Journal*.

Boland, T.P. (1963–64) 'The Queensland Immigration Society'. A Notable Experiment in Irish Settlement. JRHSQ 7(2): 307–21.

Bolton, G.C. (1963) *A Thousand Miles Away. A History of North Queensland to 1920*. Brisbane: Jacaranda Press with the ANU.

Borrie, W.D. assisted by D.R.G. Packer (1954) *Italians and Germans in Australia. A Study of Assimilation*. Melbourne: F.W. Cheshire for the ANU.

Borrie, W.D. (1958) Immigration to the Australian Colonies 1861–1901. A seminar paper, ANU.

BPP British Parliamentary Papers, House of Commons.
Annual Report of the Registrar-General for England and Wales (1861–1905).
Annual Report of the Emigrants' Information Office (1886–1900).
Select Committee Report on the Causes of Shipwrecks (1836 xvii 373).
Royal Commission Report on the Unseaworthiness of Ships (1873 xxxvi 315, 335).
Royal Commission Report on the Loss of Life at Sea (1884–85 xxv 1).

British India Register of Surgeons, NMML.

BS *British Statutes*

BT Board of Trade. Records of the Registrar-General of Shipping and Seamen, PRO.
BT 27 Passenger Lists, Outwards (1890–1900).
BT 99 Agreements and Crew Lists, Series II.

BT 158 Registers of Births, Deaths and Marriages of Passengers at Sea.

BT 159 Registers of Deaths of British Nationals at Sea.

BT 160 Registers of Births of British Nationals at Sea.

Bushby, F. (1865) Letters written to his sister during his residence in Australia. MS 253, ANL.

Carrier, N.H. and Jeffrey, J.R. (1953) *External Migration. A Study of Available Statistics 1815–1950.* London: HMSO.

Carrothers, W.A. (1929) *Emigration from the British Isles.* Reprints of Economic Classics (1969) New York: Augustus Kelley.

Census of England and Wales, General Report (1861, 1871, 1881, 1891, 1901, 1931). London: HMSO.

Chadfield, P.B. (n.d.) *Out at Sea; or, The Emigrant Afloat, being a handbook of practical information for the use of passengers on a long sea voyage.* Derby: Chadfield & Son.

Chandler, G. (1973) *The Merchant Venturers.* Liverpool: Rondo Publications.

Charlwood, D.E. (1981) *The Long Farewell. Settlers Under Sail.* Ringwood, Victoria: Allen Lane.

Chisholm, A.H. (ed.) (1958) *Australian Encyclopaedia.* 10 vols. Sydney: Angus & Robertson

Cilento, R. and Lack, C. (eds) (1959) *Triumph in the Tropics. An Historical Sketch of Queensland.* Brisbane: Smith & Paterson.

Clark, C.M.H. (1978) *The Earth Abideth for Ever 1851–1888.* Volume IV of *A History of Australia.* Melbourne: Melbourne University Press.

Clark, M. (ed.) (1957) *Sources of Australian History.* London: Oxford University Press.

CO Colonial Office. Land and Emigration Commission Papers 1833–94, PRO.

CO 386/76, 386/78 Letters with Replies to Colonial Office from Queensland (1854–76).

CO 386/120 Colonial Office Letters to Emigration Agents, Colonial Secretaries, etc. (1852–60).

CO 386/164–67 Registers of Correspondence with Public Officers Abroad (1869–78).

CO 386/171–72 Register of Deaths of Emigrants at Sea. Ships to Queensland.

CO 386/179, 182–85 List of Ships Chartered (1847–69).

CO 386/186 Register of Surgeons' Appointments (1854–92).

Coates, W.H. (1900) *The Good Old Days of Shipping.* Bombay: The *Times of India* Press. (Reprint edn 1969.) London: Cornmarket Press.

Coghlan, T.A. (1904) *A Statistical Account of Australia and New Zealand 1903–1904.* Australia: NSW Government and Commonwealth of

Australia publication.

—— (1918) *Labour and Industry in Australia.* 4 vols. London: Oxford University Press.

COL/A1–807 Colonial Secretary's Correspondence, Queensland: Letters Received (1859–96). QSA.

Coleman, T. (1972) *Passage to America. A History of Emigrants from Great Britain and Ireland to America in the mid-nineteenth Century.* London: Hutchinson.

Cook, Mrs A.M. (1883) Letters to her mother written on board the *Scottish Hero,* December 1883. MS 849, ANL.

Cotton, H.J. (1957) Discovery of the *Scottish Prince* Wreck. JHSQ 5(5): 1283–294.

Course, A.G. (1963) *The Merchant Navy. A Social History.* London: Frederick Muller.

Cox, N. (1972) The Records of the Registrar-General of Shipping and Seamen. *Maritime History* II: 168–88.

Crawford, R.M. (1970) *Australia.* (Rev. edn. First published 1952.) London: Hutchinson.

Creighton, C. (1891–94) *A History of Epidemics in Britain.* Vol. 2. Cambridge: Cambridge University Press.

Crowley, F.K. (1951) British Migration to Australia 1860–1914. A Descriptive, Analytical and Statistical Account of the Immigration from the United Kingdom. D.Phil. Thesis, Balliol College, Oxford.

Cumpston, J.H.L. (1927) *The History of Diphtheria, Scarlet Fever, Measles, and Whooping Cough in Australia 1788–1925.* Canberra: Commonwealth of Australia, Dept. of Health. Service Publication, No. 37.

Cumpston, J.H.L. and McCallum, F. (1927) *The History of Intestinal Infections (and Typhus Fever) in Australia 1788–1925.* Canberra: Commonwealth of Australia, Dept. of Health. Service Publication, No. 36.

Cunliffe, M. (1974) *The Age of Expansion 1848–1917.* History of the Western World Series, John Roberts (ed.) Springfield, Mass.: G. & C. Merriam.

Davies, A.G. (1935) Immigration and the Immigrant Ships. JHSQ 2(6): 304–26.

—— (n.d.) Arrivals at the Port of Brisbane 1848–1924. QSA.

Dicken, C.S. (1900) Queensland. In *Australasia,* vol. 4, British Empire Series. London: Kegan, Paul, Truebner.

Divine, D. (1960) *These Splendid Ships. The Story of the Peninsular and Orient Line.* London: Frederick Muller.

Donaldson, G. (1966) *The Scots Overseas.* London: Robert Hale.

Dow, H. (ed.) (1966) *Trollope's Australia.* Melbourne: Thomas Nelson.

Dunlop, E.W. and Pike, W. (1960) *Australia, Colony to Nation.* Melbourne: Longmans, Green.

References

ECR *General Report of the Emigration Commissioners* (1859–72). London: Eyre & Spottiswoode.

Edelstein, T.J. (25 June, 1981) From 'The Deserted Village' to 'The Last of England'. The Influence of Goldsmith on Victorian Images of Emigration. The British Library, Special Evening Lecture.

Edwardes, A.D. and Parsons, R. (1975) *Sail in the South*. Adelaide: Rigby.

Erickson, C. (ed.) (1976) *Emigration from Europe 1815–1914*. London: A. & C. Black.

Fairburn, W.A. (comp) (1945–55) *Merchant Sail*. 5 vols. Center Lovell Maine: Marine Education Foundation.

Farnfield, Jean (1974) Problems of Early Queensland, 1859–1870. In D.J. Dalton (ed.) *Lectures on North Queensland History*. Townsville: James Cook University.

Fitzgerald, R. (1982) *From the Dreaming to 1915. A History of Queensland*. Brisbane, University of Queensland Press.

Fitzpatrick, B.C. (1969) *The British Empire in Australia. An Economic History 1834–1930*. Revised edn. Melbourne: Macmillan.

Foote, W. (1977–78) Queensland Immigration and the Black Ball Line. JRHSQ 10(3): 21–49.

Gandevia, B. (1978) *Tears Often Shed. Child Health and Welfare in Australia from 1788*. Oxford: Pergamon.

Gibbs, P.N. (1903) *Australasia. The Britains of the South*. London: Cassell.

Good, A. (1863–68) Diary written while on board the sailing ship *Beejapore* from England to Queensland 28 February 1863 to April 1868. MS 513, ANL.

Government of Queensland (1921) *The History of Queensland: Its People and Industries. An Epitome of Progress*. 2 vols. Brisbane: States Publishing Co.

—— (1909) *Our First Half Century. A Review of Queensland Progress*. Brisbane: Government Printer.

Hale, H. (1867) 'Memory Pictures'. The Pilgrimage of an Ordinary 'Padre', 1867–1930. 2 vols. By courtesy of Mrs F. Folliott, Bath, England.

Halls, C. (1978) *Australia's Worst Shipwrecks*. Adelaide: Rigby.

Henning, R. (1963) *The Letters of Rachel Henning*. David Hume (ed.) with a Foreword by Norman Lindsay. Sydney: Angus & Robertson.

Hinshelwood, Mrs T. (1963–64) Diary and Notes on *Nebo*, Glasgow for Rockhampton, 1883. *Port of Melbourne Quarterly* Oct.–Dec. 1963, Jan.–Mar. 1964.

Hitchins, F.H. (1931) *The Colonial Land and Emigration Commission*. Philadelphia: University of Pennsylvania Press.

Hume, W. and Fowler, A.K. (1975) *A Victorian Engagement. Letters and*

Journals of Walter Hume and Anna Kate Fowler. Bertram Hume (ed.). Brisbane: University of Queensland Press.

Huntington, E. (1927) *The Character of Races*. (Reprint edn 1977). New York: Arno Press.

Hurle, H.H.C. (May 1967) *Queen of the Colonies*. A Few Remarks on the Voyage from London to Brisbane, 1865. *Queensland Heritage*. 1(6): 30–5.

IMM/112–127 Immigrant Registers, 1855–1900, QSA.

ISS *Instructions to Surgeon-Superintendents of Queensland Ships Sailing Under the Direction of H.M. Government of Queensland* (1875). London.

Jones, I. (1935) The Floods of the Brisbane River. JHSQ 2(6): 288–95.

Jose, A.W. (1901) *Australasia, the Commonwealth and New Zealand*. London: J.M. Dent.

Kleinschmidt, M.A. (1951) Migration and Settlement Schemes in Queensland 1859–1900. B.A. Honours Thesis. University of Queensland.

Knox-Robinson, R. (1978) *The Twilight of Sail*. Melbourne: Hutchinson.

Koutsoukis, A.J. (1966) *Topics from Australian History*. Sydney: Whitcombe & Tombs.

L *The Lancet*.

Lack, C. (ed.) (1959a) Queensland, *Daughter of the Sun. A Record of a Century of Responsible Government*. Brisbane: Jacaranda Press.

—— (1959b) The Taming of the Great Barrier Reef. JRHSQ 6(1): 130–54.

Lacour-Gayet, R. (1976) *A Concise History of Australia*. James Grieve (trans.). Harmondsworth: Penguin.

La Meslée, E.M. (1883) *The New Australia*. Paris: E. Plon. Translated and edited with a critical introduction by Russel Ward (1973). London: Heinemann.

Lawson, R. (1963) Immigration into Queensland. B.A. Honours Thesis. University of Queensland.

Leach, H. (comp.) (1868) *The Ship-Captain's Medical Guide*. London: A.M. Walker.

Lewis, G. (1973) *A History of the Ports of Queensland. A study in Economic Nationalism*. Brisbane: University of Queensland Press.

Lloyd's List (1 January, 1860–30 June, 1884). Amalgamated with *Shipping Gazette* and published as *Shipping Gazette and Lloyd's List* (30 June, 1884 – 1 December, 1900).

Lloyd's Register of British and Foreign Shipping (1860–1900). London.

Lloyd's Weekly Shipping Index (9 January, 1880 – 1 December, 1900). Commenced as *The Weekly Shipping Record* (1 January, 1880).

Lumb, M. (1885) Diary of daily events occurring between Oldham, England and Maryborough, Australia, 1885–86. Copied from the original by his brother. By courtesy of Mrs G. Hustwit, Brisbane, Australia.

Lyng, J.S. (1939) *The Scandinavians in Australia, New Zealand and the Western Pacific.* Melbourne: Melbourne University Press.

McCanee, R.A. and Widdowson, E.M. (1960) *The Composition of Foods* Medical Research Council, Special Report Series No. 297. London: HMSO.

MacDonagh, O. (1961) *A Pattern of Government Growth. The Passenger Acts and their Enforcement.* London: Macgibbon & Kee.

MacGinlay, M. (Nov. 1974) Irish Migration to Queensland, 1885–1912. *Queensland Heritage* 3(1): 12–20.

Maddick, I. (1973) A study in Teething. Dissertation for Diploma of Dental Public Health, Royal College of Surgeons (England).

Madgwick, R.B. (1966) *Immigration into Eastern Australia 1788–1851.* Sydney: Sydney University Press.

Mayne, E.G. (1860–61) Remarks on the Colony of Queensland as a Field for Emigration. *Journal of the Royal Dublin Society* 3: 341–45.

The Medical Directory and General Medical Register (1860–1909). London: A. Churchill.

The Medical Register (1860–1909). London: The General Medical Council of Medical Education and Registration of the United Kingdom.

The Mercantile Navy List and Annual Appendage (1857–1864). 8 vols. London. Continued as *The Mercantile Navy List and Maritime Directory* (1865–   ). London.

Mitchell, B.R. and Deane, P. (1962) *Abstract of British Historical Statistics.* Cambridge: Cambridge University Press.

Morris, E.E. (ed.) (1890) *Cassell's Picturesque Australia.* Vol. III. London: Cassell.

Morrison, A.A. (Nov. 1966) Colonial Society, 1860–1900 (Queensland). *Queensland Heritage* 1(5): 21–30.

Musgrove, F. (1963) *The Migratory Elite.* London: Heinemann.

Newell, P. and White, U. (1967) *Brisbane Sketchbook.* Adelaide: Rigby.

Official Logs, Agreements and Crew Lists: MS 2569, ANL; NMML; BT 99, PRO.

Palmer, M. (1971) *Ships and Shipping.* London: Batsford.

PD Eng. *Parliamentary Debates*, England.

Parrington, J.H. (1869) On a voyage from London to Brisbane, the ship *Storm King* 1869–70. Photographed from the original letter in the Bodleian Library, Oxford, 1951. MS 1384, ANL.

Passenger Lists: IMM 112–127, Microfilms Z 31–33, COL/A98:67–3308, 111:68–2855, QSA BT 27, PRO.

Peter, J.-P. (1975) Disease and the Sick at the end of the Eighteenth Century. In R. Forster and O. Ranum (eds) *Biology of Man in History.*

Baltimore: Johns Hopkins University Press.

Pike, D. (ed.) (1966) *Australian Dictionary of Biography*. 3 vols. Melbourne: Melbourne University Press.

Plarr's Lives of the Fellows of the Royal College of Surgeons of England (1930). London: Royal College of Surgeons of England.

Pownall, E. (1975) *Australian Pioneer Women*. Melbourne: Melbourne University Press.

QGG *Queensland Government Gazette* (1859–1901).

QPD *Parliamentary Debates,* Queensland.

QS *Queensland Statutes.*

Qualtrough, J. (1859) Voyage to New Zealand, 1859. By courtesy of Hilary Jex, Saltdean, England.

QVP *Votes and Proceedings of the Legislative Assembly, Queensland* (1860–1901).

Randall, G. (1868) A diary kept during a voyage from England to Australia (London to Brisbane) in the ship *Planet*, 1868. MS 2107, ANL.

Recommended Daily Amounts of Food Energy and Nutrients for Groups of People in the United Kingdom. Report by the Committee on Medical Aspects of Food Policy. DHSS Report on Health and Social Subjects 15.

RHSQ Royal Historical Society of Queensland, Brisbane, Australia.

Immigration File: Press cutting (n.d.) Jordan's Lambs. By One of Them.

Immigrant Ships File: Press cutting. Fifty Years Ago. *The Courier* (16 May, 1914).

Shipping File: Moxon, T.F. (n.d.) Life in the Colonial Clippers of the Eighties. Reprinted from *Australian Coal, Shipping, Steel and the Harbour.*

Shipping – Black Ball Line File: *The Mainstay. A Weekly Journal* (1863). Edited by A.B. Robinson and published on the *Light Brigade.*

Shipwrecks File: Press cutting (n.d.) *re* arrival of the *Maulsden. re Utopia.* History in Ships. *Capricornian* (January 1930). Quoted from *The Morning Bulletin*, Rockhampton (12 November, 1862).

Rickard, J. (1981) Psychohistory. An Australian Perspective. *History Today* 31: 10–13.

Ricou, J.P. (1872) Diary of the voyage of the barque *Indus*, London to Brisbane, 1872. MS 469, ANL.

Robson, L.L. (1965) *The Convict Settlers of Australia*. Melbourne: Melbourne University Press.

Roddis, L.H. (1941) *A Short History of Nautical Medicine*. New York: Paul B. Hoeber.

Rogers, J.D. (1907) *Australasia. A Historical Geography of the British Colonies*, vol. 6. Oxford: Clarendon Press.

Saunders, H. St G. (1948) *Valiant Voyaging. A Short History of the B.I.S.N. Co. in the Second World War 1935–1945*. London: Faber & Faber.

Schindler, C. (1916) Non-British Settlement in Queensland. JHSQ 1(2): 64–75.

Serle, P. (ed.) (1949) *Dictionary of Australian Biography*. 2 vols. Sydney: Angus & Robertson.

Shaw, A.G.L. (1961) *The Story of Australia*. London: Faber & Faber.

Stammers, M.K. (1978) *The Passage Makers*. Brighton, Sussex: Teredo Books.

Taylor, I.C. (ed.) (1969) *Sophy Under Sail*. London: Hodder & Stoughton.

Thomson, F. (1882) Journal of our voyage in the ship *Selkirkshire* from Glasgow to Rockhampton. MS 1025, ANL.

Thornton, R.H. (1945) *British Shipping*. Cambridge: Cambridge University Press.

Towson, J. (1854) Great Circle Sailing. *Mercantile Marine Magazine and Nautical Record*: 101ff.

Trollope, A. (1875) *New South Wales and Queensland. Australia and New Zealand*, vol. 1. London: Chapman & Hall.

Upher, J. (1863–65) Letters to his family in England, 1863–65. MS 1420, ANL.

Villiers, A. (comp.) (1962) *Of Ships and Men. A Personal Anthology*. London: Newnes.

Wakefield, E.G. (1829) *A Letter from Sydney and Other Writings*. (Reprint edn 1929.) London: Everyman's Library Series.

Walker, M. (1964) *Germany and the Emigration 1816–1885*. Cambridge, Mass: Harvard University Press.

Ward, J.M. (1966) *Empire in the Antipodes. The British in Australia 1840–1860*. London: Edward Arnold.

Waterson, D.B. (1968) *Squatter, Selector and Storekeeper. A History of the Darling Downs 1859–1893*. Sydney: Sydney University Press.

Watson, E.L.G. (1968) *Journey Under the Southern Stars*. London: Abelard–Schuman.

Watt, J. (1979) Medical Aspects and Consequences of Cook's Voyages. In Robin Fisher and Hugh Johnston (eds) *Captain James Cook and His Times*. London: Croom Helm.

Watt, J., Freeman, E. and Bynum, W.F. (eds) (1981) *Starving Sailors. The Influence of Nutrition upon Naval and Maritime History*. Greenwich, England: National Maritime Museum.

Weedon, T. (1898) *Queensland Past and Present. An Epitome of Its Resources and Development, 1897.* Brisbane: Government Printer.

Welch, J.H. (1969) *Hell to Health. The History of Quarantine at Port Phillip Heads 1852–1966.* Port Phillip, Victoria: Nepean Historical Society.

Wilburd, C.R. (1945) Notes on the History of Maritime Quarantine in Queensland. *JHSQ* 3(5):369–83.

Woolcock, H.R. (1983) Health Care on Queensland Immigrant Vessels 1860–1900. PhD Thesis, University College, London.

NAME INDEX

Acton, H.W. 8, 182, 200, 241, 298, 306
Appleyard, R.T. 25
Armstrong, W. 57
Austin, C.G. 73

Baines, J. 70
Bancroft, Dr 107
Barclay, E. 109, 289
Barry, Dr 238
Bateson, C. xii
Beaumont, T.E. 197, 227
Bird, J. 78
Blaikie, G. 261
Blainey, G. 4, 9, 55, 57, 211
Blake, G. 163, 188
Blasdall, M. on accidents 240; on activities 208, 209, 307; on bad behaviour 311, 312, 314; on berths 194, 195–96; on boredom 306; on diet 96, 203, 206; on hygiene 94, 198, 200; on surgeon and health care 134, 140, 253; on upper classes 318; on weather 182
Boland, T.P. 55
Bolton, G.C. 11
Bonthron, Dr 124
Borrie, W.D. 41
Bushby, F. 227, 300
Byrne, Dr T. 119, 222

Cambell, Dr 140
Carrothers, W.A. 29, 299
Cass, Rev. Mr 135

Chadfield, P.B. 80, 87, 97
Chandler, G. 75
Charlwood, D.E. xiv, 55, 60, 100, 115, 135, 194, 317
Chase, J. 108, 187
Clark, C.M.H. xi, 9
Clark, M. 22, 298
Coates, W.H. 59, 86
Coghlan, T.A. 4, 82, 257, 264, 322
Coleman, T. xiv
Collins, Dr 319
Collis, Mr 117
Cook, Captain 60
Cook, A.M. on accidents 241; on alcohol 205; on children 210, 262, 263; on diet 105, 107; on health 250–51; on landing 212; on mess system 104–05; on sailmaker 166; on social classes 87–8; on social life 306–07
Cotton, H.J. 63
Course, A.G. 146, 153, 177
Crawford, R.M. xiii, 1
Creighton, C. 107
Crowley, F.K. 34, 43, 319
Cumpston, J.H.L. 23, 231
Cunliffe, M. xi
Cunningham, Dr 229

Darwin, C. x
Davies, A.G. 63, 165
Dicken, C. 290
Divine, D. 51
Donaldson, G. 32

367

SUBJECT INDEX

Subject index

phthisis *see* tuberculosis

Plymouth 75, 76, 78, 100, 183, 243, 272, 300, 310

Polynesians *see* Kanakas

population growth 2, 23, 25, 31, 256, 258, 261; *see also* birth rate

ports in Europe *see* Belfast; Cork; Glasgow; Greenock; Hamburg; London; Liverpool; Plymouth; Southampton

ports in Australia 5, 7, 79; *see also* Bowen; Brisbane; Cairns; Cooktown; Gladstone; Mackay; Maryborough; Moreton Bay; Rockhampton; Sydney; Townsville

poverty 21, 29; *see also* economic

privies on ships 93–4, 156, 197, 199; *see also* hygiene

Prussia, birth rate in 257; *see also* Germany

public health legislation 107, 108–09, 115, 143; *see also* hygiene

'pull factors' *see* emigration, reasons for

punishment *see* discipline

'push factors' *see* emigration, reasons for

quarantine: arrival time and 80; births during 259; complaints about 181, 211–12, 243; legislation 107–08, 143; life in 109–10, 321; mortality in 259, 267, 269, 288; numbers of ships in 230–32; stations 108–09, 211–12; surgeons and 124, 143; time spent in 81; *see also* morbidity

Queen of Nations 233

Queen of the Colonies 228, 313

Queensland: separation from New South Wales 3, 7; *see also* mortality; ports in Australia; *and* preliminary note

Queensland Emigration Service 71

Queensland Immigration Society 11, 12

Queensland Office in London 10, 14–15, 18, 34, 37, 39, 70–3, 130, 143, 172, 295; *see also* Agent-General; emigration agents

Queensland regulations *see* regulations

Queenstown *see* Cork

railways 8, 78–9

recruitment *see* selection

Red Sea *see* Suez Canal

refrigeration 60, 86, 159

Reichstag 311

Registrar-General (England) xiii

Registrar-General (Queensland) xiii; on birth and death 258–59, 285

regulations 329; and birth and death 266, 268–70; and crews 149, 151, 154, 160, 163, 166, 169; and life at sea 183, 187, 189–91, 195–200, 203, 214; and morbidity xiii, 55, 107–08, 143, 212, 216–18, 220–21, 231–32, 236, 242, 250; and passenger arrangements 83–4, 86–7, 91–3, 98–103, 106, 110–11, 115; and passengers' behaviour *see* discipline; and selection 1–22, 24, 26–7, 35, 37–40, 45–6, 291, 294; and shipping organization 64–80; and surgeons 115–16, 118–19, 122–23, 125–26; *see also* legislation; passenger acts

religion 33, 106, 209

remittance passengers *see under* subsidized

Renfrewshire 168, 262, 291

respectable immigrants *see* selection, good character

rheumatism 175, 219, 222, 224, 280

Rockhampton 7, 8, 79, 213

Rockhampton 81, 84, 209

routes of ships 55, 57, 61, 73–8; and mortality 272

Royal Commissions on shipping disasters 61, 148–49

Royal Dane 53, 297

safety *see* accidents; passenger acts; welfare

sailing ships 50–1, 53–5, 60, 75, 189; crews on 155, 161, 162; length of voyage 88; mortality on 269, 271, 297; space on 85

saloon passengers 42, 85–6, 88, 274, 317–18

sanitary arrangements *see* hygiene; privies

Scandinavia, immigrants from 16, 22, 27, 316

schoolmaster *see* education

Scotland: immigrants from 7, 11, 12,